The

Real

Vampires

The
Real
Vampires

RICHARD SUGG

AMBERLEY

Acknowledgements

For reading, encouragement, comment and data I am very grateful to Michael Bell, Jana Britton, Susan Clancy, Anthony Hogg, Francis Hornyold Strickland, Raymond McNally, Simon Mays, Steve Schlozman, and Katherine Skaris. Many thanks to Connor Stait at Amberley for his patient and thorough help, assistance and enthusiasm.

First published 2019

Amberley Publishing
The Hill, Stroud
Gloucestershire, GL5 4EP

www.amberley-books.com

British Library Cataloguing in Publication Data.
A catalogue record for this book is available from the British Library.

ISBN 978 1 4456 9028 5 (hardback)
ISBN 978 1 4456 9029 2 (ebook)

Typesetting by Aura Technology and Software Services, India.
Printed in the UK.

Contents

Introduction: Vampire Terror

A few years ago, I began a journey. It started with a simple question: 'why vampires?' Why have vampires meant so much to us in the past two hundred years, from John Polidori's early tale, through Sheridan Le Fanu's *Carmilla*, Bram Stoker's *Dracula*, and the almost limitless range of films that have crimsoned the silver screen since the days of Nosferatu and Bela Lugosi? 'I decided that, if I was going to answer this question well, I had better find out where vampires had come from. And so I began my journey into vampire country.'

In many ways it was much stranger and more disorienting than the journey that Jonathan Harker makes at the opening of *Dracula*. True, I did not go to Transylvania; did not sit trembling in some wild forest pass as my coachman climbed down to deal with the gleaming eyes of wolves in the frozen darkness. But I did have to draw my own map as I went along. The actual countries were abundant and varied enough: Romania, Hungary, Bulgaria, Albania, Montenegro, Silesia, Poland, Serbia, Bohemia, Germany, Russia, Moravia, North America, the Ukraine and Greece. Yet what was stranger, wilder, and much harder to navigate was vampire country *as a state of mind*. In Europe and North America, anytime between 1150 and 2004, ordinary people really *believed* in vampires; they really *did* that to vampires...

At times the surprises were amusing ones. Greek vampires, for example, were often not remotely bothered about sunlight. And one man from this bright yet vampire-haunted corner of Europe stated plainly, 'No, I never heard of a vampire drinking blood...' – while other Greeks told of them feeding on apples, nuts and grapes, grazing on beans in open fields, or drinking the milk of goats. Real vampires, I began to suspect, were not sanguinary gourmets. They did not sip blood from fine wine glasses, ruminating with epicurean discernment on 'the genuine taste of human fear'. Far more simply, they just needed to eat.

But there were much bigger surprises in store. In parts of vampire country where I might have expected to breeze comfortably by, taking a few notes from the train window, the landscape grew so bizarre that there was nothing for it but to jump off, hack into the deepest thickets and pitch camp while I puzzled, long days and nights, over just what I was actually looking at, and just where I really was. Unsurprisingly, the vampire's tracks often led into the graveyard. Yet this itself was... well, like death, but not as we know it. One reason why vampires haunted people for so long was that it was remarkably *hard* to die in real vampire country. For between three and forty days you were dead, but only slightly dead. During this period a rogue soul might breeze into your mouth and set up squatter's rights in your only slightly dead body.

As with many journeys, there were moments when the sheer fatigue and difficulty of foreign travel became almost too much. At times, it seemed as if all this was just too strange, too horrifying – that the only option, after all, was to pack up and go home, to the dull but safe realities of 21st century Britain. And if I seem to exaggerate, well... think again of the iconic staking of the vampire. Try to imagine *really* doing this: after finally striking your stake into a patch of chest where you did not hit a rib, or simply find that the point rebounded, repelled by a hide swollen taut with corpse gas, you, the successful vampire staker, could well be rewarded with a face full of blood or stinking corpse fluids.

But that is the easy version of vampire staking. The really tough thing is to stake the *live vampire*. For reasons which will become clearer below, numerous living people in Bulgaria, Russia and Greece were identified as vampires while they were still alive. As a result, they could be ostracised, forbidden to marry (and thereby produce vampire children) – even burned alive. And then there were people who were *thought* to be dead, but were not. Partly owing to a widespread peasant custom of burying a body while still warm, many people were actually buried alive. Rather than being undead, they were simply not dead. The lucky ones merely suffocated in the ground. For in Bulgaria, just over a hundred and fifty years ago, this was what might happen if someone dug you out.

In the 1860s two British army officers, Stanislas St Clair and Charles Brophy, stayed for many months in the small Bulgarian village of Derekuoi.[1] Pitched on the slopes above the Black Sea (nearest landmark, the port of Varna, which features in *Dracula*), Derekuoi was a place soaked in magical terrors and superstitions. Not least of these was fear of the undead.

St Clair tells us of how, in the nearby village of Emekli, 'the child of a woman died, or rather fainted, and of course was immediately buried. Shortly afterwards the mother went to the fountain, which is close to the burying ground; in passing by this she heard moans issuing from the fresh grave of her child; she then disinterred it and found it to be alive, took it home, and brought it to health secretly.' While this kind of accident has long been impossible in our own world, we can nonetheless imagine the kind of astonished relief with which all friends and neighbours would greet such a miracle. But in Emekli, what happened was this:

> About that time some of the villagers saw the child, the council was assembled, and the child was condemned to death as a vampire. The sentence was executed in this most cruel way: the mother was held down by four or five old women, but so as to be able to see the torture of her child – this being deemed necessary to exorcise the vampire. The child was then killed according to the following process: one woman held the poor little thing's hands and another the feet, and a third ran it through the abdomen with a bit of thin pointed wood. The person who stuck the child, in relating to me this murder as an act of virtue, said that she had rarely had such bother with a vampire before – it took a full quarter of an hour to kill it, and its screams were most dreadful. The woman who killed the child is still alive, and can be brought to court, if needed.

You may begin to see, now, why even the most hardened traveller might at this point long for his familiar fireside.

Yet at the same time as I sat blinking in horror, I found myself looking, equally, at one more puzzle. The question was not just, 'how could people be so barbaric?' but also, 'how could people be so terrified?' All across vampire country, for hundreds of years, people were so terrified that they staked and beheaded and burned and reburied the living and the dead – from friendless strangers to their own family. They were so terrified that they had nervous breakdowns, became paralysed, and in some cases, actually died of fear. They were so terrified that the wild energy of their terror caused the supposed vampire to behave like a poltergeist. For yes: one reward of my tramp through this hostile territory was to learn, not just that many vampires acted like poltergeists, but that poltergeists themselves are real.

Forcing ourselves to look a little harder at that scene, we begin to realise that almost everyone in the village agreed on the necessity of this live vampire staking. And, for another, that it was not the only one they had seen or participated in. Here is our evidence. From the very start, the woman nursed her child secretly. She knew what the general belief was, and she almost certainly knew what the procedure would be upon discovery. And the woman who killed the child, 'said that she had rarely had such bother with a vampire before'. This was not the first live vampire that she had killed. We cannot easily put a number to the slayings, or say how many of the victims were children or adults. But the word 'rarely' offers a ghastly clue. She evidently *had* had 'such bother' at least once or twice in the past. And for something to be rare, it presumably needs to be one incident among several – perhaps even as high as double figures. To make matters just a little stranger, we can add that the woman who killed the child was probably the local witch: someone who commanded immense respect and power in places like Emekli and Derekuoi, where she was both a revered authority and a kind of salaried doctor-cum-priest.

Terror of vampires caused these live stakings. Ironically, the live burials were themselves essentially the result of such terror: if at all possible 'the dead' were buried while still warm, in order to prevent vampirism. Accordingly, the fear of vampires, which prompted hasty burials, must in turn have effectively *produced* vampires on the occasions when comatose people revived and managed to escape from their graves. In such cases, the supposed revenants would have then reinforced already powerful fears of vampires. Such was the tight and neatly sealed circle of superstition.

Admittedly, not everyone who escaped live burial was promptly slain. Brophy recalled how, 'some years since a man contrived to rise from his shallow grave, came back to his home, and gave his wife a tremendous beating to prove his identity, and to punish her for being in such a hurry to get rid of him.' But even here the anti-vampire precautions took over soon enough: 'A few months afterwards he died again, and that time his disconsolate widow took precautions which prevented him ever reappearing to trouble her', namely the driving 'of a nail under the left armpit into the heart'. Given that this then became Standard Vampire Procedure in the area, villagers must occasionally have been murdering their own kin, who were, at times, only comatose.

Before we touch down in the vampire-haunted isles of Greece it is worth emphasising how very well hidden that little region of Bulgarian vampire territory is. You certainly do not chance on historic gems like those while hurtling down the main roads in your hired jeep. Rather, as you stalk along through the undergrowth, ears pricked for the snuffling of any ill-tempered wild boar, you first need to spot a badly overgrown footpath, and then decide to force your way through it. By which I mean that the startling incident with which we began was not in the first, more widely available edition of the officers' book; and that, bizarrely enough, even in the second edition it is buried (as it were) in a footnote.

Greece, Montenegro and Romania

'Listen to me. She is *not* dead. She is in – is sleeping. Sleeping deeply. We may be able to save her. To make her well.' Imagine that you are the speaker in this scene. You are a doctor on one of the Greek islands. The young girl you have been treating has recently lapsed into coma. Opposite you, her parents are stubbornly uncomprehending – the mother tearful, the father stony-faced. And then – with a fearful glance at the child lying on the bed to their right, the word finally comes, in hushed and awestruck tones: 'vrikolax'.

The most you can do, in face of this, is to get the funeral delayed until the following day.[2] The girl's body is watched obsessively, according to local custom, for every intervening moment, in communal vigils further aimed at protecting her from demonisation. The day of the funeral is full of warmth, colour and life. And so too – as only you are aware – is the dark-eyed girl who is finally sealed into her coffin and lowered into the earth. No one around you realises that your tears are for the living, not the dead.

Night falls. But the village is still astir. You force yourself to wait, agonised as you are. Finally, under a yellow half moon, you creep down the lane, around the tiny white church, and into the burial ground. The smell of fresh earth hits you even before you see it. Stabbed by a spell of panicked breathlessness you pause a moment; recover, and lean down. The shovel flashes in the moonlight as you rapidly scatter off the covering dirt. Minutes pass. At last, just over a foot below the turf, the new pine cover of the coffin gleams up through the soil. You scrabble wildly through the remaining dirt; pluck a chisel from your bag; prise open the coffin lid... No sound. No movement.

But in your arms, the small body is warm... a surge of joy as you feel the tiniest breath strike your cheek. For a full two minutes, with the girl's nose pinched shut in your fingers, you breathe into her mouth. Under the rising moon, sweat runs down your face. You strike her chest, praying ceaselessly. But now, nothing stirs against your cheek. And finally, with one kiss on the pale face above the rumpled shroud, there is a last prayer offered into the pine-scented night: this time not for the girl's life, but for her soul – which is all that now remains of her as it hovers in some uncertain region in or near her lifeless body.

This is a true story. It was told, in the early 1960s, to a researcher in rural Greece. As the informant was the grandchild of the helpless doctor, a rough guess dates the incident at some point between 1890 and 1920.

For a long time, premature burial was a real danger in and beyond vampire countries. Those who seemed dead were sometimes anything but. 'By the late 1700s', writes Jan Bondeson, 'premature burial had become one of the most feared dangers of everyday life'.[3] Harry Ludlam tells of how, in Pembury, Kent, a woman called Ann West lived in such terror of live burial that she made obsessive provisions for her post-mortem existence. Accordingly, on her death in 1803 she was placed in a special tomb, with her coffin lid unscrewed, and a small window inserted in the coffin above her face. Not only that, but 'the lady's bailiff was ... instructed to bring, each evening, a little before sunset, a small basket of food and a flask of wine, and place it near' a grille in the vault, which could if required be opened from inside by Mrs West. Every evening for a year the servant was to take away the old food, and bring fresh supplies to replace it.[4]

Those lacking West's wealth could benefit, adds Bondeson, from the invention of the Bateson patented life revival device, with its underground cord and over-ground bell. If, in France or Britain, you had occasion to use this valuable post-mortem accessory in your coffin and thereby secured help, you would probably be traumatised but ultimately grateful. In Bulgaria or Greece, however, you would perhaps have thought twice before you rang that bell.

Here is another Greek, also speaking in the early 1960s:

On my mother's island a man was very ill and became unconscious. The people thought he had died, and so they prepared the funeral.

After the ceremony there was a movement in the coffin and slowly the man began to arise. Well, the people there believed he was becoming a vrikolax; in their fright they threw everything they could find at him – sticks, rocks, anything. In that way they did kill him when before he had only been in a coma.[5]

Notice, here, that the mode of killing was probably directly related to the level of terror this startling revenant inspired in the funeral gathering. Onlookers hurled sticks and stones, not just to kill the man, but because they were too terrified to *go near* him. Interestingly, this terror may in part have been catalysed by the noted *slowness* with which the corpse began to arise. To us faintly zombie-like, that aspect could also have looked suitably uncanny to the assembled mourners. In this kind of environment, any intrepid salesmen who got off the boat with a suitcase full of Bateson patented life revival devices was likely to get stoned to death himself.

Returning to the comatose girl and that helpless doctor, we can now begin to grasp that we risk getting matters the wrong way round. We can hardly begin to imagine the degree of outrage and legal action which would fall on any doctor who had allowed this to happen in Europe in recent times. But on that Greek island the danger to the doctor's reputation was strikingly different. In a small, tightly knit community with a more or less general belief in revenants, he risked being ostracised or worse if he tried to resist the parents' wishes. We can put this, indeed, even more strongly. It is very likely that the parents acted out of *love* for their daughter. The folklorist J. C. Lawson was able to conclude of Hellenic vampires that although 'during their periods of resuscitation they act as reasonable human beings', ultimately 'their whole condition is *pitiable*, and the *most humane* way of treating them is to burn their bodies' (my italics).[6] Or, in the above case, bury your dead quickly, before they become undead.

Staying in Montenegro between 1807 and 1813, the French officer L. C. Vialla de Sommières rivalled Brophy and St Clair as a pioneer in one of the remotest corners of Europe. As one reviewer of his book notes, the country was then so obscure to most other Europeans that it commanded no more than seven lines in a standard geographical work of the day.[7] Montenegrin burials were again hasty affairs, typically occurring 'eight to ten hours after death'. Sommières heard of an incident that occurred in 1813, just after his departure. 'A man named Zanetto, returning home one evening in a state of intoxication, threw himself on his bed, and was soon seized with horrible convulsions'. Although only comatose (or insensible), he was supposed to be dead. 'In carrying him to church, it was necessary to proceed by a very uneven road, intersected by rocks and stones. The frequent jolting, occasioned by the irregular motion of the corpse-bearers, soon revived Zanetto, and starting up he poured forth a volley of abuse upon the afflicted mourners. The bearers immediately threw down the coffin and ran off, and the mourners fled to the neighbouring village, where their strange story filled the people with terror.' Interestingly, and to their credit, the priests were the only ones who dared remain with this lively coffin. Rewarded by Zanetto's shouting at them, '"Living demons, you shall account for this; carry me back again instantly, or I'll throw you into the hole that has been dug for me", the priests accordingly conveyed him back in his coffin, with all due humility and patience.'[8]

Naturally, we should expect the vampire heartland of Romania to be no less severely afflicted. This was certainly the case in the capital, Belgrade, in the winter of 1888. Here 'the police found ... lying in the street, the body of a man apparently frozen to death.' Failing in their attempts to revive him, the officers presently handed the man over to the family for interment. As the bereaved were travelling to the cemetery, 'the driver of the hearse told the priest ... that he heard some noise in the coffin.' All those assembled, including a priest, agreed that they could hear it too. Scared witless, everyone except the driver fled into the snowy night, terrified 'lest a vampire should issue from [the coffin] and attack them.' Left alone, the traumatised driver spun around his carriage and whipped the horses at double-speed to the nearest police station. By the time he reached it, 'a knocking was distinctly audible. The coffin was forced open, and the man was found alive and in a very exhausted state.' He had, it transpired, got drunk with some friends and presently fallen unconscious, temporarily numbed by the cold.

The moral of these stories, perhaps, is that if you decide to get so drunk as to lose all semblance of humanity, you'd best not do it in Romania. There you could wake up not just feeling like a zombie, but looking like a vampire.

Back in Greece, we find vampire terrors reverberating on across hundreds of years, from island shores to the industrial mainland. The volcanic island of Santorini was once so notorious for its vampires that the phrase 'sending vampires to Santorini' meant roughly the same as 'sending coals to Newcastle'.[9] Living there in the seventeenth century, the Jesuit priest Father François Richard heard of numerous vampire cases throughout the islands and of how, whenever an attack occurred, all those in the neighbourhood would at dusk group together in one house or building (presumably the largest) so that 'they might spend the night a little more securely in the confidence of companionship.'[10] When Santorini was infested by a vampire named Jannetis Anapliotis, 'one woman was so frightened in broad daylight as to lose the power of speech for three days, and another whose bed he shook suffered a miscarriage.'[11]

Vampires certainly died hard in some parts of Greece. If the adolescent females who heard Marc Bolan, in 1971, singing to them, 'girl I'm just a vampire for your love', were afflicted by hormonal rather than metaphysical tremors, matters were rather different around this time in the Greek mountain village of Ambéli. Staying there intermittently, on the island of Evia (or Euboea), between 1966 and the 1980s, the anthropologist Juliet du Boulay heard tales of the last vampire that had haunted the tiny community – an event vividly recalled by all the older villagers. On that occasion only the bravest of souls would dare to look into the tainted coffin and 'see the gleaming eyes of the vampire in its depths' as they prepared the rituals of destruction. Come 1982, du Boulay observed a 'still living fear of the vampire' in Ambéli.[12] Although the village had suffered no vampirism for some years, meticulous precautions were observed after a death in order to prevent the corpse being transformed into a revenant.

We have now spent quite a few pages marvelling at the behaviour of people caught up in the hysterical vortices of vampire terror. Most of the following chapters will show us that they had their own good reasons for believing the things they did. But let us turn for a moment from their behaviour, to ours. Our own attitude to fear and to the supernatural probably has less harmful results than the worst excesses seen above. But is it entirely reasonable? Or even comprehensible?

We pay to be terrified. As a society, we go to a staggering amount of expense and trouble (count the film budgets, the special effects, the stuntmen) to entice fear into our homes. Scaling down these costs appropriately, we find that people from the communities above went to a similar lot of trouble and expense to fight terror and to destroy it. Putting it another way: it is as hard to reconcile these two radically different worlds as it is to imagine some vampire-struck village of deepest Hungary, outside which the inhabitants had hung a sign reading: 'Tonight! Genuine vampire attacks! Admission 100 forints. Certificate 12...'. Or, put it this way: however strange and unreal all those vampire-struck people now look to us, we have to take very seriously *their* likely view of *us*. They would, almost certainly, consider us mad. And, if they could confront us about our peculiar love of invading aliens, hurtling monsters, ghost-ridden mansions (and much more) could we really explain to them what all this is about? Could we, in fact, quite explain it to our*selves*?

Once, you made not just your own entertainment, but your own terror. (And the two were not the same.) As we track the vampire through the darker chambers of the human mind, we will meet a species of terror so extreme that people could die of it. We will meet nervous hysteria so potent that it may have caused spontaneous telekinesis – or, in villagers' belief, vampire-poltergeist attacks. In the first case vampire victims died of a fear which catalysed a chronic hopelessness, a radical shutdown of the whole organism. In the second, this organism went into wild overdrive. Like some febrile psychic electricity, that now extinct species of terror shot from one extreme to another: from despair to mania, all in the same village, and perhaps within a matter of hours.

Our map through vampire country looks like this. Chapter One gives us a roving, helicopter view of the territory, using both history and archaeology. It also offers some working definitions of just what a vampire is (or was). And it raises one central, overarching question: just why do people *like* the idea of vampires drinking blood?

Chapter Two takes us down to look in some detail at the revenants of three different eras: beginning with medieval Britain, and ending much more recently in Transylvania. Chapter Three jolts readers away from the vampire stereotypes of the past 200 years. Here we meet revenants which go by day, feed on milk, apples, nuts and beans, and wear shabby shrouds over their often bloated and reddened corpses. In Chapter Four we probe to the very heart of folk vampirism. Just what *made* a vampire? Vampires could be produced for many religious reasons (especially sin and excommunication) but also for magical ones (a cat leaping over a corpse, for example). Central to all of this was the human soul. For most of history, the soul was a startlingly physical, mobile and unpredictable entity. A vampire was typically a body whose soul remained after death – a surprisingly common problem in cultures where the soul watched its own funeral, sat down at the funeral supper, hovered in the house for three days after death, and lingered on earth for forty days. Having in this way seen the problem from the believers' point of view, we go on in Chapter Five to see it from that of modern science. Why did corpses fail to decay? What were the post-mortem processes that made them bloat, bleed at the mouth, grow their nails, eat themselves with audible smacking sounds, scream when staked, and spurt fresh blood weeks after burial? Why, in the words of one veteran Romanian vampire-killer, did the vampire's heart sometimes 'squeak like a mouse and try to escape'?

Readers who make it to the end of Chapter Five will be used to seeing the strange as normal, and the horrific as an occupational hazard. But at this stage we are at least within sight of the frontiers of normality – a point where the border police of the mundane are still patrolling, and able to usher any especially nervous travellers back into more homely lands. Be warned, then, that once enticed into the darkest forests of vampire country, there is no turning back. In Chapters Six to Eight we enter the realms of the vampire nightmare, and the vampire-poltergeist. Anyone who has actually had a sleep paralysis nightmare will not need to be told that it is at once real and uncannily evil. Vampires are not real. But the nightmare is, and it has proved sufficiently compelling to persuade millions of people of the reality of demons, witches, vampires, and alien-abductors. In Chapter Seven, by splicing together folkloric and hard medical evidence, we realise, indeed, that the nightmare has at times quite literally scared people to death. These two chapters are in many ways a dark alternative history of human emotion – showing that so much metaphysical terror, from hell through to horror fiction, is born within our own bodies and minds. Chapter Eight examines a version of the vampire which forces us to realise that the powers of human emotion are stranger than almost anyone has ever suspected. For, across continents and centuries, the vampire has also been a poltergeist. Fear of the vampire has produced terrors so great that these emotions seem to have caused poltergeist phenomena. I will show you not that the vampire is real, but that the poltergeist is real, and that the two were frequently indivisible. Here, amid noises and voices from nowhere, invisible beatings, and levitated crockery and furniture, folklore meets astrophysics, and the terrified villagers of vampire country find themselves in a laboratory of human nature that modern science has as yet barely begun to recognise.

'Versions of the Vampire' (Chapters Nine and Ten) shows us how many extraordinary types of the undead there once were. In Europe, first of all, we are faced with a strange puzzle. In Greece, Yugoslavia, Romania, Slovenia and the Ukraine, vampires often return to their widows or marry new wives. They sometimes beget children, and can blend into the community temporarily. Elsewhere, we have Romanian and Bulgarian vampires that not only rise from their graves but, after an allotted time span, become fully human again. Certain luckless people, meanwhile, were *predestined* to be vampires once dead, and could suffer severe ostracism in life as a result. And in Russia, Greece and Bulgaria we have a definite category of 'live vampires' – that is, people who are vampires before death, not after.

Chapter Ten turns to the distinctive undead of North America. For more than 200 years, families struck by consumption had believed that the most recent victim of this disease might be 'feeding', from their grave, on living relatives. In many cases they exhumed this corpse, examined its heart, burned it, and drank the ashes in water (all without ever using the term 'vampire'). Drawing on the pioneering research of Michael Bell, these encounters with American vampires lead us to a number of very concrete sites, events and characters, including the aged Everett Peck, a surviving descendant of the family of an 1892 'vampire', Mercy Brown. They also show us a type of revenant who was thought able to devour the living *from a distance*, without leaving its grave. Across all these centuries and countries, vampires terrorised countless people, while drinking surprisingly little blood. Our Conclusion shows that many ordinary people have drunk blood, and for an intriguing variety of reasons. Some still do.

One final thought before we begin our quest for the real vampires. As hard as we may struggle to grasp the reality of this vampire-terror, we are still likely to misunderstand it in another basic sense. Think again of those aliens, monsters, and Victorian or Edwardian ghosts that rivet us to television and cinema screens. In many cases, film scares us by drawing on things that are strange, distant, extraordinary... But all the evidence we have suggests that this was not quite the case with the fear inspired by vampires. In one sense, these revenants *were* uncanny. They were from the world of the dead – or from some limbo close to it. Yet in numerous other ways they were remarkably ordinary, everyday beings. And the special conditions which produced them were as robustly practical as any hard-working, hard-pressed rural community. We are dealing, then, with fear of a very peculiar kind: fear that is cosmic, religious, dark, and as deep as hell itself... and yet, at the same time, as ambient and local as the wind rattling through the trees, or the electricity which secretly animates our modern homes. Welcome to vampire country.

1

What, When and Where

What is a Vampire?

In many ways the revenant – one who returns – is almost synonymous with 'vampire'. Revenants are often said to be undecayed; to have fluid blood in their body; and indeed to *have* a body in which they return. They also bring death in many cases. Finally, they are very often treated like full-blown vampires: staked, mutilated, or burned, and subject to forms of religious exorcism. The main difference, though, is a big one. Although they bring death, revenants are rarely accused of *feeding* on the living. This vampiric quality, of feeding illegitimately, like some ghoulish parasite, is clearly one which has long caught and held the popular imagination.

Most of the cases in this book conform to the following definition. A vampire is any undead human being which feeds on life. As with the revenant, it is almost always quite solidly embodied – although it certainly can change into much less substantial forms. The now familiar motif of vampiric contagion is present at times, though not as frequently as we might expect – more often than vampirism as a transferable disease, contagion tends to be the transfer of death itself.

We will be meeting a few revenants amid the vampires. This is partly to broaden our geographical and historical scope, and partly because some revenants may have been viewed as vampires. In cases without written data, this is often an open question.

When: Archaeology

How old are revenants? We have good reason to believe as old as fear itself. Take, for example, the 'vampire skeleton' found in Mikulovice, in the Czech Republic, in summer 2008. In a 4,000-year-old grave in east Bohemia, archaeologists discovered that the man's body had been weighed down with two large stones: one on the chest, and one on the head. Radko Sedlacek, of the East Bohemia Museum, explained that 'remains treated in this way are now considered as vampiric. The dead man's contemporaries were afraid that he might leave his grave and return to the world.'[1]

The precise attention to head and chest may well have been no accident: both these sites have been prime contenders for the location of the soul throughout history. Paul Barber tells of numerous Celtic sites from the Iron Age in which the living had secured the dead by 'tying the body, prone burial, displacing parts of the skeleton, partial cremation, weighing the body down with large blocks of rock, orienting or positioning the grave differently, special burial places, placing wooden stakes across the body', and 'including charms in the grave'. At one particular site 'thirty-two of eighty-nine skeletons were missing the skull' (again, think soul). In many such cases, archaeologists did not believe the graves to have been disturbed.[2] Certain people were treated in this way not because they were thought to be escaping from their graves as revenants, but *in case* they should do so. The precaution was taken at first burial.

In the early nineteenth century, the parish priest Dean Lyons excavated graves on the island of South Inishkea, off Ireland's Mullet Peninsula. Here he 'found skeletons [buried] with their faces downward and ashes on their feet'; while legend has it that, on the nearby Connacht coast, the body of King Eoghan Beul was 'buried upright in the rampart of a ring fort' in 537AD. Subsequently, the king's spirit frustrated all attacking raids from Ulster, until some shrewd person had the body moved and reburied 'face downwards in wet soil'.[3]

As Jacqueline Simpson points out, restraint or deviant burial was found in Britain in the eleventh century – notably at the Anglo-Saxon burial site of Sutton Hoo, near Woodbridge in Suffolk.[4] It is also possible that it occurred in Scotland in 1405. In the present day, the grave of Farquhar Shaw on the Rothiemurchus estate is enclosed beneath a metal cage. This has been fitted to stop people removing any of the five stones placed on the grave – the legend being that misfortune will befall anyone removing them. But this legend may have been a conveniently Shaw-friendly rewriting of history. For Nan

Shepherd tells of how Shaw 'troubled the neighbourhood so that when he was dead they set five heavy stone kebbucks upon his flat tombstone, to keep him under.'[5]

Another British discovery occurred accidentally in Royston Church, near Barnsley in Yorkshire in 1869. Visiting the church around 1898, the folklorist S. O. Addy noticed that part of the lid of a stone coffin had been built into the church tower. Puzzled, he made inquiries. The gravedigger 'spoke ... with horror' of how during renovations they had found beneath the floor two heavy stones covering 'a stone coffin, in which lay a skeleton. The skeleton was perfect, but the head had been removed from its natural position, and lay between the thighs, near the pelvis.' The 'cross crosslet' carved onto the coffin lid implies that the body had been buried no later than 1400. This would mean that the deviant burial was made inside the church itself (rather than on the site it came to occupy). Here, purely by chance, the light of discovery struck upon what must have been a body of considerable status, doubly restrained, not in some tabooed burial zone, but beneath the official sacred space of Christian worship.[6] In the Icelandic Grettis saga, such treatment had its own label: 'thigh-forked'.

Meanwhile, in spring 2009, a find on the island of Lazzaretto Nuovo, near Venice, gave a more precise edge to the use of rocks. Here, the female skeleton unearthed by archaeologists was one of many medieval plague victims. It had had a brick forced into its mouth. In this case, Matteo Borrini, leader of the Italian team, thought that the grave *had* been re-opened. This was common enough when mass deaths made space underground a precious commodity. But during this initially routine procedure, medieval Italians probably saw that the corpse appeared to have been chewing on its shroud. Here, as in so many other cultures, an active dead person spelt trouble – not surprisingly, when you were surrounded by an onslaught of death which no one could explain. The brick could have been simply to halt the chewing; or to stop a demon spirit possessing the site of the soul – or both.[7]

In summer 2012 Bulgarian archaeologists digging in the Black Sea town of Sozopol 'found two medieval skeletons pierced through the chest with iron rods.' These were far from unique. Back in 2004, archaeologist Petar Balabanov had discovered six nailed-down skeletons (again, medieval) at a site near the eastern Bulgarian town of Debelt. Bulgaria as a whole hosts about 100 similar burial sites;

and Balabanov added that 'the pagan rite had also been practised in neighbouring Serbia and other Balkan countries.' Bozhidar Dimitrov – head of the National History Museum in the capital, Sofia – explained that 'these skeletons stabbed with rods illustrate a practice which was common in some Bulgarian villages up until the first decade of the twentieth century.'[8]

Pausing a moment here, as we peer down into graves which – in some cases – transport us 4,000 years back into the past, we find that the sheer stubborn persistence of magical belief is at least as eerie as any modern horror film. From the days when you could make your tent frame out of the skeleton of a woolly mammoth, through to The Beatles and beyond, attitudes to death across much of Europe were just the same. The dead could return. You must sometimes treat them with violence, lest they inflict it on you.

If all this still seems slightly distant for British, French or German readers, try these two cases. In February 1824, labourers digging a sawpit near Tintern Abbey found a skeleton buried face down in an orchard. An elderly local woman suspected this to be the remains of a man her father had spoken of, thought to have been murdered after he mysteriously disappeared from his house about a century ago. If the man's murderer feared that he would return, then prone burial would have been used so that the corpse dug itself deeper into the ground, rather than out of it.[9]

In July 1915 an officer saw two British soldiers burying a German face down. The officer evidently knew that this was a precaution lest the dead man should try to escape. If the corpse did so, he would (again) only dig himself further *into* the ground. The officer seemed to consider this a general superstition among ordinary soldiers. And the very act of *burying* your enemy in these conditions was of course remarkable (and often perilous). Another officer told of a sniper who, after making a kill, 'took the risk of going for a spade and returning to bury his foe' – almost certainly because he was just as afraid of a German revenant as he was of a live German soldier.[10]

Most of these were clearly revenants but some may also have been understood to be precisely feeding on the living, as well as killing them. The brick in the mouth of that Italian skeleton offers us the strongest clue. And it may be that, in other cases, the dead were believed to sustain their uncanny half-life just because they still drew on the vitality of the living.

When: The Written Evidence

Armed with these reasonably definite photofits of our vampire and revenant, we are now in a position to try to track down the first sightings of these miscreants in European texts. At this point, anyone who has just called out – or even thought – 'eighteenth century' will need to go and stand in the corner until Chapter Five. Admittedly, it may need to be quite a large corner, given how many people seem to have laboured under this illusion. As I write, even the Oxford English Dictionary gives the first known English use of 'vampire' from 1741. In fact, as Katharina Wilson has shown, the earliest use dates from 1688 – by which time the word had already been elevated to the status of metaphor.[11] As metaphors almost always develop after literal uses of a word, we can reasonably assume that in its literal form 'vampire' was in use before 1688.

Apart from this mistake, a lot of people also seem to believe that educated *awareness* of vampires arose only in the eighteenth century, with the publication of the 1733 *Dissertation on Serbian Vampires* of John Heinrich Zopfius, or the accounts published in 1746 by the French abbot, Augustin Dom Calmet.[12] This too is wrong. Both John Donne and Ben Jonson give the impression that, as Shakespeare's plays appeared on London stages, educated Britons could at least understand *how* a vampire came into being.

In 1616, the year of Shakespeare's death, Jonson penned a comedy called *The Devil is an Ass*. The play opens in Hell, where a junior devil named Pug is pleading with the Devil for a mischief-making trip on earth. Presently granting him his wish, Satan explains:

> But you must take a body ready made, Pug,
> I can create you none ...
> ... So, this morning,
> There is a handsome cutpurse hanged at Tyburn,
> Whose spirit departed, you may enter his body:
> For clothes employ your credit, with the hangman,
> Or let our tribe of brokers furnish you.[13]

With Pug directed into this very solid body, we meet three basic principles found in full-blooded vampire territories. First: the idea that the Devil or some demon spirit could possess and reanimate a corpse was well known. Second: most people would have agreed that the body needed to be *unsouled* before it became vulnerable to such demonic invasion – hence Satan's reference to the 'spirit departed'. Third, and most important of all, is what Jonson implies by 'this morning'. Crucially, this thief's body is dead, but only recently dead. Recall what we said earlier about those vulnerable corpses which were only *slightly* dead.

Next, we have Donne. He and Jonson were sometime friends, and were also known to exchange books. In December 1626, preaching at a funeral, Donne opposed the belief that 'the body of the dead should become the body of an evil spirit, that that spirit might at his will, and to his purposes inform, and inanimate that dead body.'[14] At first glance, it might look as if Donne is simply talking about ghosts. But, whatever he was describing here, it was something in which he did *not* believe. And other writings suggest that Donne did believe in ghosts. Not only that, but he tends to refer to ghosts as things which are markedly *in*substantial.[15] In the funeral sermon, it is 'the *body* of the dead' person which (supposedly) comes back to life. Was Donne in fact referring to the vampire? It is certainly no surprise that he did not use the actual word: so far as we know, it did not exist in English at this time. But if any Englishman would have managed to root up the idea of such a rarity, it would have been the voraciously curious, learned, and multi-lingual Donne.

Over on the Continent, vampires were far more active and easily recognised. We begin, aptly enough, with a reference from that great German occultist, Henry Cornelius Agrippa. True to the character of one believed to raise demonic spirits, thought to have sent out a satanic black dog into the countryside on his death, and consistently associated with the Faust legend, Agrippa had delved up details on Greek vampires in his 1531 *Occult Philosophy*. Agrippa tells of how, in Crete, 'the ghosts which they call *Catechanae* were wont to return back into their bodies, and go in to their wives, and lie with them; for the avoiding of which, and that they might annoy their wives no more, it was provided in the common laws that the heart of them that did arise should be thrust through with a nail, and their whole carcass be burnt.' Brief as it is, this is remarkably accurate. We have bodies, burning, and the staking of the heart.[16]

In 1653 the philosopher Henry More set out two vampire stories in detail: one, the 1591 exploits of a suicide, the shoemaker of Breslau in Silesia, and the other the still more spectacular assaults of Cuntius, from Pentsch, also in Silesia. Come 1658, Thomas Bromhall recounted the tale of Stephen Hubener, a revenant who had terrorised the citizens of Trawtenaw in Bohemia in 1567.[17] Although the English versions of these incidents appeared after the deaths of Donne and Jonson, Continental accounts (by the German physician Job Fincelius and the Italian philosopher Pico della Mirandola) were circulating in the early Elizabethan period.[18]

Further south, vampires were gnawing the pages of a Latin work of 1645 by the Greek theologian, Leone Allacci. Allacci seems these days to be more famous for his belief that the foreskin of Christ might have divinely ascended to space to form the rings of the planet Saturn. Although modern astronomers appear sceptical of this theory, we will soon see that Allacci was far more reliable as a source of vampire beliefs. Not only that, but as regards dating, he asserts that 'this belief is not of fresh and recent growth in Greece; in ancient and modern times alike men of piety have tried to root it out of the popular mind.'[19]

In the 1670s Sir Paul Ricaut, English consul in Smyrna, was asked by Charles II to produce evidence of 'the present state of the Greek and Armenian churches'. He did so in 1678, publishing his findings in the following year. In these we meet, again, a consistent and relatively accurate picture of the Greek vampire. In almost every country village, writes Ricaut, one can hear stories of these creatures – stories which 'they tell with as much variety as we do the tales of witches and enchantments.'[20]

Here we have three clear English references to vampires (More, Bromhall, and Ricaut); one probable one (from Donne); and Continental awareness from Agrippa, Fincelius, Pico, Allacci and Richard. Taken as a whole they span the period 1531–1678. Why, then, has everyone been so fixated on the eighteenth century? What was so important about these particular vampire accounts? There are three answers. One is that in this newly enlightened, increasingly scientific age, vampires were becoming more and more *extraordinary* for French and British readers. The nocturnal terrors and subsequent gruesome butcheries of vampire-country now found their way into the drawing-rooms of Paris and London, where a bewildered gentry sat with their coffee going cold before them as the fabulous reports trembled in well-manicured fingers.[21]

By contrast, when More and Bromhall wrote of revenants Europe was in the grip of what now appears one of the greatest periods of general insanity ever seen: the witch hunts. In this context, the works of the devil were surprisingly ordinary matters. The first 18th-century reports from central-eastern Europe flew off the presses as the newly rational Enlightenment was attempting to stamp out such backward superstitions across Britain and the Continent. Moreover, Britain in particular was struggling to come to terms with a history of witch beliefs that the educated now furiously opposed. To sum up the likely implications: vampires were probably going to get far more attention when your own supernatural demons had been banished from polite society. You – the educated reader – no longer believed in witches; but it was, all the same, rather *exciting* to know that *some* people believed quite fervently in vampires.

Linking this to our second answer, we have to consider an interesting possibility: although these 18th-century accounts were factual (i.e., they were believed by those involved, if not by the authors who described what happened), they might well be considered as the first serious phase of 'vampotainment' – that strange realm of ambiguous thrills which still captivates us in the present day. Interestingly, this factual vampotainment precedes the general rise of horror as a form of literary or theatrical entertainment. The first Gothic novel appeared only in 1764, in the form of Horace Walpole's *The Castle of Otranto*. And two other big examples, *The Mysteries of Udolpho* and *The Monk*, were not published until 1796. (By this later date, vampires were prowling the stages of France – and stylishly, too, as we hear of the periwigs worn by theatrical 'ghosts, vampires and devils'.[22])

The third answer concerns the question of blood. In recent times this element has for many people overtaken numerous of the older defining features of a vampire. In the context of modern vampotainment, many people will accept that an undead being which drinks blood *without* doing harm is a vampire; and a good number will also accept that a live human who drinks blood is a vampire. This second definition of course extends into real life – whether involving psychopathic killers or consenting sanguinarians.

David Keyworth has argued pretty convincingly that, far from being typical, the 18th-century vampires were quite an anomaly. It was only now that we had repeated claims of vampires – such as Peter Plogojowitz in 1725 – drinking their victims' blood.[23] Here, then, we need to raise another crucial question: do we *like* the idea of vampires drinking blood? Is this why the 18th-century vampires were such a hit, and why they have so often mistakenly been seen as the *first* vampires? For the time being, we will have to leave this weighty question dangling (or dripping). At this point we need to meet the vampire – or, to be more precise, to meet a selection of vampires from across the International Vamping Community. Before we do so, let us briefly scan the territories in question.

Where

In Europe, vampires were relatively common in Romania, Hungary, Bulgaria, Albania, Montenegro, Silesia, Poland, Serbia, Bohemia, Moravia, the Ukraine and Greece. Although they are not now associated with Germany, they were known there – at least in areas which were *once* German (as can be expected, border changes across time naturally complicate any easy division between countries.) Vampires were also a very real danger in Russia – although from around the seventeenth century they mutated into a specialised, hybrid form peculiar to this region. Michael Bell has shown that in North America, vampire exhumations were still occurring at the end of the nineteenth century, while ghostly echoes of these rituals continued in the United States until at least 1949. And in Macedonia during the First World War, a British army officer encountered Turkish beliefs and burial customs which looked very much like those found in typical vampire cultures.

The Italian find seen above is something of an oddity for that country, otherwise thought largely free of vampires. Here as elsewhere, it is rash to try and assume that what written culture has left us accurately reflects popular, non-literate beliefs. But it is at least worth mentioning a crucial point about undecayed corpses. Time and again, vampire corpses are said to be either wholly uncorrupted, or at least relatively fresh and undecayed. This can happen naturally – sometimes due to soil types or a distinctive atmosphere. The important point here is that in Catholic Italy, an undecayed corpse was a sign of special *sanctity*, rather than of the uncanny or of demonic possession. This is in part where the phrase 'odour of sanctity' comes from. It once referred to the allegedly sweet-smelling cadavers of especially pious, privileged Christians. A quite recent example is that of Padre Pio, the Franciscan friar canonised as St Pius in 2002. This figure was claimed by certain of his numerous followers (writes John Hooper) to have possessed '"the odour of sanctity", a fragrance like roses'.[24] As Piero Camporesi notes, the 13th-century saint, Beatrice II, of Este in Ferrara, was allegedly both fragrant and undecayed.[25] This specific

Italian belief may have tended to supress vampire beliefs in that country: if you saw an undecayed corpse you were more likely to pray to it than flee from it.

In following pages we will not, however, be spending much time in Italy. We are now going to move up close and personal to a small selection of vampires. However much you enjoy their company, please: do *not* try and sniff their less-than-sanctified corpses.

2

Vampire Stories

In order to make some sense of the potentially bewildering beliefs which (as it were) kept vampires alive, we will ultimately have to take this creature to pieces. Given how often the vampire was quite literally dissected by terrified villagers, however, it seems fair to delay the anatomy a little longer. Let us first meet the vampire in one piece, in a range of settings, both expected and unexpected.

Britain

So far as we know, Britain has been remarkably free of vampires of the blood-drinking variety. But there have been a number of British revenants who fulfilled most criteria *other* than blood-sucking. A number of cases were recorded in the twelfth century by the Yorkshire churchman William of Newburgh (d.1198?). One of these occurred in Buckinghamshire. During the reign of King John, sometime during or before 1196, a man died, and was buried on 29 May. The very next night, however, 'he suddenly entered the room where his wife lay asleep and, having awakened her, he not only filled her with the greatest alarm but almost killed her by leaping upon her with the whole heaviness of his weight and overlying her. On the second night, also, he tormented the trembling woman in just the same way.' Amply warned by now, the woman stayed awake upon the third night, also bringing several people to watch with her. Although the revenant came once again, he was soon frightened away 'by the shouts and cries of those who were keeping watch.'

Thus thwarted, the man now began to trouble his brothers. They too followed their sister-in-law's example, however, by staying awake and keeping a household guard around them. Faced by this obstacle, the revenant 'made his appearance' again, but did not actually attack. For, 'it seemed as though he ... only had the power to molest those who were asleep.' Presently, the animals of the town were discovered in a state of panic and terror, and before long, 'in every house there were certain of the family who kept awake and mounted guard all night long,' with the whole town now 'anxious and fearful lest they should be subjected to some sudden attack.' It was at this highly charged juncture that the revenant, which 'for a good while ... had harried people during the night alone ... began to wander abroad in plain daylight.' Interestingly, though 'dreaded by all', he was actually 'seen by but a few. Very often he would encounter a company of some half-a-dozen and he would be quite clearly discerned by but one or two of the number' – although, we are told, all the others 'very perceptibly felt his horrible presence'.

Nearly 'scared out of their senses' by this time, the townsfolk sought ecclesiastical permission to exhume, and burn, the man's body. The request passed to the Bishop of Lincoln, who, balking at this, instead wrote out a formula of absolution and had it laid upon the breast of the corpse. When this was done the body was found to be as uncorrupted as it had been on the day of burial. After this, the visions and attacks at last ceased. Notice that no stakes or silver bullets were needed to kill this revenant; it was wholly laid to rest by just one piece of paper. The crucial point was that this paper had sacred authority.

Around the same time another British incident occurred in border country, at the monastery of Melrose Abbey. Here there lived a priest of a notably worldly, even decadent character, so notorious for his hunting that he was known as 'Dog Priest'. After his death, the priest sought for several nights to force his way into the cloister where he had lived. These attempts being unsuccessful (possibly because of the monks' great piety) he presently 'appeared at the very bedside of the lady whose chaplain he had been and uttered the most piercing shrieks and heart-rending groans.' This uncivil behaviour was promptly reported to one of the monks, who then organised a party to watch for the return of the revenant. Heavily armed, these four men waited together until past twelve o'clock at night, 'in that part of the graveyard where the unhappy priest had been buried.' But soon three of them, chilled by this open-air vigil, went indoors to warm themselves by the fire.

The reader gains no prizes for guessing that just as he found himself alone in these forbidding circumstances, the remaining monk was approached by the uncanny monster. Despite feeling an understandable 'thrill of horror' at this sight, the monk's 'courage returned', and, 'as the horrible creature rushed at him with the most hideous yell, he firmly stood his ground, dealing it a terrific blow with a battle-axe which he held in his hand.' At this, the revenant 'groaned aloud with a terrible hollow noise, and swiftly turning ... fled away' at great speed. The monk chased him to his grave, which 'seemed promptly to open to him of its own accord' and then 'quickly closed over him', leaving the ground undisturbed. Right off cue, the three companions returned from their pleasant toasting by the fire, and hearing the news decided that at first light the corpse must be disinterred. On doing this, they found the body 'marked by a terrible wound, while the black blood that had flowed from this seemed to swamp the whole tomb'. They accordingly took it well beyond the bounds of the monastery, burned it, and scattered the ashes to the winds. This story, William added, had been told to him by the monks themselves.

Keyworth makes some plausible arguments for the very solid quality of British ghosts down into the late seventeenth century (even claiming, interestingly, that Hamlet's dead father is essentially an 'undead-corpse' rather than any kind of insubstantial wraith.[1]) But it does seem telling that Britain's likeliest suspects hail from our Catholic past, before the Protestant reformation so drastically altered ideas of the afterlife and the spirit world.[2]

The Vampire of Blow

Leaving Britain, we come next to the Bohemian village of Blow (or Blau), north-west of Prague. Here in about 1336 a shepherd named Myslata, who had recently died, reappeared and 'called upon several persons, who all died within eight days. At last the inhabitants of Blow dug up the herdsman's body, and fixed it in the ground' with a stake. Nothing daunted, the vampire of Blow responded with impressive cheekiness. For,

> the man even in this condition laughed at the people, [and] told them they were very obliging to furnish him with a stick to defend himself from the dogs. The same night he extricated himself from the stake, frightened several persons by appearing to them, and occasioned the death of many more, than he had hitherto done. He was then delivered into the hands of the hangman, who put him into a cart, in order to burn him without the town. As they went along, the carcass shrieked in the most hideous manner and threw

about its arms and legs, as if it had been alive: and upon being again run through with a stake, it gave a loud cry, and a great quantity of fresh, florid blood issued from the wound. At last, the body was burnt to ashes, and this execution put a final stop to the spectre's appearing.[3]

Even to the hardened vampirologist, this is quite a tale. We should remind ourselves, perhaps, that here we are in the Czech Republic – a place where they had been tackling revenants since around 2000BC. This indicates that the Czechs took these beings seriously. Indeed, the level of terror they generated here is probably the key to the seemingly improbable backchat of the Vampire of Blow. What was actually heard (what you or I would hear if we had the dubious benefit of a tape recording) was the sound of post-mortem gases and oxygen responding to the sudden staking. To this relatively mundane sound, just add sheer witless hysterical terror and... presto! You have some surprisingly precise vampire repartee.

The Vampire of Kring

In 1672 there dwelt in the market town of Kring, in the Archduchy of Krain, a man named George Grando, who died, and was buried by Father George, a monk of St. Paul, who, on returning to the widow's house, saw Grando sitting behind the door. The monk and the neighbours fled. Soon stories began to circulate of a dark figure being seen to go about the streets by night, stopping now and then to tap at the door of a house, but never to wait for an answer. In a little while people began to die mysteriously in Kring, and it was noticed that the deaths occurred in the houses at which the spectred figure had tapped its signal. The widow Grando also complained that she was tormented by the spirit of her husband, who night after night threw her into a deep sleep with the object of sucking her blood. The Supan, or chief magistrate, of Kring decided to take the usual steps to ascertain whether Grando was a vampire. He called together some of the neighbours, fortified them with a plentiful supply of spirituous liquor, and they sallied off with torches and a crucifix.

Grando's grave was opened, and the body was found to be perfectly sound and not decomposed, the mouth being opened with a pleasant smile, and there was a rosy flush on the cheeks. The whole party were seized with terror and hurried back to Kring, with the exception of the Supan. The second visit was made in company with a priest, and the party also took a heavy stick of hawthorn sharpened to a point. The grave and body were found to be exactly as they had been left. The priest kneeled down solemnly and held the crucifix aloft: 'O vampire, look at this,' he said; 'here is Jesus Christ who loosed us from the pains of hell and died for us upon the tree!'

> He went on to address the corpse, when it was seen that great tears were rolling down the vampire's cheeks. A hawthorn stake was brought forward, and as often as they strove to drive it through the body the sharpened wood rebounded, and it was not until one of the number sprang into the grave and cut off the vampire's head that the evil spirit departed with a loud shriek and a contortion of the limbs.[4]

This tale has often been transmitted through a later figure, the German pastor Johann Christoph Harenberg (1696–1774), from Brandersheim in the Duchy of Brunswick.[5] Harenberg wished to banish belief in vampires. But what seems to be the earliest surviving account of the tale was written in 1689 by a baron, Johann Weichard Valvasor, who took vampirism very seriously.

Here we meet a quite early reference to the drinking of blood, and an impressively dramatic assault: the stake bounces helplessly off until someone (who no doubt drank out on the feat long after) leaps down into the grave and hacks off Grando's head. Perhaps most interesting, though, are the discernible hints of *personality* which Grando exhibits. He has 'a pleasant smile'; and he weeps. Both features were doubtless imposed by onlookers: they probably saw a face contorted by the processes of decay, and some of the common post-mortem fluid which Barber has so thoroughly detailed in his forensic analyses. But the tendency to imagine some kind of personality is itself striking, given the long-running oscillations between vampire-zombies and more humanised vampires of style and character.

The recent history of Kring (now Kringa) nicely underlines the point made in our introduction: for most of history, no fool was going to advertise such incidents on a big sign outside the village. But this is now precisely what welcomes you into the Croatian tourist spot: '*Legenda O Vampiru Jure Grando 1672*', reads the black and white name board on its outskirts... If this does not deter you, you can then stroll on to the Vampire Bar for a Bloody Mary once you reach the village centre.

Arnod Paole

Arnod Paole was a Serbian ex-soldier who (in Barber's words) 'fell off a hay wagon and into history in the first quarter of the eighteenth century.' In this seminal episode we find blood-sucking; a kind of vampiric contagion; and an impressively long-running vampire saga, playing out across several years after Paole's actual death.

We also have some useful witnesses. With Austrian soldiers called into the vampire-struck village of Medvegia, on the Morava River, a medical officer named Johannes Fluchinger produced a detailed report. Signed on 26 January 1732, it tells of how Paole, 'about five years ago ... broke his neck in a fall from a hay wagon'. While alive, Paole had 'often revealed that, near Gossowa in Turkish Serbia, he had been troubled by a vampire, wherefore he had eaten from the earth of the vampire's grave and had smeared himself with the vampire's blood' by way of cure. Twenty or thirty days after Paole's death, 'some people complained that they were being bothered by [him] ... and in fact four people were killed by him.'

When Paole was exhumed forty days after his death, it seemed all too clear to the villagers what he had been up to. 'He was quite complete and undecayed, and ... fresh blood ... flowed from his eyes, nose, mouth and ears', while his shirt, shroud and coffin were all 'completely bloody'. As if this was not sufficient sign of an uncannily persistent life, Paole seemed to have new fingernails and toenails, and when staked, 'gave an audible groan and bled copiously'. With typical thoroughness, villagers then burned the corpse and threw the ashes back into the grave.

Given the amount of detail the Paole episode asks us to absorb, we may want to pause a moment here and see what this first stage tells us. As Barber emphasises, Fluchinger was not present at Paole's exhumation. But the details are certainly consistent with other cases of vampirism. The corpse is swimming in blood – or, at least, something which looks like it. What, though, of the four people Paole had allegedly killed? We cannot, on this evidence, say for certain how they died. But we can make two informed guesses (based, again, on related cases). Most importantly of all, people had been primed to fear vampire attacks the moment Paole died. Not only did he die an unnatural death, but he had told them about the vampire attacks he had suffered near Gossowa. So we have, first of all, a state of pre-existing fear. Next come the deaths. If the victims died of ordinary disease, the seemingly axiomatic conclusion for villagers was, nonetheless, that Paole had killed them. But there is also another, more intriguing, possibility.

This is that, before their deaths, one or more of those four people saw Paole in their rooms at night, and afterwards died of sheer terror.

Meanwhile, the vampire victims continue to pile up in Medvegia. We hear of how the first four were disinterred (but with no more detail on their condition or treatment). Next we cut to the time of Fluchinger's visit, in January 1732. At this point, enter Vampire Contagion... Villagers now recall that 'Arnod Paole attacked not only the people but also the cattle, and sucked out their blood. And since the people used the flesh of such cattle, it appears that some vampires are again present here, inasmuch as, in a period of three months, seventeen young and old people died, among them some who, with no previous illness, died in two or at the most three days'.

There follows a long and careful analysis of the many bodies exhumed, with much focus on fresh blood and undecayed organs. Fluchinger and fellow officers are now eye-witnesses. Accordingly, when we are told that a corpse over ninety days old has 'much liquid blood' in the chest, we can probably trust what we hear. In all, eleven bodies are considered to be vampiric, and four to be properly decomposed. As Barber shrewdly points out, these carefully noted differences probably persuaded villagers that they had real vampires before them, rather than just a mass of wholly undecayed corpses, perhaps preserved by the rigours of the Serbian winter. This impression must have been strengthened by the fact that, whereas the ninety day corpse was preserved, a mother and child who died about fifty days and twenty-one days before the exhumations were properly decomposed.

Amid Fluchinger's careful repetitions about the state of organs and flowing blood, certain details stand out. A 20-year-old woman named Stana, for example, had died in childbirth at least two months ago. Since she 'had painted herself with the blood of a vampire ... both she and her child' (which had died immediately after birth) 'must also become vampires'. This presumably means not that the blood-painting *caused* her vampirism, but that her doing so indicated her own fear that she was already vampirised (as with Paole himself). Presumably her attempt at cure was deemed to have failed.

Also interesting is the corpse of a 60-year-old woman, Miliza. It is this body that is more than ninety days old; and, as well as the liquid blood and well-preserved viscera, the body is startling because of its 'plumpness'. In life, Miliza had been 'very lean and dried up'. The simple conclusion was that she had been feeding on villagers since her death. And – as we will soon see at length – associated beliefs in fat vampires were far from uncommon in such contexts.

Finally, and most important of all, we have those who, while previously healthy, had died in a very short space of time – after two or, at most, three days. These included a young man of 16, and another of 17 – the latter being called Joachim. They also included a young woman of 20, Stanacka, stepdaughter of a hajduk (soldier) named Jowiza.[6] We hear that she 'lay down to sleep fifteen days ago, fresh and healthy, but at midnight she started up out of her sleep with a terrible cry, fearful and trembling, and complained that she had been throttled by the son of a hajduk by the name of Milloe, who had died nine weeks earlier.' She then 'experienced a great pain in the chest and became worse hour by hour, until finally she died on the third day.' It was actually Stanacka's death which catalysed the mass exhumations, with the decision being taken that same afternoon.

While Stanacka herself was not inspected until eighteen days after burial, we learn that, 'as she was being taken out of the grave a quantity of fresh blood flowed from her nose', and that 'there was also to be seen, on the right side under the ear, a bloodshot blue mark, the length of a finger'. These words come straight after Fluchinger's repeated reference to the throttling by Milloe. Putting all this together, we can be almost certain that Stanacka died of fear, three days after seeing and being attacked by Milloe in her bed. Details of the attack, along with subsequent pain in her chest, and the time between the assault and her death, all support this probability. So too does that striking finger mark on her neck. As we will see, it was almost certainly real, and had almost certainly been produced by that midnight attack. There is a good chance that Joachim and the other male victim died of fear too. The timespan fits, and it may also be significant that they, like Stanacka, were both young, and therefore perhaps more easily nervous than older villagers.

One final word on the destruction of the vampire corpses. As far as we can tell, they were all burned at the same time. Imagine that, driving a cartload of goods across the muddy lanes near Medvegia one evening, you round the brow of a hill and suddenly see fire. As you come nearer, you can also smell something powerful. A little nearer still, and you find yourself looking at a small vampire holocaust. Blazing madly in the dusk on the outskirts of the village are eleven corpses. They have all been decapitated, and later eleven piles of ashes will be hurled into the Morava River. The digging up of all those corpses was itself probably less onerous than the burning of eleven bodies. Corpses do not burn easily without specialised technology, and it may well be that villagers, safe as they now were, shivered by meagre firesides in coming weeks after this mammoth expenditure of fuel.[7]

Peter Plogojowitz

Just around the time of Paole's death, another part of Serbia was gripped with vampire terror, after one Peter Plogojowitz died in Kisilova in 1725. If you ever organise a European vampire tour, Kisilova should be a high point of the trip. While the Serbian tourist board is probably now grateful for Kisilova's vampire past, Hungary can at least feel glad that various people still imagine the village to be Hungarian territory (which it once was, in times of frequent warfare and political instability).[8]

With Plogojowitz dead and buried some ten weeks, nine of the residents of Kisilova died in the space of eight days. These people lingered for up to 24 hours on their deathbeds, and in this time were able to report the nocturnal horrors inflicted on them by Plogojowitz. He had 'come to them in their sleep, laid himself on them, and throttled them ('squeezed their throats') so that they would have to give up the ghost.' In some versions of the tale it was also stated that Plogojowitz would bite his victims' throats and 'suck the blood out of the wound.'[9] Moreover, Plogojowitz's widow also 'deposed that she herself had been visited by him since his death, and that his errand was to demand his shoes, which frightened her to such a degree, that she left Kisilova, and went to live somewhere else.'

Back in Kisilova, the villagers demanded of the local Imperial officer that they be allowed to exhume Plogojowitz, warning him that 'if they were not permitted to dig up this cursed carcass ... they should be forced to leave the village, and settle where they could.' The officer therefore came to Kisilova, with the minister from the nearby town of Gradisca, and both were able to see for themselves that Plogojowitz's body was 'free from any bad smell, and perfectly sound, as if it had been alive, except that the tip of the nose was a little dry and withered.' The beard and hair had grown, and there was a new set of nails. Moreover, 'under the former skin, which looked pale and dead, there appeared a new one, of a natural fresh colour' – and the hands and feet 'looked like those of a living person'. The officer saw, also, 'that the mouth of the vampire was full of fresh blood' thought to have been 'sucked from the persons he had killed'. Now 'fired with fresh indignation', the peasants 'ran immediately to fetch a sharp stake', which, on being driven 'into his breast' prompted 'a great quantity of fresh, ruddy blood' to spurt from the wound, and from nose and mouth. Not only that, but 'something which indicated a sort of life, was observed to come from his private parts. The peasants then laid the body upon a pile of wood, and burnt it to ashes.'

Just what was this 'sort of life'? As I will probably not satisfy all readers by delicately noting that it was the kind of thing you would not see in a female vampire, it may as well be stated plainly: as far as we can tell, on being staked, Plogojowitz's corpse sustained an erection. We might, at first, suspect this claim to have originated with male descendants, who felt that such evidence of family virility surpassed the wildest boasts of drunken rivals. But our report derives, of course, from the Austrian officer at the graveside. And, while I have mainly quoted the account as given by Calmet, we have also a very close translation of the original German, as rendered by the redoubtable Barber. In that version, the officer talks of certain 'wild signs' prompted by the staking, which 'I pass by out of high respect.'

Despite this frustrating euphemism, we can be fairly sure that Plogojowitz did indeed gain an odd burst of pleasure from the violent treatment inflicted on him. On inquiring into these 'wild signs', Barber learned from various coroners that the bloating of the sexual organs can indeed naturally occur during decomposition of a corpse. Moreover, Calmet's phrase 'observed to *come from* his private parts' must indicate the ejaculation of some kind of fluid. This would match that which was ejected from mouth and nose at the same time – with the staking surely being the common stimulus.[10]

It is hard now not to find some of this rather comic. But we should remind ourselves before we hit the road again of just how much profound terror was in evidence here. You do not lightly abandon your home village: if the officer had not finally agreed to the exhumation, modern visitors to Kisilova might indeed be wandering around the ruined shell of a deserted settlement. Again, in Barber's translation, the officer openly excuses what he has permitted because 'the rabble ... were beside themselves with fear.'

Sharp-eyed readers may have noticed that Plogojowitz, like Paole, attacked and throttled his victims at night (again, he was *in their rooms*) and that they consistently died in the same 24-hour period after the assaults. It seems almost certain, given the characteristic throttling, that some of these people again died of fear.

Marotinu de Sus

In this remote Romanian village, a man named Petre Toma died shortly before Christmas. Not long after, Petre's 'niece suffered nightmares and appeared seriously ill. She claimed that her uncle was visiting her at night and feeding from her heart; that he was a strigoi.'[11]

> After the niece became ill … Petre's brother had to wait, because he could not act within the 12 days of Christmas. On 8 January, the corpse was checked and deemed to be a strigoi. At midnight the next day, six men disinterred it and cut open the chest. I asked Niculae what they used for this and he looked at me as if I was mad, before brandishing his scythe again. Apparently, the chest was cut crosswise with a scythe tip, and the heart removed through the ribcage. Again, I asked what tools had been used. It was with a growing image of James Whale's 1931 classic Frankenstein that I understood Fifor to say, as neutrally as possible, 'He says it was with a pitchfork. Yes.' The subsequent description utterly failed to dispel my horror-film image. The men took the heart, spiked aloft, to the crossroads outside the village. There they roasted it over a brazier and, as far as I could understand, stuffed glowing coals into the ventricles. Held up in the night sky, the heart shed charred flakes that were caught in a tea towel. These were taken to the niece's house, ground up and mixed in a glass of water. 'The niece drank it,' Fifor confirmed, 'and in the morning she said she felt better … in this way she was cured.'[12]

This seemingly fantastical account derives from a very reliable authority. The first-person speaker is British archaeologist Timothy Taylor, who personally visited Marotinu de Sus. If I add that Taylor was there to research a television documentary, you might well be a little surprised. And in fact all this occurred in the winter of 2003–4 – just weeks after Stephenie Meyer signed her contract for *Twilight*.

Sometimes, truth is indeed stranger than fiction… It is hard to think of many horror stories or films which rival that image, of a human heart, spiked on a pitchfork, pocked with eerily glowing nuggets of light, the coals in its ventricles like some strange parody of vampiric life after death. At the same time this method is again typical of the homely pragmatism of real vampire territory – something confirmed by the mundane tea towel that no Victorian Vampire Hunting Kit would ever deign to include.

We will hear more about this extraordinary time capsule of a village below. Before we leave it we should be aware that, world-famous as this case became, it might easily have never become public, even within Romania. As Taylor further explains: 'None of this would have come to public attention had it not been for a family rift. One of Toma's daughters, who had married an urbanite, was outraged. She alerted the police who dug Toma up again in full view of the public and media. His body was examined in a procedure one would be hard-pushed to call forensic ... the court found Toma's brother guilty of [desecration], and he received a prison sentence.' It was only through the intervention of Taylor's companion, the Romanian social anthropologist Mihai Fifor, 'who was able to articulate the logic of peasant traditions, that this [sentence] was commuted, although not quashed.'[13]

We will return in detail to these stories throughout this book. It is now time, however, to examine the surprising ways in which the real vampires lived, and indeed sustained their undead lives.

3

The Free Range Vampire

Appearance

It is time to hunt the vampire. Equipped with garlic, stakes, and a clutch of European phrase books, you are just stepping out of the time machine and into some remote and spirit-haunted village of the Carpathian Mountains. You have, of course, a clear photofit of your quarry, which you politely show to the villagers. Being well aware that the film vampires of recent years have grown rather creatively varied, you are sticking to the good old aristocratic stereotype of Stoker and the more classic film Draculas of Lugosi and Christopher Lee. But reactions are not what you expect. All those questioned seem puzzled by the pale, gaunt, haughtily chiselled and aquiline figure in his cape and evening dress. And this is not merely because of your rudimentary command of Romanian. It is because your picture looks nothing like a real vampire.

The real vampires were not pale, but strikingly red, as one would expect of a creature full of the blood of others. And they were certainly not thin: their bodies were frequently bloated as though pumped full of air or gas, the skin stretched as tight as a drum. As for style and poise? They were as shabby and unimpressive as the impoverished dead of any small rural community.[1] If a figure resembling Christopher Lee's patrician Dracula were to swirl his cape through your Greek or Serbian mud streets any time between 1650 and 1930, there was only one reason to be frightened of him: namely, because someone so unusual and aristocratic must surely be your distant landlord. He was certainly powerful and dangerous, but his cruelties and his blood-sucking were very much of this world, not the next. Ironically, as uncanny as the vampire of your local cemetery may have been, it was probably in many ways far less alien than one of the gentry or upper classes.

In terms of appearance, the real vampire has to be split into two forms. First, we have the relatively human one seen in the opened grave. Second, we have the shape-changing vampire. To get out of the grave, the vampire would have mutated into one of many possible forms, and might well also be in some non-human shape once they began creeping unpleasantly around your sleeping chamber. At a quite basic level, these two forms clearly contrast. The first is a real entity (a corpse), viewed in a supernatural way. The second appears to be *just* a supernatural belief – in reality corpses cannot leave their graves, transformed or otherwise. But, in fact, matters are slightly more complicated than this initial contrast suggests. This is because, in many cases, vampire victims did actually see some kind of vampire entity in their houses. Often this thing crept up their bed, got on top of them, and proceeded to almost choke the life out of the traumatised person.

For now, however, to the graveside. Lest you are still reluctant to part with your misleading photofit, let us be clear about the vampire's physique. One early British revenant from Alnwick was (in Montague Summers' especially memorable translation) 'florid and chubby', and of 'frightful corpulence'. Now, politically correct our time may be. But the fact remains that anyone involved in casting a vampire film is still going to briskly reject any applicants for the lead role whose CVs describe the actors as being of 'frightful corpulence' and with faces 'florid and chubby'. However creative writers and directors are, they seem universally to shun The Fat Vampire. So rigid is this law of physique that Roy Kinnear or John Candy, for all their acting skills, were never going to be asked to audition. The vampire must be more or less lean, chiselled, gaunt, aquiline, and so forth. Any actors who tried to sue casting for fattism would probably find their lawyers presented with a small-print disclaimer, excluding this area from discriminatory codes, and referring explicitly to the necessary exclusion of actors celebrated for their frightful corpulence.

Well... to all chubby, round-faced, red-cheeked actors I can now give welcome news: your time has come. Step forth from the shadows, don your oversized cloaks, and enter the coveted graves of which you have so long been cheated. Real vampires were fat. Time and again, the bodies found in suspect graves were as bloated as if they had been mere skins pumped full of air and blood. Outside of Britain, we find our early Greek informant, Allacci, saying much the same thing. 'Such bodies ... become swollen and distended all over, so that the joints can scarcely be bent; the skin becomes stretched like the parchment of a drum, and when struck gives out the same sound.'[2] Allacci had indeed seen such a body at the church of St Antony on Chios: 'the skin was distended, hard, and livid, and so swollen everywhere, that the body had no flat surfaces but was round like a full sack.'

Not all vampire corpses displayed the impressively 'frightful corpulence' seen by Allacci or the British monks. But by definition, the bigger they were, the more likely they were to be identified as vampires. Why? The most basic key to appearance is this: the corpse was alive, and it was *feeding* on you or your neighbours. So the bigger it looked, and the less decayed, the more suspect it was. As we have just seen, in the Paole case the corpse of the 60-year-old woman, Miliza, was suspect in part because of its 'plumpness' – even though, in life, Miliza had been 'very lean and dried up'. Confronted with a coffined Lugosi or Christopher Lee, villagers would be likely to murmur sympathetically that the poor chap looked half-starved, and in need of a good square meal.

Almost all the common signs reported at the exhumations in vampire outbreaks fit the suspicion of a still *living* corpse. It might have hair, longer nails, and sharper teeth (although these last, Vampire Classicists should be warned, are surprisingly rare in the authentic literature). Its skin, if not ruddy, can look oddly glowing and fresh. In some cases its limbs will be flexible. It may have blood at its mouth, or the coffin might be positively swimming in it. All this uncanny vitality tends to be confirmed in many cases once the Vampire Hunters get *inside* the vampire. When staked, it can shoot out quantities of blood (sometimes in jets: villagers often know to use sheets during this operation, lest they be splashed with the dangerous fluid). It might scream. If the heart is actually eviscerated as part of the ritual, this too will often look undecayed, and may contain blood. As we saw in Medvegia, in cases where surgeons thoroughly autopsied the corpse, organs might be surprisingly intact and healthy.

Types of post-mortem decay (or lack of) are surprisingly varied. The corpse from Chios, for example, was livid – an annoyingly fluid word, historically, but one which there almost certainly means dark, roughly resembling the early colour of a bruise. (This matches what Keyworth has noted of medieval Scandinavian revenants, where the *draugr* was an undead corpse typically described as black or very dark.[3]) Yet again, the last thing this Greek revenant was, was pale. All in all, this monster (whose bloating could also be a sign that the devil had blown up the body with an evil spirit) looked as if it had been feeding on the living, and would continue to do so unless checked.

But here we may seem to hit a snag. Just how had it been getting *out* of its grave, in those preceding days when the coffin was sealed, and the grave still intact? Enter, now, the shape-changing vampire. Readers of *Dracula* will probably recall the Count's ability to metamorphose into a bat or a dog at different points in the story. Those who haven't re-opened the novel for some time might be forgiven, however, for forgetting that Dracula also takes the form of mist at various times. With these three variants, Stoker broadly captures the protean abilities of the real vampires: they could take almost any form, so long as it was at least barely tangible. (Hint: even a spirit needs *some* kind of body in which to transport itself...)

Let us attempt a brief Crime Scene Reconstruction in our traumatised vampire village. Someone has suffered nocturnal attacks – been half-smothered, half-throttled, scared three-quarters to death... In the cemetery, at the most recently dug grave, there is a tell-tale hole, probably 'about the size of a serpent'.[4] With the villagers assembled, someone reports seeing a strange dog loping about the fields last Tuesday evening. Someone else has seen a hare. With these distinctly chilling phenomena established, the rest of the story is too obvious to state... The vampire got through your keyhole or down a chimney, through another keyhole (assuming that you had a luxury executive-style bedroom with a door, and the even greater luxury of a lock) and next thing was on your chest while you lay helpless, oddly paralysed and unable to scream...[5]

At the start of the twentieth century many rural Greeks would tell you that 'the dead can assume the shape of dog, weasel ... pig and other things.' This ability was so closely associated with the Greek vampire that such shape-changing powers were even named after him: 'this is called *vrykolakismos*.'[6] When interviewed in 1934, an American Greek named Antonios stated of the vrykolakas that 'he looks like a man, like a dog, like anything'.[7] That 'anything' slides down the scale of non-human creatures, from dogs, cats, pigs and hares, on to birds, and through to reptiles, moths and insects. When burning a vampire corpse, for example, bystanders would ensure that any worms, snakes, lice, beetles or 'birds of horrible and deformed shape' were driven back into the fire as 'it may be the vampire embodied in one of these.'

In certain cases, the protean abilities of the vampire could mean that its destruction was less grimly visceral than the butchery of a blood-filled corpse. 'In Transylvania', writes Agnes Murgoci, 'it is thought that many people can project their soul as a butterfly.

In Vâlcea souls of vampires are considered to be incarnated in death's-heads moths, which, when caught, should be impaled on a pin and stuck to a wall to prevent their flying further.'[8] Murgoci adds that certain people were – even when alive – marked out as fated to become vampires; and that, 'when they sleep, their soul comes out of their mouth like a little fly.'[9] As well as mist, in some variant beliefs the vampire could take the form of 'straw or a fluff of down' in order to pass through the keyhole and attack [its] sleeping victim.'[10]

By this stage, vampire connoisseurs may be feeling not just disappointed, but positively bewildered. It is, perhaps, a little like sneaking onto the film set of your favourite superstar, only to find he or she is so terribly shabby, unpolished, and off their guard that they are temporarily unrecognisable. Is there any logic behind this wayward vampire, so reluctant to take any stable form that he seems, indeed, defiantly *anti*-iconic? On closer inspection, it seems that there is. First, at the most orthodox supernatural level, we know that the ability to change shape is a classic trait of the Devil himself. In the time of Shakespeare or Milton, educated Christians would not only assert this but genuinely believed that his Sooty Highness or his lesser devils could actually shrink down, get into your body, and swim about in your blood. Much later, writing of the emphatically vampire-haunted Ukrainians in 1938, Samuel Koenig learned of how the Devil could again take almost any form, including those of a baby, a pig, a cow, an insect, a worm or a piece of straw.[11] Montenegrin witches had a similar ability. There the traveller Edith Durham saw people kill moths because they might have been mutated witches – and in this case the witches were also held to suck blood and cause deaths.[12] While we now tend to remember witches *having* familiars (such as cats, dogs, toads, or flies) in most witch cultures they were just as likely to take these shapes themselves.

A second way of understanding this is to take a more homely, less theological viewpoint: that is, to try and see all this through the eyes of the villagers themselves. For there is indeed an underlying feature which links all these potentially bewildering vampire creatures. Simply: they were all *familiar*. Another way of putting this is to say that, when you and everyone else were so *ready* to believe in a vampire, then it was surprisingly easy to find so many things which did indeed look like one. The tell-tale hole above the grave; the uncanny hare; the strange dog... In this kind of world, almost anything could be soaked in evil or in magic. Or, we might say, everything was oddly natural and supernatural at the same time.

An intriguing story from vampire territory nicely underlines this point. This one comes from Greece, in a Peloponnesian village near Caritaena. Another New England Greek, Bill, related the tale to folklorist Dorothy Demetracopoulou Lee in 1934. As it was told originally by his mother, it presumably occurred some time between about 1880 and 1910. Trying to cross a river one day, a young man slipped and drowned. Possibly because of his sudden and unnatural death (and, crucially, the fact that he died alone) he was held to have become a vrykolakas. 'He would go to the house [and] would destroy whatever they had; flour, and other things. He even had the power ... to go by day ... there where his brother was, who had many sheep. So he would go, and call his name there, where the sheep had been left in the shade.' The problem grew so bad that litanies were said (presumably over the grave). But these failed. For, one evening, the vrykolakas 'went to the house. And there was a big noise. In the midst of the noise, the brother went to see what it is'. In pitch darkness, 'as he was feeling about, his hands caught hold of a man's leg. But he was so strong, that he could not hold it'. The vampire escaped, all of this having occurred without any door having been opened.

Presently, during another invasion of the house, the living brother shot at the vampire. After this, it confined itself to the fields. The brother took his gun, ready to shoot at it once more. But finally it was undone by a storm. Lightning fell near the brother's house. 'There was a tree outside the house and the lightning struck it. And there was a dog there, and it killed the dog. And from then on the vrykolakas disappeared.' 'Apparently', Bill concluded, 'the vrykolakas was in the dog, and the lightning burnt him, whereas his brother's gun had been unable to do so.'[13]

This belief may have been assisted by traditional ideas about lightning and the demonic. Rather than just a vague association of horror with storms, we find that many people held the Devil, for all his powers, to be vulnerable to thunderbolts. But what is most striking of all here is how impressively, neatly *self-contained* the whole incident is. After all the sinister phenomena, all the insubstantial and subjective signs, we have that very real, very solid animal lying dead beside the blasted tree. End of vampire, end of story. We can be fairly certain that no one, however long they sat and reasoned with this community, could have talked it out of its belief. What looks natural and accidental to us looked unmistakably supernatural and meaningful to them.

The fact that the Greek vampire can look 'like a man, like a dog, like anything', and that its Romanian cousin might lurk in the most innocent moth is, in the end, fundamentally practical. Every being, every spirit, needs a body. When we move from the appearance of the vampire to its habits and lifestyle, the same kind of practical logic often applies.

Lifestyle and Hours of Business

The Free Range Vampire

Let us imagine that, visiting my Greek farm shop, you find me offering vampires for sale. You might at first imagine this to be a glaring example of how, pitched down in the remote Mediterranean, certain parts of Europe still flout EU directives on agriculture. Let me assure you that the reverse is true. I am charging quite a high price for these vampires, and I am doing so just because they are free range and organic. Lest you remain still unwilling to part with your money, I should warn you that the vampires you might watch cheaply via online film sites have been shamefully mistreated: kept in the darkness all their immortal lives, in boxes barely six foot by two, and forced to feed on nothing but blood. (Small wonder they have grown so pale.) The authentic vampires of Greek life, by contrast, were omnivorous creatures, ranging freely in the fields both night and day. Now that you seem rather more ready to consider a purchase, I myself am concerned that the creature will continue to be well-treated once it leaves my shop. (They make better pets than food, in truth; killing them is a lot of trouble.) A few words of advice, then: let us begin with diet.

The Food of the Vampire

The earliest known vampires, in fact, seem to have been more overtly cannibalistic than their fictional descendants. They were often famed not so much for a precise desire to drink blood, as for a general voracity which would consume any available material to sustain their demonic lives. So we are told of how, during church services, corpses buried under the floor could be distinctly heard munching just below the worshippers.[14] (This, I must say, would have livened up my Sunday mornings no end.) In some cases these were in fact auto-cannibals, chewing on their own limbs. In others they were alleged to somehow eat up all the bodies in the immediate vicinity of their coffins. Summers tells us how, in Greece, 'it was not infrequently seen that the dead person in his grave had devoured all [corpses] about him, grinding them with his teeth and (as it was supposed) uttering a low raucous noise like the grunting of a pig who roots among garbage'. According to Calmet, it was widely believed in Germany 'that there were corpses which chew in their graves, and devour whatever lies near them. Some go so far as to say, they may be heard munching, like hogs, with a sort of grunting, grumbling noise'.[15] This claim was precisely echoed, around 1601, by a north German preacher who found his sermons disturbed from below the floor by a smacking noise, 'like a sow when it eats'.[16] In Russia, one type of vampire was said to gnaw on itself in the grave. Only when it had exhausted this home-grown food supply would it rise and go off to eat cattle.[17] Certain burial practices also support this idea of the vampire as dining alone in its own grave. Barber notes that, in one Slavic medieval burial ground, thorns, knives and nails have been found in skulls, their position suggesting that they were used to pin down the corpse's tongue, and thus prevent it from chewing.[18]

It is interesting to compare this greedy, hog-like vampire with the more iconic figure of novels and films. For all his faults, Count Dracula appears to have good table manners. The image of a noisy pig snuffling through its unnatural meal seems to intensify an implicit distinction between cannibal and vampire. Subtly yet crucially, there is something more grossly visceral about the *eating* (and perhaps especially the chewing) of human flesh. Or compare, more recently, the suavely besuited Sam Neill, in the film *Daybreakers*. Savouring human blood in a wine glass as though it were old Bordeaux, Neill remarks to the helpless 'donor' opposite him that only this kind of blood (as opposed to artificially manufactured substitutes) has the authentic taste of human fear. This may be repellent to connoisseurs of Margaux, but it is perhaps also intriguingly stylish.[19]

We might wonder, too, if there is indeed something tellingly *scientific* about the vampires which stalked the realms of fiction and film in and after the nineteenth century. Dracula's blood drinking has a certain surgical precision and efficiency. He consumes the most vital life force of a body without needing to laboriously grind his way through raw sinew and tissue. And it is not merely whimsical to add that in his literary or celluloid images, he rarely seems to appear soaked in gore. A neat line of blood might trickle from his mouth, but never goes so far as to stain his shirt.

Another way of putting this is to compare the vampire and the zombie. In terms of typical cinematic horror, these two beings are sharply distinguished. One is poised, well dressed, often suave, and infinitely clever and devious. The other is lumbering, grotesque, clad in torn and filthy rags, and with a soul-less automatism visible in its blank and inhuman gaze as much as its ill-co-ordinated movements. It scarcely needs adding that before it sinks its undead teeth into your quivering flesh, the zombie is not going to ask for a menu (still less a wine list). Summing up this kind of sharp difference in the social hierarchy of the undead, we might say that the cinematic zombie is, above all, strikingly *unselfconscious*. But the same goes, as it turns out, for many of the real vampires of Romania or Greece. Once again, the sheer practical drive for food triumphs over any aesthetic considerations or social niceties.

The real vampire did not feed on himself in order to satisfy the ghoulish delight of cinematic horror fans. He did so because he was hungry. And if there had been any other food to hand in the coffin, this would have done equally well. Take, for example, the 17th-century Vampire of Milo. After the body of a highly suspect, excommunicated man was buried on the island, 'the peasants and islanders were every night affrighted and disturbed with strange and unusual apparitions, which they immediately concluded arose from the grave of the accursed excommunicant.' On opening its grave, the terrified Greek islanders witnessed two grim indices of vampirism. First, they 'found the body uncorrupted, ruddy, and the veins replete with blood'. Second: 'the coffin was furnished with grapes, apples and nuts, and such fruit as the season afforded.'

Grapes, apples, and nuts... from a modern perspective, the Vampire of Milo, quietly attempting to enjoy his subterranean picnic, is an almost touching creature. (Once again, it seems that an animal had managed to enter the coffin, and was storing the food down there.) Far from cannibalistic, this tame vampire is indeed a vegan. He seems, at the very least, to be in need of a good PR man if he is ever to capture the interest of sensational authors and film directors.

From another viewpoint, however, the Vegan of Milo very much typified those authentic vampires who had not been stylised and aestheticised for fictional (as it were) consumption. Such a creature is organic insofar as it is far more at one with its environment – in more than one sense, far more natural. He is, simply, a creature which has not died, and as a consequence, he needs to eat. When we look at those lines above, identifying the suspect corpse as ruddy and replete with blood, we automatically leap to the standard conclusion: this demon has in its veins the blood of last night's victims. But in fact that account gives no mention of such assaults, or of blood drinking of any kind. Most basically, the blood is a sign of life (i.e., the corpse is a revenant and needs to be destroyed). And, secondly, to the watching islanders it was probably a sign that the corpse had a well-functioning digestive system, having turned the apples and nuts into blood, just like any other human being.

Much later, in the 1960s, a Greek from Samos recalled a vampire which drank the milk of the goats at night-time (the creatures being always dry in the morning).[20] We can see that this, unexciting as it might be, has a certain common-sense advantage: in this way a vampire can maintain a regular source of food, as he could not do if he killed off the animals by drinking their blood. Anyone who has seen the Swedish film *Let the Right One In*, with its grimly realistic portrayal of the difficulties of getting regular blood meals, should understand the advantages of the lactarian vampire.

Although the Romanians were more familiar with the blood-drinking vampire, they would typically look for broader markers of vampirism than the tell-tale signs of blood. 'If relations have died,' explains Murgoci, the corpse's mouth 'will be red with blood. If it has only spoilt and ruined things at home, and eaten what it could find, the mouth will be covered with maize meal.' Again, one of the means of combating the Romanian vampire was not so much to attack it as to bribe it: 'millet may be put in the coffin, or in the mouth and nose, so the vampire may delay many days till it has eaten the millet.'[21]

Back in Greece, a sure sign of the vampire was often a wrecked kitchen rather than a punctured vein. Among the New England Greeks, both Bill and George portrayed the vampire as a kind of poltergeist addicted to midnight feasts. Those who believe in him (states George) say that 'the vrykolakas does mischief ... he goes to the house and eats different kinds of food, of dough.'[22]

By now you should have a fairly good idea of what to buy if you ever invite a vampire to supper. As only the meanest readers are likely to offer it a napkin and leave it to eat itself, we should perhaps add just a few more tasty hints for those fond of meat and protein. As we saw, once it had finished chewing on its own limbs, the Russian vampire would go in search of cattle. The long-running saga of Arnod Paole involved his having attacked and killed 'several beasts', which then transmitted vampirism to others. In Bulgaria, around 1839, a vampire was believed to have scavenged dead horses and buffaloes, without ever attacking or killing humans. Summers, meanwhile, tells of a vampire from the island of Naxos which was known to rob eggs, and 'even poultry and cattle'.[23]

So much, then, for *Dracula*... Even those readers very slightly addicted to vampire-cinema will probably recall the superbly arch delivery of Coppola's Gary Oldman, who declines Harker's invitation to join him at supper that first night in the castle with: 'I have already dined. And I never drink. Wine.' Dracula, of course, is never seen to eat normal food because he cannot. Unlike the hapless vampire of *Let the Right One In*, he ghoulishly exults in this dietary constraint, rather than suffering any disgust or qualms of conscience. But that, we might add, is aristocrats for you. They can afford to be fussy. Hungry peasants cannot, and their vampires are made in their own image.

There are, admittedly, regional variations on the matter of blood. In Greece in particular, blood drinking was very rare. We have heard one Greek state quite definitely: 'No, I never heard of a vrykolakas drinking blood.'[24] According to Lee, the scholar who conducted these interviews, a Greek vampire was more likely to eat someone's liver and inner organs than to drink their blood.[25] Of Bulgaria, we learn from St Clair and Brophy that here the vampire 'does not seem to have that peculiar appetite for human blood ... only requiring it when his resources of coarser food are exhausted.'

In other parts of Europe vampires certainly did drink blood. But even there we occasionally hear of them tearing up their victims, and devouring the entire carcass in a voracious frenzy, like some nightmare hybrid of werewolf and cannibal. Again, this would make excellent sense to any peasant. If you wanted to really horrify them, on the other hand, try butchering a pig, draining the blood into a bucket, and then *throwing the rest away...*

The notion of a vampire as surviving solely on blood is again a much later one. Its modern popularity reflects a desire to stylise the vampire, to give him or her an easily distinct identity. And it comes, too, from all those fictions in which the uncanny, the undead, the magical, are no longer as readily natural as they were to the demon-haunted peasants of Romania or Serbia or the Ukraine. If anything, such fictional tales seek to artificially expand the distance between the human world and that of this increasingly fantastical demon. Should anyone remain in doubt about the often homely dietary requirements of their vampire pet, they may like to recall Barber's findings on the Croatian vampire. In this region 'one may propitiate him with hospitality'; for, 'if his hunger is satisfied, he does not attack anyone.'[26]

With the Vampire Menu established, we can move on to another enduring myth. Whatever you may have heard, a candlelit supper is not *de rigueur*. For those who would prefer lunch al fresco – read on...

The Noon-day Demon

Before you take away your free-range vampire (along with several bags of millet and muesli) you should indeed be aware that it is far less purely nocturnal than your average hamster. In 1645 Allacci wrote of the Greek vrykolakas that it 'actually makes its appearance in the daytime, even at high noon, nor does it then confine its visits to houses, but even in the fields and in hedged vineyards and upon the open highway it will suddenly advance upon persons who are labouring, or travellers as they walk along, and by the horror of its hideous aspect it will slay them without laying hold upon them or even speaking a word.'[27] We will learn later what the lone death and the 'hideous aspect' meant in that context. What we can readily see here is that this vampire is wholly devoid of two supposedly essential markers of his kind: he kills without drinking blood, and (like the Buckinghamshire revenant) he goes by day. As we saw, on Santorini, 'one woman was so frightened in broad daylight' by the revenant Jannetis Anapliotis 'as to lose the power of speech for three days'.

In a culture where religious terror grew wild and unaided in any hedgerow, the vampire did not require the special medium of darkness in order to flourish. In real vampire country, it was not a question of night versus day, but of sacred versus secular. Ask any child now about vampires, and they will tell you that they can be killed in daytime, when their powers are suspended, and they are wont to rest in their coffins. Better still, they should be attacked just after daybreak, as the first rays of the sun shoot a deadly power toward a revenant that has not fled to the safety of its tomb. A few decades ago, however, you might have learned from any child in Greece or Serbia that the vampire was compelled to remain grave-bound only for one short period in a whole week: 'between the hours of Vespers on Saturday and the end of the liturgy on the Sunday morning'.[28] What matters in that context is not a physical environment, but a sacred one.

Yet again, for the Greeks at least, this kind of supernatural hysteria is at the same time consistent with scenes of organic rural mundanity. So Richard also tells us of how, on the island of Amorgos, between Santorini and Mykonos, 'these vrykolakas have been seen not only at night but in open day, five or six together in a field, feeding apparently on green beans.'[29] We could scarcely be farther, in this serene vignette, from the image of the lone nocturnal ghoul. These creatures indeed are almost herd-like, as if some hallucinating Greek had actually been looking at half a dozen sheep or cows placidly grazing. Perhaps even grouping together for their own safety, these peaceable vegans are supremely well integrated into their natural environment. If we were to pass quickly by a painting of this scene in an art gallery (failing to read the caption, 'Six Vampires Grazing on Green Beans') we could easily be forgiven for thinking we had just glimpsed one more homely view of pastoral life in the pre-industrial world.

It is true that the noonday demon is far more typical of Greece than of other vampire lands. Yet it was certainly not unknown elsewhere: the vampires of Russia and Poland were said, at least in the seventeenth century, to 'appear from midday to midnight and suck the blood of men and beasts', and in Romania a certain category of vampire could be found wittily entertaining the girls at a summer's evening party.[30] We might also wonder, though, if the Greek vampire got more nocturnal as time went on: the references above, after all, come from the seventeenth century. It is tempting to conjecture, accordingly, that the vampire donned the cloak of night in later times, as even the Greeks grew less religious or less superstitious. This accords, again, with the sense that we are here witnessing an extinct species of human emotion. Once fears like these stalked by day, their wild vibrations of terror running far off the scale of modern sensibilities.

We now have a much clearer idea of the looks and habits of the vampire. This gives us a better chance of hunting it down, so that we will not, in future, idly pass by six grazing vampires without a second glance. When we find it, what do we do? To this in Chapter Five. The following chapter, by contrast, is less concerned with destroying the vampire than with understanding how it came to be created in the first place. Much of what has been said above may have raised as many questions as it has answered. Perhaps most basically, ringing through the head of the bewildered reader there now echoes one burning query: 'How on *earth* did they be*lieve* all this?' Those readers who have the nerve to make it to Chapter Nine will realise all too clearly that they certainly did not believe all this for fun. In fact, they needed to; and at times such belief was literally a matter of life and death. First of all, however, we need to understand what life and death *meant* in these cultures. Before science, ideas about these primary matters were quite as strange as anything in all the annals of vampire folklore.

4

How to Make a Vampire

How do you make a vampire? The basic ingredients are very simple: a body, and a soul. The body needs to be dead, and the soul needs to be the sort that people really believe in: it is something, and it does things. Both of these basic ingredients turn out to be quite strange when we get closer to them. Before we do so, we need to grasp just how *useful* the soul was to ordinary people throughout most of the last two millennia. Although you could not read, and had no grasp of anything approaching modern scientific biology, you *knew* what life was. The soul was life. The soul gave the body life. The idea is still lodged in everyday speech. To move, to breathe, to be alive, is to be animated. And 'anima' means 'soul'. Accordingly, if souls were real and were the basic root of life, then you did not require a higher degree in complex biochemistry to understand how a revenant might be produced. You simply needed to be a Christian.

Before you eagerly run off to find a dead body and rummage out its soul, I should warn you that you will also need some kind of yeast or starter culture to get the process going. Otherwise, your corpse will not rise nicely into the bloated and undead monster we met above. Here, then, are nine key types of Vampire Yeast, given by J. C. Lawson in his classic work on Greek folklore. Likely vampire suspects include:

1) Those who do not receive the full and due rites of burial.
2) Those who meet with any sudden or violent death (including suicides), or, in Maina ... those murdered who remain unavenged.
3) Children conceived or born on one of the great Church festivals, or children stillborn.

4) Those who die under a curse, especially the curse of a parent...

5) Those who die under the ban of the Church, that is to say, excommunicate.

6) Those who die unbaptised or apostate.

7) Men of evil or immoral life in general, more particularly if they have dealt in the blacker kinds of sorcery.

8) Those who have eaten the flesh of a sheep which was killed by a wolf.

9) Those over whose dead body a cat or other animal has passed.

We will return to some of these categories later in this chapter. These examples are all Greek ones, and are by no means exhaustive. But most of them fit vampire culture in general. Moreover: almost all of them are religious. In the climate of holy terror, the vampire was in every way a sacred demon. Religion defined him. Religion gave him life, and priests and prayers took it away. This very basic fact lingers on, of course, in the vampire's terror of the crucifix. But in many ways it has been diluted, distorted, or forgotten. For all that, the hackneyed image of the Vampire Hunter clutching cross in one hand and garlic in the other does have one basic grain of truth. The cross stands for religion, and the garlic stands for magic. Any of those causes given above which are not religious are indeed magical. But, as we will find, the average peasant of Vampire Country habitually saw religion, and actively exploited religion, in a magical way. Similarly (as Emma Wilby has emphasised) outside typical vampire country, people in Britain and Ireland used holy wafers or holy water to make their crops grow – and were still doing so, in some places, into the twentieth century.[1]

Excommunication

In a culture which really believed in the soul, the failure to *fully die* was far more terrifying than death itself. Many vampires were trapped in their bodies as a result of formal religious punishment. As Allacci explained:

> The *vrykolakas* is the body of a man of wicked and debauched life, very often one who has been excommunicated by his bishop. Such bodies do not like other bodies suffer decomposition after burial nor fall to dust, but having, so it seems, a skin of extreme toughness become swollen and distended all over, so that the joints can scarcely be bent; the skin becomes stretched like the parchment of a drum, and when struck gives out the same sound.[2]

To many of us, Christian or not, the thought or image of the decaying corpse is grim and repellent. If the skeleton is somehow cleaner and less disgusting, it too is a traditional icon of horror or morbidity. But for the Greeks, it was the *failure* to decay which was horrifying. This was why they so obsessively exhumed and inspected corpses, even going so far as to take careful notice of the colour and smell of the bones (which should, G. F. Abbott tells us, be 'yellow [and] redolent'.) As late as the 1960s, Greeks would talk of how the earth should 'help' the corpse to decay.[3]

As a cause of vampirism, excommunication takes us back to what is probably the earliest surviving example of a Greek revenant. In the fifteenth century, the effects of Christian excommunication were so notorious that they had even come to the attention of the head of the Ottoman Empire, the Sultan of Constantinople, Mehmed I (1413–1421).[4] Being generally curious about Christianity, Mehmed decided to arrange an experiment which would put these claims to the test. His assistants found for him a girl who had been excommunicated, 'a shameless wench' who had not only had many lovers, but who had even had the nerve to accuse the Greek Patriarch of being one of them. Though she had been long dead, when they opened her grave they found that she still had all her hair, and that her body was 'black and swollen like a drum'. This suspect corpse was sealed in a chapel and presently removed so that the Patriarch could read over it the letter of forgiveness which lifted the woman's excommunication. Even as he was doing so, 'the joints of her hands and feet began to dissolve, and those who stood close to the remains heard the noise'. The corpse was returned to the chapel, which was 'sealed carefully', and three days later, when they broke these seals 'they found her completely dissolved and in dust, and were astonished at the sight.' So much so, indeed, that Mehmed 'marvelled greatly and believed that the faith of the Christians is a true faith.'[5]

In this case the corpse had not caused any terror, mischief or death (and we ourselves can reasonably infer that its crumbling was due to the sudden change of atmosphere when its home was unsealed). In all other respects, however, this woman fulfilled the criteria for a revenant. And come the seventeenth century, such a corpse would be quite definitely identified by the Greeks as a *vrykolakas*.

In Chapter One we briefly met Sir Paul Ricaut, Charles II's consul in Smyrna from 1669 to 1678. While he was there Ricaut found that almost every country village boasted stories of the vrykolakas.

One of these tales was indeed that of the suspect, excommunicated corpse which was deviously squirrelling away apples, grapes and nuts in its coffin. Ricaut explains, more fully, that after this damning evidence was seen, the islanders 'resolved to make use of the common remedy in those cases, which was to cut and dismember the body into several parts, and to boil it in wine, as the approved means to dislodge the evil spirit, and dispose the body to a dissolution.'

The dead man's family, however, intervened. They managed to obtain from the Church a reversal of the excommunication held responsible for vampirisation. A decree to this end was written by the Patriarch in Constantinople, including (at the family's request) the exact date and minute of its signature. Back on the island, where the vampire corpse lay in its coffin, Ricaut's priest was 'himself ... performing Divine Service', when 'on a sudden [there] was heard a rumbling noise in the coffin of the dead party, to the fear and astonishment of all persons then present.' Upon opening it, 'they found the body consumed and dissolved as far into its first principles of earth, as if it had been seven years interred. The hour and minute of this dissolution was immediately noted and precisely observed, which being compared with the date of the Patriarch's release, when it was signed at Constantinople, it was found exactly to agree with that moment in which the body returned to its ashes.'

Other Greek cases echoed this remarkable tale very closely. The Jesuit Richard, our man in Santorini, recalled a case seen as the work of the Devil, who had effectively possessed a corpse. Once exorcised, and 'with the departure of the Devil' the body 'begins to decompose and gradually to lose "its colour and its *embonpoint*, and is left a noisome and ghastly lump".' On another occasion, moreover, 'so rapid was the decomposition in the case of a Greek priest's daughter, Caliste by name, that no one could remain in the church, and the body was hastily reinterred; from that time she ceased to appear.'

It is hard for us now to grasp how radically horrifying excommunication was in these cultures. For people so saturated in religious piety, the ex-communicant was far, far beyond the realms of ordinary sin – even beyond any murderer who still remained *part of* the Christian Church. It is hardly going too far to say that they did not really exist. All the basic laws and habits of Christian life (confession, prayer, forgiveness) no longer applied to them, and this terrifying limbo was perfectly underlined by the strange stasis to which the body was then subjected in its state of suspended post-mortem life.

Little wonder that this terrible 'ban of the church' was taken so seriously. In 1877 the English author Joseph Brown could still assert that 'the belief in *vrykolakas* or vampires is widely spread among the Greek Islands, in Thessaly, Epirus, and Turkey.' And, moreover, 'the terror caused by this superstition is intense' – so much so that 'in some cases priests have actually been killed for fear they should inflict' the decree of excommunication.[6] And it was only a few years before this that, in the Ionian Islands, excommunication was used as a kind of literal religious *policing*. Thomas Gallant points out that in cases where terror of criminals was too great for anyone to dare inform on them, priests habitually used the threat of excommunication: 'may the earth split and swallow them ... let iron and stones be dissolved, but not them; may they remain indissoluble and distended for eternity.' Strikingly, these terrible religious curses were directed not just at the criminals, but at 'each and every person who has knowledge of this [crime] ... and who does not come forward and tell the truth.'[7]

This last case is especially interesting for two reasons. One, it shows how central and practical religion was to such communities. In this instance, it was arguably stronger than the official police force or legal system. And little wonder... Because – secondly – it knew... *everything*. Notice how the threatened excommunication, here, applies to anyone who has withheld information, even if no one but *themself* is aware of this. The power is indeed godlike.

But so too is the general logic of excommunication in all the other cases. Quite simply: your mere words can make and unmake reality. Like God when he says 'Let there be light', the priest's mere speech controls matter, either suspending its decay or completing it. If any readers remain particularly incredulous about this power of words over things, it is worth reminding ourselves that it goes on all across Europe and the Americas every week. A priest consecrates wine and bread, and they *are* Christ's blood and body. Whether or not we believe this, it tends to go unremarked simply because we are used to it.

How else might you make a vampire? Especially (I hear the reader asking) if you are not an archbishop? Well: if you want a more democratic method, you might curse your own child. Notice that this closely resembles excommunication: you say something, and it affects reality. (And of course excommunication itself is really only a curse, dressed up in many syllables and religious respectability.)

This way of making a vampire is a typical example of something which hovers between religion and magic. And so too does category number three above, the luckless child conceived or born on one of the great Church festivals.[8] After all, you could say it was sinful for the parents to have sex on such a day, but it was surely just bad luck to be *born* on one – especially given how many such festivals there are in Greece. Equally blameless were those babies who happened to be born with a red caul (amniotic membrane), or with teeth, a split lip, an extra nipple, a lack of cartilage in the nose, or 'a tail-like extension of the spine (especially if it is covered with hair)'.[9] We will see in Chapter Nine just how serious that lack of cartilage in the nose could be.

Gathering similarly poisonous fauna on the Greek island of Chios in the 1940s, Philip Argenti and H. P. Rose heard from one woman of 60 in the village of Chalkios that 'girls born during the 12 Days [from Christmas to Epiphany] became shrews or witches'. But, she added, the midwives could recognise such babies, and always strangled them at birth. Intriguingly, these slain 'witches' thus effectively became *vampires*, as they would then 'come back at night and suck the blood of anyone they can catch.'[10] This kind of cruel bad luck is broadly echoed by category number nine: the cat that crosses over the corpse before its burial.

The Corpse with the Demon Soul

For some reason, the cat has most commonly been singled out as the chief or worst culprit as regards crossing the corpse. This may be because cats have been objects of superstition in many cultures. It is also probably because they are most likely to be inside a house, roaming freely, and are far better than dogs at leaping over things in general. As well as being widespread in past centuries, the cat taboo still lingers on in Marotinu de Sus, where reporter Matthew Schofield was told: 'Vampires are humans who have died, commonly babies before baptism or people unfortunate enough to have black cats jump over their coffins.'[11]

In most vampire countries, however, pretty much any living thing could do the same damage. In Russia, the corpse could be vampirised not only by a cat but by a leaping pig, or even if a bird flew over it.[12] At first glance this second case would appear to mean that the corpse in question was outside. 'Over' could also possibly mean 'over the roof'. For in Russia, vampirism could occur 'because the wind from the steppe had blown over the body'.[13] In either case the crossing over was not very direct, and would be pretty much impossible to prevent.

In some cases, a far less nimble and indeed wholly inactive animal could do the damage. Among the many things which bewildered Brophy and St Clair in Bulgarian Derekuoi were the seemingly innocent errors that the villagers considered grave sins. It was, for example, a sin (or taboo) to let 'a dog sleep on the roof of a house, as this gravely imperils the soul of any defunct member of the family.' In this case the danger presumably lies in a person *happening* to die while Fido is up there snoozing; in such a context it seems very unlikely that he would be allowed to doze on the roof if someone was already known to have died. Anyone who has actually committed this sin may be consoled to know that it was also, among these villagers, a sin to wash a child before it reached the age of seven. For all the local colour of the dog taboo, the basic logic is the same: any living thing can absorb the soul of the dead as it seeks to make its surprisingly hazardous voyage to the next world.

There again, almost every corpse had to be outside when it was buried. And, when commanding his battalion in Macedonia, a British officer, F. B. Welch, heard of a man who died after the Balkan wars of 1912–13. The man's friends were just about to lay his corpse in the grave when 'a large cat ran up and jumped across the body, which promptly vanished.'[14] Noting the prohibition on cats as a Greek superstition, Summers adds that it extended as far as China.[15] Barber emphasises how widespread this fear was in Slavic territory, stating specifically that certain Romanians spoke of black hens leaping over, and others of a bat. He also cites a Greek from the 1960s whose grandmother had told them that 'nothing, specifically nothing animal, bird, insect, or candle, should be allowed to fly over, jump over, or be carried over the corpse because it will become a *vorkalakas*.'[16] A little more vaguely, one of these Greeks said of an unguarded corpse, 'some cat or dog would *go by* and give him a demon soul.'[17] So widespread was this taboo that even in the Scottish highlands a version of it could be found in the 1760s: 'It was regarded as such a bad omen for a cat or a dog to pass over the corpse, that the poor creature must immediately be killed.'[18] In parts of Ireland, such an animal could still meet the same fate in the 1890s.[19]

Just about all of these different causes are in fact united by one crucial factor. You must not let *live* things cross over a dead body.

Again: 'anima/animal' are useful terms here, encompassing a broad spectrum of life which might include animals, birds, flames or lights, and (at least for some Russians) even the wind. Significantly, many ancient words for 'soul' also mean 'wind', with breath being a natural link between the two. In a few moments we are going to learn some surprising things about soul and life in vampire culture. Before we do, let us look in a little more detail at just how serious the crossing taboo could be, and how recently its effects were felt in Greece.

It is a late, warm night in the Greek mountain village of Ambéli. Twenty people are crowded into a single room. Some are drowsy; some already sleeping. Cicadas stitch their incessant tapestry of sound across the still night behind the windows. Cigarette smoke mingles with the steam from coffee cups. In the centre of the room a woman's corpse lies on a low table, a solemn straight line bisecting the loose circle of watching kin and villagers. A small child begins to cry. A woman speaks quietly to him; tries to soothe him. The crying only worsens. Presently his mother nods from across the room: the helpful woman picks up the boy to pass him to her. He is lifted over the corpse and into her arms. Suddenly, the room is shot through with an electric charge of horror. The bristling air of fear and disbelief is so powerful that the child instinctively stops his crying. In sickened confusion, the mother passes him back again to the woman, as if she might by this means undo the terrible damage. But a few moments' fevered discussion with the oldest villagers confirms their fear. The damage is irreversible. The corpse has been vampirised.

Burying it makes no difference. For several nights after her funeral 'the dead woman returned as a great heavy woolly apparition, terrifying her husband and children.' Presently the tell-tale hole over her grave was discovered. 'For three Saturdays the villagers poured boiling oil and vinegar' into this cavity, 'while the priest read the service'. Finally, the evil departed and the village was quiet once again. But the cost of this exorcism was impressively high.

This is a true story. It was told to du Boulay in the early 1970s, and was then remembered 'by all the older villagers'. This means that the event itself must have occurred not much earlier than the '30s (at which point the priest still happily connived in the belief and the associated ritual). And these fears persisted in 1982, when du Boulay published an article on them. At this time the same obsessively cautious rituals were still observed around a corpse.

Although 'Ambéli' is a pseudonym, we know that the actual island in question was Evia (or Euboea). This belief, then, persisted in Europe when I was 13 years old, just over 50 miles from Athens. It is indeed possible that, had I (at age 19) gone island-hopping to the east of Athens in 1988, instead of southwest to Poros and Aegina, I might well have found myself in vampire country during my first-ever visit to the cradle of civilisation.

If all this isn't strange enough, we need also to bear in mind that for the Evians, the taboo was even more obsessively rigid than in most vampire cultures. Du Boulay found that while a cat was seen as especially dangerous, *nothing whatsoever* must pass over the body. A cup of coffee, a cushion, a chair would all have the same devastating effect, and all were treated with appropriate caution whenever they were manoeuvred around the corpse. Not only that, but the revenant which was produced by that luckless child, was, for these villagers, the very worst type of Greek vampire. Other types of revenants which wandered after death might, even if 'depraved or sinful', be regarded with pity, but not with terror. But the vampire produced by the crossing taboo was very different. It would return at once to attack its victims and – most strikingly – would drink their blood. In Evia, the typically mutable vampire accomplished its blood drinking by going up the nostrils of its victim. This action, 'often described as "suffocating"', would eventually cause death'.[20]

We can already see that all this was terrifying to the Evians. It produced not only a general fear but precise hallucinations of that 'great heavy woolly apparition'. The reality of this demon was further attested when, at the graveside, 'those who could bear to' looked into the tell-tale hole in the earth and saw 'the gleaming eyes of the vampire in its depths'.[21] And it was at this ritual of destruction that the most staggering part of the whole tale occurred. The villagers poured into the hole about four kilos of boiling oil and vinegar, a process which was actually known as '"boiling" the vampire'. (If anyone tries this at a dinner party, I take no responsibility.) Typically, this had to be done at a sacred time: 'between the hours of Vespers on Saturday and the end of the liturgy on Sunday morning' – the only time when the vampire was compelled to remain in its grave. As du Boulay rightly emphasises, 'the effect of these actions is dramatic, for they cause the soul, with its demonic power, to "burst" (*skazei*) or "be lost" (*hanetai*); it is extinguished in a moment, and neither heaven nor hell knows it thereafter. Nothing avails, therefore, to undo the harm that has been done, and henceforward no candles are lit for the soul, no remembrance food is made, the long sequence of memorial customs lapses utterly.'[22]

Consider this for a moment. Throughout the last 2,000 years of Christian history, nothing was more indestructible than the soul. At Judgement Day, the entire world would erupt in flames and be annihilated. Yet every single human soul that had ever lived would live on: for eternity. For most of those two millennia, pious Christians accepted that you did not even own your own soul: God did. Yet here, in a little mountain village perched almost outside of time, the humblest Greek peasants could destroy the Christian soul. We can assume that they did not do this lightly. Yet again, the extreme terror they felt can be measured by such an act, which condemned to utter oblivion a friend, son, father, brother or neighbour of this small and tightly knit community. Quietly defying the most sacred, most central atom of Christian belief, the Evians used oil and vinegar to effect a heresy so radical that, in more than twenty years' research on the Christian soul I, for one, have never met it elsewhere. Notice, too, that this was actually *worse* than excommunication. That decree put the soul into a state of limbo; but it could at least be reversed.

As we saw, the vampire's shape-changing powers could be described by the Greek word '*vrykolakismos*'. Similarly (as Katherine Skaris explains) although vampires do not seem to be a great source of fear in Greece today, it is still the case on the island of Lefkada that 'if someone doesn't have a funeral their soul "*vrikolakiazei*"', i.e., 'he/ she becomes a vampire.'[23]

The 'boiling' of the vampire's demonic soul in Evia is remarkable for the way that it so beautifully brings together the wholly ordinary and the utterly extraordinary: a cat, a child, a coffee cup might all flow seamlessly into a demonic realm of mind-numbing terror and of unprecedented heresy. As so often in vampire territory, the supernatural was surprisingly natural. This was a world which was not only animated, but animistic – densely inspired with supernatural beings and powers. And at the heart of this world we now encounter one especially strange entity – a corpse which was not *quite* dead...

The Animate Corpse

For most of us, few things are as clear-cut as the difference between life and death. You can be an atheist, a Catholic, a Muslim or a

Jew: but in any case, you accept that absolute divide between the living and the dead, regardless of where the soul might be headed after this life. Even if the exact instant of death cannot be determined, once medical science has pronounced a person dead, it is as if that person has been switched off. And, if they had a soul, then at that moment it has gone at once, automatically, to heaven or hell or purgatory. But in fact this view of life and death is, historically, very much a minority opinion. For most people, across most of time, the line between life and death was oddly blurred. It was possible to be:

a) alive,
b) slightly dead,
    or
c) very dead.

Clearly this belief is important as regards vampires, who above all things are classed as 'undead'. Across continents and centuries, versions of the animate corpse are clearly visible. In the New Testament world, this was evidently a standard belief. Take, for example, the initial three-day mourning period for the deceased. As Frederick Paxton points out, this 'had its roots in a popular Near Eastern belief' – namely, that 'the soul lingered near the corpse for three days after death, hoping to re-enter the body. Only when the soul observed the face of the corpse begin to change in the process of decay did it give up hope and go on its way.'[24] In the New Testament era, then, it was the body which effectively told the soul to leave.

At the level of biochemistry this makes pretty good sense. Despite our absolute notions of life versus death, a dead body is indeed chemically very active for some time. And the idea of this intermediate period of three days is so widespread across time and space that it clearly must be founded, in part, on basic processes of decay. Under most conditions, a four- or five-day-old corpse starts to look (and probably smell) rotten.

Another piece of evidence sits right there in the Bible itself. In John's gospel, Christ raises Lazarus. When he first proposes this, Martha objects to him, 'but Lord, he hath been dead four days, and stinketh.'[25] Even by New Testament standards, Lazarus seems to be very dead. For the people around Christ, the raising of Lazarus was therefore the biggest miracle the Saviour performed – bigger, even, than his own resurrection, which occurred just *three* days after the crucifixion.

In the New Testament, those who were slightly dead (three days or less) were raised surprisingly often. In the Apocrypha, indeed, a dead person raised just moments since raises another dead person, who in his turn is markedly *ungrateful* for this miracle, wishing that he had been left in peace in the grave.[26] And at that time, for many observers the risen Christ was probably just one among many brought back from the dead.[27]

There is good reason to think that the view of life held by Shakespeare, or by Charles II, was much closer to the New Testament view than to that of educated people in the eighteenth century. First of all, every educated Christian accepted that basic idea about body and soul: the soul gave the body life. It was for this reason that people like Donne and Ricaut could at least begin to *understand* vampire beliefs, which they themselves did not hold. Thus Ricaut stated that the Greeks 'believe that the bodies of the excommunicated are possessed in the grave by some evil spirit, which actuates and preserves them from corruption, in the same manner as the soul informs and animates the living body'.[28] Similarly, Donne had talked in 1626 of how an evil spirit was supposed (by some) to 'inform, and inanimate [a] dead body'. By contrast, Joseph Pitton de Tournefort, the French botanist caught up in a vampire panic on Mykonos in 1700, gave no sense of beginning to understand this. He commented, at one point, that the revenant 'had the severe defect of not being quite dead.' Tournefort was of course a scientist. But more importantly, he was writing in the eighteenth century, when the educated medical understanding of life was increasingly cutting the soul out of the equation.

This still leaves Donne and Ricaut at some distance from full-blown vampire cultures. But there is also very good reason to think that a lot of their peers accepted a graded scale of life and death. Why? Because for over two hundred years, educated Christians made *medicine* out of the dead. There were various reasons why they thought that cures made from corpses would work. But one popular one was simply this: there was still *life* in the dead. And, if you knew how, you could get life from the dead, and swallow it. The best example here is the three-day old corpse. One big advocate of corpse medicine, the medical reformer called Paracelsus, insisted that 'if doctors were aware of the power of this substance ... no body would be left on the gibbet for more than three days.'[29] Just as in the time of Christ and Lazarus, a three-day corpse was only *slightly* dead.

Yet these relatively fresh corpses were far from being the only source of medicine. Bones and skulls were also extremely popular, and Charles II was so fond of making a fluid from human skull for his own medical use that it became known as 'the King's Drops'. Typically, bones and skulls were a lot older than the flesh of a freshly gibbeted criminal's corpse. Yet even these could be held to have some residual life force in them. This was because, in general, northern Europeans believed in the animate corpse. Katharine Park has shown that 'while Italians envisaged physical death as a quick and radical separation of body and soul, northern Europeans saw it as an extended and gradual process, corresponding to the slow decomposition of the corpse and its reduction to the skeleton and hard tissues, which was thought to last about a year.'[30] For the Italians, life cut off absolutely, as if at the flick of a switch. For the French, the Germans and the English (and probably also for the Danes) it gradually smouldered into extinction, like the coals of a dying fire.

The Vampire Corpse

Seen in this light, vampire beliefs are not as outlandish as they may appear at first glance. Both they and the educated Christians of Europe, c.1500–1700, held to a kind of scale of life and death. Ironically, the educated Christians made the belief useful and got medicine from it, while the vampire believers found it terrifying and went to much trouble to fight the consequences. (Notice, though, that however abhorrent all the staking and burning and dismemberment might seem, it was the 'civilised' peers of Shakespeare and Charles who were the cannibals.) What we can also see, quite precisely, is that the dead of educated Europe are divided into at least two basic categories: there is three days, and then there is a year. This again matches vampire territory very closely, save that vampire believers add one more division: forty days after death.[31]

The most definite link between the animate corpse and vampirism comes from Ambéli, where du Boulay was living and researching in the early 1970s. 'There exists in rural Greek thought ... a ... belief that the rupture between the body and the person who inhabited it is not made absolute on death, but is only finally completed when the flesh, as villagers say, had "dissolved" from the bones.'[32] In Ambéli this was expected to have happened within forty days. This timespan was indeed a kind of metaphysical quarantine: after that the body was considered safe from vampirisation.[33]

Why? It is here that the soul hovers back into view. For these mountain villagers held that the soul of the dead person travelled with an angel 'around the scene of its earthly life' for forty days before being 'taken up to God for the judgement.'[34] Such a belief was fairly widespread in vampire territory. Elsewhere in mainland Greece a person speaking in 1962 recalled what their grandmother had told them about the period after death: 'The soul only leaves this world after forty days, after the memorial service at the grave.'[35] Even today on the island of Lefkada, 'although there are memorial services held on the first 3 days, and the first 9, the most important is the one held on the Sunday closest to the first 40 days of mourning … Because it is believed that the spirit lingers around the house for the first 40 days, it is only when the memorial service is held, that they believe the spirit goes on to heaven.'[36]

In Russia, meanwhile, there was no doubt about the persistently animated state of the corpse. For – as Elizabeth Warner points out – 'in Russian, the word for corpse (*pokoinik*) is an animate noun.'[37] Warner found that until quite recently Russian peasants gave religious readings over the corpse for three days – presumably to protect it – and then held the funeral. Moreover, the soul there remained on earth for a total of forty days, 'during which time it is carried by an angel around all those places where it has committed some sin in order to pray for forgiveness.' Although fears of revenants had evidently vanished by the 1990s, one speaker interviewed in 1996 described the forty-day period as though it were a current belief: 'they say the soul flies about until the fortieth day' after which it is 'allocated its place'.

Writing in 1938 Samuel Koenig found severe terror of vampires still prevailing among the Galicians of the Ukraine. In their belief, the soul also remained on earth for forty days, during which time it made nightly visits to its home. The Galicians also considered the corpse to be dangerous for a year after its burial.[38] One Bulgarian version of these ideas – cited by Barber – held that 'the soul wanders on earth for forty days and tries to get back into its corpse, but seeing it in a condition of decay, flies off.'[39] Here we have forty, not three days. Save for that, it is remarkable how closely this belief – apparently still current in the twentieth century – reflects that of the New Testament, where the soul hovered hopefully over the corpse, until convinced it was really dead.

There again, the souls or demon spirits of Derekuoi were evidently far more persistent than those that Barber cites. For St Clair and

Brophy were able, during their stay in this Bulgarian region, to assemble a strikingly detailed vampire calendar. First, 'nine days after his burial' the vampire suspect 'returns to upper earth in an aeriform shape'. This shape might take the form of sparks in the darkness, or a shadow in the daytime. At this stage, the vampire 'is comparatively harmless', merely playing various poltergeist tricks. But, 'when the Bulgarian vampire has finished a forty days' apprenticeship to the realm of shadows, he rises from his tomb in bodily form, and is able to pass himself off as a human being, living honestly and naturally.' Interestingly, in this case the vampire seems to be *more* dangerous after forty days than he was earlier on. And the seemingly odd notion of his passing 'himself off as a human being' is, we will find later, all too horrifyingly real.

In virtually all vampire cultures, essentially the same ideas about death and the soul persisted for hundreds of years. The soul was *something*, and it had to leave the body. But it would not always do so quickly or easily. Even when it had, it might return to its house. In the funeral customs of these regions, everything was done to ensure that the soul left the body and the house within allotted timespans, and – crucially – to ensure that it did not *come back* after any permitted stay had elapsed. As there is nothing like a little detail to make strange beliefs real, let us now accompany the souls of vampire territory on their oddly protracted – often hazardous – journeys to the next world – following them in natural sequence from the deathbed, to the house of mourning, and on to the funeral.

Breathing your Last

The phrase 'to give up the ghost' may now be so hackneyed as to seem merely a phrase. But if you dig down a little, it means precisely what it says: to breathe out your spirit. This was just what Christ did on the cross, 'he ... cried out, and gave up the ghost' (Mark 15.39) and what Christians on their deathbeds did across the world for the next two millennia. Notice, too, that Mark's verse could, to some, give the impression that *the cry itself* physically expels the spirit.

In rural Greece in the early 1980s many people believed that, 'at the moment of death a person's soul (*psihi*), which is described as a breath of air (*mia fisi, enas aeras*) located in the area of the heart, leaves the body through the mouth.'[40] In Ambéli in the early 1970s, du Boulay found that 'to die was (literally and semantically) to "ex-pire"'.

The word 'commonly used for the act of dying' was *xepsycháo*, meaning 'to "un-soul", indicating the process by which the soul is thought to come out of the mouth with the last breath, "like a baby".'[41]

In Macedonia, G. F. Abbott heard of those final moments when the dying man 'is breathing his last, or to use the local phrase, when "his soul is breaking out of his mouth".' At this stage, he adds, 'only one or two of the nearest relatives are allowed to remain by the bedside. Upon them devolves the duty of closing the eyes and mouth of the deceased.' Again, that habitual post-mortem gesture is so familiar that we no longer wonder if it ever had practical motivation. It now seems obviously respectful; perhaps makes the corpse look more dignified; saves any one being frightened by its deathly gaze... But was it, in certain times and regions, actually done to *prevent* the soul re-entering through eyes or mouth? Lawson had noted the custom – still extant in Greece *c.*1900 – of 'paying the ferryman', Charon, with a coin in the mouth of the dead. This, he believed, was 'really a charm designed to prevent any evil spirit from entering (or possibly the soul from re-entering) the dead body.' He also found that in both Chios and Rhodes the habit was still consciously associated with *vrykolakes*. On the island of Lesbos around 1895, before burial of the corpse 'the priest takes a taper, makes the sign of the cross, and lays the taper on the dead man's mouth; else he would become a vampire.'[42] In that case it is pretty clear that the taper blocks the mouth to the potentially invading soul. Barber cites other, less obviously sacred objects or substances fitted into corpse orifices, in places as diverse as China, Australia, the Balkans and Peru.[43]

If the Greek belief about a soul within the heart seems strikingly precise, the Ukrainians managed to be even more exact. Here death (explains Koenig) 'occurs at the moment the soul leaves the body, where it has its permanent seat in a little cavity at the back of the head or neck'. The soul is conceived of as a white lamb (presumably a very small one), a fly, or a golden bird. And, 'when a person is at point of death, the little cavity in his head opens up, allowing the soul to leave, and closes again instantaneously; the dying person, therefore, experiences an extreme headache.'[44]

All of this is practical – typical, we might say, of people highly attuned to the natural world and natural laws; in short, people who deal with *things*, not abstractions. The soul is a thing, and it has to leave at death. So real was this belief among the Ancient Romans that, when someone was dying, the next of kin put their mouth down to suck out the last breath, thereby swallowing and recycling the soul itself.[45] There the fabled 'kiss of death' was a wholly positive thing.

Even on the deathbed, the soul of peasant culture may not leave the body easily. For the Greeks, there would ideally be a clear, clean break. Hence (writes Loring M. Danforth) phrases such as: '"he breathed out heavily three times, and his soul departed"'. Whatever the case, 'the ease with which the soul is separated from the body is carefully noted. It is highly desirable for the soul to leave the body quickly and a smooth passage is interpreted as a sign that the dying person has led a good life.'[46] 'A good man', notes Margaret Alexiou, 'dies easily, his soul leaving the body "like a lamb".' If we set such notions in the context of vampirism, we can see by extension that a soul might linger precisely because the person has *not* led a good life. Alexiou adds, indeed, that 'a protracted and agonised death' could occur because the dying man had 'committed some wrong which is unconfessed and unforgiven.'[47]

Elsewhere, there were other dangers lingering about the deathbed. In the Vologda region of Russia in the 1960s and '70s, people would still refrain from ritual keening in the first hours after death, precisely because, during this time, it was 'considered possible ... to "howl back" .... the deceased. Here, they recount terrible instances of how, when this rule was broken, the dead man was "called back" ... and thrashed about in convulsions for days afterwards.'[48] Alexiou found that a similar belief was current circa 1974 in Greece, as 'weeping and wailing ... remind the dying of the grief he is causing, and so prevent the soul from leaving the body.' On one occasion when women began this ritual lament too soon the supposedly dead man 'with great effort ... raised himself and told them to stop.'[49]

Much of this now looks startling and counter-intuitive to us. But here, as elsewhere, what the uneducated believed in the nineteenth or twentieth centuries was often just what the very highly educated had believed a few decades back. Take the Ukrainians' notion about a little cavity in the head to house the soul. In the time of Donne and Shakespeare, even as a newly scientific anatomy was struggling into existence, various people thought the soul to be in certain ventricles (or cavities) of the brain.[50] Walter Raleigh, meanwhile, wondered if the dying turned up their eyes because the soul was leaving through them;

and on 21 February 1648 the Puritan minister Ralph Josselin recorded the death of his infant son (also Ralph) with poignant exactitude.[51] The boy, Josselin writes, 'died quietly without sobs, or shrieks or sad groans, it breathed out the soul with nine gasps and died.'[52]

A Holiday for the Soul

Once out of the body, the soul was often in no hurry to leave either its house, or the earth in general. In Romania, 'after the burial a candle is still kept burning, incense burnt, and bread and water placed where the dead man breathed his last, for the soul is supposed to linger round the place of death for three days.' After this first phase, 'the soul is supposed to find its abode above the door lintel, and accordingly a piece of linen is put for it to rest on.'[53] Although this account is not absolutely clear as to the second stage, it seems that the soul rests on the lintel until the forty-day span has elapsed. On Lefkada, mourners still today credit this lingering soul with consciousness and sensitivity: 'On the first three days of mourning, family and friends are supposed to congregate at the house and discuss their loved one. Because the spirit is said to be in the house until the first forty days, if they don't do it, they believe that their loved one is watching them and will thus complain.'[54]

There is some sense, however, that the soul's *activity* seems to dwindle across these two periods. At first it is close by, evidently moving around, and requiring food and drink. But after three days it retreats slightly, and evidently does not move. Aptly, it is more restless for three days, and less so afterward. Similarly, in Naxos in the 1890s it was believed that 'when a man dies, his soul goes about inside the house for three days; so you must put a jug of water beside a lighted candle, in order that the soul may find the water when it is thirsty.'[55] And in the Ukraine the soul ate the post-funeral meal with the mourners. Possibly for reasons of economy, it was given just bread and brandy; but these were also put out for several days after the feast. We have no idea who, if anybody, touched them. But Koenig adds that the mountain-dwellers of the area would use a classic mode of detection to capture the soul's footprints, scattering flour on table and windowsill, and, 'in the morning even prove that the soul has touched the flour by pointing to traces which have unquestionably been left by cockroaches and flies.'[56] Over the border in Russia, Warner found that a knife might be placed in the water container to prevent a corpse drinking from it; that a woman might offer her husband food on the day after his death; and that bread, pies and drink were often placed in coffins.[57]

In certain cases, it is clear that the soul had to be actively encouraged to leave its old home. A Greek speaking in 1962 hinted at this, explaining: 'my grandmother used to say that the soul comes out of the body when one dies, but it only leaves the house when the priest comes to read the funeral prayers. The soul may be on the floor, in the air, or it may take different forms.'[58] Given the importance of a priest's ritual prayers in such a community, it seems certain that these (at least for the laity) were seen as a means of *telling* the soul to be on its way. Such a belief was quite explicit in the Ukraine in the 1940s: 'The soul leaves its dwelling place with great reluctance, remains in the vicinity of the body as long as the church bells have not rung; it usually sits beside the head of the corpse, or else perches on some object in the room, such as the frame of a sacred picture hanging on the wall. Consequently, as soon as death has occurred, the priest is notified to have the bells rung.' Koenig adds that, even after this warning (a modern version might be: 'All souls to departure gate 14. Final boarding for flight 156 to heaven and associated regions'), 'the soul, nevertheless, does not start immediately on its journey to the other world, but wanders about on earth for some time.'[59]

Some Galicians thought that the soul lingered for a full seven years, revisiting 'all the places where during its lifetime it did anything good or bad.' It seems likely that there was another, more human motivation at stake here. Simply: death is a big change. Naturally, you need time to adjust – to say goodbye to the world, and to prepare for your voyage. For the Galicians, indeed, the soul had to make a journey of several days on horseback to reach heaven, along a difficult road strewn with obstacles and thorns. It then also had to cross a fathomless sea.[60]

Soul Holes and Corpse Doors

But we are leaping ahead a little. The next stage is the exit from the house. For this, special procedures were often followed, both within and beyond vampire country. Even today, in some parts of Northern Ireland, mirrors are covered in the house after a death. Various explanations are given for this custom, which was seen by Murgoci in Romania *c.*1919, on the Serbo-Romanian border within the last fifty years, and (beyond vampire country) in Brittany just over a century ago.[61] But Murgoci makes it very clear why the Romanians did so:

'When the man is dead, a window is opened or a pane is broken so that the soul may fly out' and 'any mirrors which may be in the house are covered up.'[62] The custom prevented the soul being trapped in a mirror – probably because it had mistaken it for an open window and tried to fly through it.[63] In Derekuoi, the Bulgarians had their own precautions: 'At the moment of death, all pots, kettles, and other utensils are turned upside-down, in order to prevent the soul of the departed taking refuge in one of them, and therefrom commencing a system of annoyance against the family.'[64] Similarly, the Bretons covered or emptied receptacles containing liquids, lest the departing soul should be drowned in them.[65]

The practice of making a special opening for the soul's exit goes back a long way. Piero Camporesi reminds us of how, in 16th-century Italy, the Church officially warned Catholic peasants that it was not 'proper to make an opening in the roof of the house, in the belief that otherwise the soul would not escape from that dying body.'[66] In some cases, the motivation here was simple: you were just trying to make sure that the soul could leave the building. Hence, in Elgin County, Ontario, in the nineteenth century, they had a custom 'of opening the door of the room in which a corpse was lying, to let his spirit depart into the unknown.'[67] For some people in Kansas this lasted into the twentieth century – and, tellingly, was found among those who had originally emigrated from Russia or Germany.[68]

But for those who actively feared vampires or other revenants, matters were a little more complicated. There, the last thing you wanted to do was let the soul out through an open door. Why? Because that door would often be open, and the soul was very likely to re-enter in the way it had left. This was almost certainly why those Renaissance Italians made a hole in the roof: that aperture could then be closed, and the soul could not use it to return. The same went for the broken window in Romania. Once it was replaced, the soul's re-entry was barred. Why else, in either case, would you damage roof or window when many simple exits were available?

The Danes, meanwhile, left the mark of this custom on their houses. Looking at the picture, (*see* plate section) you could be forgiven for thinking that it was the result of some type of Scandinavian window tax. H. F. Feilberg, who first saw one of these bricked up openings in the late nineteenth century, initially assumed that it was the site of an old bread oven. But when he asked the house's inhabitants, they explained to him that this was 'a corpse door'. 'In olden days it had been the custom that the coffin ... was carried out through this opening, which was bricked up again as soon as the procession had started for church.'[69] Although, when writing of this in 1907, Feilberg found the reason for the custom forgotten (people stated simply, 'we have always done so') he rightly concluded that it was to prevent the return of the soul into the house.

The amount of trouble involved in making and then resealing this door attests again to the fear of revenants. Yet we might also add that it was perhaps less trouble than being haunted. Equally, it was less trouble than sealing your ordinary door and moving it, which was what you might have to do when beset by a revenant. Feilberg found that versions of this custom existed among the Swabians, the Russian Slavs, the Ojibway Indians, the Ostiaks, the Chinese, Siamese, Greenlanders, Hottentots, and Caribbees.

There were several other versions of the corpse-door principle – some less troublesome than others, but all with the sole aim of confusing a returning body or soul. In some places a piece of turf or a tile was taken from the roof, just as had been done in Italy. In Mecklenburg in north Germany, houses often had a loose doorstep; the coffin was thus passed *under* the door before the step was replaced. In Sweden, meanwhile, 'all the gates along the road through which a corpse has been carried to the churchyard are hung upside down, so that they open the opposite way.' Koenig adds that in the Ukraine they would shut all doors and windows tightly as soon as the coffin had been carried out.[70]

Like much else in vampire territory, corpse doors are the kind of clue that can be easily missed if you do not know precisely *how* to look at the evidence. Take, for example, the case of Cuntius, from Pentsch in Silesia. Once this notorious revenant had been identified as such (sometime around 1600), it was decided to burn him. Having been originally an Alderman of the town, Cuntius had enjoyed the honour of a burial inside the church. Accordingly, 'there were masons provided to make a hole in the wall near the altar to get his body through.'[71] Neither Henry More, who states this, nor Summers, who cites it, attempt any explanation of that remarkable desecration of a church. But the hole was clearly a corpse door. Cuntius' body could easily have been carried out of the main doors, just as it had been carried in. And everyone in the town must have known about the damage: this was not some private house in a remote country village. But clearly the majority, including those in authority, agreed that a corpse door was essential to Cuntius' destruction. Here as elsewhere, a basic terror of the supernatural won over ordinary Christian reverence or piety.[72]

Attending your Own Funeral

During the First World War, F. B. Welch, the British officer we met earlier, was heading a Turkish labour battalion in the Struma valley in Macedonia. Welch found that there, some way into the twentieth century, 'practically everybody, Turk and Greek alike, believed in the power of human beings to change themselves into animals.' By this, he appears to mean the power of *living* human beings, not dead ones. There were two such men from the village of Homondos who could change themselves into dogs, hares or cats, and who were believed, when in animal form, to carry off cattle or children. The ability to change shape in life is more typical of a witch than a vampire. But these men, like certain vampires, could not cross running water. And interestingly, like the vampires of fiction, they also had sharp white teeth.

Whilst staying in this quasi-vampiric territory, Welch saw the following Turkish burial custom: with the grave still open, the priest (the hodja) laid a plank on the dead body, touching its face.

> He then knelt on the plank; at the same time the bystanders shouted out the dead man's name; and the hodja put his face down close to the dead man's ear, and seemed to whisper something. This happened three times; then the grave was closed. The people say that when the dead man's name is shouted he tries to sit up, but the plank hits his head. The hodja also whispers to him that he is dead; at the third time the corpse realises that he really is dead. The idea evidently is to keep the dead man from rising and haunting people.

Here at the funeral we find an echo of the special prayers or church bells used elsewhere to get the soul on the move. In this ritual, it is told in no uncertain terms that it is dead. Or rather – that it is time to die. As we have seen, there was evidently a surprising amount of choice at this stage, when one was only slightly dead.

In Romania around the very same time, the corpse also took a relatively active part in its own funeral. Murgoci explains that 'during the procession, in all Romanian countries, the dead person is either carried uncovered to church, or holes are made in the coffin, so that he may see and hear what is going on.'[73] Unlike Tom Sawyer and Huckleberry Finn, Romanians did not need to play special tricks in order to attend their own funerals. It is obvious enough, here, that the corpse is still very much animate. But just *why* did the Romanians want it to 'see and hear what is going on'? Readers may have noticed that many of the above customs are actually for the benefit of the living, rather than the dead. They are not motivated by sentimental concern for the dead person, but by fear of him or her haunting their old home. And this is probably also the chief reason behind that uncovered coffin. As with the Turkish funeral, it is important for the corpse to see the proceedings, so that it *knows that it is dead.*[74]

The same logic applied elsewhere in Macedonia. Abbott noted that at Greek funerals, 'the coffin is carried uncovered, a custom said to be due to an old decree of the Turkish Government, issued in order to prevent the clandestine transmission of arms and ammunition in a closed coffin.' But, Abbott adds, 'this explanation is rendered improbable by the fact that the same custom prevails in Russia, where the decrees of the Turkish government would be of little avail.'[75] What, *c*.1910, linked both Macedonia and Russia? It was of course not the Turks, but fear of revenants.

Interestingly, on Lefkada today, 'the coffin remains open in the house and in church until the loved one is buried; the lid always remains outside the door of either the house or the church.' Though uncertain as to the reason for this, my Greek-American informant adds: 'My mother said that it might be to verify that they really are dead.'

Ukrainian funerals, meanwhile, show the marks of one of the most vampire-haunted communities of the twentieth century. The dead person's soul accompanies mourners to the graveyard and returns home with its relatives.[76] After this, the most dangerous period follows. Even though the corpse has been buried, the night after the funeral is the most perilous of all. Accordingly, the funeral vigil persists. Everyone must remain together and not sleep. Next comes the forty-day period. On its nightly visits to the old house, the soul 'enters the room quietly, even though the doors and windows be shut, uncovers the children and rocks them, and sometimes plays practical jokes on the members of the family.' As we saw, after a year, the soul has lost its power to do harm. And at this point its final departure is marked when the priest reads a special memorial prayer, and in return receives a few loaves of bread. These loaves 'must be piping hot, because the soul of the deceased rises to heaven on the steam.' If to us this ritual looks poetically beautiful, to those concerned it was not a symbol, but a practical method – one more extension of all those special doors, holes, or broken panes. Throughout, the logic is the same. The soul is some*thing*, and it has to get some*where*.

An especially unusual illustration of this occurred in 1903 in Hungary. Here the villagers of Tharros risked their lives en masse, apparently inspired by the belief that a rogue soul was going to set up home among them. In early spring,

> a peasant named Barjas, living at Nosztany, died of heart disease while attending the market at Kurd. The relatives started to take the body home, but were forcibly prevented from going through the village of Tharos, the inhabitants believing that the passage of a strange corpse would bring misfortune on the whole place. The procession then returned to Kurd, and next day, escorted by gendarmes, started again for Nosztany. On reaching Tharos the mourners found the entire population gathered in the street, armed with pitchforks and hayrakes. The gendarmes tried to force a passage, but were driven back. They thereupon fired twice upon the crowd, killing two, and wounding many others.[77]

As so often in vampire country, everyone agreed on the danger involved in allowing this alien corpse passage through Tharos. What we cannot exactly infer from that account is the precise nature of their fears. But one fair assumption is that Barjas, in local perception, was at this stage only *slightly* dead. Perhaps if he had been left resting at Kurd for four days, the people of Tharos would have been happy to let him pass through on the fifth.

Surprisingly, another example of such fears comes from Devon, around 1820. Having recently moved down to this corner of south-west England in 1845, the Reverend W. H. Thornton heard of a ghost which had terrified one Mary Stenner the previous night. The sexton of Selworthy Church, John Hobbs, had his own theory on the origin of this restless spirit. It was, he explained to Thornton, exactly twenty-five years since that he and others had been carrying a corpse from Horner Mills to Selworthy. During this journey, 'the handle of the coffin against the head came loose, just exactly to the very spot where Mary Stenner met with the ghost last night.' Accordingly, Hobbs had 'picked up a stone and knocked it in again, and no doubt it [the handle] went into the poor thing's brain, and let the spirit out. Oh, yes! I know all about it.'[78] The people of Somerset and Devon may not have feared vampires, but they certainly understood the dangers posed by a slightly dead corpse, as well as the exact location of the soul still lodged within it.[79]

By now we should have a much better sense of how a real vampire was made. You needed not just a body and soul, but a certain *kind* of body, and a certain kind of soul. That body had not been alienated by medical science. That is to say, any peasant could tell you how it gained its life: namely, through the soul. And the soul itself was remarkably physical and mobile. Not only was it material, but it was to a surprising extent part of the material world: either at risk of being trapped in mirrors and drowned in coffee cups, or inclined to return and haunt its old earthly dwelling-place.

There was of course one other way of making a vampire in such communities. For the spirit which reanimated the corpse was not necessarily *always* the vampire's own immortal soul. In some cases the Devil, or a demon, had reanimated the body. This was sometimes held to explain the bloated state of the corpse, which the Devil himself had blown up.[80] That kind of belief – terrifying as it might be – had one advantage: it allowed the soul of the dead person to have made it to heaven, hell, or purgatory, in accordance with orthodox theology.

But in Romania, as Murgoci emphasises, a vampire was always reanimated by its own soul, not by the Devil.[81] This belief fits with the especially animate quality of the Romanian corpse: both its keen attention to the proceedings of its own funeral, and its evident reluctance to leave the earth. It also helps to explain why Romania had so many vampires. Even to people steeped in magic and the supernatural, visits from the Devil himself were no doubt considered rare. But if every ordinary corpse harboured within it the seeds of a vampire... Given what we have already heard of the death customs of the Ukraine, it is also interesting to find that there too the soul is highly active and (as it were) homesick immediately after death. Within living memory, Ukrainian mourners *expected* the dead person's soul to make 'nightly visits to the house' for forty days: this was the rule, not the exception.

Weighing the Soul

What do all these startling beliefs tell us about the kind of mindset in which vampires thrived? Overall, they show that people whose worldview included vampires did not emphatically split the physical and the metaphysical. These people were surrounded by spirit forces, but these forces were strikingly active and tangible. This kind of mentality often maddened or enraged educated theologians, who derided such beliefs as crude, a gross affront to Christian religion. In fact, when the New Testament is studied rigorously, we find that there the beliefs of ordinary people about spirits were equally practical and materialising. And another way of viewing vampire communities is to say that their beliefs about the soul were in fact relatively scientific.

We can underline this by recalling a famous scientific attempt to *weigh* the soul. Even today, when we are less likely to assert that the soul is in the heart or brain, a surprising number of people will tell you one definite thing about it. The soul weighs 21 grammes. A few years ago this idea was made still more widespread by the 2003 film *21 Grams*, in which Sean Penn's character reflects on the fact that, at death, each body loses exactly 21 grammes. The truth is a lot more complicated. Between April 1901 and May 1902 a New England medical doctor, Duncan MacDougall, did indeed attempt to weigh the soul. At a charitable home for dying consumptives in Dorchester, Massachusetts, he placed patients on a beam scale when they were considered close to death. MacDougall deliberately chose consumptives, as their typical exhaustion made them likely to die quietly, without disrupting his scales. He was also careful to recognise that a body could lose weight naturally at death, through expulsion of faeces or urine (something which he verified by further experiments on fifteen dogs).

Having allowed for this, MacDougall, after weighing a total of six patients at time of death, felt he had enough evidence to at least suspect that a person lost a significant amount of weight at death. But he also stated emphatically that more experiments needed to be made – not least because he wholly discounted the value of subjects four and six: in the first case because nurses evidently interfered with his experiment on ethical grounds, and in the second because the subject was so selfish as to die before the scales were properly set up. MacDougall himself was inclined to think that the weight loss (which, tellingly, did *not* occur in the dogs) was 'the soul substance'. Later scientists wasted few words in stressing how crude the scales were, and how many subtle chemical channels there are through which a corpse can naturally lose weight. Moreover, even MacDougall himself was reluctant to actually publish his (self-confessedly slight) findings. He did so, in 1907, only because someone had unofficially leaked out his ideas, and he wanted to clarify what he had done.[82] The final blow for the 21 gramme soul, though, is even more decisive. Why? Because 21 grammes was actually just the *average* weight, derived from all experiments, combined and then divided by four.

If these really were departing souls, they in fact had *different* weights. It is not for me to say whether a fatter soul was more heavily burdened with sin, or more stuffed with holy goodness. But what we can see from this account is that for probably hundreds of years, vampire-haunted peasants had been taking MacDougall's scientific attitude to the soul. It was something. It obeyed the universal laws of matter (or, at least, the laws of nature as you knew them; and peasants knew these well, because their communities depended on them). To be absolutely clear about this: although MacDougall was open to the existence of the soul, he was defiantly scientific about its nature. If it existed, it must be a substance. A substance had mass, and therefore also weight. So: when it departed, there would be weight loss...

MacDougall, then, had far more in common with illiterate peasants than he did with word-spinning theologians. The latter would tell you, in so many words, that the soul was something and not something; that it was in the body but not in any part of the body... And when they abandoned their ambiguously physical soul, they only did so because medical anatomy had pretty much disproved its existence. In their intolerance of these kinds of scholastic theories, both MacDougall and the peasants of Romania or the Ukraine showed a healthy impatience with words that failed to connect to reality. As MacDougall himself put it: 'One ounce of fact more or less will have more weight in demonstrating the truth of the reality of continued existences ... than all the hair-splitting theories of theologians and metaphysicians combined.'

Having learned how body and soul were kept together in vampire country, we are now going to see how much trouble terrified peasants went to, in order to get them apart.

5

Vampire Scene Investigation

I. SIGNS AND CAUSES

What started a vampire panic? There were three key reasons. One, someone died, and shortly afterwards, they came back. They were seen creeping up to someone's bed in the dead of night. As they did so, they might call the victim's name. But they could also be heard in various other ways. They might knock on doors or windows and call the occupants' names. Not only that, but time and again, from Germany to Bulgaria to Greece, the vampire acted like a *poltergeist*. Two: you made a routine exhumation (as was common in Romania or Greece for religious reasons) and found the corpse to be undecayed. Three: people became sick, usually seriously so. Perhaps several people died in short succession – possibly three or more in the same family.

It is not that easy to separate these three causes, as they would often overlap. But if we do so, a little artificially, we have firstly a cause which, in many ways, must have looked and felt intensely supernatural. As we will see in Chapters Six to Eight, it was probably only partly supernatural – but in such contexts almost no one could be expected to understand the true nature of these bizarre phenomena. The second cause is more or less accidental. The third, like so much in real vampire territory, is robustly practical. It offers a scapegoat, an explanation, and an agreed course of action in response to the crisis and the culprit behind it.

This last was probably the biggest cause of vampire panics, just as it was in cases where the witch was scapegoated for death and disease. But in reality the causes were not so neatly separated. What did a vampire panic actually *feel* like to those involved? Perched comfortably up here in the well-fed, plate-glass, dotcom twenty-first century, we can only feebly recover such a reality. Yet we can certainly see how the different factors might interact. Suppose that the vampire came back *before* any other signs had appeared. Came back, that is, to visit you, up close and personal, in your bed one night... It looked real. It felt real. Sometimes, it even seemed to have teeth. Once you told people about such menacings, there was a good chance that *they* would start to see or hear the vampire too. Evidence also shows that this could often make them sick.

You now had two clear signs, and the next stage was obvious to the dimmest schoolchild. *Find* the vampire... Down in the cemetery, if you kept looking, there was a good chance of hitting upon something which looked suspiciously undecayed (especially if it was winter – which in central Europe is impressively cold, and was colder in the past, during the period known as the Little Ice Age).[1] You now dealt with the vampire – in ways which are partly familiar to us, and in some which are not. In many cases, this *did* make the vampire go away. Several well-documented cases show that people who had performed appropriate rituals then stopped seeing or hearing it, and also stopped being ill.

Another possible combination was more accidental. In certain vampire cultures, corpses or bones were routinely exhumed after a number of years. If one corpse was found undecayed (or considered to be undecayed) then you may have a vampire panic spring from almost nowhere, without any sickness, death, nightmares or poltergism. Beyond these central three signs, there were a number of others – some of which you would be hard-pressed to guess without specialist knowledge. Let us first inspect the three main areas in a little more detail.

The Appearance of the Corpse

We have already seen that the vampire of the peasant world stubbornly refused to conform to the stereotypes of revenant cinema. What was most important in these folk perceptions of the undead was, simply, the impression of persistent *life*. It is precisely for this reason that red skin is more suspect than white, indicating either general vitality, or blood in particular. We then have hair, teeth and nails – all at times alleged to be growing in the coffin of the suspect corpse. As Barber points out, however: 'in reality, neither hair, nails nor teeth grow after death, they merely *appear* to do so. This is because the skin shrinks back as it becomes dehydrated.'[2]

The often cited bloating of the corpse, again, was not a sign that Bela Lugosi, Christopher Lee, or Edward Pattinson had broken the severe dietary clauses in their film contracts, but just one more misunderstood feature of post-mortem chemistry. 'The bloating occurs because the micro-organisms of decay produce gas, mostly methane, throughout the tissues, and this gas, lacking an escape route, collects both in the tissues and in the body cavities.'[3]

Finally, of course, the vampires of certain areas would satisfy the stereotype of the blood-gorged monster. At times the corpse was said to be swimming in it. At others we have the neater, more stylised trickle of dark fluid from those grim yet oddly ruddy lips. This was clearly happening in some cases, given the account of a non-vampire-believer who, in 18th-century Wallachia, saw 'a foaming, evil-smelling, brown-black ichor' welling from the 'mouths and noses' of the exhumed dead.[4] And Michael Bell has emphasised the 'bright red blood' produced by the lung haemorrhages of consumptives. Given how many people died of this epic disease, and how quickly the dead were often buried in vampire country, it is not impossible that this sometimes produced the impression of a blood-drinking revenant.

There is also another possible source of real blood within a corpse. Discussing the notorious 'Blood Countess', Elizabeth Báthory, Tony Thorne carefully examines the behaviour of human blood, in light of the (probably mythical) belief that Báthory actually bathed in the stuff. First noting that a bathtub full of blood should swiftly become very sticky and uncomfortable, he adds, however, that: 'when a victim undergoes a sudden and violent death, the extreme stress experienced just before dying may trigger an overproduction of fibrinolysin, a powerful anti-coagulant agent. The result is that, even hours after death, the blood in the victim's cadaver remains perfectly liquid, so much so that it has been possible to transfuse blood taken from a corpse successfully into a living patient.'[5] This would probably not explain *many* bloody vampire corpses, given that witnesses would have to view the body relatively soon after death. But the physiology Thorne describes does, of course, fit one important type of suspect fatality: the person who had died a sudden, unnatural death, whether through murder or accident.

Decay is in the Eye of the Beholder

A vampire corpse was one which was not fully dead. And one common reason for believing this was that it *looked* undecayed. In certain cultures this was important because failure to decay was a religious and moral matter. It was what you might expect from someone who had been sinful; or, more extremely, someone who had actually been excommunicated. Even if you had no such belief, you could still be sure that the corpse was not dead for a basic physical reason. It was feeding on something, and that something was you, your child, or your neighbour.

Once we start, however, to look more closely at the actual accounts of some of these undecayed corpses, we realise that people sometimes saw what they *expected* to see. On reflection, this is hardly surprising. Villagers were sick or dying. There were strange noises, things thrown around your house. You didn't just suspect a vampire. You more or less wanted to find one, so as to put a stop to all the chaos. So, to some extent, you also saw what you wanted to see.

Sometimes, admittedly, the body did look almost entirely undecayed: some corpses decay very slowly, some spontaneously mummify, some are influenced by the kind of soil or air, or periods of extreme cold. A corpse undergoing the fatty degeneration known as adipocere may appear undecayed to people predisposed to this belief.

But at least five examples suggest that decay was indeed in the eye of the beholder. First we have Ricaut, our British ambassador to Greece. He tells us:

> I had once the curiosity to be present at the opening of a grave of one lately dead, who, as the people of the village reported, walked in the night, and affrighted them with strange phantasms; but it was not my fortune to see the corpse in that nature, nor to find the provisions with which the spirit nourishes it, but only such a spectacle as is usual after six or seven days burial in the grave.

As far as Ricaut is concerned, this 'vampire' looks merely like a partially decayed corpse.

Secondly, and also in 17th-century Greece, we have the vampire named Jannetis Anapliotis, from Santorini. With another Jesuit, and some Greek priests, Richard himself presently viewed Anapliotis' body when it was exhumed. His opinion of the roughly two-month-old corpse was this: 'The head was all black and desiccated, and both eyes and nose had fallen quite away ... the hands were whole' but shrivelled, and 'the entrails also had entirely suffered putrefaction'. Accordingly, Richard said to one of the Greek priests that he could 'see nothing extraordinary in the condition of the corpse, and that certainly it did not appear to me to resemble that of a *vrykolakas*. Another Greek priest standing by responded that, if the heart alone '"were whole and entire"' that sufficed to afford the devil lodgement'.

Not long after this, we have the Mykonos vampire panic, detailed so vividly by one more outsider, the French botanist de Tournefort. Watching the public opening of this troublesome corpse, he tells us:

> the body stank so terribly that incense had to be burned, but the smoke, mixed with the exhalations of this carrion, did nothing but increase the stench, and it began to inflame the minds of these poor people. Their imagination, struck by the spectacle, filled with visions. They took it into their heads to say that a thick smoke was coming from the body, and we did not dare say that it was the incense.

Tournefort and his companions, meanwhile, 'almost perished from the great stench', and tried to assert that, to them, the corpse appeared 'quite adequately dead'.[6] Yet again, for almost everyone else, terror warped this ordinary corpse into some undead supernatural demon. Ironically, even the incense – lit to hide the smell of death – suddenly became a sign of *life*...

In Clausenburg, Austria, about the beginning of June 1844, 'an old woman having died after several other aged persons, the people conceived that she was a vampire, and to convince them that she was mortal, the authorities and the Clergy, exhumed the body, and exhibited it in an advanced state of decomposition. Even then, however, the ignorant crowd were not satisfied, and it was with great difficulty that they were prevented from running stakes through the body to make sure of her destruction.'[7] Although we do not know how long the woman had been buried, we can assume that she would have decayed relatively quickly in late spring weather. What these would-be vampire-killers at the exhumation thought they saw, or thought they feared, we can only guess. But one possibility, again, is that the heart alone was considered enough to harbour a demon spirit. The number of deaths mentioned reminds us, of course, that these people had urgent practical reasons for finding a vampire scapegoat.

Perhaps strangest of all, however, is a Greek case which must have occurred around the 1880s. Eutychia was a New England Greek, interviewed as a grandmother in 1934. 'Some people,' she explained, 'come out of the soil in three years with flesh on, black and half-decayed. And I saw one, and how could I sleep after that?'[8]. This one sight of an undecayed corpse, decades before, stayed with her all her life. But what had actually happened here? In fact, there were no nocturnal attacks or terrors – not even the poltergism seen elsewhere. The man in question was originally discovered through the routine exhumation, three years after burial. But once his suspect state was seen, 'there was no doubt as to his being a *vrykolakas*'. Accordingly, 'the priests had the corpse put in the court of the church for three days, as a fearful example to sinners. The people went by and saw and took warning. People gossiped and soon endowed the man with all sorts of undiscovered crimes. In shame, his relatives had him buried again, after the priest had read many liturgies and prayers over his body.'

This account is remarkable for many reasons. For one thing, even though Eutychia no longer believed in vampires by the time she was interviewed, the *vrykolakas* of her youth 'still haunted her, as one of her most vivid memories of horror'.[9] Most basically, her story is invaluable for the way it so sharply reminds us what Vampire Country was like. It was another country, and this country was not your friendly sunny holiday destination. It was often a place of terror, sin and shame, where the priests, *circa* 1880, actively promoted belief in vampires, and where they took an innocent man out of his grave and laid out his corpse in public so as to increase their own power, compelling the youngest, most terrified children to behold it along with every other villager. Perhaps the most startling thing about Eutychia's memory is this: the supposed revenant had his entire life history *rewritten*, his sins retrospectively invented and applied, just because of the chemical accidents of his corpse.

Sickness and Death

The third main reason for suspecting a vampire was that people fell sick and died. A full list of examples of this would make up a book in their own right. But a brisk scan across time and space is perhaps in order, lest anyone is resistant to this more mundane explanation for vampirism.

Contagious Disease

In Britain, we have a 12th-century revenant from Alnwick castle. With 'this fetid and corrupting body wandered abroad ... a terrible plague broke out and there was hardly a house which did not mourn its dead.' The town's population rapidly shrank and survivors began to flee to neighbouring areas. Although this occurred before the era of the Black Death, various pestilences (often connected with famine) were recorded throughout the twelfth century. This was probably one. The fact that, after destruction of the revenant, 'the pestilence which was rife among the people ceased, as if the air, which had been corrupted by the contagious motions of the dreadful corpse, were already purified by the fire which had consumed it' must (if true) have been pure luck.

Other communities were not so fortunate. David Keyworth notes another 12th-century case, in which the population of Drakelow, in Derbyshire, was wholly annihilated by two supposed revenants. Later, in the Tyrol in 1343 vampirism was suspected during a devastating outbreak of plague. Although the worst of this apocalyptic contagion was over in Britain before 1700, come 1738 we hear of how, in the plague-struck Palatinate of Kamieniec in Poland, inhabitants ascribed the pestilence 'to a cause which is perfectly ridiculous'. Having 'a mighty notion of the power of the vampires, and being persuaded that these bloodsuckers are the only authors of the mortality', they would dig up friends and relatives in order to stake and behead them.[10] Despite these measures, 47 people here died of the vampire plague in just three weeks.[11]

Toward the close of the nineteenth century, vampires apparently still stalked the islands of Greece, carrying fatal disease with them. Paraphrasing popular local beliefs in 1888, the head of a Cretan monastery talked of how 'this monster, as time goes on, becomes more and more audacious and blood-thirsty, so that it is able completely to devastate whole villages.' Between the gloomy plague-struck town of Alnwick, *c.*1200, and the sun-dazzled peaks and shores of the southern Mediterranean 700 years later, little had changed in this respect. The same applied on the island of Evia, where, in January 1895, a recently dead woman was held to have 'caused many deaths'. Meanwhile, over in New England the last-known ritual destruction of a vampire took place in Rhode Island in 1892. The alleged culprit, a young woman called Mercy Brown, was believed to be feeding on her surviving family. In reality, the vampire was scapegoat of choice for the devastation inflicted by consumption – a disease which was held responsible for a quarter of deaths in the North-eastern US *c*.1800, and 'remained the leading cause of death throughout the nineteenth century and well into the next.'[12]

Vampire Bite Marks
We have seen that real vampires could be both fatal and terrifying without needing to bite their victims or drink their blood. But in cases where they *were* thought to puncture their prey, the bite marks, at least, may often have been real. There seem to have been three main causes of these marks. One was psychosomatic: a strange fusion of mental and physical terror produced them spontaneously, without anyone or anything actually touching the body. (More on this in Chapters Six, Seven and Eight.) The second was disease. This can of course leave marks on the body. In the eighteenth century, that early vampirologist, Augustin Dom Calmet, heard of an uncannily preserved corpse that was supposedly destroying its kin near Belgrade, some time between 1711 and 1740. A letter written by a Lieutenant de Beloz stated: 'At the place where these persons are sucked a very blue spot is formed.'[13] Clearly, then, these blue spots were real. And the victims themselves were dying. As we will see when looking at self-produced bite marks, however, it is difficult to be absolutely sure if these 18th-century Romanians died of disease. They may in fact have been killed by fear itself.

The third cause of bite marks was, neatly enough... that something had bitten you. In the early twentieth century the intrepid Edith Durham trekked fearlessly across the wilds of Albania and elsewhere, at a time when many well-domesticated females would not dare ask for the vote. Durham found that in Montenegro villagers would habitually kill moths or flies, in the belief that they were witches (*vjeshtitzas*) in another form. Like vampires, these were held to come through the keyhole and suck a sleeper's blood. The victim grew pallid, caught fever, and ultimately died. As Durham shrewdly points out, in this case the humble mosquito and malaria were probably the real culprits. Something was indeed sucking your blood, and it could indeed kill you...

Other Signs
Greedy Corpses, Nervous Animals
Beyond this central set of signs we have a looser assortment of others. One of these again relates to the quite basic notion of the vampire

needing to feed itself. Perhaps on apples and nuts; perhaps on green beans; occasionally, on blood... but most essentially, on *life* in general. In this it was often more like a hungry animal or zombie than like Count Dracula – not least because Dracula, in stark contrast, would never eat ordinary food. Real vampires were omnivorous, and less than fussy. Beware, then, of any corpses which seemed to be *eating* in their graves...

There were various reasons why people might get this impression. Recall, for example, the rare Venetian vampire we met earlier, with the brick wedged into its mouth because (we can infer) medieval witnesses believed it to be chewing on its shroud. In reality, the shroud probably just collapsed into the corpse's face as it decayed, and the chemicals of decay themselves ate into the material. And, once you had polished off your shroud by way of a tasty appetiser, what next? Well, I think for main I shall eat up the other corpses in the vicinity of my grave, and to finish I shall begin chewing on my own tender limbs. (After which, one wafer thin mint and a stake... *crack!* through your chest to punish you for your greediness.)

Just occasionally, the idea that someone in their grave was eating themself could prove to be true. Calmet recalls how, 'a few years since, a man being buried in the churchyard at Bar-le-Duc, there was a noise heard in the grave; and next day the man, being dug up, was found to have ate the flesh off his arms. This I had from several eyewitnesses. The man, it seems, was stupefied by drinking a great quantity of brandy, and was taken for dead.'[14] Although Calmet's phrasing is not wholly clear, it appears that the man actually *survived* this ordeal (no one else, presumably, would have known about the brandy, so he must have been alive to tell that part of the tale). Then there were those buried hastily in times of severe contagion. During an epidemic of cholera in Florence in 1855, one man escaped from a mass grave, and later claimed that he had felt several other bodies moving around him. Although all dead when disinterred a few days after his escape, several were found to have chewed their own fingers.[15] Beyond such cases, however, it is also clear that the truly dead were up to some strange tricks in their graves.

As we heard, the nourishing repast of shroud, personal limbs, and fellow corpses was often on the menu for the cannibalistic vampires of days gone by. Now and then they could even be heard during church services, munching just below the worshippers.[16] Recall, too, that north German preacher who, *c.*1601, found his sermons disturbed from below the floor by a smacking noise, 'like a sow when it eats'.[17]

This, take note, was a sign which people *heard*. Not only that, but they heard it very precisely – in such communities, who would not know what a greedy pig sounded like? This exactitude alerts us to the probability that churchgoers really were hearing *something*. And, as Barber has pointed out, this was in fact probably the gaseous percussions of ordinary corpse decay, in contexts where there was only very basic, if any, embalming.

Such perceptions, then, make a certain sense. Yet the other sign of vampire feeding is one which again drops us, with a jolt, into the intensely superstitious, demon-haunted past. For as Summers informed us earlier, in Greece 'it was not infrequently seen that the dead person in his grave had devoured all [corpses] about him, grinding them with his teeth and (as it was supposed) uttering a low raucous noise like the grunting of a pig who roots among garbage.' What does this mean? It seems, ironically, to be little more than a bizarrely slanted description of the ordinary processes of decomposition in any given burial ground. To us this process of explanation looks hopelessly irrational, and hopelessly uneconomical. The body which does *not* decay is a vampire; and the bodies which *do* decay are also being eaten *by* the vampire. Not only that, but when the vampire itself started to decay, rather than breathing one great village-sized sigh of relief, the locals were likely to shake their heads and conclude that, having guzzled up the other bodies, it was now reduced to eating itself.[18]

There again, even if we believed that something was eating the corpses, our most likely choice would be an animal. These graves were fairly shallow and insecure, with coffins being rare. A dog or a wolf would have no trouble smelling the body; and the freshly turned earth would be a useful sign for those animals with less sensitive noses. Yet here we are perhaps failing to give sufficient credit to the Vampire Scene Investigators of bygone Greece or Hungary. Animals which fed from graves naturally had to leave signs of disturbance. And, when investigators saw this ruptured earth they, of course, knew *exactly* what was going on – the vampire was leaving its grave in order that it might come and visit them, extending its gourmandising from the lowly realm of corpses into that great human restaurant known as the village (Opening Hours: 11p.m. to dawn – i.e., when all the food is sound asleep...). The chief signs to watch for would be a small hole over the grave, shifting of the earth, and/or tilting of the cross or headstone. Given the vampire's effortlessly protean abilities it could easily have found some form which would allow it to escape through the slightest of gaps.

If there was nothing obviously amiss in the cemetery, those who already suspected a vampire would know how to follow up their fears. You could, for example, take a white or a black horse and get a young virginal boy to ride it around the graves. The grave which the horse refused to cross was home to your vampire. (Yet one more reason, we might add, for young boys to lie about their virginity.)

Interestingly, this procedure seems sometimes to have worked. Murgoci tells of how, around the late nineteenth century, a luckless Romanian peasant, Dimitriu, from Vaguilesti, had more than seven children die. Suspecting a vampire, the villagers took a white horse to the cemetery one night, 'to see if it would pass over all the graves of the wife's relations. This they did, and the horse jumped over all the graves, until it came to the grave of the mother-in-law, Joana Marta, who had been a witch, renowned far and wide.' Now the horse 'stood still, beating the earth with its feet, neighing, and snorting, unable to step over the grave. Probably', the villagers concluded, 'there was something unholy there.' (Cue bad mother-in-law joke.) Accordingly Dimitriu and his son returned with candles and 'went to dig up the grave. They were seized with horror at what they saw. There she was, sitting like a Turk, with long hair falling over her face, with all her skin red, and with fingernails frightfully long. They got together brushwood, shavings, and bits of old crosses, they poured wine on her, they put in straw, and set fire to the whole. Then they shovelled the earth back and went home.'

Even at our safe distance the genuine horror of father and son at that uncanny spectacle is enough to pitch us back into the flesh-crawling candlelight of the graveside. But what of the horse? *Why* did it stop? As even non-equestrians know, horses are sensitive animals. Given their typical duties, it is not surprising that they should respond very finely to human cues and behaviour. Recall, for example, the famous counting horse, Hans, trained by German farmer Wilhelm von Osten in the late nineteenth century. Hans attracted international celebrity for his mathematical feats. These were performed by tapping a hoof the correct number of times in response to von Osten's questions. But investigators presently found that Hans was not the mathematical wizard he seemed. He was in fact responding to the minutest involuntary cues, given unconsciously by his owner. These, such as a tiny bend forward, were so slight that even von Osten was not aware of them. They were enough, however, to let Hans know, time after time, when to stop tapping.[19] If we now map this piece of horsey sensitivity onto the Romanian incident, the answer is simple.

The person leading the horse *knew*, like everyone else, that Marta had been a notorious witch in her lifetime. Inevitably, they gave the slightest restraining cue to the horse, and it responded accordingly. Versions of this must have happened in other cases – as, for example, when the horse's handler or rider knew that such a grave housed a suspect character, or just the last person buried.

Dogs, of course, seem to most of us the obvious creatures for sniffing out trouble, whether from this world or the next. Barber notes, however, that rather than howling instinctively at some supernatural presence, dogs in such conditions might be expected, by villagers, to fall eerily silent.[20] Meanwhile, in the human realm we have that special category of people who could allegedly see vampires, even when the latter were invisible. Sometimes described as 'light shadowed', they had perhaps been born on a Saturday, the one day on which the vampire could not leave its grave.[21]

II. PREVENTION AND CURE

Prevention

We should have realised by now that, when faced with an actively predatory vampire, people were not squeamish about the mutilation, staking, or burning of a sometime friend, child, parent or other relation. Recall, here, the seemingly traumatic duty of Arthur Holmwood in *Dracula*, obliged to personally drive the mercy-bearing stake deeper and deeper into the body of his undead fiancée, Lucy Westenra. In real vampire territory, variations on this task seem to have been a pretty common occurrence. Yet such destruction could certainly be difficult and time-consuming. Not surprisingly, then, there were a large range of measures aimed at preventing the vampirisation of a corpse. Alternatively, there were some surprising methods of merely *tricking* a vampire once it was on the loose. There were also some intriguing ways of curing those among the living who had been potentially vampirised by the revenant.

At certain points, methods of prevention overlap with methods of destruction. For the most part, what we are concerned with here are tactics aimed at: preventing vampirisation in the first place; preventing the vampire getting out of its grave; or preventing the vampire getting into your house in particular if it does get out of its grave.

As we have seen, one tactic was to give the dead man something to feed or chew on. Murgoci found that this was definitely the case in Romania in the 1920s, where small stones and incense might be put in mouth, nose, ears, navel, and under fingernails, 'so that the vampire may have something to gnaw'. Here the navel and fingernails look like convenient receptacles as much as anything; the corpse itself becomes a kind of post-mortem larder, keeping chewable scraps in places where they will not be lost.

Summers tells, meanwhile, of Hungarian peasants arrested in 1912 for mutilating a corpse. After a boy of 14 died in a small village, a farmer who had employed the lad 'thought that the ghost of the latter appeared to him every night.' 'In order to put a stop to these supposed visitations, the farmer, accompanied by some friends, went to the cemetery one night, stuffed three pieces of garlic and three stones in the mouth, and thrust a stake through the corpse, fixing it to the ground.'[22] This case looks like a mixture of practical restraint and magic – the garlic providing the latter element, as it did in many other ways; in the Ukraine, for example, it was routinely hung up to protect a young baby or infant.[23]

As well as garlic, millet seed might be stuffed into the corpse's nostrils, ears and eyes in Bulgaria.[24] Rather more forcefully, Romanian or Bulgarian villagers described by Murgoci used *preventative* staking of a suspect corpse. In Romanian Vâlcea they pierced the heart with a needle, and in Bulgaria thrust a red-hot iron into it. Here the heart may well have been viewed as seat of the soul, or at least as the basic centre of life. But in other cases – as in Hungary in 1912 – a key aim was simply to fix the corpse into the grave, and prevent it getting out. Barber describes Romania as 'the home of ... the "automatic vampire piercing device", which is a sharpened stake, or group of them, driven into the grave, so that if the body seeks to rise up, it will be punctured and "killed".'[25] It is possible that there is a certain open-minded compassion built into this method, for it evidently avoids the trauma of staking your loved one without good reason. If the corpse is not a vampire, it is left to rest in peace, and if it is, it gets what it deserves (loosely, the equivalent of leaving a pre-sprung man-trap for burglars in your hallway at night).

Clearly, though, vampire villagers were often fiercely practical, rather than sentimental, about beings which they considered very real and very dangerous. We can be sure of this because, in that remote enclave of Transylvania in and around Marotinu de Sus, preventative staking may still be happening as I write. Questioned by journalist Daniel McLaughlin about the notorious vampire exhumation of Petre Toma in January 2004, 76-year-old Maria

Dragomir, in nearby Celaru, recalled 'hearing about scores of similar events. A child born feet first or with bits of placenta still attached,' for example, 'carries a lifelong mark of a potential strigoi and, when he dies, knitting needles must be forced through his heart and navel to stop him haunting the living.'[26] Notice that here, the 'scores' of preventative stakings are a kind of Standard Vamping Procedure: the deceased has not done anything evil, or even committed suicide, and no one has been attacked. This kind of guiltless 'potential strigoi' recalls those Greek children, cited by Lawson, who were merely born on the wrong day of the year.

Moreover, while Dragomir was old (and therefore possibly recalling events spanning around sixty years), there seems little doubt that such stakings continued to occur well into our own century in this demon-haunted corner of Romania. In fact, they may even have increased. For, ever since traditional vampire destruction was threatened by the 2007 prosecution of Toma's attackers, in the nearby village of Amărăştii de Sus, people instead drive a fire-hardened stake through the heart or belly of the dead as a *'preventative'*.[27] The implication is very clear. When something is important, people usually find a way around official obstacles. And in this shadowy time warp of Europe, where most villagers 'had learned to kill a vampire while still children', ignorant legal outsiders would not easily be allowed to interfere with time-honoured matters of life, death, and un-death.[28]

One other preventative staking is especially memorable. Carefully respecting the traditional calendar of vampirism (three days, forty days, a year) a young man goes, in the dead of night, to the tomb of the suspect corpse, just before the one year anniversary of death. The stake is about a metre long, and again obeys local tradition, being made from hawthorn. It is driven through the heart. All this, taking place one night in the Serbian town of Požarevac, could have been lifted neatly out of innumerable vampire fictions, or inserted snugly into scores of folklore histories.

Yet when we look more closely at certain details, we start to frown and scratch our heads. For the vampire hunter, as he stood there in the clammy shadow of the vault with the sharpened stake beside him, did not display quite the secretive urgency of Van Helsing or his accomplices, that night in Highgate. With the corpse as yet still unmolested, he took out a mobile phone, and ... rang the police. Stranger still, the police were rather blasé about the whole matter: 'They said "be careful or Milosevic's hand might get you from the grave".'

The corpse was that of Slobodan Milosevic, former Serbian dictator and alleged 'Butcher of the Balkans'. He had died in his cell on 11 March 2006, of a heart attack, during his prolonged trial for war crimes. His attacker, Miroslav Milosevic (no relation), had been a student member of OTPOR, a key Serbian resistance group, whose demonstrations helped topple the dictator back in 2000. As well as being strikingly open about his actions, Miroslav also seems to have been notably practical in his motivations, rather than merely vengeful: 'Entering the Milosevic vault and driving a hawthorn stake through the grave was my duty carried out in the name of the Požarevac Resistance. I wanted to do it painlessly, without conflict with the people who would be at the grave on the day of the anniversary. After I drove the stake through the grave I presented myself at the police station and made a statement to the chief.'

Like hundreds before him across Europe, Miroslav evidently felt this to be a grim and necessary duty. He wanted, we are told, 'to pre-empt the return of the Undead Milosevic's evil spirit to this earth.'[29] Coming to this story cold one morning, those who have not, like ourselves, trodden the darker byways of vampire country could be forgiven for spluttering out their cornflakes. But as we have seen, hundreds of Romanian villagers would have understood Miroslav's actions, and taken what he said quite literally. We might also wonder, however, if the restless spirit of a man seen by many as irredeemably evil had helped to super-charge beliefs that would otherwise be weaker than in past eras. In real vampire territory, a child born feet first, or on the wrong day of the year, was dangerous. An excommunicant or a suicide was still more dangerous; and a murderer still more... So, with a man who had died a sudden and relatively early death, after being allegedly complicit in the massacre of hundreds or thousands, it was probably best to be on the safe side.[30]

Anyone belonging to that much-maligned subgroup, the Vampire-Hunting Pacifists Association, may finally be interested in some non-violent ruses aimed at disarming the revenant by cunning. Barber explains how numerous seeds, including millet, mustard and poppy, might be strewn along the path to the grave, as well as left in the grave itself. 'Usually what is at issue is a harnessing of the revenant's compulsions: he must collect the grains one at a time, and often just one grain per year. This so engages his attention that he is obliged to drop all other pursuits.' He adds that 'the revenant is similarly obsessed, in northern Germany, with untying knots. Often nets or stockings were buried with corpses to provide them – at a rate of one knot per year – with many years of what was apparently an utterly riveting occupation.'[31] Writing of Bulgarians who, not long before 1988, were still painting crosses in tar on their doors as protection against vampires, Mercia MacDermott adds that they would also leave sunflower heads, sieves or fishing nets in or outside their houses – hoping that the vampire, counting in his obsessional manner, would still be adding up when the first cock crowed and sent him home.[32]

Does this kind of tactic say anything about the vampire himself? It seems to imbue him with a certain amount of human personality, albeit a limited and fairly autistic one. We might also, in this light, return to our perennial questions: human or animal? Vampire or zombie? Can zombies count? From what the films suggest, not even calories; while the original Count Dracula, readers will recall, was certainly very good with money.

Cure
Smoking the Vampire
Murgoci found that, in the Romanaţi district of Romania (and evidently not long before the 1920s), the precise destructive ritual went like this:

> The vampire was disinterred, undressed, and put in a bag. The clothes were put back into the coffin and sprinkled with holy water, the coffin put back into the grave, and the grave closed. A strong man carried the body to the forest. The heart was cut out, and the body cut up, and one piece after another burnt. Last of all the heart was burnt, and those present came near so that the smoke passed over them, and protected them from evil.

At one level, this looks like a kind of magical cancellation or reversal. It also has a certain satisfying economy about it. Not only does the burning destroy the vampire, but the smoke of destruction has a further use, whether curative or preventative. Whatever the case, a burning vampire suddenly becomes anti-vampire medicine.

This smoke cure also seems to have occurred in New England. A few years ago Michael Bell interviewed Margery Matthews in her house in the town of Foster. Margery was a descendant of the Young family. In 1827, after she was stricken like so many other New Englanders with consumption, the Youngs buried their daughter Nancy. When other children fell sick, they treated Nancy as the vampire who was feeding on her kin. She was exhumed, and her heart taken out and burned.

From this point accounts vary. But one of them states that, as the body burned, 'all the members of the family gathered around and inhaled the smoke from the burning remains, feeling confident, no doubt, that it would restore them to health and prevent any more of them falling prey to that dread disease.'[33]

Here there is a little detail which gives a slightly greater edge of cannibalism to the ritual. The family, it is said, *inhaled* the smoke, rather than merely allowing it to pass over them. For those who do not see this as cannibalism, try a basic definition: 'cannibalism is the absorption or consumption of another human being.' Or, try this: would you smoke a cigarette made out of human organic matter?

Human Vampires?

Ask almost anyone what vampires do, and the answer will be, 'They drink blood'. The vampires of folklore did not do this, because they were not real. And even those who fervently believed that vampires *were* real often had no idea about this demon drinking blood. Yet at the level of fiction and fantasy, the fascination with vampiric bloodlust must have something to tell us. The very fact that folk vampires were rarely said to drink blood makes the popular image all the more interesting. Do people, for some dark uncertain reasons, actually *want* to believe in this blood-drinking demon? Whatever the exact motivation behind this fantasy, there is no doubt that it gives the revenant of vampotainment a very definite identity. For he or she violates two firm boundaries or taboos. One: they cross or blur the nominally hard line between life and death. Two: they break that basic, age-old law: people do not feed on other people. Those who do are either vampires or cannibals. The vampire may, in the past two centuries, have become far more stylish, well-spoken, well-dressed and desirable; but in many contexts, to be labelled a vampire, even polemically, is just as serious and negative as being labelled a cannibal.[34]

It is now time to meet some cannibals and vampires whose existence you had probably never suspected. For, as Barber neatly put it some time back, 'whether or not vampires drank the blood of human beings, we have most persuasive evidence that human beings have drunk the blood of vampires.'[35] What does this mean? The vampire's blood, or the vampire's ashes, were drunk by way of cure.

If you had mentioned to a European anthropologist in 1827 or 1899 that people were drinking human ashes in water, they would probably have nodded knowingly. But they would assume that you were talking about the cannibalistic rituals of a tribe in South America or Africa.

They would have been far more surprised to learn that this was going on in New England or Romania – right through the nineteenth century, and almost certainly some way into the twentieth. The first instance is again that of Nancy Young. While Bell and his assistant Joe Carroll were discussing the ritual destruction of Nancy's body, there arose not only the question of the curative corpse-smoke, but of exactly what happened to the ashes of the heart. Tellingly, this matter was shrouded in uncertainty. Margery Matthews stated: 'I can remember my mother saying something about the ashes, but I don't remember what that was.' Bell explained to her that, 'in some cases they fed them to someone in the family who was sick.' Margery's husband Charles was surprised by this, and – Bell suspected – 'maybe disgusted'. This in turn makes us wonder if Margery no longer remembered what her mother had said because she preferred *not* to remember it...

There was a similar failure of memory with the otherwise very clear-headed Everett Peck, descendant of the family of our 1892 'vampire' of New England, Mercy Brown. Questioned by Bell about this, Peck could only say that 'they burnt the heart, took the ashes and done something with 'em. I don't remember that stuff there.'[36] Bell himself could only conclude that Mercy's sick brother, Edwin, 'was said to have drunk the ashes in water'. But one thing about this case gives us another clue. In these New England rituals, it was usually only the heart which was burned. Yet in 1892 the family, we are told, burned both the heart *and the liver* to ashes.[37] This was probably because they needed the organs not just for destruction, but for cure. The subsequent drinking was then evidently far less public than the burning – an interesting detail, as it suggests some shame about the swallowing of ashes, while there was none about the mutilation of a family corpse.

Yet there is no such uncertainty or secrecy in Romanian accounts of this practice.

In Amarasti in the north of Dolj [*c*.1899], an old woman, the mother of the peasant Dinu Georghita, died. After some months the children of her eldest son began to die, one after the other, and, after that, the children of her youngest son. The sons became anxious, dug her up one night, cut her in two, and buried her again. Still the deaths did not cease. They dug her up a second time, and what did they see? The body whole without a wound. It was a great marvel. They took her and carried her into the forest, and put her under a great tree in a remote part of the forest. There they disembowelled her, took out her heart, from which blood was flowing, cut it in four, put it on hot cinders and burnt it. They took the ashes and gave them to children to drink with water. They threw the body on the fire, burnt it, and buried the ashes of the body. Then the deaths ceased.

In this account, rather than any sense of shame, we perhaps even have a certain hint of pride: 'We were being cut down one after another, slaughtered by a vampire; but... we knew what to do. And it worked.' Here, as in other cases of scapegoating, the people involved must have felt *empowered* by what they did. They believed they were doing something effective, and they were now active aggressors, not passive victims.

Just in case anyone is still sceptical about the words of those now dead, let us hear from those who are living. As we know, the 2004 assault on Romanian vampire, Petre Toma, caused an international sensation. And to underline the kind of scapegoating psychology seen above (the empowerment, the purely magical worldview) there is no better illustration than this. Writing in *The Seattle Times* in 2004, Matthew Schofield cited villager Ion Balasa, aged 64. Balasa explained that there are two ways to stop a vampire, but only one after he or she has risen to feed. 'Before the burial, you can insert a long sewing needle, just into the bellybutton,' he said. 'That will stop them from becoming a vampire.' But once they've become vampires, all that's left is to dig them up, use a curved haying sickle to remove the heart, burn the heart to ashes on an iron plate, then have the ill relatives drink the ashes mixed with water. But... be warned: 'the heart of a vampire, while you burn it, will squeak like a mouse and try to escape,' Balasa said. 'It's best to take a wooden stake and pin it to the pan, so it won't get away.' If, in all the fact and fiction of vampire destruction, you have ever seen (heard?) anything more vivid than this twitching, squeaking heart, pinned like a frightened mouse to the red-hot plate, then... congratulations. I have not.

Petre's brother-in-law, Gheorghe Marinescu, went on to explain to Schofield that, 'after Petre died, Marinescu's son, daughter-in-law, and grand-daughter fell ill. Marinescu knew the cause was his dead brother-in-law. So he went to the cemetery. The first time, he was frightened, so he had a little graveside drink, for courage. He ended up with a little too much courage and couldn't use the shovel. So the next night he returned, and with a proper amount of courage, was successful. Marinescu said he found Petre on his side, his mouth bloody. His heart squeaked and jumped as it was burned. When it was mixed with water and taken to those who were sick, it worked.' At this point, Schofield adds, Marinescu's wife, 'Petre's sister, interrupted his story with a broom, swinging it at him and a stranger. She was worried that he would incur the wrath of the police, who would jail him. But then his son Costel called what happened next a miracle. After weeks in bed, Costel got up to walk. His head wasn't pounding. His chest wasn't aching. His stomach felt fine. "We were all saved," he said. "We had been saved from a vampire." But how could he be sure his illness came from a vampire?' asked Schofield. The response has the ringing clarity of purely magical belief, its chime as rich as any heard from the sixteenth century onwards: '"What other explanation is possible?" he asked'.

And in a sense, Costel was right. They believed in a vampire. This belief made them sick; and their attack on the vampire, along with the ash drinking, made them well. There is some reason to think that Marinescu, rather carried away with the excitement of talking to an American reporter, may have altered certain facts – partly for added drama, and partly to set himself at the heroic centre of the tale. But the squeaking heart, evidently drawn from decades-worth of previous vampire slayings, was probably authentic. For a heart can certainly exhibit startling behaviour when burned. Some time before 1622, for example, Francis Bacon saw 'the heart of one that was [disem]bowelled ... for high treason' leap, when cast into the ritual fire, 'at least ... a foot and half in height; and after, by degrees, lower and lower; for the space, as we remember, of seven, or eight minutes.'[38]

Although Francis Bacon was a careful observer, it's somehow reassuring to hear what a living doctor thinks of the mousey squeaking vampire heart. When I relayed this story to Dr Steve Schlozman at Harvard, he explained that the heart had probably acted, 'through the confluence of trapped air and teeny valves, as a whistle. As the stake pierced the heart, the thick muscles were pressed down. They are rather unporous, forcing that air therefore out of the only exit it can find, in this case the one way valves of the heart's chambers.'

If Balasa was inventing certain things, then, he does seem to have been on the level about the squeaking heart. It is quite possible, indeed, that he and others noticed this phenomenon just because they thought it to be another sign of residual *life*. Notice, for example, the apparent link, in the above account, between the exhumed Petre, 'on his side, his mouth bloody' and the fact that 'his heart squeaked and jumped as it was burned'.

No less authentic were the sicknesses. We can be confident about these because the sickness of the grand-daughter was also cited in one of the most reliable accounts of the incident, gathered by Timothy Taylor on a 2007 trip to Marotinu de Sus. Taylor stated that, after Toma's death, his niece (Marinescu's grand-daughter), 'suffered nightmares and appeared seriously ill. She claimed that her uncle was visiting her at night and feeding from her heart; that he was a strigoi.'

As for Costel: his symptoms (pounding head, aching chest, bad stomach) hardly sound vague. Again, indeed, they sound in part like a highly nervous imaginative reaction. And Costel, like Toma's niece and Marinescu's daughter-in-law, was cured by drinking the vampiric ashes. Just over ten years ago, satellites gazed down, jet planes passed over Marotinu de Sus – a village in which fear of vampires was so great that it could make you seriously ill. It is possible, in fact, that this uncannily preserved species of fear – one extinct in most of Europe – had the potential to be more extreme even than that. 'What did we do?' pleaded Flora Marinescu, Petre's sister and the wife of the man accused of re-killing him. 'If they're right, he was already dead. If we're right, we killed a vampire and saved three lives. ... Is that so wrong?'. She may in fact have been right about saving those lives. For the kind of fear I am talking about is the kind of fear that could scare people to death.[39]

For much of history, the potency of such fear was also demonstrated by the extremes to which people would go to avoid or cure vampirism. As we have seen, sometime before 1733, Arnod Paole believed that he had been 'tormented by a Turkish vampire, in the neighbourhood of Cassova, upon the borders of Turkish Servia'. For the Heydukes, this meant that Paole had been a 'passive vampire' while alive. Accordingly, he had tried to cure himself by 'eating some of the earth upon the vampire's grave, and by rubbing himself with his blood'. If we pause to think for a moment about this attempted cure, it looks fairly drastic. If you doubt that, try covering yourself in the blood of a corpse (bearing in mind, too, that this blood may well be mixed with other, more or less putrid post-mortem fluids). As far as I know, this has never been seen or imagined in even the most luridly creative vampire film or fiction.

As for drinking the vampire's blood? Given what we have seen of the relatively furtive drinking of ashes, it is possible that curative blood-drinking was often equally secretive. But the examples which exist are certainly vivid.

Vampire Snacks and Cocktails

First (for those who find actual *drinking* especially repellent) we have the tasty Vampire Loaf. This food is high in iron. You will need: 8 ounces of flour, 1 tbsp of oil, 1 tsp of salt, half a glass of vampire blood, and the usual quantity of yeast. Writing in around 1750, Calmet states clearly that: 'it is common in Russia, to eat bread, kneaded up with the blood of vampires.' Ironically enough, while it was probably Russian Christians doing this, Christians had been accusing Jews of such habits for centuries: the idea of ritual bread baked with the blood of murdered Christian children was a fundamental motif of the Blood Libel.[40]

As Bell has shown, the vampirising of the vampire went on a good deal later than the 1750s. A German source of 1835 states:

> In East Prussia when a person is believed to be suffering from the attacks of a vampire and suspicion falls on the ghost of somebody who died lately, the only remedy is thought to be for the family of the deceased to go to his grave, dig up his body, behead it and place the head between the legs of the corpse. If blood flows from the severed head the man was certainly a vampire, and the family must drink of the flowing blood, thus recovering the blood which had been sucked from their living bodies by the vampire. Thus the vampire is paid out in kind.[41]

Here the human vampirism exactly replicates that so often attributed to the vampires of fiction. Flowing blood is drunk directly from the body. The idea of the vampire thus being 'paid out in kind', however, is an educated imposition, and probably a little wide of the mark. Such actions were far more basic than personalised notions of 'revenge'. They were magical, and they were matters of life and death.

In Prussian Poland in late 1870 or early 1871, after a country squire at Roslasin, in Posen, died, his death was 'speedily followed by that of his eldest son, and the dangerous illness of several of his relatives ... The deceased was at once suspected of being a vampire, rising from his grave and sucking the blood of his surviving friends. To prevent further mischief his second son determined to chop off the corpse's head' and paid some peasants to assist him. 'The head was to be laid with the feet, while an assistant collected the blood dropping from the neck in a vessel, to give to the relatives to drink.' Interestingly, there was a clash here between an evidently powerful family and the parish priest, for the latter interfered with the son's plan. It was presently carried out one night, but not without a witness seeing the mutilation and reporting it. The vampire killers were sentenced to three months by the local court, and protested this judgement, around May 1871, to the Prussian Court of Appeals.[42] Can a son commit parricide upon his undead father? This I must leave to a lawyer such as Van Helsing.

For anyone unhappy about quaffing such medicine straight from the corpse's neck, Barber offers a handy alternative from Pomerania: 'dip part of the shroud in the blood of the revenant, leach the blood out into brandy, and drink the mixture to protect oneself against revenants.'[43] One assumes that this tasty aperitif is best drunk with some of the Russian anti-vampire bread mentioned above. It is not clear whether your anti-vampire cocktail should be shaken or stirred. But the brandy, at around 40 per cent proof, would at least have had the benefit of sterilising the blood.

III. DESTRUCTION

Should you ever find yourself in Doylestown, Pennsylvania, with some time to kill, you may want to visit the Mercer Museum. Here you can see a rare Victorian Vampire Hunting Kit. The wooden box contains 'a pistol, two silver bullets, a cross attached to a wooden stake, a magnifying glass, some garlic, and several "serums" especially formulated by the kit's manufacturer, reputedly a Dr Ernst Blomberg. The kit', adds J. Gordon Melton, 'was reportedly designed for nineteenth-century English-speaking travellers going to Eastern Europe.'[44] Reportedly, indeed... For it has also been 'reported' that just such a traveller, Englishman Mark Woodpecker, *shot* a vampire in Transylvania and had it mummified. A glance at the museum's website confirms that this particular kit was certainly a fake. Upon examination by 'the Winterthru Museum Analytical Laboratory' it was found that, 'while most of the components of the kit date to the mid-19th century, certain elements suggest a later timeframe. These include the paper label (*c.*1945), hand-held magnifier, aspects of the cross, [while] the "silver bullets" are composed of pewter. It has been concluded that the kit is actually a product of the 20th century.'[45]

If *c.*1945 is correct, then the kit was probably also a product of the growing rage for vampotainment. Are any of these kits genuine? Solving that question might well be harder than slaying the most resilient of vampires. The trail (points out Anthony Hogg) could lead you to an antique gun dealer, Michael de Winter, who claims to have invented the kits in around 1970, as a way to shift less profitable firearms and spice up his stall in London's Portobello Road. Or it could lead you to people who paid startling prices for such kits at auction.[46]

The good news is that we do not need to solve this conundrum just here. Even if the kits were genuine, they still come under the heading of vampotainment. Why? Because, if any were made in the nineteenth century, they were for wealthy playboys who did not actually believe in vampires. If you showed such a kit off in the village bar in Kring or Kisilova or Derekuoi a hundred odd years ago, there was a slight chance that you may win a few murmurs of approval or curiosity. But when you explained that it – with its wood, leather, steel, brass, ivory, glass, iron, mother-of-pearl, and felt – had actually *cost* more than the entire village... (which itself of course is nothing to paying vastly more for such a kit *c*.1980 or so, and never taking it out of your house). There again, even if it cost no more than a good bottle of local plum brandy (for which you were of course paying as you propped your tweed-clad elbow on the bar) there would be further problems. Where were the millet seeds? Where were the tools required for heavy-duty decapitation and dismemberment? Where were the flint and the vast quantity of wood and pitch needed for igniting and burning eleven corpses? And the bottle for bottling the vampire...? The brandy would be long gone before the questions were over.

What use, then, is a Vampire Hunting Kit? For us, it is at least a very useful symbol. One neat compact box, with everything you need to kill a vampire... Wrong. The items required would often fill a Vampire Hunting Truck (or cart), and they would vary considerably from one region or epoch to another. Not only that, but in places where a fair-aged adult might see scores of vampires despatched in their lifetime, there was one central rule of Vampire Destruction. It had to be *practical*. You, the unaided, probably isolated villagers, had to be able to achieve it effectively with the materials you had to hand. You may call on a priest, but they could be expensive. (Compare the Greek who *c*.1962 remarked that a bishop 'must kneel in front of the grave while reading the exorcisement', adding: 'but a bishop does not kneel easily; indeed, he needs £15 to do it'.)[47] And as time wore on, the last thing you were going to do in the midst of a life-or-death crisis was wait for the next auction, travel three days to buy the kit, and draw unwanted attention to your activities amongst those outsiders who viewed your handiwork as criminal mutilation. But the fact that such rituals were often relatively homely should not distract us from a second key rule: if need be, you were certainly prepared to be ruthlessly thorough. If the problem persisted... so did you.

And this brings us to a third basic rule. *Why* did the problem persist? In some cases, it was because there was an epidemic of fatal contagion cutting down your family and friends. In others, the initial fears of vampirism might have arisen because villagers had been having nightmares about the last dead person. During this highly nervous communal terror, there could also be vampire poltergism exploding across the village. After the first staking, most people recovered (because they expected to), and the poltergism more or less stopped (because fear had been causing it). But for some especially nervous sufferers both the nightmares and the poltergism continued. So they kept going, and these last victims were finally reassured; finally calmed down; and thus finally caused the problems to stop. So our third rule, interestingly, is that, in a lot of cases, the Vampire Destruction could *actually work*. Stake, chop, burn, drown, bottle... If it seemed convincing, then it might well do the trick – not least, as we have said, because it also gave them a sudden feeling of power.

Staking

Let us begin with probably the most familiar method, before going on to decapitation and dismemberment, and thirdly to cremation. After these three (sometimes overlapping) techniques we will find a surprising number of others. We shall try to get through them briskly.

At least the staking is straightforward. By now there can scarcely be a modern child who has not seen it done on film or cartoon. There again... are you going to use ash, oak, hawthorn, aspen, or wood from a wild rose tree?[48] (And if there is an argument about which type as you stand in the midst of some especially well-timbered glebe, which know-all will claim that their stake is made from the same wood as Christ's cross?) Or – if in Dalmatia – perhaps a consecrated dagger, thrust into the vampire by a youth who has just taken confession and Holy Communion? And where exactly is it going? Heart, head, or navel? If it is the head and you are in Russia, you may need to check first that the vampire's mouth is open. If it is, you then thrust the stake into the mouth – something which (Barber found) various Russian peasants did to a dead girl called Yuschkov in 1848.[49] In Zărneşti in Romania you would jam iron forks into the heart, eyes and breast, and bury the corpse face down for good measure.[50]

In the matter of personal corpse staking, I will assume readers innocent unless proven guilty. But one does not have to have actually attempted this to realise that even a quite well-decayed corpse has a ribcage. And, as we saw in the town of Kring in 1672, when the hawthorn stake was raised, 'as often as they strove to drive it through the body the sharpened wood rebounded, and it was not until one of the number sprang into the grave and cut off the vampire's head that the evil spirit departed with a loud shriek and a contortion of the limbs'. This may have been a stubborn rib, or possibly just a body peculiarly swollen and stiffened with corpse gases. During the vampire panic on Mykonos, the butcher had trouble enough even finding a heart. We have other evidence, moreover, that staking through the heart was often not the satisfyingly stylised process shown on celluloid. It was often asserted that the vampire must be killed by a *single* blow of the stake, as a second would reanimate it. This almost certainly implies that villagers quite frequently failed to achieve this clean fatal thrust on first attempt.

One's Vampire Staking Standard Procedure would probably also be affected by another basic question. Just *why* were you staking the corpse? Perhaps to drive out the soul or the Devil. Perhaps to pin the vampire into its grave. Or possibly just to make the body unfit for further vampirising: 'In Serbia and Bulgaria a nail should be put in the back of the neck, as well as a stake through the heart, so that the Devil who means to use the body as a vampire may not be able to distend the skin.' Barber cites the same motivation among the Serbo-Croatians, who aimed simply to wound the corpse, thus 'frustrating the intention of the Devil to blow up the corpse and cause it to become a vampire'.[51] This logic nicely captures the now vanished mixture of homely pragmatism and otherworldly terror once fused into the body of a vampire corpse; on one hand, the Prince of Darkness himself; on the other, a technique as easy as puncturing a football...

Forensics and Folklore
From the whys, we come next to the question of what happened during the staking. Ever since the 14th-century Vampire of Blow offered cheeky backchat to those who staked him to the ground, witnesses have claimed to hear cries from the ruptured corpse. When the villagers of Kring were thwarted in their attempts to puncture Grando's unhallowed chest, 'one of the number sprang into the grave and cut off the vampire's head', at which point 'the evil spirit departed with a loud shriek and a contortion of the limbs'.[52] A few decades later, the corpse of Arnod Paole gave 'a hideous cry' when staked.

We have heard from a highly reliable clinical source that a vampire heart could indeed 'squeak like a mouse' when punctured. Those staking Paole may have produced this kind of sound when the stake pierced the heart; or the noise may simply have resulted from the sudden rush of escaping corpse gases. And Grando? Although the heart cannot have been involved, the sudden severing of the neck was again a kind of puncture. If we assume that a lot of trapped gas then shot out 'with a loud shriek', we can also see why this was accompanied by 'a contortion of the limbs'. Far from doing anything supernatural, the body was merely obeying ordinary laws of action and reaction as the gases were displaced, and muscles and tissues experienced sudden changes of pressure and tension. Recall, too, another possibly significant detail about Paole. His corpse was then decapitated after the staking. At this point no cry was recorded. This could be seen as implying a certain accuracy on the part of bystanders: terrified and superstitious as they are, the 'cries' they describe seem to happen when they ought to. By contrast, at the beheading Paole's corpse does *not* cry, because the gases have *already* escaped.

Those readers who managed to figure all this out without being told (and are eagerly thrusting up their hands) must be warned that this alone would not secure one a Vampire Hunter's BSc. Back in the eighteenth century even Calmet had worked out that the sudden expulsion of air could easily produce this kind of sound.[53]

Having said that, we perhaps need to think a little bit harder about *precisely* what kind of sound the corpse would make in Vampire Country. Ultimately, this depended on who was listening. Just as a perhaps badly decayed body *looked* 'undecayed' to terrified villagers, the audible response to staking almost certainly sounded very different if you believed that beneath you was one of the Undead. This kind of auditory gestalt may even partly explain how highly nervous onlookers claimed to hear the Vampire of Blow actually *speaking* to them.

To recover that exact vampire cry, then, we would need the actual mind of a traumatised vampire hunter between our ears. But we can readily guess that this rush of ejected air made sweet music for the bystanders. All else aside, it *proved* that you had a vampire before you, not just any harmless corpse. And the same of course went for the spurt of blood that might also greet the thrust of the stake.

We saw this in Kisilova, where the staking of Plogojowitz prompted 'a great quantity of fresh, ruddy blood' to spurt from the wound, and from nose and mouth. Again, there was apparently some subjective perception here: did they see blood, or was it just some suitably coloured post-mortem fluid which answered for it? As Barber astutely points out, real corpse blood *could* be unusually dark, owing to its lack of oxygen.[54] But at another level what mattered was that the bystanders *thought* the spurting fluid to be blood, whether it splashed from the chest or the ruptured neck. This mattered not just because it offered proof, but because this blood in particular was powerful. It could be positively powerful, given its medicinal use when drunk; or it could be negatively powerful. Before staking or decapitation, a corpse might be covered with earth or a cloth, given that, in some parts of vampire territory, anyone splashed with it would either be killed or go mad.[55] Yet again, we find here that Vampire Life is less stylised than Vampire Art: blood does not obediently jet out in neat convenient patterns (perhaps, in the lower sort of vampire B-movies, splashing the camera but not one's face). It is messy, and could be deadly.

Before we cast aside our stake and gather up the tools of decapitation we should note the famous 18th-century assault on the figure now claimed to be Serbia's first vampire, Sava Savanovic. Some of you may have heard of him fairly recently, as he was said to have become newly restless in December 2012, some time after his watermill home in Zarožje fell down. But *why* was he still haunting people, more than 200 years after he was staked? It was said that, just as the stake pierced him, a butterfly shot from Sava's mouth. Given the vampire's shape-changing abilities, a mere butterfly had to be taken seriously – at least as seriously as those vampire moths which, in Transylvania, were carefully pinned (or staked) to the wall.

Decapitation

Here as elsewhere, no Vampire Hunting Kit required (even if it had contained an axe, which most apparently did not). Barber notes the use of spades for beheading, and the same kind of rule evidently prevailed with other kinds of dismemberment.[56] We can well imagine that beheading with a spade was not a clean or stylish piece of work. But ultimately, after some hacking, sawing and straining, it was pragmatic and effective. Get the job done, with whatever tools you have to hand. In this respect, matters perhaps changed little over hundreds of years. When Timothy Taylor asked Niculae Pedescu in Marotinu de Sus what they had used to extract

Toma's heart, his informant 'looked at me as if I was mad, before brandishing his scythe again'.[57]

The main things one needs to behead a corpse, in reality, are strength and determination – bringing us back again to a second key rule of Vampire Destruction: if necessary, be ruthlessly thorough. And this, at times, means that you cannot afford to be squeamish or sentimental. Witness two remarkable cases, both from Prussia. Writing in 1895, the American author George Stetson relates how, fairly recently, '"at Peukuhl, a small village in Prussia, a farmer died last March. Since then one of his sons has been sickly, and believing that the dead man would not rest until he had drawn to himself the nine surviving members of the family, the sickly son, armed with a spade, exhumed his father and cut off his head"'.[58]

Next, we have Barber, reporting from vampire-struck Posen. Here in 1913 a man was brought to court after beheading his own dead mother, Eva, and putting the head at her feet. This had occurred around two-and-a-half years before the trial, when, in the aftermath of her death, seven more family members died, and the defendant himself fell badly ill. After the beheading, the son recovered. The court heard that 'he believes firmly that by doing so he saved his life.' Here, then, the solution worked, if only by luck (and thin luck from an outsider's point of view, after seven deaths). But that perception would have been shared, also, by the evidently large 'number of people … especially of evangelical faith' who had first advised the son of the appropriate remedy.[59]

Another case from the same year suggests slightly more squeamishness. At Putzig near Danzig, 'on midsummer night two relatives of a woman who died three years ago persuaded some workmen to exhume the corpse, decapitate it, and lay the head at [the] feet. Their belief was that by this means they would stay mortality in the family, of which nine members have died during the last three years.' Here the unnamed relatives (who could have been male or female) appear to lack the determination to carry out the beheading themselves – although they may, of course, merely have been elderly and infirm.[60]

The Posen case reminds us of our third central rule: sometimes, the Vampire Slaying *works*. Such cases of partial luck were perhaps relatively rare. But they would probably be remembered in the way that superstitious or religious people tend to remember exceptional positive cases: that is, out of proportion to their statistical significance. These successes stood out in village memory, while the many failures faded into oblivion. But if the vampirism in question involved nightmares and poltergism, the attack often worked because you expected it to work. And in the precise case of beheading, there was probably a common-sense feeling that even a demon soul could not operate a corpse without a head. At very least, it would have to find another one: whether or not the film exists, we can be pretty certain that there were no Headless Vampire Horsemen in real vampire country.

And this is fairly surprising, given how fanciful certain accounts of vampire decapitation could be... Calmet heard, for example, of a Moravian village called Liebava, in which, during the 1740s, a vampire 'had often disturbed the living in their beds at night ... had come out of the cemetery, and had appeared in several houses'. Finally, the vampire's

> troublesome visits had ceased because a Hungarian stranger, passing through the village at the time of these reports, had boasted that he could put an end to them, and make the vampire disappear. To perform his promise, he mounted on the church steeple, and observed the moment when the vampire came out of his grave, leaving near it the linen clothes in which he had been enveloped, and then went to disturb the inhabitants of the village. The Hungarian, having seen him come out from his grave, went down quickly from the steeple, took up the linen envelopes of the vampire, and carried them with him up the tower. The vampire having returned from his prowlings, cried loudly against the Hungarian, who made him a sign from the top of the tower that if he wished to have his clothes again he must fetch them; the vampire began to ascend the steeple, but the Hungarian threw him down backwards from the ladder, and cut his head off with a spade. Such was the end of this tragedy.[61]

Indeed. Were this ever filmed, we must hope that the censor would stamp a resounding 18 certificate upon it – horror is one thing, but naked vampires, in the lingering Puritan territories of Britain and America, are quite another.

Prudery aside, what does this tale tell us? First, it shows us that there are limits to vampire forensics. Yes, the corpse screamed when staked; had blood inside it or at its mouth; had oddly long nails, and so forth. But certain things that vampire villagers tell you about simply *did not happen*. At the same time, this does not mean that we should simply ignore such wayward claims. For other evidence suggests that *something* did happen to prompt this story. What was it? The second use of the tale is that it shows how powerful certain skeleton keys can be when seeking to break into the otherwise hermetically sealed corridors of the great Vampire Mystery Mansion. Even a tale as fanciful as this can be unlocked and understood, if you know the way into it. The basic point to grasp is that, first, the villagers probably *did* see something in their rooms at night. They had very good reason to be frightened of it, and you too would be gibbering with terror if it came into your room. (Don't argue – at least not until you have read Chapters Six and Seven.)

Next, enter the Hungarian. There are two plausible ways of looking at his tall tale. One: everyone was so utterly terrified of the vampire that they were all locked indoors (was it day or night? we are simply not told) and saw nothing. The roving Vampire Killer was therefore free to make it all up when they crept out of their houses. Two: they all gathered at a suitably cautious distance to watch the exploits described above. Yes, really. There really was a ladder, and the Hungarian really did have the grave clothes, as well as that (notably authentic) spade. But: the vampire was … *invisible*. This would have been readily accepted by the villagers. Recall that 'light-shadowed' people could see invisible vampires, for example. The Hungarian may well have claimed to have had such powers.

Whichever line we take here, we can readily guess that the Hungarian's biggest skill, aside from sheer invention, was a gift for drama. If he merely told the tale, he had to be dramatically convincing. And if he really *acted* it, he had to be even more convincing. (It is just possible, of course, that he actually believed the whole thing himself – in which case he would have been effortlessly convincing.) Throughout history, successful magicians have had charisma. An early example was Christ. Like the numerous other magicians around him claiming to drive out devils (almost always held responsible for sickness at that time) he was often effective just *because* people believed in him.

Another application, then, of our third rule. Sometimes the killing *works*. In this case we might be surprised that something so ludicrous could work. But we should also remind ourselves that, if the villagers had seen this apparently farcical Vampire Pantomime (catch line – 'where are my vamping trousers?') then, for them, the sheer breathless daring and elaborateness of the spectacle may also have been usefully cathartic (which, in a strange way, is after all what horror films are for us.)

I hope that anyone about to interview for the job of Travelling Vampire Killer has gained some useful tips from the above. One other interesting thought before we quit Liebava and rummage out the matches, wood and pitch. Whatever we might believe about this story, we can tell that it was plausible for the villagers. And this means that their vampires perhaps had a certain strange degree of *personality* – they could get either angry or embarrassed about the stealing of their clothes. Here, then, the vampire has enough human character to wrench himself away from the dehumanised zombie. Admittedly he does not have enough sense to see what is coming: namely, that anyone rushing up a propped ladder is highly vulnerable to the person at the top.

Burning

Ever since the discovery of fire, any criminal or victim of magic could tell you that, if you really wanted to get rid of something, you should burn it. In the first case there is little left for the forensics men; and in the second there is the magical power of purification, on one hand, along with a sense that now the witch or Devil has nothing left to work with.

And yet... there is more than one way to burn a vampire. At times immediate and outright burning was indeed the standard procedure, as with the revenant of Melrose Abbey or the Bohemian Vampire of Blow. But around these impressively decisive wholesale cremations, vampire country was littered with circling fires of a far more modest or reluctant character. On Mykonos, on New Year's Day 1701, the traumatised islanders were driven to burning after all else had failed. Only then, when 'whole families ... were packing up, with the intention of retiring to Syra or Tinos' did the Greeks carry the vrykolakas, 'by the order of the administrators, to the tip of St George's Island, where a great funeral pyre had been prepared, with tar, out of fear that the wood, as dry as it was, would not burn fast enough for them on its own'. Once convinced of the necessity of this cremation, the islanders were cautious enough to now burn the revenant on a different, uninhabited, island.

A similar cautionary thoroughness was often on display further north. As we heard from Murgoci, the Romanian vampire might first be carried away to the forest before burning. Even then, 'the burning must be complete. If the smallest piece of bone remains unburnt, the vampire can grow up again from it.'[62] This idea was consistent, of course, with the mobile resilience of the demon soul that galvanised the revenant. A spirit could easily inhabit a scrap of bone – just as it could make its home in any of the birds or insects which, during a wholesale cremation, would be ruthlessly driven back into the fire, lest the vampire lurked in one of them.

As Barber has rightly emphasised, it is very hard to burn a whole body without modern industrial technology – not just because of the inferior heat of an open-air fire, but because it can be difficult to burn the lower part of the corpse, where oxygen is not circulating.[63] Hence the way that the Romanians, in the above case, cut the corpse up beforehand. And hence, too, the common technique of burning only the heart (and perhaps liver and lungs). As we will see, this was pretty much the universal destructive method in New England. When it was used in Romania, the vampire killers usually drank the ashes; but if they did not, they would be sure to cast them into a river.[64] Again, even after the catharsis of fire, it is crucial to get any remnants as far away as possible.

It has been stressed that the burning of the revenant was a particularly Greek habit; and these destructive fires were still being torched in the early twentieth century. Having spent around two years in Greece between 1898 and 1900, Lawson could state that he had 'heard *vrykolakes* mentioned ... with a very present and real sense of dread' in 'villages on the west slopes of Mount Pelion, the village of Leonidio on the east coast of the Peloponnese, Andros, Tenos, Santorini, and Cephalonia'. At Santorini in 1899 he was told that the inhabitants of Therasia had lately burnt a *vrykolakas*; while another such case occurred near Patras in 1902.[65]

Writing in 1923, Edith Durham found that a vampire had been incinerated a few weeks before in Bosnia. By that stage, both civil and church authorities would often be less co-operative about such rituals. But if you did feel the need to be cautious, or simply lacked the resources for a full burning, there were interesting variants on offer. The Greeks tended to use the word 'burn' for other destructive practices. The priest's formula, reversing an excommunication, could be described as 'burning' the corpse. Alternatively, as we saw in Ambéli, around the middle of the twentieth century, you might 'boil' the vampire.[66] Recall that this involved pouring a mixture of boiling oil and vinegar through a hole in the grave.[67] This had at least two advantages. One: it suited the homely limits of people without great resources. Two: you did not have to even look at, much less touch, the evil corpse within. This was clearly no small matter, given that few villagers would dare even peer through the hole to see 'the gleaming eyes of the vampire in its depths'.[68]

Anyone who feels rather disappointed with this kind of low-key annihilation might like to hear about an impressively high-profile, daring and dramatic vampire burning that took place in the Carpathian Mountains in 1909. And anyone still not satisfied will hopefully be appeased when they learn that the vampire in question was also (wait for it) a *Count*... Although detail (the Count's name or that of the adjacent village) is sadly lacking, the report, from a Viennese newspaper in June that year, looks authentic. As Summers informs us, the incident arose, not because the locals had got their hands on a copy of *Dracula*, but because people were dying like flies. The dead 'Count B---', reputed as a vampire, was believed to be haunting the castle, and this was burned accordingly. Dramatic as this must have been, it seems that no one was hurt: by this stage the lonely fortress sheltered just a caretaker and his wife, with the usual number of bats, rats and spiders. Summers fails to tell us what was done with the castle's ashes.[69]

Bullets, Bottling, and Bread Monitors

If anyone is still under the illusion that vampires can be killed only by silver bullets or sunlight, a brisk dash through other methods of disposal might be useful. You could try to hasten decomposition by using quicklime, or dispose of the body in water.[70] This last custom was said to be typical in Russia, while Barber notes that the 'bog bodies' recovered by archaeologists may also have been suspected revenants.[71] Others believed that the vampire could not cross water, or – in the case of the Greeks – salt water. Recalling the Greek habit of taking the corpse to another (presumably uninhabited) island, Murgoci compares it to the practice, in Romanian Mehedinți, of simply carrying the body away to the mountains.[72]

One source claims that in the Crimea revenants were disabled by either decapitation or shooting into the body, and Barber cites a Hungarian custom of firing rifles into the grave.[73] In Bulgaria we have the much-beloved silver bullet shot into the vampire corpse; but MacDermott, mentioning this, lists it as just one of many things which, when added up, one would have trouble cramming into the neat and polished Vampire Kit. Rather like some Greeks, the Bulgarians might pour boiling water, or boiling wine and oil into the grave. They might put in blackberry, thorns or hawthorn, or deter the vampire with wild roses, garlic, tar, salt or salt grinders, or various Christian objects.[74] Fans of Stephenie Meyer may be pleased to hear that wolves were powerful enemies of Bulgarian vampires. Another enemy was thunder or lightning. As in Greece, a thunderbolt (i.e., lightning) could kill a vampire, while a good late spring storm offered a kind of wholesale Vampire Clear-out, destroying all of them, so that 'they presented no problem in summer.'[75]

Two other particularly interesting Bulgarian practices are found in the ever-startling collection of habits encountered by those veteran Balkan travellers, Brophy and St Clair. First: any really determined Victorian vampire-hunter would need to somehow carry with him on the slow and arduous journey through central and southern Europe not just stakes, gun and mallet, but... a load of old shit. For this was a key ingredient in the 'Ilatch (literally, medicine), administered by the witch or some other wise woman' of the Bulgarian village. Having detected a vampire by the hole in his grave, she then 'stuffs it up with human excrement (his favourite food) mixed with poisonous herbs'. At one level this seems to obey the simple logic that the vampire is undead, and must be killed. If poisonous herbs kill ordinary people, they will kill him. At another it very possibly follows the logic of so many vampire-killing confidence tricks: people believe in what the witch is doing, because, in reality, animals come and eat the excrement, giving the impression that the vampire has actually done so.

For the second trick you will need that brandy bottle which the locals emptied so efficiently while peering into your Vampire Hunting Kit. And, before you start applauding this much cleaner method of destruction, you should be aware that you will also need to fill it with excrement. For, as St Clair explains:

There is yet another method of abolishing the vampire, that of *bottling* him; there are certain persons who make a profession of this ... the sorcerer, armed with a picture of some saint, lies in ambush until he sees the vampire pass, when he pursues him with his Eikon; the poor Obour [vampire] takes refuge in a tree or on the roof of a house, but his persecutor follows him up with the talisman, driving him away from all shelter, in the direction of a bottle specially prepared, in which is placed some of the vampire's favourite food [i.e., excrement]: having no other resource, he enters this prison and is immediately fastened down with a cork, on which is a fragment of the Eikon. The bottle is then thrown into the fire, and the vampire disappears forever.

St Clair takes this to mean that the sorcerer has bottled and burned the vampire's spirit. He goes on to object indignantly that 'this method shows the grossly material view of the soul taken by the Bulgarians, who imagine that it is a sort of chemical compound ... destructible by heat.'

Like many other gentlefolk of his day, St Clair knew little about the real beliefs of the British lower orders – or, indeed, those of certain British priests around the time of his birth. For – permitting ourselves a well-earned detour out of vampire country – we must here remind him that ghosts were being bottled up some way into the nineteenth century in Shropshire and Montgomeryshire. Speaking not long before 1883, Sarah Mason of Baschurch recalled 'a woman hanged on a tree at Cutberry ... who came again so badly that nine clergymen had to be fetched to lay her.' These men 'read and read until they got her into a bottle' and 'buried it under a flat sandstone in the road'. Passing this en route to school each day, Mason would wonder what might happen if the stone should be moved.[76] Though it was not made quite clear, it seems that this woman hanged herself, meaning that in vampire territory she would have been no less suspect.

Still more startling than this apparent suicide's ghost was that of Elizabeth Browne, of Stanton-on-Hine-Heath, 9 miles north of Shrewsbury, who died naturally at age ninety-two in January 1777. This old lady 'had first been buried in the dingle adjoining her father's house, but "she came again", so that they were forced to take her up and bury her in the church.' With even this fairly drastic reburial of the body failing to quiet the ghost, villagers next 'got all the parsons in the country together, who prayed her unquiet spirit into a bottle, which was buried in the nave of the church'. Over a century later, in spring 1882, workmen re-tiling the church floor would not dare disturb the bottle, 'lest the ghost should again take to annoying the waggoners' lads on dark winter evenings'.[77] So much, then, for the rarefied soul of British popular belief. Notice, too, that the standard phrase 'she came again' sounds much like 'revenant'; while the quasi-material spirit, when bottled up, is permitted space in the church, just as was the mutilated corpse in Royston centuries before.

Let us close with some valuable information for those on a very low Vampire Hunting Budget. Having been cruelly thwarted in your attempt to steal a genuine Victorian VHK from the auction rooms, and spent your remaining money fleeing to deepest Bulgaria, where internet alerts for your capture are little heeded, you now find yourself obliged to outwit a vampire with a) a loaf of bread, or b) nothing at all. Despair not. Help is at hand. MacDermott explains that Bulgarian vampires 'were thought to be very naïve and easily tricked'. Hence,

> one could get rid of a vampire by approaching him with a warm loaf and inviting him to go to some distant place on the pretext of a fair or a wedding, and then abandoning him there. Alternatively, one could send him to get fish from the Danube, where he would fall in and be drowned, or one could wrap a newly baked loaf in a cloth, put it in a red bag, leave it on someone else's land, and ask the vampire to stay there and look after it.

This sounds, again, rather like the showmanship of the professional Vampire Killer (or: professional Vampire Detainer). If nothing else, it is inventive, and might appeal to the imagination of frightened villagers. A friend who grew up in a farming community assures me that the detail about 'someone else's land' sounds particularly authentic.

By now some of us could be forgiven for not taking this demon very seriously. When not picnicking quietly on apples, nuts, or green beans, he might be found starring in what look uncannily like out-takes from Carry on Vamping, or (as Chapter Nine will reveal) singing at Greek parties. All in all, he hardly seems capable of masterminding some grandiose apocalyptic plot to transform the earth into a dark Vampire Kingdom (Note on vampire's door: 'Vampire Apocalypse postponed. Am minding loaf of bread.') But: be warned ... just as we are lured into this false sense of security, we will find one long, gaunt chill finger tapping our shoulder from behind the sofa. And when you turn around, be quite aware: you are about to meet a vampire which can scare people ... to death.

6

Vampire Nightmares

A few years ago, I woke up during the night. I was lying on my back, in a strange room, in a strange house. I could not move, and there was something on top of me. It was neither human nor animal. It had the rough outlines of a human figure, but seemed to be made of a kind of fuzzy static – what some of my older readers might recognise as 'television snow'. I was not only paralysed, but also unable to speak. Along with this doubly helpless loss of voice and motion, I was beginning to feel stifled. I had, too, a sense of unreality that was not quite dread, but which I can still recall quite powerfully now, in the clear early sun of a December morning.

This was the first time that I had ever had a sleep paralysis nightmare. It is hard to be absolutely sure what caused it, but many of the classic catalysts were there. I had recently been pretty overworked: I had only just come away on holiday after weeks of researching and writing this book. I was in a strange house (or rather, a holiday cottage), and I was alone in a strange room, having been unjustly turfed out of a nice double bed with slanderous accusations of snoring. As mentioned, I happened to be lying on my back. And, in the best traditions of a well-deserved holiday, I had had plenty to eat and drink quite late in the evening, not long before going to bed. A more general cause may well have been my deep, at the time almost obsessive, immersion in the whole topic of the nightmare. After all, I had at that point lived more than forty years without ever having a single one.

Armed with a useful framework of knowledge about the condition, I swore silently but vigorously at the aggressor, and off it went. I got off quite lightly. By contrast, across history thousands of otherwise very tough characters (hardened soldiers among them) have found this easily the most terrifying experience of their lives. At this stage, my own brush with the nightmare was not quite over. Some time later, I had a second attack, quite a lot milder than the first. And later still I had a third and (one hopes) final nightmare experience. This one had a special twist. My eyes seemed to be open, and I could definitely see my room (my usual one) and bed. There was nothing odd or indistinct about any of it. Most notably of all, I could see one hand lying outside the blankets, hanging over the edge of the bed. From this point I must beg you to draw on the most potent resources of your imagination – it is hard to get this across in writing; much easier to act in person. My other hand was on the other side of the bed, and at no point seemed to move. Having become somewhat blasé after my first two attacks, I lay there mentally saying to myself, yes, yes, sleep paralysis... and waiting for it to finish. At this moment, seemingly from nowhere... well – try letting your left hand dangle over the arm of your chair. Then, lift your right hand, hover it open, and bring it down...

SNAP!

around your left wrist. It felt and looked as real as that, albeit *much* more unexpected. Try imagining, say, one of those expertly executed shock scenes from a good horror film – and then, that you are starring in it yourself.

Yet here is the strange thing. No cameras required. No make-up, no music, no dry ice or special effects of any kind. But there certainly does appear to be a powerful link between the nightmares of the pillow and those of fiction and cinema. To many nightmare sufferers it indeed seems as if the roots, the mythic archetypes of horror tales and films lie *inside* the human body. In my case, it felt uncannily as if the body and (some part of) the mind were playing nasty games with me. Just when you thought you were ahead of the whole experience, the nightmare upped the stakes. And even though I do not believe it was anything external to myself, it certainly did feel as if something was playing an evil game, daring me to be so blasé on the *next* occasion...

In these two chapters we are going to journey into the darkest heart of vampire terror. From this point on, our journey will be rather different from that taken so far. Walking boots can be greased and reboxed, sticks hung up, sturdy donkeys put out to graze. Where we have ventured through lands of increasing strangeness, we are now going to tread in a world which threatens us with one of the most potent qualities of all good horror – that deeply unsettling combination of the strange *and* the familiar. For this part of the trip occurs in our own bedrooms, and in the more mysterious spaces of our own bodies and minds. It offers a kind of basic archaeology of vampire terrors. As we will see, much of the map for this uncanny journey has been drawn by medical science.

Some of you will know all too well what I am talking about when I say the word 'Nightmare'. It may have happened to you this very week, and if so you will be hoping and praying that it does not happen again tonight. But you, this first class of reader, do have a certain grim advantage – a hard-won personal sense that this is very, very real. (You are able to believe in this *emotionally*, as well as intellectually.) Those readers who have never experienced a nightmare (and indeed possibly never heard of it until now) have the opposite set of gains and losses. You will need to make some especially strong leaps of imagination in order to get into a space that others try very hard to get out of.

Along with these two broadly opposed groups, a couple of others should be added before we begin. For a surprising number of people will probably have had this experience and simply *not known what it was*. When I was teaching my MA course, Literature of the Supernatural, just weeks after my first nightmare, I found that three of fourteen students had had severe and repeated attacks. Until I discussed the subject with them, they had not fully known what was happening. One woman, Amber, had told her parents but found that, entirely ignorant of the condition, they were unable to take her seriously. It is not my aim to act as a kind of proxy medical doctor. But I do have the reasonable hope that the information given will demystify and clarify experiences which, here in the plate-glass, dotcom, super-clinical twenty-first century, are often not merely terrifying, but unjustly *lonely*. There is a very good chance that some of you will have had nightmares, and been too traumatised and puzzled to tell anyone. And there is an equally good chance that those of you who did tell someone will have been met with disbelief, incomprehension, hostility, or even diagnoses of mental illness from family, friends or doctors. If so, you will shortly be able to tell these unhelpful sceptics that this condition is very real, and very powerful – so powerful, in fact, that it has made thousands of people believe in vampires, witches, and alien abductors.

The Nightmare and Sleep Paralysis in Medical Science

Why does this happen? Let us start, first, with the simplest level. We are *all* paralysed every night. Sleep paralysis happens to everyone, routinely and necessarily. But usually, we are not aware of it. During REM sleep, you are paralysed for a specific reason: namely, so that you cannot start acting out your dreams. Acting out your dreams can be dangerous. Witness, for example, the case of Lord Longford. In November 1994 Longford – reports *The Times* – was seen with three sticking plasters on his forehead. He explained that he had been dreaming of playing tennis against Martina Navratilova. He was leading 3–2 in the second set when Navratilova returned serve so hard that Longford knew he could not hit the ball with his racket. Having decided to head it instead, he was woken by Lady Longford, who told him that he had been banging his head on the furniture.[1] Leaving aside any dark Freudian implications of this affair, we find the sober voice of modern science responding sympathetically to Longford's experience. In a letter to *The Times* on 17 November, Adrian J. Williams (Co-Director of the Sleep Disorders Centre at London's St Thomas Hospital) confirmed that 'inhibition of muscle activity' was designed to stop us acting out dreams, and cited an experiment on sleeping cats. When their REM paralysis was artificially 'switched off' under lab conditions, the animals would indeed begin stalking in their sleep.[2]

If cats have this artfully designed paralysis too, then it probably has some basic evolutionary functions. Why should we not shout and scream during our sleep (even if it is only at the umpire and not the vampire)? A fair guess would be because, napping safely in your well-hidden cave, it is not a good idea to attract a sabre-toothed tiger to your bedside when you are at your most defenceless.

As you will by now have realised, the problem with sleep paralysis occurs if you wake up. If you do, you are actually in some very strange – and still poorly understood – state, somewhere between sleep and waking. In such cases, you may not sense anything nightmarish or supernatural. But if your sleep paralysis episode is combined with a nightmare, you certainly will. At this point the technical details are best told by some experts in the field. First, the enterprising historian of ghosts, witches, and much else, Owen Davies.

'Sleep paralysis is not rare. Surveys around the world suggest that 20–45% of people experience at least one sleep paralysis episode in their lifetimes ... The condition is associated with the disturbance of rapid eye movement (REM) sleep, and usually occurs immediately before sleep onset or upon awakening, most often in the early hours. Those affected by sleep paralysis can see and hear, because under REM sleep there is intense central nervous system activity, but they are unable to make significant movements, because muscle activity is suppressed. Likewise, only inarticulate sounds can be made.' While 'most episodes last under ten minutes ... sufferers may feel their paralysis has lasted much longer.' Notice the implications of that phrase 'in the early hours': there is a very good chance that, if you have this nerve-shattering experience, you will do so at the very weakest point of the night, with food, blood sugar and body temperature all at their lowest ebb.[3]

Adding that the nightmare seems to occur in only 'about 5–20% of people', Davies further explains that, 'with the nightmare, sleep paralysis is accompanied by the feeling of a heavy pressure on the chest, choking sensations, and hypnagogic (accompanying falling asleep) and hypnopompic (accompanying waking from sleep) hallucinations.' These 'usually concern a sense of a physical presence in the room, which manifests itself either visually or aurally, or both', and involve 'a strong sense of fear or even terror'.[4] Clearly, while one can have bad dreams without sleep paralysis, it is hard to rival the experience of a nightmare when combined with it. The American scholar Shelley Adler uses 'Nightmare' to cover the two conditions together, and in what follows I will do likewise, as most of the accounts we will meet below include both parts of the experience.

Precisely because of the ignorance surrounding this problem, exact numbers of sufferers are uncertain. Interestingly, where Davies (published in 2003) has a maximum of 20 per cent suffering nightmare and sleep-paralysis, Adler has 25–30 per cent.[5] This higher figure may well reflect much greater awareness of the condition in the period between 2003 and 2011 (this last being the year when Adler published her book, *Sleep Paralysis*).[6] Certainly the rise of internet culture has played an important part in developing a supportive community of sufferers. This change is confirmed on one hand by the experience of one of my recent students, Laura, who had suffered SP Nightmares in the 1990s, when the internet was in its infancy. At that time she knew nothing about the condition, and emphasised that in the present day it would have been much easier to learn. Secondly, we have recent statistics. When Adler made a google search for 'sleep paralysis' on 21 April 2010 she got 527,000 hits; when I repeated that on 9 October 2014, I got 1, 550,000.

Searching again in July 2015, I found that whereas previously the opening entries would often be from teenage sufferers, traumatised and isolated, Wikipedia now had a clear entry coming in at first place, with the NHS not far behind, and a side-bar from the Mayo Clinic offering medical advice, and estimating more than three million US sufferers per year. An update in August 2018 gives the NHS in first place, with a total of 1,740,000 hits. In 2014 and 2015 Chris White and Carter Andersen published dedicated self-help books on the subject for sufferers, while 2015 also saw the release of a notably high profile documentary film, *The Nightmare*, directed by Rodney Ascher.

Adler's broad outline of symptoms is a little fuller than that of Davies. She identifies:

1) a sense of an evil presence accompanied by various sounds (footsteps, whispering);
2) breathing difficulties, feelings of suffocation, bodily pressure, sense of doom; and
3) sensations of floating, flying, and falling (including out-of-body experiences and viewing one's body from an external perspective).

These first two often co-occur and are characterised by 'intense terror'. The third, she adds, is sometimes associated with fear, but 'tends to be correlated with feelings of bliss'.

Like Davies, Adler makes clear how universal the basic symptoms are. In numerous languages the words denoting the attack include terms which involve weight, pressure, crushing, and choking or strangling. Other symptoms might include bad smells ('when a rat is dead'; 'a wicked smell, stench in the room'); and a range of sounds: 'a door opening or closing, bedsprings creaking, an animal growling, approaching footsteps, rustling, or scratching ... The individual may distinctly hear his or her name being called or may only be able to discern unintelligible – but clearly malevolent – whispering.' As we will see, the sufferer who reported 'a cold, cold feeling running through me' was not alone.[7] Even from just these few, relatively detached lines it is striking how very close much of this seems to the best horror films: uncertain hints of menace, dark suggestion, sudden violent drop in temperature – even the foetid breath of evil...

In the early nineteenth century the Scottish physician Robert Macnish was himself a sufferer, and wrote extensively about the nightmare in his 1827 work *The Philosophy of Sleep*. Those habitually prone to attacks, Macnish noted, experienced 'a certain degree of giddiness, ringing in the ears, tension in the forehead, flashing of light before the eyes', with some also having a bad taste in the mouth after the attacks.[8] Tellingly, MacNish's ringing has since been updated to fit modern electric or electronic sounds: victims now also report 'buzzing or beeping noises'.[9] The sufferer imagines (Macnish adds) that they are shouting or screaming at the top of their voice, and that the whole house will be roused. In fact, just stifled groans are made – no one comes because, 'in the Nightmare, no one can hear you scream...' This last horrific feature was made especially vivid for me a few months ago, when I spoke to a current sufferer, a friend of one those former MA students. Trapped in the depths of a nightmare, she had always felt, she told me, that she was positively screaming at the top of her lungs.

Across history, one other important feature has been the tendency to construe the attack as erotic. We will catch some interesting glimpses of this uncanny (and usually undesired) form of love in following pages.

We now have some idea of what a nightmare is. And we know that, in medical terms, it is essentially a mix-up of states (sleep paralysis and consciousness) which should normally remain separate. As Alexis Madrigal explains, 'during sleep paralysis, a person experiences an "out of sequence" REM state. In REM sleep, we dream and our minds shut off the physical control of the body; we're supposed to be temporarily paralysed. But we are not supposed to be conscious in REM sleep. Yet that is precisely what happens during sleep paralysis: it is a mix of brain states that are normally held separate.'[10] As we will see, that 'mix of brain states' has more or less cosmic implications.

But what causes this mix-up? Perhaps the most common reported cause is simply sleeping on your back – something which is of course associated with the more routine sleep disorder known as snoring.[11] (A bawdy joke made by Mercutio in *Romeo and Juliet* shows us that Shakespeare was aware of this alleged catalyst.[12]) Other common catalysts are a heavy meal or too much alcohol shortly before bedtime, stress, overwork, disturbed sleeping habits, and sleeping in an unfamiliar place or room.[13] It also appears that certain groups of people are especially prone to attacks. Macnish claimed that men suffer more than women, unmarried women more than married ones, and pregnant women most of all among women.[14] Davies noted the same point about pregnancy almost 170 years later, citing a Finnish medical study, and suggesting that pregnant women are indeed more likely to sleep on their backs.[15]

The Origin of Evil?

Time and again, from Britain to Germany, from Hungary down to Greece, nightmare symptoms show up during vampire outbreaks. And, although the nightmare has been briefly linked to vampire incidents by Davies and Adler, no one as yet seems to have realised just how precise that connection is. Nightmare attacks explain the creature on your chest, trying to get at your throat, and sucking the life out of you (choking, suffocation). Part of this link involves the very basic fact that, in vampire nightmares, people did actually *see* their vampiric attacker. It may have looked exactly like the last person who had died. It may have been in one of those many 'animal shapes' vampires often used ('he looks like a man, like a dog, like anything').[16] Nightmares can also explain repeated claims that the vampire was calling its victim's name, and the tell-tale bite marks on throat or chest. Most strikingly of all, study of the nightmare makes us realise that, in certain vampire attacks, human beings actually died of fear.

But the supernatural horrors of the nightmare go well beyond vampirism. We might indeed say that vampires are just one planet in a whole cosmos of supernatural terrors, with the nightmare flowing through the dark void that links other worlds of demonic evil. For the nightmare also lies behind the figure of the witch. For others, the attacking agent has often been Satan himself. Much later, with just that notorious shape-shifting ability long credited to The Prince of Darkness, nightmare figures made a curious quantum leap into hyperspace, and began stalking out of spaceships. From the 1960s, your nightmares came not from the depths of hell, but from the depths of outer space: in the past fifty-odd years, such demons have frequently taken the form of the alien abductor.

During the worst of these attacks, the human body and mind are filled with a raw surge of pure evil. But the more precise form which this charge takes is very much open to the local interpretations of period or culture. As Davies explains, in the midst of this bewildering trauma, the human central nervous system actively strives to make sense of what is happening.[17] In doing so, it does something rather ironic. It produces an entity which is at once terrifying, and yet at least *more familiar* than the rawly disembodied, faceless terror which initially hovers through the dark. Our own brains give terror its peculiar shape. And it is for this reason that the history of the nightmare looks oddly like a grimly epic video game – witch versus vampire... For yes, the two biggest demons of pre-modern culture are at least partly *interchangeable*. Nightmare witch or Nightmare vampire? To a large extent, the answer depended on where you lived.

Anyone who has even briefly studied the witch hunts or the accounts of vampire outbreaks will often have a sense of looking in on another world. At a casual glance, we might imagine that this is a kind of dreamlike realm, loosely resembling ours, yet defying many of its basic laws. In fact, the nightmare shows us that one central truth of this world lies in a strange space between sleep and our conscious lives. Recall what Madrigal says above about that 'mix of brain states'. You are not quite awake, nor quite asleep. Rather, you are in a peculiar *third space*, which somehow feels both utterly real, and utterly bizarre. So... take our two familiar worlds, of sleep and waking, mix them up, and there, cutting its dark shadows down through ordinary life, is that third world: the supernatural.

Valuable as they are, medical explanations and accounts offer us only the driest paraphrase of true nightmare experiences. It is time to get up close, now, in the company of some actual sufferers.

Personal Nightmares

In 1753 the Scottish physician John Bond published the first full study of the nightmare. Bond was motivated, in part, by his own severe nightmare attacks. 'I have often been so much oppressed by this enemy of rest, that I would have given ten thousand worlds like this for some person that would either pinch, shake, or turn me off my back.'[18] Come 1816 the horror remained undiminished. 'It would be impossible by any words' (wrote the surgeon John Waller), 'to convey an adequate idea of the terror felt during this affection: the patient continues to feel it for several minutes after he is awake.'[19] By 1834 nightmare terror was spiralling into a vortex that seemed to end only in the floors of hell itself:

> Imagination cannot conceive the horrors it gives rise to, or language describe them in adequate terms. They are a thousand times more frightful than the visions conjured up by necromancy or *diablerie*; and far transcend everything in history or romance ... [including] the hidden tortures of the Spanish Inquisition. The whole mind ... is wrought up to a pitch of unutterable despair ... and the wretched

victim feels as if pent alive in his coffin ... The modifications which Nightmare assumes are infinite; but one passion is almost never absent – that of utter and incomprehensible dread. Sometimes he is involved in the coils of a horrid, slimy monster, whose eyes have the phosphorescent glare of the sepulchre ... Everything horrible, disgusting, or terrific in the physical or moral world, is brought before him in fearful array. He is hissed at by serpents, tortured by demons, stunned by the hollow voices and cold touch of apparitions ... [if he closes his eyes] still its icy breath is felt diffusing itself over his visage, and he knows he is in the presence of a fiend...

Thus Macnish, who (like Bond and Waller) was at the same time a hard-headed man of science. Clearly no amount of cold reason could douse the raw inner flame of horror which ignited this fantastic experience. Admittedly, this did not stop people trying. That excerpt from Macnish goes on for several more pages. It is as though, where Waller flatly states, 'it would be impossible by any words...' Macnish *keeps* hurling words at the experience, desperately trying to make them stick, to somehow get rational control of the attack and kill it dead. Listening to accounts like this we begin to get a sense of some kind of dark ultimate meanings, the secret realities that lie beneath or beyond mere language. Small wonder, then, that so many film directors should have been inspired to recreate the experience through atmospheres of silent menace. And long before the age of cinema, Macnish tellingly adds that, if the sufferer has been reading Gothic novels such as *The Monk* or *The Mysteries of Udolpho*, suitably Gothic terrors will then invade their nightmares.

Jumping ahead to the time of living memory, we hear (via Davies) a particularly arresting description from one American sufferer. This man 'had fought for thirteen consecutive months in frontline combat in Korea, but said of his one nightmare attack in 1964, "Never, before or since, have I experienced the fear of that night".'[20] More recently, an anonymous Christian woman tells us: 'One Saturday morning, I woke up tired, cranky, irritable and just did not want to work. I did not feel like packing any boxes [to help my sister move] or cleaning or sweeping ... So as I'm laying there on the bed ... I suddenly could not move. I could not scream and I could not think. One thing I could do was HEAR and I heard two distinct voices: one was a demonic woman that said "we should have never let you get away from us" – then a demonic man's voice that said "this time you will not get away from us".'

Writing in 2011, Madrigal tells of his own attacks in a way which is far less religious, but no less memorable:

> I experienced sleep paralysis twice in college. I can vouch for the sheer terror that attends the experience. I saw – no, felt – an evil presence to my left. I can't tell you what was evil about it or how I knew it was so nasty. But I did. As the experience progressed, it came closer. It didn't feel like my life was at risk. That was, in fact, too small. It felt like the presence was after something else, probably what you'd call my soul or my being, even though intellectually I'm a straight materialist. I woke up more scared than I've ever been in my life. Overwhelming fear. Overwhelming dread. Overwhelming fear and dread.

Madrigal, 'a straight materialist', perfectly evokes that sense of supernatural evil: 'it felt like the presence was after something else, *probably what you'd call my soul...*' Similarly, David Hufford, one of the pioneers of sleep-paralysis research, tells of how, back in 1967, 'I had heard the footsteps, sensed the terrifying presence and felt it climb onto *my* chest, all the while unable to move or cry out. I didn't talk with anyone about it ... I had no idea that it had ever happened to anyone else ... My experience had felt "spiritual", although I had not believed in malevolent spirits'. An anonymous internet post cited by Adler tries to explain how the emotion is '"beyond" fear or terror, like the evil is trying to reach my soul', while another American posting, from 2001, talks of 'feeling completely immobile, in fear of my life, and afraid that something is in the room trying to pull out my soul.'[21]

We seem here to have a kind of perfect storm of physical and psychic terrors. But beyond the impressive force of evil there is also something else. Three people here (one a definite atheist or agnostic) talk about *the soul*. Even from these brief references it is easy enough to recall all those innumerable vanished Christians who had once felt Satan or God fighting for *their* souls across Europe and America, down so many centuries. One other question arises here, then. Is the nightmare attack one basic originating force, not merely of evil, but of the spiritual world itself?

The Reality of the Nightmare
In other accounts cited by Adler, there is certainly no shortage of the uncanny: '"overwhelming sense of dread/evil closing in" ... "black

horror" ... "the fear progressed from foreboding to absolute panic" ... "feelings of dread/bad/evil".' Yet equally potent is the victim's sense that all this is, indeed, *absolutely real*:

> I am 52 years old. My [night-mares] started in my mid-20s. I remember the first time it happened. I had a new baby and was napping in the afternoon because I also worked in the evenings. Suddenly, I was wide awake except for the fact that my eyes were still closed and I was completely paralysed. I have never been so terrified in my life. I KNEW someone else was in the room. I could hear them moving around. I felt like I was in grave danger. Then I KNOW I felt someone sit down on the bed right next to me! I tried to scream ... I was struggling and struggling but I couldn't even move a finger. Finally, the episode passed and I woke up perfectly fine. I thought I was going crazy and never mentioned it to anyone. I still don't bring it up much because I get THAT LOOK from people who don't know what you're talking about. I have had several episodes since then ... I have never opened my eyes ... and that is a blessing because if I ever did and saw something looking back at me I would probably die in my sleep...

Try to imagine a horror so intense, and so real that to actually see it would kill you... For those of us who cannot, Adler supplies numerous supporting witnesses: 'I have suffered from sleep paralysis and it was the most scary thing in my life. The first time it happened I thought it was a dream but I know I was awake.' 'Each time is terrifying. I suddenly am awake and aware of the bed and my situation, but realise I cannot move. It is not a dream.'[22] Time and again, across widely separated centuries, continents, cultures and classes the emphatic message screams out. An Inuit victim interviewed sometime before 2001 insisted: 'to me, it is never going to stop being scary. I think when you experience this you are scared every time ... when I was still a child, I thought I was going to die.' And London professor Margaret Kammerer states in 1996:

> To the victim, figures in the room seem completely real ... The frightening sensation that 'a thing' is touching one's body also seems real ... Many years passed before I realised that the alarming heavy breathing coming ever closer and louder from the dark was my own – magnified and growing more threatening and rasping as

I struggled to break the paralysis. During these episodes time stands still and the paralysis seems interminable. In real time the episodes probably last for less than a minute.[23]

Most recently of all, my sometime student, Amber, said the same thing when interviewed for a short television trailer in the suitably Gothic setting of Durham Castle: 'Each time, it feels equally real.' Her memory of this had not softened, 15 years after the experiences themselves.

Thinking for a moment about the repeated power and repeated reality of these incidents, we might wonder if the closest parallel for non-sufferers would be the effects of sex, alcohol or other, less legal narcotics. Every time, it seems convincing. And every time, you think (or feel): 'yes – this is what life is *really* about...' To put it another way: all the very good things and the very bad things seem to hit us at some level beyond words.

Like Macnish, the experts have tried to contain and define the nightmare state through language. For all that, one has the sense that these descriptions are ultimately inadequate. Davies talks about 'hallucinations', and Adler of how 'a person experiencing a night terror is actually not awake, but in an altered state of consciousness between slow-wave sleep and a waking state.'[24] There is some sense, here, that these phrases are mere words, failing to define the actual state in question. Perhaps the most useful thing about Adler's description is 'altered state of consciousness', with its hint at the drug-like condition of the nightmare.

One of the most vivid examples of this nightmare reality is given by Macnish. And it is all the more convincing because, unusually, it occurred in daylight:

During the intensely hot summer of 1825, I experienced an attack of daymare. Immediately after dining, I threw myself on my back upon a sofa, and, before I was aware, was seized with difficult respiration, extreme dread, and utter incapability of motion or speech ... During all this time, I was perfectly awake; I saw the light glaring in at the windows in broad sultry streams; I felt the intense heat of the day pervading my frame; and heard distinctly the different noises in the street, and even the ticking of my own watch, which I had placed on the cushion beside me. I had, at the same time, the consciousness of flies buzzing around, and settling with annoying pertinacity upon my face. During the whole fit, judgement was never for a moment suspended.

Almost 200 years later, other sufferers echo this seemingly mundane and detailed reality: 'I woke and saw the room as I would normally when I was awake. The lights were still on, the TV I could lightly hear off to my left and I could see the length of my body lying on the couch.' Another recommends that fellow victims should check their digital alarm clock during attacks; can they see the time clearly, and see it changing? This, the writer insists, is peculiar to sleep paralysis.[25]

Look again at Macnish. Not only are all senses highly active, but his *eyes are open*. Just what are we to make of this? I certainly know that my eyes seemed to be open during my first and last attacks: everything looked just as it should from that position – save for the fuzzy man, and the sudden hand from nowhere... More recently, films of sufferers (such as Adam Segev) have shown their eyes to be open, and slowly blinking at times, though the body is otherwise motionless.

Vampire Nightmares

We saw earlier that archaeological evidence on revenants goes back, via deviant burials, to at least 2000BC. There were no doubt many reasons why – even as the blocks of Stonehenge were splashing by river to Salisbury – people feared revenants. But one of them must, again, have been nightmares. Adler finds what may be the earliest reference in a Sumerian work, *c.*2400BC. Others occurred in ancient Assyria and Babylon, while in ancient Greece the nightmare was well-known under the name 'ephialtes'.

Many revenant nightmares must of course now be lost, having long since crumbled to dust with the people who suffered them. Yet there is no shortage of details once accounts start to be committed to writing. From the twelfth century to the twenty-first, from Britain to Bohemia, Greece to Transylvania, the nightmare and the vampire are constant companions.

We begin in Buckinghamshire. The very early revenant we met there, *c.*1196, came back to his wife's room 'and, having awakened her ... not only filled her with the greatest alarm but almost killed her by leaping upon her with the whole heaviness of his weight and overlying her. On the second night, also, he tormented the trembling woman in just the same way.' Here the weight is an obvious clue. The words remind us, indeed, of how well the oft-cited weight of the nightmare attack suits an *embodied* revenant, rather than an ethereal ghost.

Over on the Continent, the 14th-century Vampire of Blow was both more destructive, and more resilient. We heard Calmet telling of how, soon after his death, the shepherd Myslata reappeared, and 'called upon several persons, who all died within eight days.' And Summers makes it clear that this indeed means 'called by name'. Along with this typical symptom of nightmare (or perhaps daymare), others soon followed. After his staking, the nightmares continued. For, 'the vampire appeared in a horrible form that night, suffocating several people to death and frightening others to death.'[26]

In the early sixteenth century Agrippa told of how those Cretan vampires, 'the spirits of the deceased husbands, would be very troublesome to their wives, and endeavour to lie with them, while they could have any recourse to their dead bodies.' Here we seem to be looking at one more sexualised version of the nightmare. It is also very likely that the wives expected to be the prime victims of their dead husbands, making them more prone to stress and to psychosomatically induced nightmares.

Later, we have the 1567 case from Trawtenaw (now Trutnov) in Bohemia. Here there lived,

> one Stephen Hubener, that gathered such great riches, built such stately houses, and was so successful that all admired. And at last falling sick, died, and was very honorably interred. But a short while after his death and burial, his body ... did pinch many men with such strait embracements, that many of them died, yet diverse recovered again, who all with one consent confessed that they were thus clasped or beclipped by this rich man, in that very habit in which they had seen him alive ... therefore the magistrate of that place, that he might void or lay this satanical sight, commanded the body of that man to be digged out of the grave, after he had lain in the earth twenty weeks, yet was not corrupted or rotten, but fat, as young and well fed bodies use to be; the body was delivered to the hangman, to be carried away to the place of execution, where he cut off his head with his axe, and anatomizing him, took out his heart, and did cleave it: there issued out of his body blood, as if he had been alive (witch-like) to sustain punishment, therefore the hangman threw the body into the fire, a great company standing by...[27]

We also learn that this ritual worked – probably because, once everyone had seen or heard of it, they *expected* the attacks to stop.

As these were at least partly psychosomatic, they did. Yet not, it seems, before several people had actually died during Hubener's assaults... Note also an early case of very definite nightmare visualisation: people do not perceive some vague shape which they take for the recently dead Hubener, but all see him 'in that very habit in which they had seen him alive.'

The Shoemaker of Breslau

Come 1591, we have the case of the suicidal shoemaker from Breslau. (Breslau was then in German territory; the modern town, renamed Wroclaw, is now in Poland). After gossip had begun as to the shoemaker's suspicious death, his figure began to appear – yet again, 'in the exact shape and habit of the deceased, and that not only in the night, but at mid-day. Those that were asleep it terrified with horrible visions; those that were waking it would strike, pull, or press, lying heavy upon them like an *Ephialtes*: so that there were perpetual complaints every morning of their last night's rest through the whole town'. Here the author explicitly likens the shoemaker's attacks to the nightmare ('like an *Ephialtes*'). And he also hints at that typically blurred line between sleep and waking, dream and reality. His attempted distinction between the two ('were asleep...', 'were waking...') probably refers to nightmares in both cases.

The Breslau incident was one of the most extraordinary supernatural terrors on record. With the shoemaker's friends suppressing rumours of his suicide, no formal action was taken until a full eight months after the burial. Meanwhile,

> no sooner did the sun hide his head, but this *spectrum* would be sure to appear, so that every body was fain to look about him, and stand upon his guard, which was a sore trouble to those whom the labours of the day made more sensible of the want of rest in the night. For this terrible apparition would sometimes stand by their bed-sides, sometimes cast itself upon the midst of their beds, would lie close to them, would miserably suffocate them, and would so strike and pinch them, that not only blue marks, but plain impressions of his fingers would be upon sundry parts of their bodies in the morning. Nay, such was the violence and impetuousness of this ghost, that when men forsook their beds, and kept their dining-rooms, with candles lighted, and many of them in company together, the better to secure themselves from fear and disturbance; yet he would then appear to them, and have a bout with some of them...

One basic fact comes through all of these seemingly bizarre occurrences: terror begot more terror. Here as elsewhere, the nightmare fed like some demonic animal on fear, sleeplessness and stress. This meant not only that at least scores of people suffered nightmares, but that, as the traumatised months dragged on from September 1591 to April 1592, victims had both bruises and finger-marks on their bodies. Additionally, even when a number of people were herded together awake at night, *something* still attacked them ('have a bout with some of them…'). Implausible as some of this might seem, it almost certainly did happen.

Before we leave Breslau let us ensure we have made the most of our visit. How did all this start? What were the mechanics of communal hysteria? Here is a plausible theory. It was rumoured that the shoemaker had committed suicide, and this at once put him into the class of potential revenant. Accordingly, it was the shoemaker's form which appeared in the first nightmare after his death (as we saw, the brain gives the nightmare the most likely shape it can find). Once this had happened, the tale went round quickly ('one heard talk everywhere…'), thus prompting other attacks, in people whose fears had now been sharply pre-activated.

At one level this psychology reveals an ironic contrast with modern nightmare sufferers. As emphasised, such people can feel highly isolated, tabooed, and stigmatised. In Breslau, you certainly had an understanding and supportive community. The last thing you needed to do was keep this to yourself. Yet, by spreading the news like wildfire, you then ensured that others suffered, and in a devastating snowball effect, yet others, as terror gained size, momentum, and increasingly unstable energy.

In Breslau as elsewhere, the horrors stopped in time-honoured fashion – with the shoemaker finally dismembered, burned, and thrown in the form of ashes into the river, people grew calm and the attacks ceased.

Cuntius of Pentsch

We briefly met Cuntius earlier, when he was passing through a particularly unusual corpse door. Early-modern Christians did not lightly smash up their own churches. But by this time, if he had done even half the things attributed to him, Cuntius had certainly deserved his fate (which, again, was burning). For Cuntius' alleged exploits are some of the most staggering in all the annals of vampire history. What is still more staggering is that most of them were probably true.

Given how severely these events stretch the ordinary limits of belief, readers may be reassured to know that their source looks very reliable. The author of the account was the parson of Pentsch. So, we have, first, another person who was on the scene, and who was attacked himself at one point. We also have a man of God. And on the whole, men of God did not lie in this period. A Protestant in particular (Silesia being an early stronghold of the Reformation) was especially unlikely to do so, given their sense of the need to set a personal example for their still insecure new faith.

The exact date of the Cuntius affair is uncertain. Henry More, however, thinks that it occurred sometime after that of the shoemaker – hence in the late sixteenth or early seventeenth century. Cuntius, aged almost 60, was himself quite wealthy and respectable, being a town Alderman and owning five horses. While he and a servant were inspecting a horse's hoof in the stable, the animal kicked them both down. Cuntius got by far the worst of the blows, and seems to have suffered some sort of brain fever as he lay on his deathbed. He began, at any rate, 'loudly complaining, that his sins were such, that they were utterly unpardonable, and that the least part of them were bigger than all the sins of the world besides'. If this now sounds like boasting, it was taken all too seriously by the townspeople. Signs were expected, and found. At Cuntius' deathbed his eldest son saw a black cat force its way through the window and dash over to scratch the face of the dying man. At his funeral there was a violent storm.

Even before the burial, with Cuntius 'not ... dead a day or two ... several rumours were spread in the town of a *spiritus incubus*, or *Ephialtes*, in the shape of Cuntius, that would have forced a woman'. Here we have the sexualised nightmare, taking the form of attempted rape. Next, 'after his burial, the same spectre awakened one that was sleeping in his dining room, saying, *I can scarce withhold my self from beating thee to death*' in the voice of Cuntius. Presently it was the turn of the parson himself. In a typically blurred description of nightmare consciousness, we hear of how Cuntius 'so squeezed and pressed' him 'when he was asleep, that wakening he found himself utterly spent, and his strength quite gone, but could not imagine the reason'. (Read: he could not move.) 'But while he lay musing with himself what the matter might be, this spectre returns again to him, and holding him all over so fast, that he could not wag a finger, rolled him in his bed backwards and forwards a good many times together.' Later the parson's wife was another victim, with Cuntius 'coming through the casement in the shape of a little dwarf, and running to her bedside,' where he 'so wrung and pulled as if he would have torn her throat out, had not her two daughters come in to help her.' There were evidently many other attacks. We hear more briefly of 'his strangling of old men' and 'his frequent endeavouring to force women'.

There is more of this affair below. We can just say, for now, that again the horrors terminated with the very costly burning of the demon corpse – a pyre which needed 'the expense of two hundred and fifteen great billets' of wood before the body was reduced to ashes.

Later Cases

Clad in its vampiric shroud, the nightmare stalked on through the bedchambers of the late seventeenth and eighteenth centuries. Recall – if you dare – the Vegan Vampire of Milo. To us, this may sound about as alarming as a tame rabbit, nibbling on its underground store of apples, grapes and nuts. But to the Greeks it bore the terror of excommunication; hence the way that 'the peasants and islanders were every night affrighted and disturbed with strange and unusual apparitions, which they immediately concluded arose from the grave of the accursed Excommunicant.'

From that great vampire bible, *Magia Posthuma* (1704), we hear of a woman who died in a certain village, and was buried in the normal way with all the usual sacraments. About four days after her death 'the inhabitants of the village were affrighted with an uncommon noise and outcry, and saw a spectre, sometimes in the shape of a dog, and sometimes in that of a man, which appeared to great multitudes of people, and put them to excessive pain, by squeezing their throats, and pressing their breasts, almost to suffocation.' Although we have no details here about date or place, we find that the female revenant not only took the form of an animal, but also, intriguingly, that of a man. (Presumably it was easy to identify the woman as supposed culprit, because she had died so recently.)

In the famous case of Peter Plogojowitz in 1725, nightmare attacks were the vampire's sole means of assault. His victims told of how he had 'come to them in their sleep, laid himself on them, and throttled them, so that they would have to give up the ghost.' In his 1733 *Dissertation on Serbian Vampires*, Zopfius confirms that victims would often 'complain of suffocation and a total deficiency of spirits, after which they soon expire'. Shortly before, in 1732, one of Arnod Paole's vampire descendants was up to the same tricks. Here in Medvegia a woman called Stanacka 'lay down to sleep fifteen days ago, fresh and healthy, but at midnight she started up out of her sleep with a terrible cry, fearful and trembling, and complained that she had been throttled by the son of a hajduk by the name of Milloe, who had died nine weeks earlier.' She then 'experienced a great pain in the chest and became worse hour by hour, until finally she died on the third day.'[28]

An advance preview of the Russian vampire reveals how, 'on 26 December 1798, in the village of Spiridonovka' in the Kiev region, 'a peasant named Kirrill Peven died and was buried in the local cemetery.' In the following year, 'after reports of numerous sightings of the dead man, who apparently caused nightmares and sickness, the villagers, together with the local priest, exhumed the body, and ... discovered the corpse uncorrupted and with blood under his fingernails.' Even with these few bare details we can certainly imagine that report of the first nightmares quickly sparked many more.[29]

Come 1888, the head of a Cretan monastery wrote of how:

The common practice of the *vrykolakes* is to seat themselves upon those who are asleep and by their enormous weight to cause an agonizing sense of oppression. There is great danger that the sufferer in such cases may expire, and himself too be turned into a *vrykolakas*, if there be not someone at hand who perceives his torment and fires off a gun, thereby putting the blood-thirsty monster to flight; for fortunately it is afraid of the report of fire-arms and retreats without effecting its purpose. Not a few such scenes we have witnessed with our own eyes.

However superstitious this may look to us, the nightmare victims of this monastery were neither lonely, unaided, nor misunderstood. Probably because of the communal sleeping arrangements of the monastery, there was indeed a good chance that someone would 'perceive [your] torment' and fire the anti-vampire gun as required (thus jolting the sufferer out of the nightmare, and giving the impression that the *vrykolakas* had fled). Looked at carefully, this tells us two interesting things. One: most people knew how to recognise someone else's nightmare attack. And two: they were quite happy with the idea that the vampiric attacker was *invisible* to all but its victim.

In certain other cases the nightmare is just lightly hinted at. It was said of George Grando's widow in Kring, for example, that he, on his post-mortem return, 'night after night threw her into a deep sleep with the object of sucking her blood.' Although a nightmare does not seem like 'deep sleep' in most respects, the term may well refer to paralysis in particular. 'Sucking her blood' could indicate the typical pressure at the throat or chest. Similarly coded is one of Barber's several references to vampire nightmares. The original account tells us only that a woman's dead husband 'came every night and tortured her'.[30] The accounts above suggest that many nightmare sufferers would consider 'tortured' a good choice for the experience, if they could use just one word to describe it. A little more explicitly, Barber also describes how, 'where the vampire is of the ambulatory type – for example, the Yugoslavian vampire – he appears before the victim in the night and either strangles him or sucks blood. In any case, the victim often complains of a feeling of suffocation before death.'[31] Koenig, meanwhile, explains that Ukrainian vampires 'sometimes enter a house by crawling under the door. Once inside, they fasten themselves on the chest of a sleeper and suck his warm blood, before hurrying back to their graves.'[32]

In Ambéli in 1982 all the older villagers still recalled the *vrykolakas* that came after the luckless child crossed over the corpse. 'For several nights after the burial the dead woman returned as a great heavy woolly apparition, terrifying her husband and children.' Small wonder that they were terrified: they were almost certainly having nightmare attacks. The word 'heavy' is of course the strongest clue; but 'woolly' is also fairly close to the figure which I saw myself during my first nightmare experience. Du Boulay also emphasises the Greek vampire's habit of 'attacking either their own family or their own flocks, damaging and eventually killing them – an action often described as "suffocating" – by going up the nose and drinking their blood.'[33] The woman's family, then, *expected* to be attacked.

In at least one part of Europe, vampire nightmares have also managed to haunt the twenty-first century. After the death of Petre Toma in Marotinu de Sus, 'his niece suffered nightmares and appeared seriously ill. She claimed that her uncle was visiting her at night and feeding from her heart; that he was a strigoi.' So explains Timothy Taylor, who on his 2004 stay in the village also heard of how the niece was cured by drinking the vampire's ashes in water. This girl's nightmares were no idle bad dreams – as with many others throughout history, they made her seriously ill. Little surprise, given that 'her uncle was visiting her at night and feeding from her heart'. This last phrase, we should bear in mind, was probably not just inspired by her beliefs about what vampires did. Rather, it was also what the nightmare *felt* like. Those words offer us just one more version of that vividly repeated claim seen above: the vampire-nightmare was sucking out one's life, one's being, soul, one's innermost core or essence.[34] As we have already seen, drinking the ashes cured this girl because her sickness was (to put it drily) psychosomatic. It was belief which made her sick, and belief which later cured her.

There is no doubt, then, that in cases where contagious disease was not in play, the major cause of vampirism was the nightmare. If we now grapple with the surprisingly exact parallels between the two, we can also see that the nightmare explains almost all other features of vampire assaults in remarkably exact detail.

Nightmare Symptoms, or Vampire Signs?
Overwork and Stress

To understand fully how the symptoms of a medical condition could be so easily misunderstood, we need first to be aware of two basic causal factors. We saw above that the American attacked by demons had just woken up 'tired, cranky, and irritable', and that another victim had a new baby, was working in the evenings, and had therefore taken to afternoon naps, during one of which she suffered her first attack. The same went for David Hufford, who had his first experience when sleeping in the day during a bout of illness at college.[35]

Davies emphasises that 'unusually strenuous physical activity ... seems to increase the chance of "attack".' Noting that extremely long working days were the norm for most people in most of history, he rightly concludes that 'we may postulate a greater incidence of the nightmare in previous centuries. The intense anxiety created by fear of bewitchment in past societies may have further increased the incidence of the nightmare. Recent biomedical research has confirmed that anxiety raises the chances of sleep paralysis.'[36] Two hundred and fifty years earlier, John Bond seems to hint at the problem of overwork when he claims that autumn and spring are the 'most fertile periods' for nightmare attacks, for those seasons would have been the busiest (most overworked) times of year on most farms.[37]

In Breslau, the nightmare-spectre was 'a sore trouble to those whom the labours of the day made more sensible of the want of rest in the night.' Ironically, in terms of disturbed sleep patterns and sheer fatigue, the ordinary death rituals of vampire territory, while deliberately aimed at preventing revenants, must actually have produced them at times. For in Greece people stayed awake round the corpse the whole night before the funeral; and in parts of the Ukraine the Galicians also stayed up during the night after the burial, as this was considered the most dangerous period for vampire attacks. As Koenig points out, people were then so exhausted that they had devised a special tradition of pranks, aimed at rousing those who fell asleep.[38]

It is obvious enough that nightmares produced stress. But in some cases it evidently took a relatively small amount of anxiety to catalyse a nightmare. Take, for example, one of Bond's patients, described candidly as a 'fat clergyman' of about fifty. This nightmare sufferer reported that his attacks would invariably occur the night after he had had to conduct a wedding or christening. Perhaps this luckless minister was the rather nervous type of officiant, prone (like Rowan Atkinson) to refer at a crucial moment to 'the Father, the Son, and the Holy Goat', or 'your awful wedded wife'. At very least, we have to imagine that, by the standards of a probably not overworked minister, these were presumably fairly demanding and stressful occasions.

It takes just a small effort of imagination to grasp how peculiarly vicious the spiralling circle of nightmares, stress, lost sleep, anxious anticipation, and further nightmares must have been in a vampire- or witch-haunted community. Terror begot more terror. Nightmares were caught like a disease. In some cases numerous people were attacked by the vampire-nightmare, and in others the same person was attacked night after night. Davies is certainly on the right track when he emphasises how 'the intense anxiety created by fear of bewitchment in past societies may have further increased the incidence of the nightmare.' But, as Chapter Eight will make horribly clear, the truth was much more radical than that. For people who believed in witches, vampires and demons not only made themselves sick, and not only caused their own Nightmares. They were gripped by a species of terror that is now largely extinct in the developed world. And this terror was so powerful that it actually *caused* supernatural phenomena. In such circumstances, exhuming and mutilating a corpse was a small price to pay to break the vicious circle of terror.

The Vampire Calls you by Your Name

We heard Adler stating that the nightmare sufferer 'may distinctly hear his or her name being called or may only be able to discern unintelligible – but clearly malevolent – whispering.'[39] By now both those symptoms are so deeply embedded in the horror film tradition as to be familiar to almost all of us. Yet they are no mere invention. In the Bohemian village of Blow, the hallucinatory name-calling was enough to terrify victims to death. In the case of Cuntius, the dead man delivered whole menacing sentences to his victims; while toward the other end of our vampire timeline we have the New England Greek, Bill. Telling of the drowned boy who later troubled his brother by day and night, Bill reported that during the day the spectre could be heard, calling the brother's name, 'there where the sheep had been left in the shade'. This could well be an example of the kind of day-mare which Macnish experienced – especially as, in the heat of a Greek afternoon, a siesta would come very naturally, perhaps unbidden.

The Vampire Sucks Your Life Out

As we have seen, the notion that a vampire only sucks your blood is yet one more stylised fabrication, mysteriously selected by the aesthetics of vampotainment. What we need to grasp here is that, most basically, the vampire fed on life. It is this that unites versions of the vampire across time and space: from the evil social oppressor or parasite of polemic, through to the Andean vampires which – even as I write – suck out your life by sucking out your *fat*...[40] At first glance this devouring of life in general might seem disappointingly vague. Yet it actually fits precise symptoms of the nightmare across hundreds of years.

The most obvious point is that, regardless of your beliefs about vampires or other demons, the nightmare does indeed *seem* to be sucking out your life. You cannot breathe. Something is on your chest (often, if visible, just inches from your face) or at your throat. In the circumstances, the idea that this thing is sucking out your breath is probably the most rational answer. In some cases, you don't need to even seek the answer (then or later) because that is exactly what it *feels* like: 'I felt him sucking the air out of my lungs,' writes one sufferer on an internet post, with another confirming, 'it does feel like something is sitting on your chest sucking the breath out of you.'[41] Again, one victim 'could feel that disgusting fucker kissing me on the lips and sucking the air out of my lungs too.'[42]

In other cases this kind of sensation shades into the feeling which Madrigal recalled so powerfully, years after one of only two attacks: 'It didn't feel like my life was at risk ... It felt like the presence was after something else, probably what you'd call my soul.' A sufferer posting under the name of Aspen Kye on 3 January 2012 states emphatically: 'I remember feeling as if a spirit or energy was sucking my energy from my body and soul.'[43] Other accounts hint at this spiritual vampirism: 'each time it has happened, it has felt like something sucking the life force out of me.'[44] When one American woman suffers some kind of three-night haunting, with a nightmare on the second evening, she writes: 'I was in the state of sleep paralysis and I could feel something sucking my energy. I wanted to scream but I couldn't move.' Although this victim recognises sleep paralysis as a medical condition, her protective rituals, going through her entire house with cymbals and burning sage, strongly indicate New Age beliefs.[45] Here, then, and in several other cases ('I try to scream or move but I can't, I know I can but I can't do it (it feels like something is sucking the energy out of me). Most of the time I hear voices in the background I hear screaming people (as if they're being tortured or something)...') 'energy' might well be a loose New Age code for what others would call 'soul'.[46]

As promised, this kind of sensation can be remarkably precise. Witness the American woman who, 'four or five times ... was caught in the paralyzed world of being able to see with my eyes closed in the dark and not able to breathe or move, and fought the peculiar ache in the middle of the brain that always accompanies sleep paralysis. Like a syringe is sucking out some precious chemical, or something is trying to be inserted, or both.'[47] How would this have felt to the Ukrainians, with their belief that the *soul* was locked up in a special chamber of the head which opened only at death? It is obvious enough that the modern experience of the syringe is highly coloured by the scientific culture of our times. But perhaps what is most interesting is this – the description is both precise and highly subjective. And this makes us realise that, when the Nightmare slid along your bed and up your chest in Romania in 1730, your own precise subjective account (vampirism) was just as reasonable.

And in fact, such an explanation was also able to encompass *both* of the broad positions seen above. Splitting them a little artificially, we have the sucking of breath, and the sucking of the soul. Among educated and uneducated Christians for most of the past two millennia, these two could well be the same thing. Most basically, the soul was the root of *physical* life, as much as it was some spiritual passport to the places Above or Below.

So... the vampire comes, sits on your chest or throat, and sucks out your soul. Believing this yourself, you die of terror. Similarly, the relatives who find you, believe that you were killed by the soul-sucking vampire. An apparent problem with this arises in all those nightmare victims who were attacked *more than once* by the predatory demon. How many souls did they have? But what actually matters most in such contexts is that people believed in 'a soul' and in 'some soul' – that is, in a spiritual force diffused throughout the body or blood. This general force of vitality was held to be a mixture of blood and breath. In Western medicine these were the 'spirits' of the body – linking body and soul, and flitting about the veins and nerves to do routine physiological work.

And tellingly, it is these spirits which show up when educated outsiders try to understand what is happening in vampire panics. Zopfius, for example, talks of how those attacked typically complain of 'a total deficiency of spirits'; and Calmet of an initial, and worsening 'lowness of spirits' in those who are dying.[48] Indeed, even *The Times* of London was able to recognise this belief in 1785, referring sardonically to those 'Polish vampires, who steal out of their graves in the night-time, and prey on the animal spirits of mortals.'[49]

In the present day, those who still believe in the soul tend to divide it very sharply from the body. It may be difficult, therefore, to truly grasp the holistic physiology which has prevailed across most of history. But modern nightmare symptoms certainly fit that psycho-physical unity. The entity is attacking your body (the weight, the breathlessness) and, even for materialists, the soul. If this was a kind of perfect storm of all possible terrors for secular sufferers, how much deeper was its thunder in Bulgaria, c.1800, when you *already* believed in a soul? One saturating your body, in a kind of spiritual vapour which the vampire was now gulping from your quivering lungs?

The Vampire Leaves Bite Marks: or, How Nightmares Can Come True

Just what had left those tell-tale marks at the victim's throat? Evidence from non-vampire believers certainly shows that these were no mere fantasy. As we saw, Calmet had heard of how, 'at the place where these persons are sucked a very blue spot is formed'. These derived from that case of the three-year-old vampire corpse near Belgrade. Adding that 'the part whence the blood is drawn is not determinate; sometimes it is in one place, and sometimes in another', the author (a Lieutenant de Beloz) makes it clear that he himself believes these to be vampire bite marks. And he then further emphasises that this spectacle of bite marks is 'a notorious fact ... passed or executed in the sight of more than 1300 persons'.[50] For a while I was stumped by this part of the vampire puzzle. But I then made two crucial discoveries.

First, re-reading Bond's nightmare book, I had one of those wonderful moments of revelation – that rare instant of sudden delight when two pieces of evidence snap together like opposite poles of a magnet. Recall Bond's 'fat clergyman' of about fifty. This unnamed minister was indeed so prone to fits of nightmare that he was forced to stint himself of his beloved beer and meat suppers. When his restraint failed and the Nightmare caught him, he groaned so loudly that he woke the whole house. More than once, this priest imagined that the Devil came to his bedside and tried to choke him. And the next day 'he observed the black impressions of his hard fingers on his neck'. To any nightmare victim in Greece, Hungary, or Bulgaria these 'finger-marks' would clearly have struck the eye as vampire bite-marks. Yet the ultimate truth about these nocturnal injuries is a little stranger still.

For what I came to realise, secondly, studying both vampire nightmares and vampire poltergeists, was this: for people who are very terrified, nightmares *can come true*. If during a nightmare you think the Devil has his fingers around your throat, you can actually wake up to find the marks he has left. Between them, your traumatised body and mind have produced these bruises. In the case of the clergyman, the link is beyond doubt. In the case of all those 'blue spots' supposedly inflicted by the Belgrade vampire, it would certainly be plausible that these marks appeared in various places, according to just *where* the nightmare had seemed to attack the victim.

In Breslau, the revenant would not only suffocate victims, but 'would so strike and pinch them, that not only blue marks, but plain impressions of his fingers would be upon sundry parts of their bodies in the morning'. Perhaps most telling of all was the case of Stanacka, who died of terror in the aftermath of the Arnod Paole case. Fluchinger, the German medical officer, states clearly that he saw, 'on the right side under [Stanacka's] ear, a bloodshot blue mark, the length of a finger'.[51] This was almost certainly produced by the woman's nightmare – an attack which would ultimately kill her.

Meanwhile, in the incident from *Magia Posthuma* which we met above, 'there were several whose bodies he bruised all over, and reduced them to the utmost weakness, so that they grew pale, lean, and disfigured.' Aside from presenting an irksome task to any *Dracula* film make-up artists, this indiscriminate bruising might seem to somehow violate the aesthetics of vampotainment, which typically requires just those two (often almost invisible) puncture marks upon the throat.

Once again, we find that the bitten throat is in part a product of this aesthetic (as it were) revamping. The idea is not straightforwardly wrong – just misleading. As Barber points out, when folk vampires suck blood, they usually attack the area of the chest.[52] Keyworth makes the same point, and interestingly even Stoker gets this right once.[53]

Recall that notorious scene in which Mina is found with head thrust down against Dracula's bleeding chest – a tableau all the more gripping for its odd mixture of melodrama and homely simile: 'the attitude of the two had a terrible resemblance to a child forcing a kitten's nose into a saucer of milk to compel it to drink.'[54]

At one level the chest makes better sense than the throat. Vampire-stricken peasants are not modern doctors, imagining that their attacker will go with scientific rigour for a main artery. If marks are seen on the chest, people naturally assume that the vampire went for the very richest, most precious blood, in the area of the heart. This again fits the holistic qualities of body and soul in such a context. Although many would believe that the blood contained quantities of soul, almost all Christians seemed to have located *the* soul in either head or heart – in the latter case, often quite precisely in the left ventricle.[55]

But this level of explanation is, in the end, only secondary. What matters most is that the nightmare – as a real medical phenomenon – *does* leave bruises. As Adler points out, this was probably recognised long ago. This feature of the attacks is embedded in the word itself: one which is apparently derived from 'mar', meaning 'to pound, bruise, crush'.[56] Wherever these bruises may be, they are, in vampire territory, a clear sign that you are being attacked.

Given how strange all this is, readers may rightly take some persuading. Let us then look briefly at some examples of this auto-injury outside of vampire territory. First, we have the region known as Locorotondo, in south-eastern Italy. When studying this area, Anthony Galt found that the nightmare was, for some peasants there, a mischievous female spirit called *ajure*. This sat on victims' chests, and pinched them and tangled their hair, with bruising cited as a key symptom of such attacks. Here the nightmare was widely construed as a spirit-being in the 1950s, and for a few people it still had this status come the 1990s. These Italians do not seem to have been as terrified of the *ajure* as others were of vampire nightmares. But what is interesting is that, in this deeply magical and superstitious culture, nightmare attacks were surprisingly common. 'The *ajure* came to many people in the countryside, and queries in separate interviews with two informants elicited expressions of wonder that she [the *ajure*] had not come to the interviewer and his field assistant, as if the experience were so widespread that it was strange to be asking about it.'[57] In Locorotondo just a few years ago, we seem to hear an uncanny echo of the demon-haunted past.

These people evidently had so many nightmares because – like those of witch or vampire country – they were more superstitious than most of us.[58]

Still more recently, an American named Jim described what seems to have been his first nightmare attack: 'I woke up in the middle of the night a while ago, which is normal because I'm an insomniac, but I was worried something had been following me because I had been playing with black magic to try and help a friend with a ghost problem. I was being held down and my vision was blurry. I couldn't move and my chest wouldn't expand, like there was a weight on it. I passed out and woke up in the daytime. I had a big raw-looking mark on my chest and what looked like a rope bruise around my neck.'[59] In another recent internet posting, an American woman reported her first sleep paralysis experiences, during which: 'usually it feels like someone sucking on different parts of my neck (kinda like how it feels when someone starts to give you a hickey).'[60] Here, though no bruises are reported, we get an intriguing sense of something sucking with just about *enough* force to leave a mark (like a love bite).

And occasionally, nightmare victims *could* also be found bleeding – both within and beyond vampire territory. Research on North American witch beliefs from 1919 tells of Pennsylvanian 'children who are hag-ridden at night' and 'found in the morning "bruised on the chest and sore, with nipples bleeding from sucking"'.[61] Almost a century later, the Washington teenager who felt a nightmare 'sucking the energy' from her tells of how, 'sometimes when I wake up I find scratches on my body (my arms, legs, chest, and my lower stomach)'. Like certain vampire victims, this modern American was marked all over. Not only that, but 'the scratches are under my clothes, how could anyone be able to do that? Nothing could have been scratching me, I don't have ANY sharp objects near my bed, and my bed couldn't scratch me (it's an air mattress).' Here the details make it especially obvious that the marks are coming from *inside* the victim's body.

Writing in 2009, a grandmother named Miriam Martinez recounts an incident which confirms with uncanny force our working hypothesis: very bad nightmares *can* come true... Martinez had experienced sleep paralysis all her life – and for most of that time without even knowing 'that there was a name for such things'. In her most recent attack, a few months prior to the post,

I was babysitting my grandsons. I was laying on my right side with my youngest grandson laying right next to me while my oldest grandson, who is eight years old, was sleeping at the bottom of the bed on his back. I was facing this door mirror just about to fall asleep when I saw my oldest grandson rise out of his body and come towards me and bite me on my neck and then he went back to his body. I could not move or even scream out but the most frightening thing was when I got up the next morning there was this big scratch on my neck in the same exact place where he had bitten me.[62]

If this was the 'most frightening part' of the incident for a modern woman, such injuries must have had a tenfold power in a traumatised vampire community. And that power, as we will now see, was sometimes fatal. During or after the nightmare attacks of vampires, people did indeed die of fear.

7

Vampire Nightmares (II): Dying of Fear

In North America in the 1980s, a strange phenomenon occurs. A number of seemingly healthy people die during the night, 'on their back, with looks of terror on their faces'. Doctors are puzzled. There seems to be some pattern to these sudden deaths; yet no physical cause can be pinpointed. Presently a detective begins to realise just how big this phenomenon is, and how eerily consistent the basic features. She starts to investigate. Her quest takes her to places that few people could ever have believed existed.

This may sound like the trailer for a horror film – but it is a true story. The victims were a series of male refugees, a people known as the Hmong, from Laos in Southeast Asia. And the detective was the anthropologist and scholar, Shelley Adler. As she explains:

On a winter morning in early January 1981, Xiong Tou Xiong, a twenty-nine-year-old man, was found dead in the bed of his Portland, Oregon home. He had not been ill; his death was sudden and unexpected. Two days later, Yong Leng Thao, a forty-seven-year-old man, died on the way to a Portland hospital after his wife found him lying in his bed, unresponsive. He had been up late watching television with an uncle and had gone to bed after midnight, briefly waking his wife. Both were soon asleep. 'Then came his laboured breathing, so loud that it awakened her. She shook him … [in the] next moments of horror, she realised that she could do nothing more.'

Adler herself became aware of these and similar deaths only in 1986. She presently learned that the first known accounts of the phenomenon were from 1977 (and here there is a genuine horror film link, as it was these early incidents which inspired director Wes Craven to create his infamous *Nightmare on Elm Street*); and that deaths were still occurring throughout the mid-1980s, having reached their statistical peak in 1981 and 1982. These fatalities became known as Sudden Unexpected Nocturnal Death Syndrome (SUNDS). Victims were all Hmong men, who died during sleep. The median age at death was 33, and 'the median length of time that they had been living in the United States before death was 17 months.' Realising that the victims all seemed to have suffered nightmare attacks, Adler began to research a remarkable possibility: that these men had in fact died of terror. After years of painstakingly interviewing Hmong men and women; studying the original Hmong cosmology and problems of adaptation in the US; and probing possible medical causes of death, Adler finally put all the pieces of this strange jigsaw into one startling picture. These Hmong men had indeed died of their fear of the evil spirits thought to cause nightmare attacks.

My own detective work on this subject began some time back. Even before I had realised the pivotal role of nightmare attacks in vampire outbreaks, I noticed that that young woman, Stanacka, seemed to have died of fear, during the episodes centred on Arnod Paole. But it was only when I began following up leads from Adler's research that I realised how precisely similar these 'fear-deaths' could be across time and space.

Fatal Fear?

The belief that the nightmare could kill went back a long way. Macnish cites the fifth-century Roman physician, Caelius Aurelianus, who had claimed that 'many people die of this complaint'; and Adler notes a twelfth-century Icelandic poem in which a warrior prince, Vanlandi, was attacked by a nightmare. Although his men sought to help him when he cried out in his sleep, Vanlandi's attacking demon shifted around and then 'pressed down on his head so that he died.' This case is interesting because it already involves the kind of magical beliefs found in vampire territory: Vanlandi's nightmare was supposedly the result of witchcraft.[1] Vanlandi himself may well have suspected this dark magic before the attack, as his friends refer to the possibility at one point in the story. If so, such fears could have catalysed the nightmare, while also bringing his fear during the attack to a fatal pitch.

Come 1746, Calmet is reviewing the possibility that supposed vampire victims died of fear. Interestingly, Calmet is otherwise rigorously sceptical about many aspects of the vampire outbreaks.

But one thing that he does think very probable is that, in such cases, fear could kill. For Calmet indeed believes that this frequently happens in his *own* country, and in the civilised world in general, during time of plague. In such cases, when 'a man finds himself indisposed in the least degree', he immediately thinks he has plague, and 'puts himself in so violent an agitation, that it is almost impossible he should get over it.' Calmet goes on to cite an instance from Marseilles, in which 'a woman … [was] literally frightened to death by a trifling illness, that her servant was seized with, which she imagined to be the plague.'[2]

In his 1816 *Treatise on the Incubus*, Waller claims to have heard of several nightmare attacks which proved fatal. One was a young carpenter known to him, who at age 30 had been subject to severe nightmares for much of his life. Working away from home for several weeks in Norwich, this young man went to bed one night in apparent good health. His landlord's family at one point heard him groan and say something; but as he quickly fell quiet, they took no further notice. In the morning the carpenter failed to appear. Someone went into his room, and 'he was found dead, having thrown himself by his exertions and struggles out of bed, with his feet, however, still entangled among the bedclothes. I have not the least doubt,' adds Waller, 'that it was Night-Mare which proved fatal to him.'[3] Just less than twenty years later Macnish, similarly, believed that, 'probably, some of those who are found dead in bed, have lost their lives in a fit of incubus, the circumstance being imputed to some other cause.'[4]

Given how startling this phenomenon might seem, it should be stressed that fear of magic and the supernatural have also produced dramatic physical effects short of death. Modern medical science recognises that this continuum of terror, even when not fatal, has caused 'paralysis … gait disorder … loss of vision, loss of hearing, and episodes resembling epilepsy.'[5] One of the earliest recorded cases has been consistently ignored. In the New Testament, Acts 13 tells of how Paul, enraged by the success of a rival magician, Bar-Jesus,

> set his eyes on him, And said, O full of all subtlety and all mischief, [thou] child of the devil, [thou] enemy of all righteousness … behold, the hand of the Lord [is] upon thee, and thou shalt be blind, not seeing the sun for a season. And immediately there fell on him a mist and a darkness; and he went about seeking some to lead him by the hand
>
> (Acts, 13.9–11).

Occurring in an intensely magical environment, after Paul has told his victim what to fear, this is a textbook case of what medicine now terms 'conversion disorder' – the physical expression of mental terror. It would later be seen in numerous cases of supposed witchcraft, where self-generated symptoms included bruising, varying degrees of paralysis, fits, and even stoppage of urine.[6] More recently, cases of shellshock from the First World War featured men who lost the power of speech. As with Bar-Jesus' loss of sight, this was real, but often only temporary.

Voodoo Death

If people in vampire territory died during or shortly after nightmare attacks, we can also say that they essentially died of their beliefs. These beliefs were magical or supernatural. And it is for this reason that other cases of 'voodoo death' make such a good match. In 1923, the missionary John Roscoe reported voodoo deaths seen during his time in East Africa. On one occasion three men were brought to him for treatment after being attacked by a leopard during a hunt. Two of them had been torn quite badly on their scalps; the third was merely scratched on his neck. Roscoe told this last man that he would soon be well. 'To my surprise he said, "I am dying."' Assuming that the man had an 'exaggerated idea of his wound', Roscoe asked him to come back with the others the next morning. Next day, only two men returned. They told Roscoe that the man with the neck wound had died. Roscoe concludes: 'so far as it was possible to discover, no complications had arisen, but he was convinced that the animal had been caused by magic to attack him and his imagination had done the rest.'[7]

Roscoe records no visible symptoms of infection, and the other two hunters, though suffering worse injuries, escaped with their lives. To us the dead man's idea might seem peculiarly quaint or tortuous. The simple explanation for the initial incident would be: leopards attack people; end of story. Or, looking at it another way, we might wonder at the sad irony of a case in which a man *escapes* the claws of a dangerous animal, only to die of the shadows in his own mind...

The leopard death was echoed by another African case in which Roscoe saw a soldier, at Lake Albert on the Sudan, who was thought to be choking on a bone in his throat. The man had fallen down and was gasping for breath. When he was examined, nothing was found there. But in a short time he died. 'It transpired that the man was convinced he was under a spell worked by another soldier.'

This second instance looks like a classic case of voodoo death. The initial seizure was something which the Australian anthropologist Herbert Basedow had seen *c.*1925, when an aborigine had had a bone pointed at him (i.e., been cursed) by a sorcerer. He collapsed in utter terror, frothing at the mouth and suffering convulsions. Presently he crawled off, resigned to die, and did so in a very short time.[8]

This last instance we owe to Walter Cannon, an American physiologist who made a classic study of voodoo death in 1942. Cannon's first known example went back to 1587, derived from a Spanish traveller, Soares de Souza. Souza saw a number of cases of death 'induced by fright when men were condemned and sentenced by a so-called "medicine man"' among the Tupinambá Indians of Brazil. Later, travelling in the Congo in 1682, the missionary Girolamo Merolla heard of a young African who, staying with a friend on a journey, was given a wild hen to eat. The host told him that the food was something else, as wild hen was, for the young, 'strictly banned'. The two met again a few years later. Rather rashly, the host asked the young man if he would eat a wild hen; to which his answer was 'that he had been solemnly charged by a wizard not to eat that food.' The host laughed and asked him why he refused now, when he had eaten one at his table before. On hearing this, the young man 'immediately began to tremble, so greatly was he possessed by fear, and in twenty-four hours he was dead.'

In that case, the victim died of his beliefs, even though he had not been directly cursed by anybody. This was because the banned food was essentially 'taboo'. Now often used rather loosely in everyday speech (e.g., 'incest is one of the last taboos') this term originally came from study of tribal groups in Melanesia in the nineteenth century.[9] Cannon also records a case from New Zealand, *c.*1845, of a Maori woman who ate some fruit and then was told that this had been taken from a tabooed place, and the chief's spirit would kill her. 'This incident occurred in the afternoon; the next day about twelve o'clock she was dead.' Around 1890 a male victim of taboo among the Maoris died 'the same day he was tapued'.

Writing around 1906, the soldier A. G. Leonard told of voodoo deaths among the tribes of the Lower Niger:

> I have seen more than one hardened old Haussa soldier dying steadily and by inches because he believed himself to be bewitched;

no nourishment or medicines that were given to him had the slightest effect either to check the mischief or to improve his condition in any way ... under very similar conditions I have seen Kru-men and others die in spite of every effort that was made to save them, because they had made up their minds, not (as we thought at the time) to die, but that being in the clutch of malignant demons they were bound to die.[10]

The point about the 'hardened old solider' underlines what is implicit in many of these accounts. Men who were otherwise fearless in warfare were nonetheless terrified of magic – so much so that their fear could kill them. The same went for the Tupinambá, known as one of the most ferocious of New World cannibal tribes. And the same also went, deep in the heart of Europe, for those hardened soldiers who had fought dauntlessly against the Turks, and who were yet childishly afraid of vampires.

These cases may seem remote from modern urban life. Yet there are in fact instances of Western, educated medical patients dying of fear – or of their mistaken beliefs – in clinical settings. Adler points out that Gerald W. Milton, 'who treated patients in an Australian melanoma clinic, became "convinced of the similarity between the westernised man dying through fear of a disease from which there is no escape and the aborigine who dies from an all-powerful spell."' Adler goes on to explain how 'Milton found that, for some of his cancer patients, "the realisation of impending death is a blow so terrible that they are quite unable to adjust to it, and they die rapidly before the malignancy seems to have developed enough to cause death."'

Still more striking is the case of a Tennessee physician, Clifton Meador. In 1974 (writes Adler) Meador 'treated a patient for cancer of the oesophagus, a disease that was considered fatal at the time. The patient died a few weeks later, but the subsequent autopsy revealed that his oesophagus was perfectly healthy.' Interviewed three decades later, Meador stated explicitly: 'he died with cancer, but not from cancer ... I thought he had cancer. He thought he had cancer. Everyone around him thought he had cancer.'[11] These people seem to have died from fear or hopelessness. We might add that, ironically, their belief in the authority of Western scientific medicine was in a way equal to a belief in magic: its power, like that of the witch-doctor, was absolute and unquestionable.

A second clinical point concerns the precise physiology of extreme fear. When attacked by a predator and seemingly facing death, a human or animal can revert to a last-ditch evolutionary mechanism,

> known as 'tonic immobility' or quiescence – in lay terms, 'playing possum'. When an animal is seized by an attacker, the caudal ventrolateral region of the vPAG (the ventral periaqueductal grey matter in the brain) generates a response that, from the outside, looks like total collapse. In the teeth of a full-blown sympathetic response, the parasympathetic system now swings into overdrive. The body, insensitive to pain, goes completely limp, often falling to the ground with limbs splayed and neck thrown back. Eyes closed, it trembles, defecates, and lies still. It looks, in a word, dead.

The quoted words are those of Jeff Wise, a contemporary adventurer and scientist of fear. Wise offers some memorable examples of this strange evolutionary response. Explaining that 'many predators will not eat prey that looks dead,' he cites the case of the missionary David Livingstone, who fell into this state when he was quite literally caught in a lion's teeth. The lion dropped the unappetising explorer and moved off after some hunters who were clearly alive. More recently, a young woman called Sue Yellowtail was saved in much the same way when attacked by a mountain lion in Colorado one December morning. First stalked by the animal, she tried to run across a stream and slipped halfway. With the cat's teeth sunk into her scalp, and death possibly seconds away, she dropped into quiescence. The animal, Wise notes, evidently reacted just as Livingstone's full-size lion had: 'momentarily, it released its grip. That was enough. In an instant she had snapped out of her dissociative dream state and was sputtering back up to the air. Without reason, without thought, she started running, flailing so hard that she ran right out of one of her hip boots.' Luckily for her, aggression very quickly succeeded passivity – in further dramatic struggles, Yellowtail had to stab the cat in the eye before she finally escaped.[12]

Even a layman's glance at this impressive emergency response shows that it is meant to be only short-term. It is nice not to feel pain when in a lion's mouth, but you are of course *meant* to feel pain for good reason, so that you can respond and get some sort of help. And there are indeed serious physiological consequences 'if quiescence goes on too long': 'heart rate and blood pressure can plunge dramatically, indeed to the point of death.' Wise concludes unequivocally: 'it's not just folklore: you really can die of fright.'[13]

Vampire Deaths

When we bring this scientific knowledge into the midst of vampire hysteria, it explains several cases of nightmare-death very precisely. In much of vampire territory, voodoo deaths of various kinds were widespread well into the twentieth century. In 1923 that great explorer of the Balkans, Edith Durham, described a vampire panic near Vlasenitsa in Bosnia. During a typhus attack a young man died, after which his wife began to sicken. She swore that her dead spouse had returned in the night and drunk her blood, insisting, 'He is a lampir!' The neighbours panicked, and begged permission to exhume the man's body. But the authorities refused. Durham adds:

> The lampir was seen and heard by many people and there were 15 deaths. It would be interesting to know how many of these died because they believed they must die. The peasants all through Albania, and Macedonia are extraordinarily affected mentally if they believe they must die. In Albania, I heard of more than one case in which a man's death having been foretold by reading the future in fowls' bones, he proceeded to sicken and die. There was no suspicion whatever of poison and the tale appeared to be true.

The Bosnian case is an ambiguous one. Typhoid fever can be fatal, and could well have been the cause of all fifteen deaths. But there clearly were a lot of nightmare attacks in Vlasenitsa during this crisis: they first hit the wife, and then her neighbours. Durham states tellingly that 'the lampir was seen and heard by many people' (perhaps thus indicating poltergeist noises), and also that 'more and more had their blood sucked by him.'[14] Unfortunately, what we don't know is how quickly those subsequent deaths occurred. If victims expired within three days of 'seeing the vampire', then we could well assume that a combination of nightmare and voodoo death was responsible.

What is clear is that the Albanian case of the fowl's bones is a classic voodoo death. And it was certainly not the only one to occur in vampire territory. As we have seen, in Derekuoi St Clair and Brophy found that all matters of health (and much else besides) were in the hands of the village witch. Far from being scapegoated or victimised, this woman was powerful and revered – and indeed more or less salaried. If someone was ill the witch took a scarf with a knot in it, measured it against her arm, and then transferred it to the arm of the patient. If the knot fell near their hand or fingers, the person's illness was 'entirely imaginary, but if it touches the elbow he is condemned to death beyond the power of the Bulgarian Pharmacopeia.' The officers add quite emphatically that: 'our late landlord Tanez was given over by the witch and had *made up his mind to die.*' Why was Tanez visiting the witch in the first place? Apparently because of hangovers, or at any rate some symptoms produced (St Clair and Brophy thought) by excessive intakes of wine. Certainly the officers managed to effect their own cure, using nothing more occult than a Seidlitz powder.

A no less striking parallel to tribal voodoo deaths derived from the villagers' belief in the magical power of the (evidently wild) Cheshmé cat. 'The brother of Marynka, our washerwoman, was bitten by one of the Cheshmé cats, and died either from the wound or from fright.' This man may well have died from the wound – what the officers say about the local sanitary habits would make blood poisoning all too likely. Yet it seems quite clear that the Bulgarians had a magical belief in the power of this animal. Hence the fact that the witch could also 'cure ... the bite of a Cheshmé cat' merely by spells. (Compare that African leopard whose bite was magically fatal.) Conversely, the village witch could also 'cast spells which will cause their object to die the lingering death of the spellbound.'

The forms of voodoo death and voodoo belief which Brophy and St Clair met in the 1860s were still serious facts in Albania and Macedonia when Durham wrote in 1923. At more or less the same time that imperial explorers were witnessing tribal cases in darkest Africa or Australia, the very same thing was going on in the heart of Europe. Although neither Brophy, St Clair, nor Durham had any idea of voodoo death as an anthropological concept, their descriptions fit the psychology and the symptoms perfectly. These people could die of their belief in magic and, as with so many tribal cases, 'seem to make no effort whatsoever to live.'

The first stage in the nightmare deaths of vampire country seems often to be a visible wasting of the victim. Calmet tells of how, among the Haiduks of the Hungarian-Transylvanian border, 'there are dead persons, called by them vampires, which suck the blood of the living, so as to make them fall away visibly to skin and bones...' Again, recalling that famous case of the 'bite-marks' seen by 1300 people near Belgrade, we hear that 'the persons whose blood had been sucked found themselves in a pitiable state of languor, weakness, and lassitude.'[15]

And when we dissect the language closely associated with the nightmare, we find this sense of physical wastage lodged within it. Drawing on Hufford, Adler points out that the word 'haggard' may well be connected to the old nightmare phrase 'hag rid' (i.e., ridden by the hag). And, as the Oxford English Dictionary reminds us, 'haggard' once had the sense of 'half-starved; gaunt, lean'. Ironically, this kind of physical effect could well have been another example of the vicious spiral of terror. Once a person believed that they had suffered a vampire attack, they began to *look* like the victim of a vampire attack. This then reinforced their desperate status, in both their own and everyone else's eyes. Accordingly, they adopted the kind of unto-death fatalism described by Durham. In such cases, even if they did have a real disease, they would probably (like certain of those cancer patients) have died far more quickly of their own fear of vampirism than ordinary patients would. Fear was the vampire that sucked their life away.

Here we already see a radical degree of mind over matter. Fear or stress eats away the victim's body. As to the actual deaths? Yet again, examples seem to go back to the very earliest documented revenants. In Herefordshire, *c.*1150, a deceased Welsh wizard became a revenant. Four nights after his death, 'he came back, and keeps coming every night, calling by name certain of his former neighbours, who instantly fall sick and die within three days.' Next comes Stephen Hubener of Trawtenaw. In 1567 Hubener, returning shortly after burial, 'did pinch many men with such strait embracements, that many of them died, yet diverse recovered again, who all with one consent confessed that they were thus clasped or beclipped by this rich man, in that very habit in which they had seen him alive.'

Later, in the more full-blooded vampire territory of Kisilova, we have Peter Plogojowitz. With Plogojowitz dead and buried some ten weeks, 'within a week, nine people, both old and young, died also, after suffering a 24-hour illness. And they said publicly, while they were yet alive, but on their deathbed, that the above-mentioned

Plogojowitz ... had come to them in their sleep, laid himself on them, and throttled them, so that they would have to give up the ghost.'

In the winter of 1731–2, during the protracted aftermath of the Arnod Paole case, the woman 'named Stanacka ... went to bed in perfect health, but awoke in the middle of the night, trembling, and crying out, that the son of the Heyduke Millo, who died about nine weeks before, had almost strangled her while she was asleep. From that time, she fell into a languishing state, and died at three days end.' These very clear nightmare symptoms prompt us to suspect that when the unnamed 16-year-old son of a Haiduk, and another, Joachim (aged 17) died here after 'a three-day illness' the cause may have also been voodoo death catalysed by nightmares.[16]

From Derekuoi we hear of a man named Dimitri who was continually harassed by a female water spirit. In part this must have involved daytime hallucinations, for Dimitri could 'never go out of his house without seeing' the spirit. Dimitri obtained a remedy from a Turkish Hodja and this proved effective (notice the probable psychosomatic basis of the cure). But presently, growing complacent, he neglected to use the remedy, 'and one evening was seized upon by his supernatural inamorata, who imprinted a fervent kiss upon his lips; a week afterwards Dimitri was dead.' Under St Clair's typically dry prose we are able to perceive yet one more version of that nightmarish sucking out of human life. Here, surely, is an incident truly meriting that hackneyed old phrase 'the kiss of death'.

In Greece, and within living memory, we have the mountain villagers of Ambéli. Du Boulay states quite clearly that here the vampires, 'coming in any guise, human or animal ... return to attack either their own family or their own flocks, damaging and eventually killing them – an action often described as 'suffocating' (*ná pníxei*) – by going up the nose and drinking their blood.'[17] Barber, finally, notes that 'the vampires of the Gypsies' may 'seek to kill them by sucking their blood, eating parts of their bodies, doing other violence to them, or simply causing them such terror that they die.'[18]

All of these look like possible or probable voodoo deaths. As we saw, the timespan for such fatalities was somewhere between one and three days. With Plogojowitz it is very clear that victims died just a day after their nightmares. And that account also has one other possible clue. Victims all stated that Plogojowitz 'throttled them, so that they

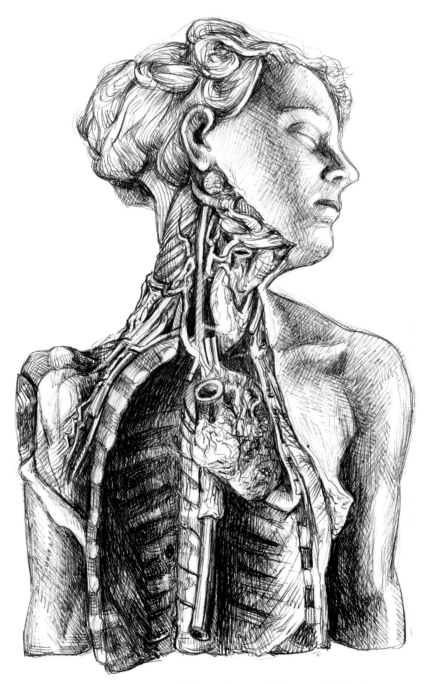

Some people believed the site of the soul was the heart, which led to strange methods of dealing with this organ when the recently deceased person was believed to be 'undead' and causing harm to the living. Drawing by R. Ennis, 2007 (Wellcome Collection.

Santorini, today a popular tourist destination, was once known as a notorious Vampire Island in Greek culture. (Picture courtesy of Trans World Productions on Flickr)

Medieval deviant burials from Sozopol, Bulgaria. (Courtesy of Wiki Commons)

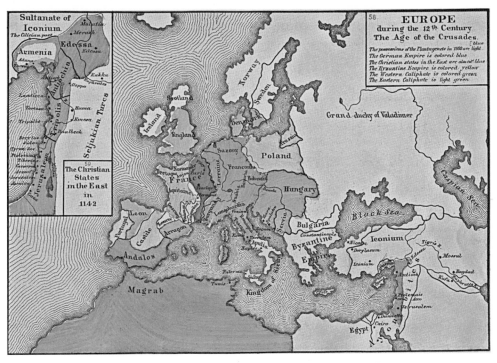

Europe in the twelfth century, showing Bulgaria just north of the Byzantine Empire. (Courtesy of Perry-Castañeda Library Map Collection)

Melrose Abbey – home of a medieval British revenant. (Courtesy of Tom Hartley on Flickr)

The Mediterranean in 1204. (Courtesy of Perry-Castañeda Library Map Collection)

The recovery of supposedly dead victims of cholera, as depicted in *The Premature Burial* by Antoine Wiertz, fuelled the demand for safety coffins. (Courtesy of Wiki Commons)

PLATE V.

CORPSE-DOOR, DARUM, WESTJUTLAND.

To face p. 364.

Above left: This 1600 work by Jacob de Gheyn represents an experience that could be all too real to people who feared that the dead would return to haunt them. (Courtesy of Rijksmusem)

Above right: An example of a corpse door, in Darum, West Jutland, as seen by H. F. Feilberg, in the late nineteenth century.

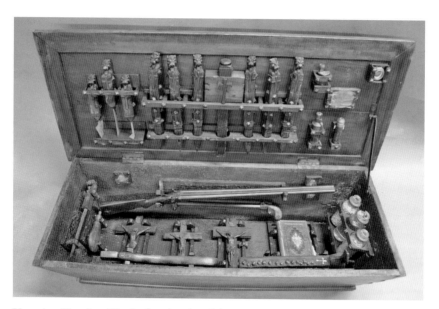

Vampire Hunting Kit in hand-painted box. (Courtesy of Anthony Hogg and Sterling Associates, Inc/Live Auctioneers)

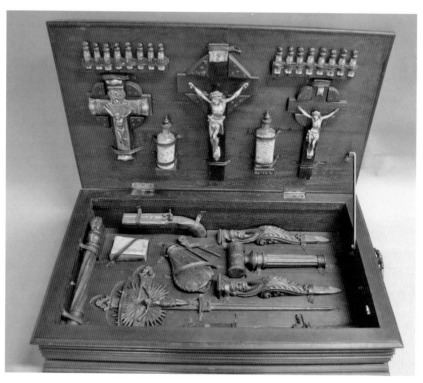

Vampire Hunting Kit in coffin box. (Courtesy of Anthony Hogg and Sterling Associates, Inc/Live Auctioneers)

Right: Everett Peck, last surviving descendant of the Brown family, pictured in 1981. (Courtesy of Michael E. Bell)

Below: The New England graves of the Brown family. Mercy Brown was believed to be a vampire who lived off the bodies of her living relatives, who died soon afterwards. (Courtesy of Michael E. Bell)

'When they dug up Mercy ... she had turned over in the grave,' said Everett Peck when he was asked about the widely-held belief that she was a vampire. (Courtesy of Michael E. Bell)

Rachel Harris died soon after her marriage to Captain Isaac Burton in 1793. People believed she was to blame when her stepsister Hulda also died a few years later, after Hulda had become Captain Burton's second wife. (Courtesy of Michael E. Bell)

would have to give up the ghost.' This seems to be their way of saying that they *knew* that they would now *have* to die, (i.e., 'give up the ghost'). With Stanacka, Calmet's 'languishing state' fits both tonic immobility and the various descriptions of all those tribespeople who simply laid down to die. Barber's (possibly more accurate) version tells how she 'experienced a great pain in the chest and became worse hour after hour.'[19] This localised pain sounds rather like the kind of psychosomatic illness which elsewhere paralysed people's legs or (in Marotinu de Sus) gave Costel a pain in the chest.

It is worth adding, lest anyone find these deaths too far-fetched, that in Britain throughout the nineteenth century a number of people died of what was effectively voodoo death, after believing that they had seen ghosts. In several cases this was the result of the crudest prank.[20]

Sudden Death: Vagal Inhibition

We saw above that Macnish's young carpenter was found dead the morning after a nightmare attack. Macnish believed that the carpenter and others like him had been killed by their Nightmares – that they had, in fact, died of terror. Clearly this is quite different from the voodoo deaths seen above. In these there is usually a gap of at least several hours between the trigger (curse, broken taboo, etc.) and the actual death, with the timespan sometimes being as much as three days. But MacNish's carpenter must have died in eight hours at most, and probably (given the typical working lifestyles of a manual labourer of that period) as little as six. Meanwhile, Yong Leng Thao, that Hmong victim of SUNDs, clearly died far more quickly than that. One possible key to the difference between voodoo death and sudden death is the medical phenomenon known as vagal inhibition.

As Bernard Knight explains, vagal inhibition refers to 'sudden heart stoppage due to excessive nervous stimulation of the heart via the vagus nerve, which is the paired (10th) cranial nerve which leaves the base of the brain and courses down the neck, through the chest to terminate in the abdomen.' The vagus nerve 'supplies many organs and structures with "parasympathetic" nerve fibres, which is part of the "autonomic nervous system". This is not under voluntary control and performs a myriad of functions concerned with the workings of blood vessels, glands, heart etc.' Knight stresses that 'any sudden unexpected stimulus to many parts of the body can cause a burst of nerve impulses to pass down the parasympathetic via the vagus, so slowing or stopping the heart. In contrast to sympathetic nerve activity (the "flight or fight" response which releases adrenaline and directly speeds up the heart), vagus impulses slow the heart, and in excess can stop it altogether.'

The most common result of vagal inhibition would be only a temporary faint. But death has been recorded in a number of cases. The condition can be triggered by more or less purely mechanical causes, such as the sudden immersion of skin in cold water, or even the sudden intrusion of cold water into the throat. The most common physical cause, however, is a sudden pressure on the neck – one which can be as light as an unexpected and well-meaning tap from an unseen friend. Interestingly, though, 'the likelihood of vagal inhibition is heightened when the victim is pre-sensitised by emotional tension ... very apprehensive patients have died instantly,' adds Knight, 'on having teeth extracted or small operations performed under local anaesthetic ... even a horrific or nauseating sight has caused sudden death.'[21]

The more mechanical side of vagal inhibition is well illustrated by the case of a batsman, killed by a ball to the chest in London in 1964, as well as by a horse which died of shock almost instantly when confronted by a troop of elephants from a visiting menagerie.[22] In 1958 Brenda Carol Holt, aged 12, 'died from vagal inhibition caused by fright after she had seen her dog run into the path of an oncoming car.' After going home with her (unharmed) dog to get a lead, Brenda collapsed into a chair and died almost immediately. The pathologist, Professor J. M. Webster, thought that the girl's fright was 'delayed'.[23] By 'delay' here Webster seems to mean longer than the few seconds or minutes of many such cases: for Brenda appears to have died around an hour after the near-miss with the car. A longer case of delay occurred in 1968 when a Pakistani man, Malik Youkb, was attacked by racist thugs who beat his car while he was in it, also throwing bricks through the back window as he drove away. Youkb later complained of backache and died in hospital.[24]

These two cases are, in some ways, very close to certain deaths found in vampire country. Although they did not occur immediately, they both seem to have produced death more quickly than happens with voodoo deaths. Most importantly of all, death occurs solely through emotional trauma, without any external physical impact on the victim's body. We seem, then, to find that people can die of fear (by voodoo death, in around 12–72 hours) or of terror. The latter, if caused by vagal inhibition, can take mere seconds or minutes, with delayed cases taking one or more hours.[25]

Terror Deaths: Vampires and Spirits

Did certain nightmare victims die of terror *during* vampire nightmares? The answer is almost certainly yes. Hubener's victims are one possible instance. He, as we have just recalled, 'did pinch many men with such strait embracements, that many of them died.' The account then carefully goes on to explain that, 'yet diverse recovered again, who all with one consent confessed that they were thus clasped or beclipped by this rich man, in that very habit in which they had seen him alive.' This essentially means, 'though the deceased died before they could tell us anything, those who survived confirmed that...'.What they confirmed were, of course, abundant nightmares.

Secondly, if we look again at that 1888 account from the Cretan monastery, we find a very strong hint: 'There is great danger that the sufferer may expire, and himself too be turned into a vrykolakas, if there be not someone at hand who perceives his torment and fires off a gun, thereby putting the bloodthirsty monster to flight.' Does the writer here mean that when a gun was *not* fired (thus ending the nightmare), sufferers died in their beds? If so, the death must have occurred no later than morning, when a body was found, making the longest timespan about five hours.

Perhaps not surprisingly, the most clinically precise accounts on this topic come from those nightmare deaths of Hmong refugees, beginning more than forty years ago. These men were found dead in their beds, often 'with looks of terror on their faces'. They had died in the throes of nightmare attacks. Occasionally, a relative would be awakened while this was happening. Yet even then, the sufferer 'died within a minute or two'.

Between 1977 and 2010, as many as 117 Southeast Asians died of SUNDS in the US. All but one of the victims were male. Between 1986 and 1992, a cardiologist called Pedro Brugada collected a number of unusual looking ECG results, their shape 'reminiscent of a shark's fin'. These findings ultimately identified a rare heart condition which became known as 'Brugada syndrome'. Brugada syndrome is an inherited condition, eight to ten times more common in men, which can 'lead to un-co-ordinated electrical activity in the heart's lower chambers'. The resulting effects ranged from fainting, seizure, and breathing difficulties, through to sudden death. By the time that

Adler wrote in 2010, it was accepted by the scientific community that SUNDS and Brugada syndrome were the same thing. Because the condition is very hard to detect or predict ('clinically silent' as Adler puts it) data on affected groups remains incomplete. But it does seem clear that many, if not all, of the Hmong fatalities suffered from this underlying condition.

Do we therefore simply conclude that they died of natural causes? Adler's answer was, in fact, no. Hmong cosmology, she found, gave the nightmare special powers of terror. Back in Laos, the Hmong had practised rituals connected to ancestor worship. Among other things, these involved animal sacrifice. Now that they were living in the US, the Hmong were unable to conduct their traditional rituals. This left them vulnerable to evil spirits – ones from which their own, ancestral spirits would normally have protected them.

For the nightmare, among the Hmong, is an evil spirit. Their term for the condition is *dab tsong*, and 'tsong' is the name of this spirit. The attacks therefore confirmed to them that they were being punished for failing their dead kin. But this was not all. The rituals were, for the Hmong, a predominantly *male* responsibility. And the Hmong interpretation of spirit attacks was quite precise. The first two nightmares which a man suffered were both serious and terrifying. But it was the third that they expected to be fatal.

In reaching her hard-won conclusion on the Hmong deaths, Adler shrewdly emphasised the kind of traumas the Hmong had faced *before* they reached the US. Those who actually escaped had come through an attempted genocide – which killed tens of thousands in 1975 – and survived the perilous crossing of the Mekong river, where many were drowned.[26] Why, then, had underlying heart problems not been brought to the pitch of cardiac arrest in these circumstances?

In the light of this striking contrast between the effects of human trauma and supernatural terror, Adler concluded:

It is my contention that in the context of severe and ongoing stress related to cultural disruption and national resettlement (exacerbated by intense feelings of powerlessness about existence in the United States), and from the perspective of a belief system in which evil spirits have the power to kill men who do not fulfill their religious obligations, the solitary Hmong man confronted by the numinous terror of the Nightmare (and aware of its murderous intent) can die of SUNDS.[27]

As we briefly noted in the last chapter, the nightmare boasts an impressive trio of central demons: vampire, witch, and alien abductor. As we are shortly about to enter the world of the poltergeist – a zone where ordinary laws of physics warp and often shatter – we can use these two terrifying icons as a kind of antechamber on our journey, bracing us for the strangest realm of all. First, the witch.

The Witch versus the Vampire

Any schoolchild can tell you a good deal about witches or vampires. But what few people realise is how peculiarly interchangeable these two figures have been throughout history. The witch was the ultimate scapegoat. On countless occasions she was blamed for death and disease in humans and animals, severe weather, crop failure and even the drying up of milk in human women.[28] In terms of a rival scapegoat, the vampire was almost certainly the closest contender. In addition to disease and death, vampires were also accused of causing severe weather, from droughts to floods to frosts. In Romania, certain 'live vampires' were complicit in such phenomena. 'When a vampire washes itself, rain will fall from heaven. Thus, when a drought occurs, nobles send all their men to wash, because any of them may be a vampire.' Moreover, male vampires in this region grow tails after death, and 'the moment any vampire wets its tail, there is rain.' Adding that 'it is usually special vampires (live) who have power over rain', Murgoci also notes (writing in 1926) that 'heavy rains in Zărneşti were supposed to be caused by a recently buried girl, thought to be a vampire.'

Meanwhile, over in the Polish village of Muszyna in Galicia in May 1893, eleven peasants were cooling their heels in the local jail. Believing that 'the recent frosts were the work of a vampire which had entered into an old man who had lately been buried,' these men had 'opened the grave, beheaded the body, and pierced the heart with a stake.'[29] Various twists on this kind of ritual could be seen in following years. When the village schoolmaster died in the Czech village of Metschin in spring 1900, he was 'buried with every mark of esteem on the part of the inhabitants.' But come the end of August, 'the villagers are one and all clamouring that he may be exhumed, owing to the long spell of drought [that] has set in, to the great loss of all the farmers in that district.' Perhaps at a loss as to how this worthy man could have caused the problem, the

165

villagers presently learned that his 'sorrowing relations were unwise enough to place under the poor man's head a cushion stuffed with feathers ... and until the feathery pillow is removed they maintain that no rain will fall.'[30]

In Hungary at the same time, the problem was not droughts, but storms. Accordingly, an elder in the village of Szuszag decided that the corpse of Joseph Zurka, interred weeks earlier, was to blame, and the villagers (for once showing some commendable sense of dramatic flair) opened the grave one stormy night, and ran a pitchfork into the heart of the corpse.[31] In Austria the following summer, 'the peasantry of the village of Kruzumar, near Czernowitz, guided by an ancient superstition, dug up a dead body from the cemetery, and flung it into the river at midnight to draw rain, as the district was suffering from long drought. When the body was found, several of the ringleaders were arrested, but as rain actually fell within a few days there is great indignation at their arrest.'[32] In Bosnian Hrenovicza, water was poured on the exhumed corpse of a recent suicide during a drought in summer 1902.[33]

Readers have probably spotted the implicit logic of some of these cases. A corpse buried with a dry feather pillow causes drought; to stop drought you fling the suspect corpse into a river... Interestingly, these habits supply a possible solution to the puzzle of a recently found deviant burial in Britain. In late January 2017 news broke of a Roman British skeleton from Stanwick, Northamptonshire, which had suffered a curious mutilation. Buried face down, the corpse had had its tongue amputated and replaced with a flat stone. 'Simon Mays, Historic England's human skeletal biologist, told the *Guardian's* Dalya Alberge that such a Romano-British mutilation was thought to be unique', adding, '"The fact that he's buried face down in the grave is consistent with somebody whose behaviour marked them out as odd or threatening within a community."'[34] This reputation meant that the dead man was later blamed for excessive rainfall. Hence the stone as magical counter-measure – something hard, dry and dead where the soft, moist, living tongue had once been.[35]

Back in the crimson heart of vampire country, in Transylvania in 1904, a severe drought in the village of Renschor was thought to be the work of a dead man named Bordas. Accordingly, 'the inhabitants of the place, acting on the advice of the soothsayer from a neighbouring village, exhumed the body at midnight, and with many incantations, hurled the body from one to another on pitchforks, at the same time violently restraining from intervention the son of Bordas, who besought them to desist. All concerned in the outrage have been arrested, and this time an example is to be made.'[36] This report needs to be treated with a little caution, given that hurling a body from one pitchfork to another would appear unique in vampire country. For all that, the broad pattern makes sense, and the 'soothsayer' sounds not unlike the revered and powerful local witch described by Brophy and St Clair.

So much for weather. Regarding livestock, we have seen that the vampires of Ambéli were held to kill both their own family, and the family's flocks; and we will soon meet a Greek vampire stealthily drinking the milk of goats. One type of Russian vampire was said, *c.*1874, to gnaw on itself in the grave before going out, more adventurously, to consume cattle.[37] The notorious Cuntius of Pentsch was wont, in his lighter moments, to suck dry the cows and devour poultry. More broadly, Summers (writing in the 1920s) states that 'in Russia ... in Poland, in Serbia and among the Slavonic peoples generally, an epidemic among the cattle is generally ascribed to a vampire who is draining them of their vitality.' Most impressively of all, the Bulgarian ustrel was a type of vampire which fed *only* on cattle:

> An ustrel is the spirit of a Christian child who was born on a Saturday and died unfortunately before he could be baptized. On the ninth day after burial he grubs his way out of the grave and attacks the cattle at once, sucking their blood all night and returning at peep of dawn to the grave to rest from his labours. In ten days or so the copious draughts of blood which he has swallowed have so fortified his constitution that he can undertake longer journeys; so when he falls in with great herds of cattle or flocks of sheep he returns no more to the grave for rest and refreshment at night, but takes up his quarters during the day either between the horns of a sturdy calf or ram or between the hind legs of a milch-cow.

Aside from the striking details of this account (penned in 1913), we are also reminded of how the Bulgarians of Derekuoi so precisely graded the progress of their vampires, from the tamer devils of the nine-day apprenticeship, to those of ten days and upwards. And the detail seen above grows no less abundant and colourful when we witness the destruction of the ustrel...

On a Saturday, before sunrise, a drummer signals to all the village that no fires may be lit. No one may even smoke. Two men go into the wood, pick two branches, strip off all their clothes, and rub the branches together (Boy Scout fashion) until they get a flame. From this they light two bonfires, one on either side of a cross-roads, which is known to be frequented by wolves. The whole herd is driven between these two fires, and the ustrel, unable to stand the heat, drops to the ground. After this no one may go near the cross-roads for several days. If they did, the ustrel would call their name and follow them back to the village. But, left alone, he is presently strangled by a wolf at midnight, so that 'the herdsmen can see the ground soaked with his slimy blood.'[38]

It hardly needs stressing that this must have been a lot of trouble. As a Cub Scout I personally spent many fruitless hours rubbing together two exceptionally dry sticks. Nothing ever happened. We can also fairly imagine that the two Bulgarian fire starters may have caught pneumonia if the ritual was enacted during the winter.

For our purposes, this kind of obsessive procedure is interesting because it attests to the very real belief in the ustrel. And this belief itself, bizarre as it now looks, was almost certainly founded on the basis of *genuine* cattle disease. For we hear of how

> beasts whose blood he has sucked die the same night ... he begins with the fattest animal and works his way down steadily through the leaner kine till not one single beast is left alive. The carcasses of the victims swell up, and when the hide is stripped off you can always perceive the livid patch of flesh where the monster sucked the blood of the poor creature. In a single night he may, by working hard, kill five cows; but he seldom exceeds that number.[39]

If we cut the ustrel out of this, the symptoms themselves could well have been detailed by a professional vet. Bloating in cattle, as Sally Hickey points out, can be caused by 'ingestion of lush green fodder' or root crops.[40] So we have here a real problem, very serious in an isolated rural economy. And we have a scapegoat. Did it work? If the problem was in fact parasites, then the heat of the fires may have driven them off the animals.

In worlds of everyday magic (which was most of the world, most of the time) there were always going to be scapegoats. The question was: who, or what? Were they devils from hell, or your neighbour from down the street? When we focus this question sharply down to the central opposition, witch versus vampire, we are struck by one of the stranger ironies of supernatural history. With unwitting chivalry, thousands of dead vampires saved the lives of thousands of living women.

During the official witch-hunts of early-modern Europe, perhaps 50,000 people were executed as witches. Citing this estimate, the witchcraft historian Richard Golden gives a possible range of 'between 40,638 and 52,738', adding that 'defensible estimates could range upwards of 100,000.'[41] The numbers who died under torture before reaching trial, and who were beaten, cut, stabbed or ostracised, may also run into many thousands. Vigilante attacks and killings went on across Europe for centuries after the legal persecution of witches had been outlawed by educated powers.[42] In 1751 Ruth Osborne was murdered as a witch in Tring, Hertfordshire; in 1860 Antonia Alanis was tortured to death in Mexico; in 1879 a Russian woman, Agrafena Ignatjewa, was boarded into her house by terrified villagers and burned alive.[43] In the west of England around 1885 two brothers were imprisoned for burning to death an old woman they believed to have bewitched their cattle. Many others, if lucky to have escaped with their lives, may never have recovered from the psychological trauma of vigilante attacks. In Great Paxton, Huntingdonshire, in spring 1808, all the pleas of the local vicar could not protect witch suspect Ann Izzard, who (as Stephen A. Mitchell explains) was dragged from her own bed one night, scratched with pins, and severely beaten.[44] George Hendricks has detailed attacks occurring in Germany and Switzerland in the 1950s and '60s.[45] And, as is well known, witch-killings still occur in parts of the world today. A 72-year-old woman was burned to death in Ghana in 2010, and Kepari Leniata, a young mother in Papua New Guinea, was doused with petrol and set alight in February 2013.[46]

Before vampotainment, there was real vampire terror. Before Harry Potter, magic was real and dangerous – not least to those suspected of it. And in this kind of world, the vampire was remarkably useful to all those women who may otherwise have been the necessary scapegoats for anything from non-laying chickens to a raging bout of fatal disease. What we realise when we look at the vampire from this new angle is, first, how much he or she was integrated into a tightly-knit web of pervasive magic (rather than cut neatly into a lean, cape-wearing icon). And we realise, secondly, by how many threads the witch and the vampire were linked across this web of everyday occultism. Two especially powerful links were the nightmare, and voodoo death.

On 14 April 1621, Elizabeth Sawyer of Edmonton was charged with various crimes performed by supposed witchcraft. On 19 April she was hanged as a witch at Tyburn. Sawyer's case is relatively well-known – with impressive speed and opportunism, Thomas Dekker, William Rowley and John Ford adapted her story into a play and had it on the stage by December of that year. One of their sources was an account published by a minister, Henry Goodcole, who had spoken to Sawyer in prison. Aside from his obvious bias (he believed in witchcraft, and that Sawyer was a witch) Goodcole's account is evidently detailed and reliable. Among other things, he tells of how Sawyer did 'witch unto death Agnes Ratcliffe', because Ratcliffe did 'strike a sow' belonging to Sawyer 'for licking up a little soap where she had laid it.'

Declaring that she would be revenged for this assault on the pig, Sawyer 'thus threatened Agnes Ratcliffe, that it should be a dear blow unto her, which accordingly fell out, and suddenly; for that evening Agnes ... fell very sick, and was extraordinarily vexed, and in a most strange manner in her sickness was tormented.' Her husband indeed swore to the court that his wife 'died ... within four days after she fell sick: and further then related, that in the time of her sickness his wife Agnes ... lay foaming at the mouth, and was extraordinarily distempered.' Also seen in this condition by several neighbours, Agnes explicitly stated that, 'if she did die at that time she would verily take it on her death, that Elizabeth Sawyer her neighbour, whose sow with a washing-beetle she had stricken, and so for that cause her malice being great, was the occasion of her death.'

It hardly needs emphasising that this is a clear case of voodoo death. Ratcliffe knew of the curse. And she was terrified of witches. Accordingly, just like all those cursed tribespeople of Australia or Africa, she died within four days, after foaming at the mouth, and openly confirming her own belief that Sawyer had attempted her death.

Much later, in the 1890s the folklorist J. Hampden Porter wandered bemusedly through the Allegheny Mountains of North America, a place where magic and superstition swarmed like flies in summer. Among many startling tales, not the least was this. 'The sister-in-law of Doctor M--, during his absence, was pressed to death by the witch, Mrs R--, sitting night after night on her chest in the form of a wild-cat'. We are told, more precisely, that 'the unfortunate girl whom [the witch] destroyed saw her under her own form when she first came into the room, and then witnessed her transformation into a wild-cat that immediately leaped upon the bed'. There is clearly a strong chance that this was voodoo death catalysed by nightmare. All details fit that hypothesis. The attacks were repeated, and the associated stress and fear probably got worse as they went on. Mrs R--, the supposed witch, had 'great celebrity in the section of country where she lived, and was dreaded by everybody.' Her awesome reputation was confirmed for Porter when she grew violently hostile to him, thus prompting his normal guides to forsake his dangerous company.[47] We might add that the witch's 'victim' could hardly have been the *most* ignorant or credulous person in the village, given that her sister was married to a doctor.

Modern Nightmares

Faced with dark scraps of history such as this, it is easy to begin thinking that everything strange or irrational happened only in the past. A brief overview of the nightmare in our own times should assure us that this is far from true. One first basic question is: what support do modern nightmare victims have?

Lonely in Your Nightmare: Sleep Paralysis without a Community
If you suffered a nightmare in witch or vampire country, you did not suffer alone. As soon as possible, you told everyone about the witch or vampire. And they, of course, acted in time-honoured fashion. In the shorter term, general knowledge of the nightmare of the first sufferer might well mean *more* nightmares across the town or village, and a good deal of hysteria. And if the culprit was held to be a witch, then this shared knowledge would often result in violence, and perhaps death for the chosen scapegoat. But in vampire territory we have an interesting difference. You attacked only a dead culprit. And, because this was very likely to calm the frenzied psychosomatic electricity supplying the nightmares, people were probably cured. Yet again, the vampire is a relatively useful and benign sort of scapegoat.

Now: contrast this with the bizarrely isolated condition of recent nightmare sufferers in the USA or Britain. 'This is the most terrifying experience I have ever had because I feel like a demon was trying to kill me. Please can someone tell me if they have been through something similar? No one understands in my family or friends!'[48] 'I thought I was the only person in the world that this had happened to,' writes a victim cited by Adler.[49] 'I am 30 years old and I have had this sleep disorder since I was about 17 ... Initially I was embarrassed by it for many years and didn't really know how to explain it to people without freaking them out and so I didn't speak about [it]!'[50] Statements such as these seem to capture the majority experience in the United States – a country that, for decades, has had the most advanced and abundant medical knowledge and technology the world has ever known.

In many cases, sufferers do not tell anyone for a very long time – not even in their immediate family. This is vividly borne out by a recent case in which a 23-year-old victim described attacks to their mother, who 'freaked out and said I was being punished for some kind of wrongdoing in the past.' Adler, who uncovered the story, adds that it was almost twenty years later that this sufferer learned the truth: 'My dad, my grandmother, and one of my uncles had it, too, but the family had been keeping it secret because they thought it was a sign of insanity!'[51] Writing to the *New York Times* in 1999, a man named Aamer Mumtaz told of suffering sleep paralysis since his childhood. Despite the fact that his attacks involved no suffocation or evil entities, Mumtaz 'always thought that these events were either psychological in origin or that, worse, something was physically wrong with me. In either event, they seemed too bizarre to discuss with any doctor. So I never mentioned them to anyone.'[52]

Since the late 1980s, David J. Hufford has been a world authority on the nightmare experience. But matters were very different when he suffered his first attack, in December 1964. His terror then was so great that, once the paralysis ceased, he leapt up and 'sprinted several blocks to take shelter in the student union building'. Even so, Hufford told no one. Ironically, it was only in 1971–2, when working as an anthropologist in Newfoundland, that he realised what had happened by hearing similar tales from local people. Although Hufford would go on to pioneer research on sleep paralysis, come 2009 he could still state: 'I suspect that millions of people in the United States are walking around never having told anybody about these terrifying experiences.'[53] When, in 2013, I made this point about community versus isolation to Professor Richard J. McNally, a veteran sleep researcher at Harvard, his response was almost identical: 'At least in America, the phenomenon is nearly unknown, yet when I mention to people, they often say how they experienced it and had no idea what had happened'.[54]

Faced with this kind of evidence, we may feel slightly less inclined to blame the unsympathetic mother who verbally attacked her suffering child, rather than reveal the dark family secret. What is rather more surprising is how ignorant even medical doctors have remained in America. One victim warned other sufferers on an internet post: 'go armed with info, as my doctor referred me to a psychiatrist.'[55] The word 'armed' is telling. Where your deeply irrational fellow villagers once offered you instant sympathy and support, in 21st-century America you were more likely to find yourself in a covert war of incomprehension with your ultra-rational, no-nonsense GP.

I am not saying, of course, that it would be better to believe in witches and vampires so as to gain a little more help and understanding. But the contrast is a strong and ironic one. Although the Hmong immigrants described by Adler have been frequently portrayed as deeply primitive by Americans, they would have had none of the problems of total incomprehension seen above. It is certainly not easy to explain the paradox of American ignorance in the midst of knowledge. One possible reason may be this: on the one hand, the actual experience of the nightmare remains, for many, almost as densely terrifying and evil as it was for witch and vampire communities. On the other, there is no general frame of reference: the experience is not only incomprehensible when it happens, but very probably unknown outside of the person's own life. It is worth wondering if, in this kind of context, some victims have even suffered an oblique kind of guilt. If they did, matters would not be helped by the secretive mother or the ignorant doctor seen above.

Alien Abduction

For some, there is of course one popular modern frame of reference for sleep paralysis. Since the 1960s, staggering numbers of people claim to have been abducted by aliens. In some cases they report being probed and examined, and not uncommonly claim to have had eggs or sperm removed. And many supposed abductees were so utterly convinced that they even convinced others – most notably, the Harvard professor John Mack.[56] Alien nightmares broadly obey the same tacit laws as those of witch and vampire communities. This experience was so strange and powerful that it simply had to have *come from somewhere else.*

This new hysteria has not produced alien victims. No extra-terrestrial scapegoat was ever burned or slashed or hanged for their crimes (and probably not even autopsied). But it is fair to describe the US version of the phenomenon as something approaching mass hysteria. And in some cases the abductees must – like certain witch-accusers of the past – have enjoyed the attention their stories brought them. Unconsciously, indeed, they perhaps also enjoyed getting such specialised attention from people who had travelled light years to bestow it: that is, their unconscious construction of the nightmare into alien abduction was (as with those once attacked by *The* Devil) a form of unwitting egotism.

Are there any other parallels? One interesting element is that of distance. In a world where many people (though in the US, by no means all) have lost an intense terror of demons or witches or the supernatural *per se*, the unimaginable distance of another inhabited planet now stands in for the older distance of heaven or hell. The otherness of the nightmare creates depths and distances. This prompts us to ask: Did the intensity of the nightmare experience, during the high Christian era, substantially contribute to the *depth* of hell itself? In asking this, we are forced to admit that we do not, indeed, know *exactly* how deep ordinary people felt hell to be. But in (say) Shakespeare's time hell must have been capacious, as most people agreed that many sinners went there, and as the centuries wore on, no one was leaving. The 17th-century German author, Heremias Drexelius, for example, calculated 100,000,000,000 residents in one German square mile.[57] The horrors of demonic torment certainly give us a potent impression of psychic depth. And for much of history, we should recall, your sense of real physical depths was probably less awe-inspiring than the kind of abysses conjured by a Nightmare attack: there were no submarines, no deep sea diving... no Jules Verne had even imagined that epic journey to the centre of the earth. A few caves and mines were all that most people had to go on.

'And there's these little demons that run around really fast back and forth with feet that are red, bony and webbed with claws (I can only see from the waist down): could this be a vision of hell? That's what I started to think but I don't know.'[58] If someone in the US could write this *c.*2010, what might the nightmare have done for visions of hell in times when everyone around you believed in it, and a minister was all too likely to tell you that you were going there after death?

On the other side of death, we have life. Vampires and witches killed people. They sucked your breath or your blood out. They attacked fertility at its core: the milk of women and animals, children, miscarriages...Later on, in a society which might seem radically distant from those cultures, aliens did something oddly similar. Albeit usually without causing harm, they went to the very core of life: eggs and sperm. Their reasons may have been very different; their technique was usually sterilised and ultra-scientific... But the underlying psychology looks very much the same.

The Evolution of Fear: a Species on the Verge of Extinction?

Time and again when researching the magical and supernatural beliefs of the past, one has a feeling of encountering, not just dead people, but dead worlds. Whole forms of experience, of emotion, have passed into extinction in Europe and North America, where once they were as common as berries in a hedgerow. Once, people died of the fear the nightmare brought. This seems to have happened much more recently to Hmong refugees. Allowing for the heart condition described by Adler, and also for the uncertainty as to sudden- versus voodoo-death, the cosmology of the Hmong is much closer to that of witch or vampire country than that of most modern Americans.

Once, it was possible to die of what you believed in the middle of Europe. The density of that belief has now been sufficiently diluted so that this almost never happens in those countries that previously comprised witch and vampire territory. Both belief and terror have undergone a kind of evolution. A hardened veteran of the Korean war can state flatly that his single Nightmare was the most terrifying experience of his life: but he did not die of it. Even in Marotinu de Sus, nightmares make people sick, but as far as we know do not kill them.

Another way to understand this evolution is to look at the case of nightmare in modern Japan. Back in 1999, one journalist could note that 'sleep paralysis research in Japan has had a head start because sleep paralysis is well-known to most Japanese, who call it kanashibari, while it is little-known and less studied in the West.'[59] In witch or vampire communities, such a framework of understanding would usually make a vampire more comprehensible, yet also more terrifying. In Japan the effect seems to have been strikingly different. As Adler explains, among many Japanese children and teenagers, 'experiencing kanashibari and subsequently sharing the terrifying details are seen as desirable.' So much so, indeed, that 'some devise strategies and techniques for luring kanashibari' – knowing, for example, that they should lie on their backs, as well as clutching toys, or going to bed crying (how you can *genuinely* make yourself cry I do not know – and Adler does not say). When one researcher interviewed these youngsters, she found that they were 'too eager to experience the nightmare to devise means for staying away from it.' On certain

Japanese websites, sufferers 'describe how much they enjoy the horror of the experience.'[60]

Something extraordinary has happened here. Once, such terrors reduced hardened adult soldiers to gibbering children. In Japan, they are now a child's idea of fun. (And it is probably no accident that this phenomenon, novel as it is, is chiefly obvious among younger generations.) Across millennia and across continents, from the Old Testament to the Internet Age, nightmare sufferers have been united in the overwhelming terror of their experience. Except in Japan... Why? The general awareness of the condition, the shared frame of reference, seems to be a factor. But that is hardly enough, given how common such a framework was in witch and vampire attacks. What seems different is that such awareness is fused with the mind-set of one of the most pragmatically rational nations on earth. Modern Japan – a country where one can travel from Kyoto to Tokyo without leaving the suburbs – is in many ways a fiercely demystified society. And nowhere is this quality borne out more sharply than in its ability to spiritually drain that event which has sat there, a squat lurking demon of unfathomable evil, at so many of the most powerful or terrifying moments of human experience. In Japan, at least, the evolution of terror seems to be well ahead of the world in general. Here not only the terror-unto-death, but nightmare terror itself, may soon be extinct.

Clearly the vampire's achievements were formidable when it stalked under the cloak of the nightmare. But they were arguably yet more startling when it assumed another alias: it is now time to meet the vampire-poltergeist.

8

The Vampire Meets the Poltergeist

'I see it and I still don't believe it. How a glass can fly at a 90-degree angle through a doorway and around a corner, or the television run with no electricity?'[1] So said John Resch in March 1984, one week into one of the most extraordinary poltergeist cases of recent decades, in his house in Columbus, Ohio. In doing so, he pithily encapsulated the radical problems of belief faced by anyone experiencing or reading about poltergeists.

Poltergeists defy belief. During a poltergeist incident, objects can hurtle about when no one is touching them. At the same time, with perhaps thousands of items flying around over a course of weeks, they rarely hurt any of the people witnessing this chaos. In some cases objects move around in different but equally bizarre ways – floating through the air very slowly; turning corners in the way described by Resch; travelling through mid-air on impossibly level trajectories. Sometimes objects may split or explode on the spot, often being seen to vibrate or 'wiggle' before they do so. The telekinetic powers of the poltergeist do have limits. We never hear of cars or lorries being thrown around by them. But a fridge, a heavy table or a bed can certainly be raised or flipped over.

Poltergeist noises range from the slightest scratchings or tappings up to explosive hammerings, audible at least 500 yards away. In a number of cases these rappings can ultimately be used as a form of communication with the poltergeist (one rap for 'yes'; two for 'no'). Actual voices, though rare, have been reliably documented. Showers of stones are widely reported. Sometimes these are violent and seemingly persecutory; at other times they fall as softly and harmlessly as snow. But in either case, they can frequently seem to appear from nowhere. It is either impossible to see the beginning of their flight, or they appear to pass through solid matter (walls, roofs, ceilings). Though stones are especially common, poltergeists are extremely fond of making all sorts of objects appear from, or disappear into, thin air. These are usually termed 'apports'. In case we still feel that we have not been shoved far enough down Alice's rabbit hole, we must also confront (or shelter from) inexplicable showers of water, oil, mud, excrement and urine (again, often apported seemingly from nowhere).

Oh – and poltergeists start fires. These certainly are dangerous. Yet they also defy the mechanics of ordinary conflagrations. Fire brigades often find them impossible to explain (no cause, no clear point of origin). When extinguished by witnesses, the burned material cannot easily be got to burn again. The outside of a book might be burned, and the inside remain undamaged. There is some evidence to show that this fire-starting is one among many ways in which poltergeists can manipulate energy. This certainly includes – as with the Resch's television – disruption of electrical and electronic equipment: pretty much any household appliance, including lights, heaters, cookers and telephones. Electric shocks are rare but not unknown. Mobile phones receive messages when switched off, even with a SIM-card removed. Modern technology offers the poltergeist a wide and playful field, and it has adapted effortlessly. But in previous centuries it had other tricks. It would repeatedly ring house or servant bells – as with the phones, even if the bells were ultimately disconnected. It could agitate a pail of water so that it seemed to 'boil' (though, in fact, remaining cold). It could turn a room, or very precise part of a room, freezing cold.

In some cases very definite smells have been reported: pipe smoke; violets; burned toast… At times the smell can be indescribably foul. It is often and rightly emphasised that serious injury is extremely rare in a poltergeist outbreak. But people can certainly be slapped, buffeted – even dragged about. In a few cases they have been levitated. In others they have been pinched, scratched or bitten, and had marks left on their bodies.

Now – our task here is to get on the trail of the vampire-poltergeists (and quickly, before they do any more damage). But this section of our vampire hunt presents a special dilemma. Can I reasonably expect anyone to follow me on such a quest when… they do not believe *a word* I am saying? Perhaps not. A few lines are in order, then, on the matter of belief, and the possible explanations for these incredible events. Readers of these opening pages will probably divide   into three groups. One group believes none of the above, and most of its members possibly never will. A second group is more open-minded. Those within it can see a certain consistency, some interesting patterns in the incidents just described. Yet at the same time, they are having trouble *fully* believing this, in the way they believe that an object will fall when they drop it. With this I greatly sympathise. And the third group? These people do believe me. In some cases, because they have read extensively through poltergeist literature, or because they are indeed parapsychologists. And in other cases, because this has happened to them.

There are more such people than you might think. Until I began researching this subject, I had met only a single person who openly admitted to (and described) suffering a poltergeist incident. But when I started talking to old friends about the research, two of them said: 'Yes – that's happened to me.' I had known them seven and eleven years. In all that time, neither a word nor a hint on the subject. Perhaps more strikingly, during a chance discussion on poltergeists with four people, it was only when I stopped and asked: 'Has anyone ever experienced a poltergeist?' that one of them spoke up and said, 'I have'. In many cases, people do not talk about the impossible. If they do, they might be ridiculed, shunned, or told they are lying. Imagine the very worst thing that has ever happened to you. And now try to imagine that firstly, nobody believes you when you tell them; or, secondly, they believe you did it yourself.

We cannot realistically tackle the problem of belief in a few paragraphs. The most I can hope for at this stage is that people will be kind enough to read on. And those who do may well be wondering: well, what *is* a poltergeist? Is it a ghost? The name certainly says so, being German for 'noisy spirit'. But the immediate cause of poltergeist events, in about 98 per cent of cases, is far more human and mundane. It is one person, who unconsciously seems to be generating or enabling the phenomena. They are usually young, aged between about 8 and 20. Historically, they were more likely to be female. There is some evidence to suggest that this gender profile was at least partly one more result of the oppression of women. Why? Because poltergeist agents (as they are often called) are very frequently unhappy, tense, stressed, or conflicted – essentially repressing something or other. And in the past these problems were more likely to affect women, who were habitually marginalised, bullied and frustrated.

Poltergeist phenomena cluster around or follow this agent. As the parapsychologist Hereward Carrington put it, we are dealing in many cases not with a haunted house, but with a haunted person. And so, if you move house to flee the chaos... the agent will simply take the chaos with them. This is one reason for believing in the mechanics of a human agent. Another is that, if the agent is removed, the problems stop in that particular location. A little more subtly, the events might stop if the problems of the agent are resolved in some way.

These details seem to limit the madness of the poltergeist to the human realm. And it must be emphasised that there are many poltergeist cases which show no hint of anything ghostly or otherworldly. But a significant number of incidents do strongly imply the agency of the dead, as well as the living. As we saw, there may be conversations, through rappings or with actual articulate voices. Sometimes these voices know things which almost no one else does. Sometimes witnesses are able to link them with a person who has died in the house, perhaps quite recently. Now and again previous occupants of the house will admit to similar problems. 'Haunted houses', then, do seem genuinely to exist; but these will not form part of this chapter, as we have no evidence of them in our vampire-poltergeist incidents.

Arguably most interesting of all in this area, we have the problem of *agency*. Whatever is doing all this, it often behaves as though it has agency, in the sense that it shows preferences, habits, choices, mischief – even a temper. Now, all this could be the very bizarre, highly complex secret workings of a troubled *human* unconscious, indirectly relieving its inner frustrations. All of it could be down purely to the human agent, somehow looking and behaving like a ghost. At this point I will only say that some very reliable people have seen ghosts – and that at times, two or more people have seen the same ghost, at the same instant. To sum up, then: the poltergeist is either a troubled, perhaps physiologically unusual human being; or they are a ghost which needs such a human agent through which to work (hence their other possible name, 'medium').

How does all this fit into the world of the vampire? There are three key points. Perhaps most intriguingly: some of the seemingly incredible claims made by vampire-struck villagers from Crete to Hungary are in fact true. If poltergeists are real, then the poltergeist labelled as vampire is also real (different name, same activities). There may or may not be ghostly involvement, but the phenomena themselves did happen. So, when such people described impossible supernatural events, they were really describing bizarre yet credible paranormal incidents. This in itself is a remarkable matter. It also suggests that, like other poltergeist victims, vampire villagers have at times been unfairly victimised as liars or fantasists.

Secondly, we have the mechanics of the vampire-poltergeist. Some kind of human energy is needed to enable the phenomena. In a few cases this may have been the energy of personal trauma and psychological repression. But in most of them, it was almost certainly the energy of sheer terror. As we will see, related to this special kind of energy, there is the question of numbers. Outside of vampire country, poltergeist cases typically involve just one agent. But within vampire country, there may well be two, three, even several – just as there can be multiple victims of nightmare, and just as, in many cases, almost everyone is scared to some degree.

The third point is that some vampire-poltergeists may have been real ghosts. In the cases we have, however, there is not enough detail to be sure of this. Let us now look at these cases in which the vampire behaved like a poltergeist. After some general evidence, I will work through chronologically, with one notable exception. This is the case of Cuntius – a poltergeist affair so prolonged, aggravated and bizarre that it seems best to acclimatise ourselves before venturing into such particularly wild and rugged country.

Vampire Poltergeists: A Very Brief History

Let us begin with a quick overview of plausible evidence, before going on to cases which offer us more detail. At times, you really have to know what you are looking for, to spot the vampireist as it goes flitting by. Citing Schertz's *Magia Posthuma* of 1704, Calmet states that vampires 'are seen ... both by day and night, and the things which formerly belonged to them are observed to stir and change their place, without any person's being seen to touch them.' Notice how the phrasing here strongly suggests the record of poltergeist events observed *in real time*, rather than people finding that things have been moved about afterwards. Writing on Bulgaria, MacDermott states more clearly that vampires 'usually return to their own homes, where they behave as poltergeists, making strange noises in the attic, breaking dishes, upsetting water, mixing jars of lentils, rice, beans and so on...'.[2]

Meanwhile, in the Ukraine, 'after visiting their homes, the vampires wander about the houses in the vicinity, rattling the doors and windows, and even calling the occupants by name.' If the sequence in this account is accurate, it may well say something about the mechanics of fear. The bereaved family expects to get the first visit, and so their pre-existing fear kicks off the poltergeist affair, before news spreads, fear spreads, and so too do the uncanny noises and voices. Koenig adds that the night after the funeral is the most perilous of all. As we saw, the funeral vigil then persists, with everyone remaining together and not sleeping. Next comes the forty-day period. Making nightly visits to the old house in this time, the soul 'enters the room quietly, even though the doors and windows be shut, uncovers the children and rocks them, and sometimes plays practical jokes on the members of the family.'

In Romania, Murgoci found that the vampire sometimes 'comes back in the night and speaks with the family.' On these visits 'he may eat what he finds in dishes and knock things about, or he may help with the housework and cut wood.' Admittedly, those last details are hardly the stuff of the most chilling horror movies: I myself could probably come to an amicable arrangement with such a useful demon, especially if it could do its chores quietly. But if these last two traits seem not to fit the devilish mischief expected from poltergeists, well – be prepared to change your mind.

Sometime between about 1880 and 1910 we have that Greek incident in the village near Caritaena. After that young man slipped and died in the river, he returned as a vampire-poltergeist: 'He would go to the house, they say; he would destroy whatever they had, – flour, and other things.' He would also call to his brother in the afternoon as the living man watched his sheep. Even after further religious rites, the drowned boy stalked his old home: 'One evening he went to the house. And there was a big noise. In the midst of the noise, the brother went to see what it is ... Darkness, you understand. And as he was feeling about, his hands caught hold of a man's leg. But he was so strong, that he could not hold it. And so he went away; no door was opened.'[3]

Here the events are catalysed by pre-existing fear (the boy's sudden unnatural death), and in the same way stop because people expect them to. They believe him struck by lightning, in the form of that suspect dog. And the poltergeist agent was almost certainly the living brother:

He, as near kin, expected trouble and got it, both by day and night. We also saw that in Greece vampire-poltergism was still happening *c.*1960, when one interviewee warned of the dangers of careless death rites. In such cases 'the corpse ... will become a *vorkalakas* (a *vrikolax*) and will pollute the flour in the house.'[4]

Barber, meanwhile, notes that 'the vampires of the Gypsies ... have been known to cause the living physical harm by beating them or destroying their property. They have been known also to disturb families by causing loud noises, setting fires, turning over caravans, [and] breaking dishes.' These typical poltergeist habits (the overturning of a caravan is impressive, but not beyond some of the physical extremes seen elsewhere) become the more interesting when we remind ourselves that Gypsy vampires could at times 'kill victims by simply causing them such terror that they die.'[5]

The Vampireist: Detailed Case Histories

Tellingly, the vampire-poltergeist is at least as old as the first known revenants. At Melrose Abbey in the twelfth century, the revenant known as 'Dog Priest' can be fingered as a poltergeist by one small but damning clue. For, after his death, this dissolute priest sought for several nights 'to force an entrance into the cloister'. He did not succeed. What can this mean? Probably, that the monks heard *noises*, which they could not explain – how else would they know about these unsuccessful attempts? Another possible answer is that things were moved or damaged. Both of course fit the poltergeist. And the belief that he would first return to his old home fits too: Those who feared him most were those who expected such a return, and who would, therefore, unwittingly produce poltergeist effects.

Breslau: 1591

Clearly there was much poltergism here. The shoemaker was said to strike and pinch people so violently that 'not only blue marks, but plain impressions of his fingers would be upon sundry parts of their bodies in the morning.' Occurring just after reference to people near-suffocated in bed, this probably indicates nightmare attacks. But it was certainly not nightmare when, after 'men forsook their beds, and kept their dining-rooms, with candles lighted, and many of them together, the better to secure themselves from fear and disturbance; yet he would then appear to them, and have a bout with some of them [i.e., hit them], notwithstanding all this provision against it.'

Santorini

From 17th-century Greece we have the case of Jannetis Anapliotis. Anapliotis had been a usurer on the island of Santorini, and this occupation already seems to have made him suspect. Before he died, Anapliotis 'repented of his misdeeds and ... left his wife an order to pay anything else justly reclaimed from him.' Six weeks after his death, however, the wife 'refused to satisfy some just claim for repayment, and immediately he began to appear in the streets, and to molest above all his own wife and relatives.' Additionally, 'he woke up priests early in the morning, telling them it was time for matins, pulled coverlets off people as they slept, shook their beds, left the taps of wine-barrels running, and so on.' As we saw, 'one woman was so frightened in broad daylight as to lose the power of speech for three days, and another whose bed he shook suffered a miscarriage.'[6]

The shaking of beds and the yanking off of bedclothes are certainly classic poltergeist tricks. A particularly well-attested case from summer 1910 centred on a young man called John Randall, in Enniscorthy in County Wexford, Ireland. The articulate ghostly voice also echoes down centuries of poltergeist phenomena, and as we have seen was frequently heard in vampire country. There is a good chance that Anapliotis' ghost really was involved in these disturbances. In a number of cases, what look like restless spirits have apparently returned because of some unfinished or mishandled business relating to their burial or finances.

Kring

We saw that in Kring, George Grando seems to have inflicted nightmares on his wife – 'she was tormented by the spirit of her husband, who night after night threw her into a deep sleep with the object of sucking her blood.' And we also heard of how 'a monk of St Paul ... on returning to the widow's house, saw Grando sitting behind the door.' Perhaps he really did see Grando's ghost. But the widow's nightmares alone would have been enough to cause genuine terror, and that terror may well have been what sparked the next phase, with its 'stories ... of a dark figure being seen to go about the streets by night, stopping now and then to tap at the door of a house, but never to wait for an answer.' Noises, and especially rapping noises, are probably the most common poltergeist phenomena. And if the agents in these cases were terrified enough to cause the noises, it is indeed probable that they then went on to die of fear: 'in a little while people began to die mysteriously in Kring, and it was noticed that the deaths occurred in the houses at which the spectred figure had tapped its signal.'[7]

The Vampireist of Derekuoi

We now reunite ourselves with those bemused officers, St Clair and Brophy, continually shaking their sceptical Protestant heads at the wayward villagers of Derekuoi. Here we are fortunate to have quite a lot of evidence. First, there is a general recognition that the local vampire typically behaves like a poltergeist. For, in its initial

> aeriform shape ... the vampire ... may be easily discerned in the dark by a succession of sparks like those from a flint and steel; in the light, by a shadow projected upon a wall, and varying in density according to the age of the vampire in his career. In this stage he is comparatively harmless, and is only able to play the practical jokes of the German Kobold and Gnome, of the Irish Phooka, or the English Puck; he roars in a terrible voice, or amuses himself by calling out the inhabitants of a cottage by the most endearing terms, and then beating them black and blue.

A surprising amount of data is packed up in these few lines. Almost all the phenomena are standard poltergeist habits. The sparks – described with the notable precision of something actually seen – match the many reports of strange lights during poltergeist incidents. They may possibly also link to the notorious fire-starting of some poltergeists, as well as to their electrical powers. Occasionally, a light can directly precede a full ghostly apparition. A striking case occurred to the broadcaster James Alexander Gordon in 1973, in the notoriously haunted Langham Hotel building in London.[8]

The daytime shadows are a little harder to pin down. They could just be subjective misinterpretations. But the phrase 'varying in density' could well echo the many ghost figures that have ranged from mist through to shadows of varying darkness, density, and more or less human shape.[9] With the roaring, taunting and beating we are on very firm and familiar ground. No less intriguing is the way that St Clair likens the Bulgarian vampireist to Puck (and his German and Irish cousins). This was no accident. For many of the pranks credited to trickster fairies such as Puck almost certainly *were* poltergeist incidents. Puck and other fairies were just poltergeists under another name (any would-be Poltergeist Hunters should be aware that our quarry is a master of disguise, going under a variety of aliases, from vampire, to witch, to ghost, to demon...). During a poltergeist incident on a remote Irish farm in 1877, the father of the house, when asked about the cause, stated: 'I would have thought, sir, it do be fairies, but them ... knowledgeable men will not allow such a thing.'[10]

The opening remarks by St Clair evidently reflect various tales, perhaps going back decades. But we then come to a very specific and recent outbreak, during which Kodja Keraz, the villager wrestler, had his jaw broken one wild night. With that injury, we are once again in those uncertain borderlands where poltergeist and nightmare blur together. Either could have been the cause. And nightmares would of course be very likely in such a situation. In around 1863, for example, Derekuoi

> was so infested by vampires that the inhabitants were forced to assemble together in two or three houses, to burn candles all night, and to watch by turns, in order to avoid the assaults of the Obours, who lit up the streets with their sparkles, and of whom the most enterprising threw their shadows on the walls of the room where the peasants were dying of fear; whilst others howled, shrieked, and swore outside the door, entered the abandoned houses, spat blood into the flour, turned everything topsy-turvy, and smeared the whole place, even the pictures of the saints, with cow-dung.[11]

Bloody flour, and houses plastered in cowshit... We have of course already met this pollution several times: while the Greeks were not as specific as we would like, they must have meant something like this when they complained of the revenant polluting flour. Both the blood and dung were almost certainly apported.

In Cuddapah in India in 1935 a family was beset with peltings of stones, spontaneous burning of clothing, movements of objects, and sprinkling with water. Moreover, 'when the inmates were at meals, within closed doors, human excreta fell near their plates.'[12] This evidence indicates that when people complain of a ghost or vampire 'polluting' food or drink, they probably mean blood, piss, or shit, and perhaps saliva. Ordinary dirt would also be a possibility, but in rural or pre-modern environments people were usually less fussy about such things; it would probably have to be a *lot* of dirt to count as pollution.

Meanwhile, a poltergeist could be found up to some very dirty tricks in Dortmund, at the home of Lutheran physician Barthold Florian

Gerstmann, in late May 1713. Discussing this case (of which a detailed first-hand account still exists), Annekatrin Puhle cites 'a spectacular throwing of faeces ... on 26 May, as the diary entry documents: "Between 9 and 10 o'clock the walls of the middle-sitting room are being dirtied by human muck as if covered by a coat of paint."' With such events persisting over several days, it is darkly intriguing to wonder how many people would sit through the most legendary horror movies rather than suffer such events themselves. Among other damage, a 'bombardment of stones ... went on for 20 days,' with a total of '760 stones and 147 broken panes' being recorded.[13]

It should be said at once that, if there is a loophole for a hoax in any of our accounts, it can be seen in Derekuoi. The houses attacked by this supposed poltergeist were 'abandoned' at the time. Yet various other pieces of evidence make the hoax explanation seem unlikely. Most basically, we need to ask: who would want to do this? and: who would get away with it? Another way of approaching the hoax theory is to re-emphasise just how much fear there was in Derekuoi in everyday life. As we know from our own strange culture of Vampotainment, people who create fear for excitement are either very secure, or outright bored. These Bulgarians, by contrast, seem to have had an abundance of natural fear all around them. They would neither want nor need to create any artificially.

The one detail which is a little hard to account for is that 'abandoned houses' would not contain an obvious agent for the damage. Lacking a detailed map of just where the assembled villagers were in relation to the affected houses, we can only assume that they were fairly close. As emphasised, Derekuoi itself was small. Moreover, there is strong evidence that poltergeist energy is often electrical or electromagnetic. Most if not all of the houses in the village would have been pretty good conductors of such energy, having bare earth floors with no mats or rugs.

As with other cases of the vampireist, the ending of the outburst is telling. St Clair explains that, 'happily for Derekuoi, Vola's mother, an old lady suspected of a turn for witchcraft, discovered the Ilatch we have already mentioned, laid the troublesome and troubled spirits, and since then the village has been free from these unpleasant supernatural visitations.' We met both the Ilatch – or anti-vampire medicine – and the witch earlier. And those who recall how powerful this woman actually was – like a tribal witch-doctor she could probably kill someone just by *saying* that they would die – will see how misleading St Clair's droll 'suspected of a turn for witchcraft' really is. The witch was 'the most respected woman in the village', and the local priest would himself pay for her assistance if one of his family was sick or if his crops were suffering from drought. Once we appreciate this, we can see yet one more clear case of how and why the vampireist (or poltergeist) is stopped. Fear gave him life. And a sufficiently powerful ritual, conducted by a sufficiently powerful person, took away both the fear and the life ('energy' of course being a word which covers both).

The vampire-poltergeist did not go away in a hurry. Summers cites the case of a Greek merchant, Patino, from Patmos, who died away from home on business. When the coffin was being shipped back, a sailor who was sitting on it thought he felt movement within. When inspected, Patino was dead, but alarmingly 'intact and incorrupt'. After his burial, Patino returned as a vampire and 'forced his way into various houses, yelling, howling and dealing blows right and left'. Not only that, but 'in a few days more than fifteen persons … took their deaths' – some almost certainly from sheer terror. When attempts at exorcism failed, sailors were asked to carry the body back to Anatolia, where Patino had died. Unsurprisingly, the sailors were too terrified to carry the corpse that far, and burned it on the first uninhabited island they came to. Given that this story was personally related to Summers, and is relatively precise in its details, there is some chance that it occurred in the early twentieth century.

A case which takes us north to Serbia certainly did. In September 1923 an *Observer* piece found by Summers described a house under siege at 61 Bosanska Street, Belgrade. Bricks and stones broke all the windows, prompting the traumatised family to barricade the apertures with boards, tables and chairs. Inside, furniture shifted violently about, and was sometimes thrown down and smashed. In Belgrade just ninety-odd years ago, the vampire was still your scapegoat of choice for almost all malign and unexplained events. For Summers, clearly rather baffled, notes: 'It was stated that the troublesome apparition was a vampire, although its activities certainly seemed to be those of a poltergeist,' and can only conclude, following his wayward belief in satanic forces, that a vampire who 'wished to annoy and molest' people 'might resort to poltergeist tricks'.[14] Again, of course, the clearest link between the two was pure fear.

It was evidently later again that the vintage vampire domain of Serbian Kisilova was stalked by a female revenant, Ruža Vlajna.

Vlajna was detected chiefly by her habit of banging on the pots and pans hung out on the roofs of houses, while the claim that she was seen 'walking on the surface of the Danube' could also indicate a ghost. It was in 2006 that a local resident recalled this revenant, who had been a villager during the time of her grandfather.[15]

Cuntius of Pentsch

How terrifying was Cuntius to the traumatised citizens of Pentsch? So terrifying that they broke a hole in their church in order to destroy his undead corpse... This, so far as I know, is unique in the annals of vampire destruction. We have now spent some time, as promised, acclimatising ourselves to the territory of the vampire-poltergeist, in the hope that what follows here will be slightly less improbable than if we were thrust into its horrors cold. One clue before we start: at times it was probably assumed that Cuntius, though present, was invisible; although in the memorable instant when he steps from the wall and creeps to the bedside, witnesses may have seen a visible apparition.

After Cuntius' sudden violent death, 'the watchmen of the town also affirmed, that they heard every night great stirs in his house, the fallings and throwings of things about.' A maidservant and some others in their beds 'heard ... the noise and tramplings of one riding about the house, who at last ran against the walls with that violence, that the whole house shaked again, as if it would fall, and the windows were all filled with flashings of light ...' We hear, too, of 'his often speaking to the Maid that lay with her mistress, his widow, to give him place, for it was his right; and if she would not give it him, he would writhe her neck behind her.'

Add to this 'his galloping up and down like a wanton horse in the court of his house ... he being divers times seen to ride, not only in the streets, but along the vallies of the fields, and on the mountains, with so strong a trot, that he made the very ground flash with fire under him ... his bruising of the body of a child of a certain Smith, and making his bones so soft, that you might wrap the corpse on heaps like a glove ... his miserably tugging all night with a Jew that had taken up his Inn in the town, and tossing him up and down in the lodging where he lay', and... we are still far from done.

Another particular victim of Cuntius was the local parson. We are told that 'he pressed the lips together of one of this Theologer's sons so, that they could scarce get them asunder'; and that the minister's house was so generally disturbed with this unruly ghost, that the servants were fain to keep together anights in one room, lying upon straw, and watching the approaches of this troublesome fiend. But a Maid of the house, being more courageous than the rest, would needs one night go to bed, and forsake [the] company. Whereupon Cuntius finding her alone, presently assaults her, pulls away the bedding, and would have carried her away with him; but she hardly escaping fled to the rest of the family ... Another time he came into her Master's chamber, making a noise like a hog that eats grain, smacking and grunting very sonorously. They could not chase him away, by speaking to him; but ever as they lighted a candle, he would vanish.

Another time about evening, when this Theologer was sitting with his wife and children about him, exercising himself in music ... a most grievous stink arose suddenly, which by degrees spread itself to every corner of the room. Here upon he commends him and his family to God by prayer. The smell nevertheless increased, and became above all measure pestilently noisome, insomuch that he was forced to go up to his chamber. He and his wife had not been in bed a quarter of an hour, but they find the same stink in the bed-chamber; of which, while they are complaining one to another, out steps the spectre from the wall, and creeping to his bed-side, breathes upon him an exceeding cold breath, of so intolerable stinking and malignant a scent, as is beyond all imagination and expression. Here upon the Theologer ... grew very ill, and was fain to keep his bed, his face, belly, and guts swelling as if he had been poisoned; whence he was also troubled with a difficulty of breathing, and with a putrid inflammation of his eyes, so that he could not well use them of a long time after.

Our author adds that: 'taking leave of the sick Divine, if we should go back, and recount what we have omitted, it would exceed the number of what we have already recounted. As for example, the trembling or sweating of Cuntius his gelding, from which he was not free night nor day: the burning blue of the candles at the approach of Cuntius his ghost: his drinking up the milk in the milk bowls, his flinging dung into them, or turning the milk into blood; his pulling up posts deep set in the ground, and so heavy, that two lusty porters could not deal with them ... his holding fast the cradles of children, or taking them out of them ... his defiling the water in the font, and fouling the altar on that side that did hang towards his grave with dirty bloody spots ... his pelting one of the women that washed his corpse, so forcibly, that the print of the clods he flung, were to be seen upon the wall...'

When I first read this whole account, I spent much of it frowning irritably and shaking my head. I pulled out anything which looked like nightmare symptoms and associated conversion disorder, and more or less ignored the rest. Coming to it again, however, with a knowledge of poltergeist phenomena, is a strikingly different experience. All the way through, poltergeist symptoms leap out at you. The noises (which elsewhere can be even more oddly precise than that hog smacking its chops); the flashing lights and sparks (mild compared to the dangerous fires lit from nowhere by some poltergeists); articulate human speech; visible apparitions; beating, yanking, plucking away of bedclothes; the stench (often equally intolerable, described at times as like that of a corpse or a septic tank); lifting of heavy objects; the pollution of food or apparently non-human drinking of liquid; humans or animals hurled around; livestock interfered with in oddly precise ways; and pelting with earth or stones.[16] It is even possible that the 'burning blue' of candles is connected with the well-attested role of the poltergeist's strange electrical and magnetic powers.

Many readers may already have noticed that it is hard to be sure, in this account, what is caused by nightmare and what by a poltergeist. Where does one end and the other begin? The nightmare can feature assaults, quite serious injuries, and aural hallucinations. That kind of uncertainty will persist to some extent throughout this chapter. It does look, though, as if some of the violence was that of the poltergeist: a child is beaten to death, and a Jewish lodger assaulted all night. We have not seen anything so extreme in cases of mere nightmare. In other areas, it is perhaps genuinely impossible to separate nightmare from poltergeist. Notice, for example, that there are two possible instances of conversion disorder here. One of the sons of the parson seems to be struck temporarily mute (they could barely get his lips apart); and the parson himself suffers various psychosomatic afflictions, with the stomach problems partly resembling what Costel experienced in Marotinu de Sus.

Again, one key thread which does link *all* of these incidents is simply: fear. Either fear made all this happen, or it supplied the energy for it to happen. It should be added that the probable level of fear experienced in Pentsch may have been related to the extreme violence of certain phenomena. It is very rare to see poltergeist violence causing death (as with the dogs and the child). But there is some evidence to suggest that the extremity of poltergeist phenomena can be influenced by people's attitude to it. It may be, then, that here we are again looking at the effects of a species of fear now extinct in most of the modern developed world.[17]

Notice, too, that while some of this could have been subjective (experienced by just one person at a time), in some cases it was undeniably collective. Numerous people heard the hoof beats, the crashing against the house; saw the sparks of fire from this ghostly rider. Equally, all of the parson's family smelt the abysmal stench.

And this phantasmagoria not only gripped the entire town; it lasted, seemingly, for months on end. It had begun just days after Cuntius' burial in February, and it ended only after the destruction of his corpse in July. There may have been some periods of relative calm. But what we have just seen suggests that any such lulls would have been brief – especially as the author openly states that he has omitted much of what actually happened. Cast your mind back, then, over the last five-odd months. And now imagine that, through all that time, your entire neighbourhood or village was haunted. If it is hard to really grasp what that must have been like, we should further be aware that some poltergeist cases have lasted even longer: Enfield in 1977–78 ran for about fifteen months, and South Shields, 2005–6, for more than eight months. While the assaults on Caroline Mitchell's family in Essex seem to have been at their height for the year beginning January 2010, less aggravated paranormal phenomena were still occurring as late as 2014.[18] As I write (in March 2019), Keith Linder of Seattle is still experiencing the attacks of a poltergeist, which has visited him in multiple locations since May 2012.[19]

Think, too, of the basic social damage which Cuntius inflicted across these wild months from early spring into mid-summer. For our author insists that the citizens' 'calamity was such ... that there was none but either pitied them, or despised them; none would lodge in their town, trading was decayed, and the citizens impoverished by the continual stirs and tumults of this unquiet ghost.'

If Cuntius had not been dealt with, the town may have been abandoned or gone bankrupt. Once we start to appreciate this, we already find ourselves wondering about the repeated claims that every reported poltergeist case was either a lie or a hoax. Just which insane townsperson would have staged this hoax? If it was a stranger, they would of course be instantly scapegoated in such a context. We would have to accept that this hoaxer was vicious enough to beat a child to death, while also producing a smell with no source, and having it follow people round a house. And finally: what was their motivation? We can easily answer – eccentricity, malice, desire for attention... But we cannot so easily say why all these motivations so neatly vanished when Cuntius' body was destroyed.

This leaves us, of course, with one very big question. What was the ultimate, absolute cause of the vampireist of Pentsch? Fear must have been the immediate, local cause. If it was not, then it would be very hard to explain why the problems stopped after the destruction of the corpse. This must have been because the energy of fear disappeared or diluted, leaving little or nothing to sustain paranormal events. But... does that local explanation finally rule out the possibility of a genuine ghost? Whether benign apparitions or rampaging poltergeists, ghosts seem to need some kind of energy to materialise or to act. It is possible, then, that if Cuntius' ghost really was responsible, it was banished that July only because, when the fear was gone, it had no fuel to power its activities.

The Mechanics of the Poltergeist

We have now covered several hundreds of miles and more than 800 years in pursuit of our quarry. This is, then, perhaps a good moment to rest and take stock of what we have learned. Before we move on to other precise links between the vampire and the poltergeist, I will share the process which brought me to it, and the unprecedented strangeness of this experience. For more than two decades, I have researched some peculiar things (arcane religious and magical beliefs, medicinal cannibalism, pre-scientific ideas of the soul). This has often involved a certain strenuous effort of the imagination. But I have never experienced the kind of mind-bending that poltergeist research has forced on me. In a word: if you think this is madness – well, so do I. But I also think it is true.

Our basic hypothesis is that fear made this happen. For those who find a 400-year-old vampire case too distant a piece of evidence, we might shift briefly from superstitious fear to modern trauma. In Florida in 1997, an insurance loss adjuster called James Holland could be seen frowning over a particularly unusual claim for water damage. Michael Clarkson tells of how, at a house in the suburb of Jacksonville, 87-year-old Lillian Barton 'said that she got light sprinkles of liquid or water on her head while she was sleeping and occasionally during the day as she walked through the house.' Later, a plumber, 'Mike Thigpin was so alarmed from getting soaked in the living room that he left the house, believing it to be haunted.' Krista, aged 11, was almost certainly the source of these incidents – her mother was absent from the household, and she was relatively neurotic. She was said to be closely watched during the attacks, and her mother doubted that she could have faked them. Yet Krista's disruptive powers ceased after she underwent the modern magical ritual known as psychoanalysis (it is no small irony, after what we have seen of vampire destruction, that the word literally means 'dissection of the soul'.[20]) Whether mass terror or personal neurosis, the same rule holds – no energy, no events.

This hypothesis is based on my study of hundreds of poltergeist cases. Time and time again, they follow the agent from house to house. In the case of Welsh miner James Craze, in Abertridwr in February 1906, several witnesses, including a vicar and police, reported that poltergeist rappings clearly followed Craze from one part of the room to another (and there, just over a century ago, Craze himself displayed the kind of terror found in vampire country).[21] Further confirmation comes from the much rarer cases in which one set of occupants find a house to be haunted, though another does not. While Lowes Cottage in Derbyshire, for example, may have had a genuine ghost, it evidently required a family with children to bring this to life.

We can see a version of these mechanics at work on Mykonos in 1700. Thanks to the observations of the bewildered French outsider, Tournefort, the extraordinary vampire panic that occurred there in late December has been unusually well documented. 'We saw a ... quite tragic scene on the same island occasioned by one of those corpses that are believed to return after their burial. The one of whom I shall give an account was a peasant of Mykonos, naturally sullen and quarrelsome – a circumstance to be noted concerning such matters. He had been killed in the fields, no one knew by whom nor how.'

Notice that the man dies a sudden, unnatural death. Accordingly, local fear is whetted before anything even occurs. And presently, 'two days after he had been buried in a chapel in the town, it was bruited abroad that he had been seen walking during the night, taking long strides; that he came into houses and overturned furniture, extinguished lamps, embraced people from behind, and played a thousand little roguish tricks. At first people only laughed, but the matter became serious when the most respectable people began to complain.' Even without knowing what 'the thousand little roguish tricks' were, we can see that the invisible assaults and telekinesis are classic poltergeist activities.

Notice, too, that this poltergeist activity looks, again, impressively general. There must be several agents. Not only that but *everyone*, from the elite to the peasants, seems to be suffering from it. And yet intriguingly, at the same time there seems to be a kind of hierarchy of fear. Tournefort makes it clear that 'the most respectable people' are affected at least a little later. Why? We can assume that, although they are slightly less superstitious than the peasants, they are superstitious enough to be terrified by what they hear from others. Indeed, they may well have heard the poltergeist themselves and even seen it throwing chairs about. This makes us suspect that Tournefort's 'at first people only laughed' is a subtle coding for 'at first the *respectable* people only laughed' – they, after all, were the ones Tournefort was most likely to talk to.

It certainly seems unlikely that any laughter could be heard once the exhumed corpse, undergoing public dissection, was deemed to be a *vrykolakas*. 'People kept calling out nothing but "*Vrykolakas!*" in the chapel and in the square before it, this being the name they give to these supposed revenants. The noise spread through the streets as if it were being roared, and this name seemed to be invented to shake the vault of the chapel.' Like a spark on the edge of a dry forest, this word catches those out in the square and spreads. Psychologists may glibly try to explain the dynamics of crowd behaviour: but finally, there is nothing like really *feeling* it. A strange, exultant, spontaneous vibration of collective *power*... If fear is exciting, then fear in numbers is vastly more so. We must then consider something strange and ironic – in such cases, the living reanimate the dead. It is they, in their collective hallucinations and communal hysteria, who spark some wild psychic electricity into an otherwise inert and rotting corpse.

And the sheer intensity of the fear crippling Mykonos is of course attested by its durability. Presently, the body has been opened, and the heart taken down to the seashore and burned. But even now, the revenant,

> in spite of this execution became less docile and made more noise than ever. They accused him of beating people at night, of breaking in doors, and even roofs; of breaking windows, tearing up clothes,

and emptying pitchers and bottles. He was a very thirsty dead man: I believe that he did not spare any house but that of the consul, with whom we lodged. However, I have never viewed anything so pitiable as the state of this island. Everyone's head was turned: the wisest people were struck like the others. It was a regular illness of the brain, as dangerous as madness or rage. One saw entire families abandon their houses and come from the outlying areas of the town into the square, carrying their pallets, to pass the night there. Everyone complained of some new insult, and there were nothing but groans at the coming of night. The most intelligent ones withdrew to the country.

We now have intensified poltergeist activity, corresponding perfectly to the greater and more widespread energy of the human terror which is causing it. Outright beatings; broken windows and hammering on roofs. Drink is interfered with and clothes are shredded. This last phenomenon occurred elsewhere. During a severe outbreak at the house of Gilbert Campbell, at Keppoch near Glasgow in 1670, 'food was polluted and spoiled', and the family's 'clothes [were] cut to pieces while on their backs by invisible hands.' Geoff Holder, meanwhile, found this category occurring in three per cent of the 134 Scottish cases he studied.[22]

But the most crucial moment here is not the phenomena themselves. It is Tournefort's typically dry aside: 'he was a very thirsty dead man: I believe that he did not spare any house but that of the consul, with whom we lodged.' This makes it indisputably clear that, despite convulsing virtually the entire town, the poltergeist did *not* attack the French consul and his guests. Why? The French did not believe in the vampire, and so the French did not produce poltergeist activity. In vampire country, fear makes things happen. Yet that fear is founded on basic and distinctive local beliefs, and the enlightened Tournefort and his companions were the last people to share these beliefs.

Clearly, in a culture where fear could kill you, a vampire poltergeist was a very serious matter. Despite this, a vampire community arguably had more effective, even more rational ways of dealing with a poltergeist than our society now does. In the modern, developed world poltergeists and ghosts have become a new taboo. We have already witnessed this kind of stigmatic secrecy in the region of the nightmare. Numerous modern sufferers initially told no one because they were at once baffled, and faintly afflicted by the sense of having something mentally wrong with them. We saw, too, that nightmare victims of witch or vampire had a community which our contemporaries lack.

And the same point applies for poltergeist victims. In this area, supernatural explanations might be terrifying. But they were actually *less* embarrassing or stigmatising than psychoanalytic ones. In blaming a vampire, you did not have to admit to some radical failure or dark secret in the emotional history of your family – or, putting it more precisely, to explain why your beloved Timmy had been smearing shit all over the holy pictures. Here as elsewhere, then, the supernatural was surprisingly useful. Given how far more likely a poltergeist now is to be blamed on personal trauma or neurosis, we can reasonably infer that modern sufferers may have a lot more reason to keep quiet than those of vampire country, whose terror was nothing if not collective and impersonal. More broadly, my own sometimes accidental gathering of poltergeist data has made it clear that a surprising number of people suffer from poltergeists to varying degrees, while many of them (probably the majority) suffer in silence. At this most basic level, we see on one hand a supportive and sympathetic community; on the other, no community at all, or a kind of anti-community of derisive pseudo-sceptics and trolls.

The Poltergeist Defies our Frames of Reference
The study of poltergeists brings us up sharply against a simple but easily forgotten fact of life: the human mind does not know what to do with pieces of information unless it has a suitable frame of reference for them. On first venturing into poltergeist territory, many normal frames of reference dissolve or seem useless. To put it another way, day after day we are constantly making sense of the world. Normally we do not think about this because it is relatively easy and unconscious. But when it goes wrong, we become keenly aware of how important this mental sorting process is. I am stressing this because it is precisely how I felt when I began reading up in detail on poltergeist cases. Large heavy objects lifted and thrown about, fires spontaneously lit, stones hurled at people without ever hurting them, objects and liquid appearing out of thin air or disappearing into it... As I said, this defies the laws of physics – at least in the every-day sense in which most of us know them.

What do we do when we are confronted with the impossible? Broadly, one of three things: we laugh; we get angry; we become afraid. In a sense these are arguably all variants of the same reaction. All three are non-rational responses. We can also add that the first two stances are more likely among those confronting poltergeists at a distance. To have a violent poltergeist blow up in your face is far more frightening. If you doubt that, then ask the men and women who are trained to keep calm in the face of danger. A woman I know hurtled out of a house where a poltergeist was throwing toys, despite the fact that by profession she was a US Air Force pilot. Called in to the poltergeist-infested home of 11-year-old John Mulvey, in Niagara in 1970, police Constable Harry Fox felt much the same. 'It was one of the scariest things I've ever been involved with. At least in your normal work, if you're confronted with a big man, you can defend yourself. But this was different, unpredictable. I think it was some sort of invisible energy, which you couldn't see.' A few years later, police Sergeant Brian Hyams recalled his experience of the notorious Enfield poltergeist, in London in 1977: '"lego bricks just started to levitate, or move about I should say, jump about like jumping beans ... and suddenly, one or two lego bricks started to fly towards us"' – at which point, Hyams 'ran out of the house ... "I'm no hero ... I went straight out of the door and I think there was a rush between us who got out the swiftest"'.[23]

Poltergeist Energy

It seems very likely that Fox and Hyams were later angry with themselves for having been so afraid. Meanwhile, at least some readers are probably angry with me for writing about poltergeists. One reason for this is, again, a kind of disorientation. At first glance, the poltergeist might seem to imply that all ordinary laws and assumptions are torn up and that virtually anything goes. In fact, this is not at all the case. At one level, we know that across more than 2,000 years of documented cases, the poltergeist is indeed startlingly consistent in its behaviour. It throws things, raps, starts fires and so forth. Given how many other things are subject to the shaping forces of different cultures, it is indeed striking how constant these basic habits are. To put it another way: in thousands of cases, very different people have said more or less the same thing about poltergeists.

To this basic consistency we can add other kinds of order. Almost invariably, poltergeists need a human agent as an energy source. The fact that events follow this agent is evidently due to a hidden law – poltergeists can only operate at a certain distance from an agent's body. The veteran parapsychologist William Roll found that events quite precisely dropped off in a falling curve when he grouped them according to distance in this way.[24] As we have seen, this may well explain the immunity enjoyed by those in the consul's house on Mykonos, as chaos and terror assailed all else around them. The agent themself can feel better immediately after discharging the negative energy which directly causes events; and there is also evidence that if they are badly injured or very ill, events cease, owing to a basic lack of energy.

These and many other details imply that, far from being lawless, poltergeists have their own laws. They interact with the physical world in some precise and intriguing ways. One especially striking example of this is the relationship between poltergeists and electromagnetic energy. In its most dramatic form, this is of course visible during intense solar storms – the influx of high levels of energy from the sun, which among other things catalyses the northern lights. With that in mind, join me for a few moments on the island of Lewis on 30 January 1938.

About 10.30 that Sunday morning, 80-year-old Mrs Macleod was sat by the fire in her cottage. The exact location was Carn Dubh, Tolsta Chaolais, and she was with her teenage granddaughter and the girl's younger brother. Lying by the hearth were some caorans, small pieces of peat used to light the fire. Like the Enfield Lego bricks, these suddenly began to dance about. One jumped into Mrs Macleod's cup of tea. Another struck her on the face.

'Although astonished, Mrs Macleod and the children finished their cup of tea,' and the girl then went into the next room, 'which serves as a pantry, and also communicates with the front door. Immediately the girl opened the door she called to her Granny in Gaelic that a tumbler had broken. The tumbler was standing on the dresser, and it was split in two, just as a tumbler breaks clean when too hot water is poured into it.' Next,

the other dishes on the shelf began to break with a loud cracking sound. The cups, which were hanging in little hooks on the dresser, fell off and smashed to pieces. The plates and saucers broke off where they lay, while the astonished girl watched them from a short distance. A jug which contained rice shot off the dresser, over the girl's head, and smashed on the floor not far from the stove in the bedroom. In doing so it had to turn the sharp corner formed by the angle of the wall, to get to the bedroom door. Another jug containing pease-meal also shot off the dresser, round the corner of the door, clean across the bedroom and came to rest on the bed.

Presently 'a tin of cocoa, tin of salts, and the salt cellar were found on the bed.' Possibly because he lacked a rigid adult frame of reference about the impossible, the young boy 'was at first delighted by the pranks played by the crockery, and as each article came flying into the room where he was, he shouted gleefully in Gaelic "Here's another!" The teapot behaved most violently of all. It left its place on the shelf like a sky rocket, shot across into the bedroom and struck the wall some feet above the bed,' leaving spattered tea leaves in sight of Mrs Macleod's family, who came in from the farm below moments later.

While the girl managed to catch one teacup as it flew, she only worsened matters by opening the door of a cupboard, aiming to put plates in there for safekeeping. Dishes in the cupboard now cracked also. Later, 'it was found that the lamp globes in both rooms had shivered to pieces. A toothbrush of celluloid, or some similar composition, which had been lying on the dresser, without moving from its original position, snapped into three pieces, as clean as if it had been chopped through with an axe.' Similarly, a bar of soap 'was split from end to end just as if it had been sliced through.'[25]

Here we have classic poltergeist activity: objects levitated and turning corners, shattered without contact, sometimes broken very cleanly. Unusually, it lasted just those few minutes, and was never repeated. Why? As Geoff Holder points out, James Shaw Grant, a local journalist who covered the story, thought that the house went live. Since the preceding Tuesday there had been brilliant displays of the northern lights, and even at the time Mrs Macleod suspected a natural cause connected with this activity. She was right. As Grant Shaw noted, the large iron stove and iron chimney were highly conductive. After a charge entered through them – first affecting the caorans – it then fled through the cottage whenever a further wooden door was opened, breaking any temporary insulation. This theory was neatly confirmed a few months later. When 'Mrs Macleod tried to darn a sock with a ball of wool that had been one of the "levitated" objects ... the wool crumbled in her hand, as if lightning had passed through it.'[26]

This apparently natural cause links to another element of the Lewis case. Compared to most poltergeist incidents, it was strikingly brief. Was it, then, purely the result of the storms, without any human agent? While it may have been, there is good evidence to show that even moderate influxes of electromagnetic energy have definite effects on the human body (and particularly on the brain); and that they may have been responsible for triggering much longer poltergeist incidents. Roll found that, out of thirty poltergeist incidents with precisely dated beginnings, 'twenty-two were during heightened magnetic disturbances. The likelihood that this arose by chance was three in one hundred.'[27]

More broadly, science has just recently begun to argue that the strength and speed of solar winds seem to influence levels of heart attack, suicide, and terrorist activity.[28] Lest any readers imagine they can flee vampires or poltergeists by heading down well south of the aurora borealis, they should be warned that such effects were found in Minnesota, Tokyo, Arkansas and the Czech Republic.[29] Findings such as this show that magnetic storms, as well as famously knocking out radio signals, power grids, and the homing abilities of pigeons, have remarkably precise effects on human bodies and human emotions. No less intriguing is the fact that, during the biggest solar storm of the nineteenth century, in 1859, the flood of energy kept telegraph wires sending messages for hours after they had been shut down.[30] This, which must have looked frighteningly uncanny to some, compares strikingly with the way that poltergeists, in the Resch home and elsewhere, have often been able to operate disconnected electrical equipment.

Turning back to the poltergeists of vampire country, we would hardly expect to find so much evidence of magnetic conditions in many cases. But two episodes are worth considering. In 1591 a startling display of the aurora borealis was seen over Nuremburg: a tapestry of the sight still exists. As we know, solar storms can have powerful effects even when not visible. Was this potent solar wind also active to the northeast, over Breslau (now Polish Wroclaw), some time after the shoemaker's suicide that September?

Secondly, we have Derekuoi. The most pronounced incident of vampire-poltergism described to St Clair and Brophy had occurred 'five years' before St Clair penned his book in the winter of 1866–7. If this was slightly loose phrasing (on the part of St Clair or his Bulgarian informants) then it would fit the striking aurora seen unusually far south in Fredericksburg, Virginia, on 14 December 1862. Although we no longer have reported sightings of this aurora from Bulgaria, it seems possible that magnetic effects were present there, on a similar latitude to Virginia itself.

Before we leave the vampire-poltergeist, it is necessary to say a few words about hoaxing. Surprisingly few poltergeist cases seem to have been complete hoaxes. We should not, of course, underestimate what skilled or determined people can do in this area. But unless an awful lot of people throughout history have been lying (with at once vast and yet oddly consistent powers of invention), then we find ourselves looking at incidents which were simply impossible to create by sleight of hand. Beyond that, there is an important historical dimension to the whole idea of the hoax. The Oxford English Dictionary's first use of 'hoax' as a verb is from 1796; as a noun, from 1808.[31] So the explicit concept of a hoax is a relatively new thing. There has doubtless been fraud and trickery through all of human history. But the novelty of the actual term 'hoax' is probably significant.

If we stick precisely to the supernatural hoax, there is another important point at stake. People who really believe in the supernatural (who live by it, minutely and habitually; kill for it and die for it) are far less likely to stage 'supernatural hoaxes'. For this you typically need some degree of irreverence or scepticism. The hoaxer needs to be someone who does not *believe* in the supernatural. Hence we find that there were a lot of ghost hoaxes in the nineteenth century, yet few or none in previous ones.

In a few moments the darker side of human psychology is going to take us into some different – though often equally horrific – territory. Before we leave the poltergeist to meet the live vampires, let us reconsider what we have just learned. When I began researching vampires, I expected to be dealing with fantastic stories under which lay various rational explanations. Some people would say that real research should always surprise the researcher just a little bit. I am very pleased, ultimately, to have had this surprise – to find that some of the most incredible things these often superstitious people said about vampires were, in fact, true.

No less extraordinary is what the vampireist tells us about the extremes of supernatural terror. As with other, more modern poltergeists, the vampireist offers us a whole alternative history of human emotion. I am a great believer in science, and constantly grateful for its many wonderful discoveries. Yet we live in an age when not only scientists but ordinary people are continually attempting to explain away human emotions in quasi-scientific terms (all just hormones, serotonin, endorphins...). Once we take the poltergeist seriously, we find that human emotions oblige scientists to more or less rewrite mainstream laws of physics. There are strange and very real powers within us, and there is much, much more to learn about them.

9

Versions of the Vampire (I)

We began our journey with a basic question: where were vampires found? Once we turn to versions of the vampire, it at times begins to seem as if a better question would be: where are they *not* found? Jan Perkowski defined a vampire as 'any being that derives sustenance from a person who is weakened by the experience.'[1] Narrowing this down a little we can remind ourselves that blood-drinking can be a central element, while the solidity of a 'walking corpse' has also been important.

If we take the first of these sub-criteria in a brief jet flight across the globe, we find ourselves catching glimpses of such creatures both in and well beyond familiar vampire territory. Corinne G. Dempsey describes the *yaksi* of Kerala as 'a kind of vampire-like female – a deceptively beautiful woman who dwells in the night-blooming *pala* tree. Lurking mainly in uninhabited areas, the *yaksi's* prey are commonly unsuspecting men whom she entices and later kills by sucking their blood.' Edgar Martín del Campo tells of how, in Central Mexico the *teyollohcuani* are living vampires, documented from 1561 to the 21st century. They are able to change into bird or animal form, and feed on human and especially infants' blood and/ or hearts.[2] Among the Mintira of the Malay peninsula we find 'a water demon, with a dog's head, and an alligator's mouth, which sucks blood from men's great toes, and thumbs, from the effects of which they die.'[3] Although this at first glance looks oddly like a rationalisation of the vampire bat, in fact these are not found in Malaysia.

Back in Europe, certain vampiric sub-types are present in Bulgaria and in parts of the Ukraine. MacDermott explains that, until it merged with other forms of vampire around the mid-nineteenth century, the Bulgarian *vurkolak* was 'a special kind of vampire originating from the blood of a robber or evil-doer killed outside the village limits in the forests or mountains. The *vurkolak* haunts the place where the person was killed, or takes up residence in derelict watermills and so on, far from human habitation, and drinks the blood of those who pass that way. The term *vurkolak* 'is derived from an Old Slavonic word, whose two components signify "wolf" and "fur" (or "pelt") respectively. Although, accordingly, 'in some countries ... the term has the connotation of "werewolf" ... in Bulgaria [it] has no association with wolves.'[4]

In the Ukraine, one version of the vampire arises from deceased wizards or witches who transform into

> vampires ... of both sexes; males are called *opyry* and females *widmy*. Their corpses are revived at night by the action of the moonbeams, for which reason they are most active during the full moon. Leaving their graves, they first turn their steps to their former homes, to visit their families. An *opyr* who is survived by a widow is said to have intercourse with her. He may even beget offspring in this way, but they are born without bones. A *widma*, on the other hand, is innately modest, and is satisfied to turn loving eyes upon her husband, or sweetheart.

Notice, here, that the *opyr's* sexual assaults recall certain of the more sexualised nightmare experiences reported above. Still more colourful than these moon-bathed revenants are the 'so-called *mawky*, the ghosts of children who died before baptism. They are pictured' (Koenig tells us) 'as girls with tall, graceful figures, round faces and long tresses. They wear garlands of flowers upon their heads, and are clothed in very thin, transparent dresses, but their backs entirely lack any covering of flesh, so that their entrails are externally visible. They roam the world begging to be baptised, and are especially active on the Eve of St John (Kupalo), on which night they entice people and suck their blood.'[5]

We have already come across many bloodless revenants. But given its location, the ghostly *jacien* found among the Luo of Kenya is worth a mention. This is a vengeful spirit, used partly as a scapegoat (to explain sickness, for example). The bones of the suspect corpse can be subjected to the kind of deviant burial we have met in many contexts (burned to ashes, which are then thrown into a lake or marsh); or, in a ritual strikingly like that seen in Ambéli, boiling water can be poured onto them through a hole in the coffin.[6]

One other 'walking corpse' is notable for the place and period in which it occurs. Writing in 1895, James E. Crombie recalled an Edinburgh murder trial of November 1889. Two young men had gone on a walking trip on the island of Arran. Only one of them returned. The body of the missing man was presently found under a heap of stones, and his friend, Lawrie, was tried, convicted, and sentenced to penal servitude for life. During the trial, the clothes of the murdered man were produced in court, but not his boots. When they were requested, it was explained that 'the local constable had buried them on the sea-shore between high and low watermark. All the efforts of counsel failed to elicit any explanation of this extraordinary proceeding. The man would only admit that by the orders of his senior officer he had put them out of sight.' Crombie believed that this was done to prevent 'the ghost of the murdered man from walking, for the removal of the shoes of a person who has either met with a violent death or is suspected of being a vampire, and making away with them, is not an uncommon northern superstition.' Given what we saw of that First World War sniper, burying a German corpse as a potential revenant some twenty years on, Crombie is almost certainly right.[7]

In parts of Bolivia and Peru, one highly distinctive version of the vampire stalks lonely mountain roads to this very day. If a white man in a long coat should approach you there, you can be sure of a very nasty surprise. Through a special pipe he will blow onto you a white powder (itself often made from human bones) to send you to sleep. He will then cut down your side with a sharp knife, remove your fat, and heal you up again. When you wake you will remember nothing. But you will gradually weaken, pine away, and eventually die.[8]

This figure, called either *kharisiri*, *pishtaco*, or *lik'i*, has a long and strange history, and a no less extraordinary present. Here we can only touch on his origins, crimes, and intriguing recent mutations. Anthony Oliver-Smith notes that the *pishtaco* seems to have arisen – or been first documented – during the Spanish invasion of Central and South America in the sixteenth century. Certain Indians believed that the Spanish would murder them, and use their fat as medicine, to heal sores or wounds.[9] Their belief may well have been true, given reliable written accounts of the atrocities which the Spanish evidently did inflict on New World natives. Human fat was widely used in this way in the Old World, where it was usually obtained from the bodies of executed criminals. Even if New World beliefs about the Spanish fat-murders were myths, they were nonetheless ones grounded in the extreme cruelties of the Spanish conquest – cruelties that more than justified that age-old sense, 'there is nothing which these people will not do to us; and that includes making us into medicine.'

As Nathan Wachtel and David Samper explain, the modern *pishtaco* is likely to sell the fat on to pharmaceutical companies, to industry, or for the founding of church bells.[10] He can also steal your blood, which he may sell to blood banks.[11] Moreover, just as witchcraft beliefs in the developing world can easily incorporate technology such as mobile phones into their web of fears, so the *pishtaco* is now likely to have a newer, relatively hi-tech instrument, equipped with a needle, for extracting blood or fat.

For our purposes, two things about *pishtaco* or *kharisiri* are especially striking. One: for a long time in these cultures, fat was a life force which rivalled or outclassed blood. To steal your fat was to steal your life. Clearly, in many cases the *pishtaco* was a classic scapegoat, used – like witch or vampire – to explain fatal illnesses, especially of the young and previously healthy. When people fell sick in this way, you realised that they had met a *pishtaco*. They had no memory of it, but the effects were all too clear.

Secondly, this peculiar demon was not just a scapegoat, but to varying degrees an *outsider*. They were not dead or undead, but a living person with special powers. A key part of their alien status was often their whiteness. In this respect the *pishtaco* can be seen to overlap with a whole startling web of Latin American rumours about powerful outsiders, especially North Americans – that they steal children for their organs, eat them in high class restaurants; or use native Indians as supports within the concrete struts of new road bridges.[12] But in some cases an Andean villager could have done enough to make him an outsider within his own community – and, therefore, a *pishtaco* or *kharisiri*. A *kharisiri* who was burned alive at Orinoca in 1983, for example, owed his fate partly to his conversion to an Evangelical sect. In 1978, in the Bolivian Andean village of Chipaya, it seemed to take even less to make a man named Gregorio into a *kharisiri*. Alleged to own the special machine which enabled one to 'do kharisiri', he was horribly tortured and interrogated, and was lucky to escape with his life. When telling this tale to Wachtel in 1989, Gregorio could only suppose that he was persecuted because he was successful and (by Chipaya standards) relatively affluent.[13]

Faced with this bewildering variety of vampire types or subtypes, the reader may well be forgiven for growing confused – or indeed hopelessly fearful, struck with the sobering realisation that there is almost no part of the world where *something* will not attempt to suck one's blood or sell one's fat. In these two chapters we are going, however, to narrow the field down to four types of vampire variant. The first two are the friendly vampire and the live vampire; the third the peculiar undead of Russia; and the fourth, the American vampire of New England.

I. Friendly Vampires
Sexy Vampires
Despite their often alien status, Greek vampires in particular were very good at blending in – at least, up to a point...

> Once a man died and left his wife widowed. During the nights following his death he continued to visit his wife and to sleep with her. From their intercourse two children were born. The woman used to leave the house early in the morning, visit different places, speak to different people, and come back to the house in the evening when she discussed the news of the village with her husband. Usually the topic of their conversation was about couples who were having intercourse illegally. Once she told her husband that she'd heard about the best man sleeping with the bride after the husband had left the village. This shocked the vrykolax so that he cried out:
>> 'This world is too immoral ... let the earth swallow all of us now.'
> At this moment the entire family disappeared. [14]

If one removed from this the small detail about the husband being dead, nothing could look more typically – indeed delightfully – Greek. Village gossip; narrow-minded righteous indignation; a healthy nuclear family... In this tale (reported by a Greek *c.*1960) sexual misbehaviour seems far more terrifying than the return of the undead.

Other cases are surprisingly plentiful. In the 1930s one of the New England Greeks explained:

They say that once a vrykolakas married. And he begot two children. But every Saturday his wife would miss him, they say ... There was a party, and he went to the party; and he was singing. All those who were there listening, said, 'This man's voice resembles the voice of So-and-so.' So all of them there said, 'This man has died. How can it be this man?' So they asked the woman, 'Where did you get to know him?' So she said, 'He is a shoemaker. He came,' she says, 'and we arranged to get married. But every Saturday,' she says, 'he disappears.' So the village made plans, because we are told that the vrykolakas does not come out on Saturday. So they went, they set out with fire and torches, they went up to the grave, they opened it and they found him inside. He begged for mercy, that they do not burn him. As a sign, he showed them how one side of his body was empty.

The sensible reader will be pleased, no doubt, to hear that they heeded him not. Instead, 'they burned him. And that was the end of the vrykolakas.'

But... the end of *what*, exactly? Clearly this was no lumbering vampire zombie. A good family man, a sociable partygoer, a busy shoemaker... And, along with all these chameleon abilities, able to try to talk his way out of the burning as he lay there in his own grave. This last, admittedly, does remind us that he was (supposedly) dead. And moreover, as any Greek knew, there was good reason for suspicion once one heard that detail about the Saturday absences. This, as we saw, was the only time when the Greek vampire was compelled to remain in his grave. One other detail is new. One side of the vampire's body, we hear, 'was empty'. This was not just a whimsical invention – other Greeks told of how, though otherwise normal-looking, the vampire was empty, or 'open' on one side. Bizarre as this sounds, the trait was found also in the Galician Ukraine. As we have just seen, the backs of those unbaptised infant vampires entirely lacked 'any covering of flesh, so that their entrails were externally visible.' For all his skills of disguise, this Greek revenant also looked odd, again, if one knew how to spot it.

For us, however, perhaps the most important clue here is the seemingly minor detail of how the wife came to know the man at all. When asked, she responds: 'He came ... and we arranged to get married.' This seems to indicate that the vampire-husband 'came' from somewhere *else*... Not that far away, of course, as people recognised his voice. But he was at least a relative outsider – clearly from her answer the woman had not known him before.

Another version of the tale confirms this suspicion:

> Someone died and he returned but to a different village where he married, even though he had already been married in his first village. In this new village he plied his old trade. He had two children with his second wife, but some people from the first village were visiting there, saw him, and recognized who he was. They went to his new wife and asked about him; she told them that he ate only liver and that every Saturday he went away to return again on Monday morning. Apparently he was going back to his grave on the weekends. Learning all this, the villagers went to the grave, found the hole that he was coming out from, and threw hot water and vinegar in there. When they did that they heard him say, 'You burned me!'

As if this were not chilling enough, we also learn that, 'when he "died", why his children in the village burst at that moment too.'[15]

Again, the man was an outsider, at first unknown to his new wife. Again, he blended in, working hard and having children. Again, the Saturday absences – this time compounded by the still more glaring dietary fondness for liver (possibly as a source of blood, although here we are of course in Greek territory, where such nourishment was less central for the vampire.) And again he talks from his grave when 'burned' in the Greek manner. Notice, though, that here the villagers do not *see* anything. They use the tell-tale hole, and only hear the desperate vampire voice from within as the mixture destroys him. This suggests an interesting possibility. Recall that those vampires who sobbed or cried or screamed when staked were making the kind of noise which a corpse really would make when gases escaped rapidly from the site of puncture. Hot water thrown on a cold corpse may well hiss, if nothing else – and given how creative people could be, in such contexts...

Whatever the vampire *said*, exactly, we also know that his children suffered a more spontaneous destruction. Dramatic and startling as this may look, it makes a certain kind of sense. What, after all, would have been the metaphysical or legal status of these offspring, had they survived? Aside from getting a hell of a time in the playground, they would probably not have been eligible for child support.

Perhaps this was why, in the first case we met, the whole family, vampire-children and all, was conveniently 'swallowed by the earth'.

Certainly the problem of revenant children was taken seriously elsewhere. Glancing back to the demon-haunted Ukraine, we can here recall those children begot by the vampiric *opyr* upon his widow, and 'born without bones'. Was this child 'without bones' actually a miscarriage? At any rate, we can see that it was not only Greek vampires who could show an abundance of fertile life – who could, indeed, seem more alive in one way than ordinary but sterile men. Barber adds of the Yugoslavian vampire that, 'when he is not sucking blood, [he] is apt to wear out his widow with his attentions'; and in the 1920s Durham heard of an interesting twist on this theme, being told of a Montenegren vampire who fathered a child on the woman he had been prevented from marrying in life. (Any women who too hastily snub male suitors may want to bear this sobering possibility in mind.) The person who told Durham this story swore that the likeness between the child and its dead father was unmistakable. As far back as 1689, J. V. Valvasor lamented the 'gullible peasants' of the Istrian countryside, these Slovenes believing 'that the wandering "strigoni" furtively creep into their beds and sleep with their wives without ever letting out a single word.'[16]

This last phrase brings us to two possible prosaic explanations for all this vampire sex. First: we saw that nightmare attacks had sometimes been viewed as the assault of an incubus or succubus – essentially, sexual assaults on both men and women. This has been reported more recently, with varying degrees of sexual enjoyment noted during certain nightmare attacks. If we imagine a man waking to find that his wife seems to be undergoing some strange kind of sexual experience with an invisible demon, then a vampire is as good a culprit as any.

The second possible explanation is more mundane. It would be surprising if none of these tales was ever motivated by the basic need to 'decently' explain extra-marital sex and illegitimate offspring. After all, this was Greece; and as our first example showed, these were small moralistic villages where everyone knew everyone else's business, and judged them accordingly. With nice irony, we then find that once again demonic sex is preferable to *immoral* sex – that is, all these women were married, and (according to the official versions) had merely been deceived, rather than acting dishonestly themselves. In such cases it is even possible that the children's supposed 'bursting' or disappearance might disguise the need to have them given away for adoption, or even infanticide.

There again, by no means *everything* in vampire country can be explained with such satisfying neatness. Try this one, for example...

Once there was a *vrykolakos* that married a girl from our village. He never brought meat into the house, but he always brought in liver to eat. The girl often complained to him, but he used to say that liver was good for them. He never enjoyed going to church very much; when he was there he would always leave before the 'holies' came out of the 'ieron' (sacred place). The girl became worried; she discussed her husband with the priest who decided to take matters into his own hands to help that poor girl. So the next time the man-*vrykolax* was in the church, the priest closed all the exits and brought out the 'holies'. The *vrykolax* tried to get out, but when he discovered that all the exits were blocked he became frantic. Wildly he ran up and down the church, when he came to the middle of the church he jumped straight up in a final effort to escape and, at that moment, he burst like a cucumber. And the girl was saved.[17]

Perhaps needless to say, this is Greece again (and was also reported around 1960). Along with that tell-tale sign about liver, we have the typical power of the sacred – here shown in highly dramatic fashion, when these most potent holy icons cause the vampire to 'burst like a cucumber' before the entire congregation (an event which, once again, would have had me clamouring to spend my Sundays at church). This may just be some kind of mythic addition, Chinese-whispered onto a story which was itself half-true. But it is telling that the revenant 'bursts' in the way that those in graves were said to; and also that the presumably over-ripe cucumber suggests a half-putrid body, splitting along its seams... As we pursue our strange detective story among the live vampires of Romania, Bulgaria and elsewhere, we will also need to keep in mind an implicit detail of this story. As with the very first case we met, here there is no sign within the story that the suspect husband had actually returned from the dead. In neither instance do we have the typical visit to the grave on the Saturday. Indeed, if there had been any grave to attack in this last story, there would have been no need for the priest's cunning scheme in the church.

The last of our oversexed vampires is perhaps the most impressive of all. To make his acquaintance, we need to take a brief detour via Highclere Castle in Hampshire. Although this might look well-suited to house its own vampire in good aristocratic style (and some of you can judge for yourself, having very possibly seen the house on television, where it doubles as Downton Abbey) the detour is a little more complicated than that. It requires us, in fact, to ask what might link this stately home with an abandoned house in the Mani, one of the wildest and remotest regions of mainland Greece. The answer is Henry John George Herbert, 3rd Earl of Carnarvon and sometime owner of Highclere in the nineteenth century. Herbert was not only a traveller but something of an adventurer – even suffering a spell of imprisonment in Spain because of his political views on the Carlist Wars. Come 1839, just before he began making extensive renovations to Highclere, Herbert was blinking his way through the dusty glare of the Mani, and at one point, 'passing by a dreary and half-deserted village, I was shown a house to which another wild legend attached, and which was said to have been once inhabited by a shoemaker's widow.'

Her husband, however, though dead, had not entirely departed; for, being a vampire, he used a vampire's privilege, and bursting the bondage of the tomb returned every night except Saturday to his old abode, and sometimes even worked at his old trade. At length the woman became pregnant. The villagers taxed her with infidelity to her husband's memory, and she in her own defence maintained that she was on the point of giving birth to no unlawful issue. At this horrifying disclosure the villagers sallied forth to attack the vampire in his tomb, undertaking the enterprise on a Saturday morning, on which day alone the vampire's devil-imparted strength forsakes him, and the grave has power to hold his body. They found him in his grave, making shoes. 'How did you know that I was a vampire?' exclaimed the still living tenant of the tomb. A villager, in answer, pointed to a youth whose cheek a month before had been bright with health, but on which the ghastly paleness of disease and coming death had fixed its mark. The vampire immediately spat at him. The moisture from those accursed lips burnt the man's capote as though it had been fire, but it could not hurt the man himself, because it was the blessed Saturday. Maddened by the failure of his attempt, the vampire imprudently cried, 'though I am nerveless now, yet you shall taste my vengeance to the full on every night save this alone.' On hearing this alarming threat, the neighbours fell upon him, tore him to pieces, and cut out his heart, dividing it into portions, and distributing the several parts among the villagers, commanding each one to eat his allotted fragment, – 'and this,' my narrator observed, 'is the only real specific against vampires; and since that event,' he added, 'no vampire had ever molested the village again, though for two months before persons had been perishing daily under their fatal influence.'[18]

Herbert goes on to add that, in this region, 'every case of gradual decline was attributed' to vampires, thereby confirming that the two months of vampirism were, typically, the work of some real but unknown epidemic of disease. It may indeed have been this outbreak which left the village 'half-deserted'.

It was not unknown for vampire-struck villagers to eat the vampire's heart when they destroyed it. But to actually tear the vampire to pieces spontaneously, rip out its heart (dripping, presumably, after its recent depredations) and eat it raw...? Here we can only hope that the Mani tale was not some disguised account of an actual murder, rather than a kind of half-myth. It is certainly intriguing to find that, where vampires sometimes have quite wild or bestial qualities, here it is the vampire hunters who, in their desperate terror, are transformed briefly into frenzied animals, and into cannibals.

It is probably no accident that such a tale should come from the Mani of all places. The wildness of both the land and the people has long been legendary. The name itself is said to derive from the Greek word which gives us 'mania' and 'maniac', and even in the 1950s the intrepid traveller Patrick Leigh Fermor found the region formidably strange, impoverished and remote. Rather irresponsibly noting a widespread Maniot belief in vampires, but failing to give any further details, Fermor goes on to tell of the ferocious and endless feuding of the area, where two key ambitions of every family were to build a higher tower than their neighbours (many of these being visible on Fermor's trip, as now) and to have male children. The towers were for attacking the neighbours below you, and male children were valued chiefly because they would soon be able to help you kill people – thus being named 'guns' in local slang.[19] Perhaps it is not entirely surprising, then, that while the Maniots believed in vampires, the rest of Greece believed that the Maniots *were* vampires... Bob Barrow cites the Greek author Evlyia Çelebi, who (writing in the 1670s) noted that the Deep Maniates drank the blood of their animals, adding that: 'if they encounter people from the Outer Mani they also drink their blood.'[20] As Lawson informed us earlier, among the suspect dead of Greece there were 'those who meet with any sudden or violent death (including suicides), or, in Maina ... those murdered who remain unavenged.'

We are now about to get on the trail of the live vampires. For this we will need a very clear head, and some deft footwork. Let us therefore take stock of what we have seen so far. Three key points stand out from the tales of these oversexed vampire husbands. One: at least to the wife, this kind of behaviour could seem to be reasonably (ahem) 'friendly'. Two: a couple of those Greek husbands did not actually show any sign of having died, and so may well have been 'live vampires'. And three: whether dead or alive, any vampire which can beget children is certainly remarkably lifelike in one very basic sense. It should by now be evident that it is not easy to draw a clear line between friendly vampires and live vampires. And at times the same can be said, frustratingly, for the divide between live vampires and undead vampires. A round-up of the available data on live vampires, then, is probably in order.

II. Live Vampires

Writing in 1894, the colourfully named Kirby Flower Smith could state that 'the belief in *living* vampires ... is still prevalent in Thessaly and Epirus', going on to add that from antiquity these regions had been notorious for magic and witchcraft, and linking Thessalian witches to the strix and the Lamia.[21] This date looks interesting when we shift north. Of her travels in the Balkans just after 1900, Durham later wrote: 'I did not hear of anyone in Montenegro being a vampire during his lifetime, though they used to be formerly.' If Thessaly was anything to go by, 'formerly' may have been pretty recently.

Not surprisingly, Romania also had its share of live vampires. Murgoci discusses these as current demons when she writes in 1926. Deep in the crimson heart of vampire country, the live vampires of Romania are part of a strikingly complex society. Noting that *strigoi* and *moroii* are the most common terms for live and dead vampires, Murgoci adds that 'usually we have *strigoi* and *moroii*' consorting together, 'but the *moroii* are subject to the *strigoi*'. Along with this vampire hierarchy, we also have a kind of Vampire Academy, for, at the boundaries of the village, 'where neither the cuckoo sings nor the dog barks, the dead vampires meet the living ones, and teach them all sorts of incantations and spells.' Showing, for once, some feeling for atmosphere, these Vampire Tutorials are also held 'in churchyards, in ruined or deserted houses, or in the forest.' To round out this obsessive vampire taxonomy, there is even a kind of well-organised Monster Bureaucracy, meeting annually to see that their vamping should run in an orderly fashion: 'It is said that *strigoi* meet *moroii* and *varcolaci* [werewolves] at the boundaries, and decide on their programme of evil for the coming year.' (I should like at this point to state categorically that this in no way reminds me of any Faculty board meetings at university. Whatsoever.)

The live male vampires of Romania are said to be bald, whereas female vampires 'are dry in the body and ... red in the face' – neither description being exactly a smoking gun, in terms of your vampire photofit. Murgoci makes very clear that this female character is alive and kicking when she adds that 'they go out on St Andrew's Eve to the boundaries even if they have just born children.' One other detail gives us an especially strong sense of the live vampire as lurking indistinguishably among the living. As you may recall, during drought, and knowing that 'when a vampire washes itself, rain will fall from heaven,' Romanian nobles would 'send all their men to wash, because any of them may be a vampire'. (At this point, presumably, all the male peasants were effecting extremely hasty ablutions, each one desperately hoping that the clouds would not break before he had finished.)

Elsewhere Murgoci cites a woman, speaking *c.*1914, who states that 'vampires are just like other folk, only that God has ordained that they should wander over the country and kill people', adding: 'there was one that wandered through ten villages, killing their inhabitants.' Two key points here. One: yet again, anyone who travels for no good reason is probably suspect. Two: this slaughtering of ten villages may well refer to some especially severe epidemic of contagion. An intriguing variation on that theme occurs when Murgoci states: 'if the [undead] vampire is not recognized as such, and rendered innocuous, it goes on with its evil ways for seven years. First it destroys its relations, then it destroys men and animals in its village and in its country, next it passes into another country, or to where another language is spoken, and becomes a man again. He marries, and has children, and the children, after they die, all become vampires and eat the relations of their mother.' As Murgoci herself notes, much of this obviously refers to severe outbreaks of disease. But what is particularly interesting to us is the remarkable belief that, after seven years, the vampire 'becomes a man again' – that is, changes from a dead vampire to a live one. And notice too that this change is also somehow linked to travel and to distance. Look at it from another angle, and you have, one fine evening, a stranger walking into town, buying some drinks, and enquiring about work. For a time he seems a valuable addition to the community. But eventually...? Eventually he has spawned a whole Vampire Dynasty of satanic brats right in *your* village. (I may have mentioned this already, but if you live in vampire country, do *not* talk to strangers.)

Predestined Vampires

Any child can tell you that people bitten by a vampire will in turn join the ranks of the thirsty undead. But those predestined to vampirism are rather different. Recalling Lawson's long list of Greeks who would become vampires after death, we might focus in on 'children conceived or born on one of the great Church festivals, or children stillborn,' since these seem notably more predestined than (say) 'men of evil or immoral life in general' or 'those who have eaten the flesh of a sheep which was killed by a wolf.'

Predestined vampires also seem to have been especially common in Romania. Summers tells us that 'in many districts of Roumania it is thought that persons are doomed to become vampires and that they cannot escape their destiny. While they lie asleep their soul comes out of their mouth like a little fly. If the body were to be turned round so that the head reposed where the feet had lain the soul would not be able to find its way back and the man dies.' This twist on the roving vampire soul already implies that such people are tainted in life – sufficiently so, indeed, to inspire fantasies of murdering them.

Murgoci gives a variation on this kind of prevention in one of her vampire folktales. After being rejected for his poverty by the parents of his beloved, a young man hangs himself, returns as a vampire, and makes love to the girl in this new form. One evening the girl secretly follows him to the graveyard, where she sees him eating the heart of a corpse. Evidently aware that he has been spied, he presently demands to know where she has been, and what she has seen. The girl lies to him about her discovery, despite threats against her parents. The threats are made good. First her father dies, and presently her mother. And before long the girl knows that her time is coming.

It is at this point that she herself takes some interesting precautions against the vampirism which she fears will seize her after death.

She tells her relations that 'when she was dead they were not to take her out by the door or by the window, but to break an opening in the walls of the house.' This of course was a form of corpse door – and although we are not told so, the point is presumably that it will afterwards be bricked up. Certainly the chief aim is to confuse the corpse, preventing it from finding its way back home. For the relations, she adds, 'were not to bury her in the churchyard, but in the forest, and they were not to take her by the road but to go right across the fields until they came to a little hollow among the trees of the forest and here her grave was to be.' In themselves all these elaborate safeguards are already interesting – showing as they do how seriously one might take the threat (and how real death customs might turn up in a folk story). What is also interesting is that here the girl seems not quite as innocent as other victims of vampire destiny. That is, she was not born with the trait, but evidently acquired it because she had sex with the vampire.

Elsewhere Murgoci shows a clear link between the live and the predestined vampire, stating: 'people destined to become vampires after death may be able in life to send out their souls, and even their bodies, to wander at crossroads with reanimated corpses. This type may be called the live-vampire type.'

We now come to those luckless individuals who, through no fault of their own, seemed born to pass vampirism down through their family, generation after generation, like some rogue demonic gene. Such beliefs were by no means limited to the poor and ignorant. Discussing the typical excision of the undead vampire's heart, Barber remarks that, 'in 1874 such an operation was proposed – to be performed on himself, on the occasion of his death – by a Romanian prince living in Paris.' This individual had actually 'been forced into exile because the members of his family were believed in their homeland to turn into vampires at death. It is evident that he himself believed this.'[22] Following up on these brief lines with some painstaking detective work, Rob Brautigam has further shown that the nobleman's name was Borolojovac, that he died on the Rue d'Amsterdam around September or October 1874, and that, as Borolojovac lay dying, he did indeed request his host to see to the subsequent evisceration. Brautigam also adds that, with arresting precision, the nobleman believed himself, of all the family, to be cursed because he was the eldest son.[23]

We can assume that Borolojovac's host was similarly privileged, and possibly himself titled. Here we are then, in Haussmann's Paris, in an élite milieu that might almost have formed a sub-plot from Proust's epic novel, *À La Recherche du Temps Perdu*. And at this point, faced with a Romanian prince who might one evening be kissing the gloved hand of some lovely young society debutante, and the next clamping his teeth just below the silk band at her throat, we seem to find ourselves offered a juxtaposition (Swann and Count Dracula together at supper) not so much strange as surreal.

And if all this, *c*.1870, was enough to exile someone with the power and education of a Romanian prince, what might the humble peasants of Derekuoi be licenced to believe at just the same time? For it was in 1869 that Brophy and St Clair first published their book *A Residence in Bulgaria*, having by that time been guests in the Balkan hill village for eighteen months and three years respectively. In Chapter Eight we heard of that nightmare attack on the village wrestler, Kodja Keraz. The supposed vampire who made this attack on Keraz was survived by his son Theodore, who in turn acted as a servant to Brophy and St Clair.

Although Theodore's father had been one of the more harmless vampire types of Bulgaria (a kind of mischievous poltergeist), Theodore himself was tainted by the family trait. As 'the son of a noted vampire,' Theodore was, *c*.1865, 'doing penance during this present Lent by neither smoking, nor drinking wine or spirits, in order to expiate the sins of his father, in order to prevent himself inheriting the propensity.' (The Lent in question must have been some time between 1865 (when the stay began) and winter 1866–7, when the book was written.) We further learn that 'poor Theodore is head over heels in love with Miss Tuturitza, the young lady next door, who fully reciprocates his affection, but her parents refuse to sanction the marriage on account of the vampire father.' The girl's parents themselves, while perhaps not highly educated, were certainly a force to be reckoned with – her father being one 'Kodja Kostantia, ex-assassin and landowner of Derekuoi.'

Here we catch a rare glimpse, not just of something approaching a live vampire, but of the poignant clash of ancient superstitions and thwarted young love – something perhaps as old as myth and as fresh as the face of any living, love-struck girl of our own times. Although Derekuoi seems not to have suffered the same class or clan prejudices as Verona, this vampire Romeo could never marry his Juliet. This may seem quaint and absurd to us, but the consequences were hardly less tragic than the star-crossed lovers of Shakespeare's play. If the prospect of his awful post-mortem destiny had hung heavy over

Borolojovac during his otherwise privileged life, how much grimmer was it for Theodore, who could scarcely leave his village, let alone the country?

The answers to that question are given in the second edition of Sinclair and Brophy's book. Looking back in 1876 on the thwarted love affair, they explain that, 'Master Theodore got himself into trouble by running away with Tuturitza's sister, Marynka.' We have no more details to explain *why* Theodore switched his attention to the sister. Certainly the choice does not seem a good one, given that the parental strictures would obviously extend to both daughters. But Theodore's most serious problem, as it turns out, was fatherhood, rather than mere sexual liaison or marriage. For, 'after the elopement, Marynka's house was burnt by the peasants, and she was pursued and put into prison, and only released, when, after delivery of the adulterous child, she had killed it, because, had her child lived, it would have become a vampire.'

As I warned earlier, sometimes Real Vampire Country can seem more like a different planet than a different territory. Here, in a scenario which many would assume to be the mere stuff of *Twilight* fantasy fiction, the dilemma of the vampire child forces a mother to kill her own infant. And notice how precise that Bulgarian belief was – the child would allegedly have '*become* a vampire' at some stage in its life, perhaps like Theodore himself, who in his youth was seeking to prevent this development by his Lenten penances. Further details on the whole affair offer us elements of farce which see the tale rivalling the wildest tragi-comedy of the Renaissance stage: 'The archbishop heard of all this, fined the couple £40, and forced them to marry in the interval. The husband of Marynka, a brigand, then in prison, was released, and so the woman had two husbands. It was however agreed that they should share the wife — such was the decision of the Ecclesiastical Court.'

If the fate of Theodore and his child seems to us sad and startling, it was rivalled by a Bulgarian incident which occurred around 1838. (In the following extract 'scavengers' evidently refers to people, not animals, being used in the sense of a person appointed to take away refuse.) St Clair and Brophy tell us that,

When the Bulgarian vampire has finished a forty days apprenticeship to the realm of shadows, he rises from his tomb in bodily form and is able to pass himself off as a human being living honestly and naturally. Thirty years' since, a stranger arrived in this village, established himself, and married a wife with whom he lived on very good terms, she making but one complaint, that her husband absented himself from the conjugal roof every night and all night. It was soon remarked that (although scavengers were, and are, utterly unknown in Bulgaria) a great deal of scavengers' work was done at night by some unseen being, and that when one branch of this industry was exhausted the dead horses and buffaloes which lay about the streets were devoured by invisible teeth, much to the prejudice of the village dogs; then the mysterious mouth drained the blood of all cattle that happened to be in any way sickly. These occurrences and the testimony of the wife caused the stranger to be suspected of vampirism, he was examined, found to have only one nostril, and upon this irrefragable evidence was condemned to death. In executing this sentence our villagers did not think it necessary to send for the priest, to confess themselves, or to take consecrated halters or daggers; they just tied their man hand and foot, led him to a hill a little outside Derekuoi, lit a big fire of wait-a-bit thorns, and burned him alive.

Among various telling details (the familiar problem of cattle disease and death; the vigilante nature of the sentence and execution; the horribly vivid identification of the 'wait-a-bit thorns') the most important is the fact that this uncanny stranger had 'only one nostril'. This probably meant that he had no central cartilage in his nose. Barber notes this as a possible sign of vampirism, along with other deformities such as an extra nipple, a split lower lip, and 'a tail-like extension of the spine, especially if it is covered with hair'.[24] Clive Leatherdale identifies the single nostril as a feature of Bavarian vampires, while Diarmuid Ó Giolláin adds that this was supposed to be characteristic of the Scottish fairies of Mull.[25]

It quickly becomes obvious, then, that this specific deformity was readily linked to the demonic or supernatural across a wide range of countries and eras. But the central point we have to grasp is far more basic than that. For all our modern obsession with cosmetic appearances, it is now generally considered in bad taste to mock or marginalise people on account of physical deformities. In this, we are very much in the historical minority. Abundant evidence shows that, in most cultures and at most times, if you looked odd, you were suspect – you looked odd because there was something absolutely, morally, supernaturally wrong with you. Accordingly, you were dangerous. And accordingly, you were very likely to be attacked, if not outrightly destroyed.[26]

A short book could be written on deformity and demonisation. If you squinted you had the evil eye. As T. P. Vukanović points out, in Rakovica, a suburb of Belgrade, cross-eyed women were witches (and had tails).[27] As Barber notes, an extension of the spine, sometimes hair-covered, is actually possible.[28] This may in part lie behind the alleged tail of that psychotic vampire we met above. Live female vampires, as we have just seen, had dry skin and were red faced.

So much, then, for appearance. In using the single nostril as a proof of vampirism, the villagers of Derekuoi were in very good company. If this is startling enough, however, there is something else buried in that Bulgarian account which is still more so. It is obvious to us that these villagers murdered a live person. Yet from what the British authors say, the Bulgarians believed that *originally* he had been dead (and in a sense probably still was 'undead'.) For, after that forty day period, a dead person was able to rise from their grave and could 'pass himself off as a human being living honestly and naturally.' At one level, this belief fits with that oddly permeable boundary between life and death which we met in Chapter Four. In one case you can be alive, dead, or slightly dead. In another you can stray across the border with surprising ease. In popular culture, the death police are remarkably lax about passport control. And the Bulgarian belief also fits uncannily well with what we heard above from Murgoci: 'If the [undead] vampire is not recognized as such, and rendered innocuous, it goes on with its evil ways for seven years' and presently *'becomes a man again. He marries, and has children...'*

At face value, what we seem to have in much of the above is a distinction between 'live vampires' and 'dead vampires'. That is: in Greece and Bulgaria and Russia, a vampire could look like a corpse, or like a more or less normal person. In reality, of course, something far more shocking was probably happening. The alleged 'vampires' of some of these accounts were actually living people who, for one reason or other, were singled out, scapegoated, and murdered.

If it were not for the unusually clear evidence of the Derekuoi story, we would probably not suspect something odd in other, broadly similar tales. And the Derekuoi story is unusually clear for one interesting reason: it is told by people who *do not believe* in vampires. If it had not been, there is a good chance that it would have looked quite different – possibly so fantastical that readers like ourselves would just have frowned and discounted it as another strange vampire myth from the impenetrable forests of folklore.

We have seen that, on the whole, there is one big difference between the witch scapegoat and the vampire scapegoat. The living witch suffers, whereas the vampire (already dead) does not. As a generalisation this is true. But it seems after all that it was not universally true.

This kind of scapegoating of living people as 'vampires' seems to have been possible in Bulgaria and Romania. Did it also happen in Greece? Recall that tale of the shoemaker who was happily married (with two children) until he was heard singing at a party. At this point his voice was identified by several people as the voice of a dead man. It may be that what we have here is a reconstructed version of an actual scapegoating, and actual murder. When asked how she knew him, the wife had replied 'he came...' He came from *somewhere else*. Another suspect outsider, who disappears every Saturday. Even in the bizarre tale of the vampire who 'burst like a cucumber' in the church, we have the phrase 'once there was a vrykolakos that married a girl from our village'. 'From *our* village'... this surely means that the 'vrykolakos' was *not* from that village, but was again a stranger.

How many other living people were murdered as vampires in Bulgaria and elsewhere? The chances of any hostile outsider having witnessed or heard of such killings was obviously very low. Yet occasionally extraordinary tales leak out. Recall the Greek informant, speaking *c.*1960, about the milk-drinking vampire of Samos. Quaintly comical as this may seem at first glance, the full version of that report tells us that it was anything but:

I come from Samos. There was a vrikolax there who used to go and suck the milk out of all the goats. Since the people never milk goats in the dark; yet, when they found their animals in the morning, they had no milk, it was clear that it was a vrikolax who was doing it. So they waited for him with gunpowder in their guns. Only gunpowder will kill one; you cannot catch him with anything else. When they saw him they shot him and cut him in four pieces and, sure enough, his intestines were full of milk which proved he was a vrikolax.

Though we do not have the speaker's age, this was evidently a 20th-century incident. What did it actually involve? The goats had a condition which temporarily stopped their milk. A scapegoat was required, and the vampire was local scapegoat of choice here. The gunmen shot a wandering vagrant, cut him open, and found in his guts a fluid (probably chyle) which they took for milk. Brief as the account is, it is telling that there is no mention of the vrikolax looking like a local person who had recently died. He did not look familiar, because he was again an outsider. Whoever he was, this man was a living person murdered as a supposed vampire. He was not the first, and he was probably not the last.

Forewarned, now, of the peculiar dangers and horrors lying in wait for any luckless stranger or perceived outsider in Greece, Romania or Bulgaria, we may at last be ready to venture to the wildest edges of the dark and frayed map of Vampire Country. Winter clothing is advised. Wolves and bears will abound, and be aware that any seemingly ordinary peasant who passes you in their woven birch shoes could easily be one of the undead. We are about to enter Russia.

III. Russian Vampires

Try, if you can, to imagine this. You wake suddenly from a deep and dreamless sleep. With a strange dislocated lurch of memory, you become aware that a heavy thud was what jolted you awake – and that now lighter, rapid percussions are falling just above you. Pitch darkness. The sweet smell of pine resin. Trying to move, you find that you can barely catch your breath, and that your face and limbs swiftly strike the limits of your wooden prison. How did you get here? This you cannot immediately recollect. But one thing is horribly clear. You are in a coffin, and you are about to be buried alive. In the midst of smothering, choking wild panic, you cling to the faintest edge of light still visible at the seams of the coffin. You cry out. You beat as loudly as you can on the wooden lid. For a bare few seconds, silence. The earth ceases to spatter down onto the pine boards in your grave. But then...

... it begins again. And now, the blows are swifter. Above you, the two men striking spades into the mounds of earth are possibly more terrified than you are. As the dirt rains down, you beg them. You promise them every last item of your worldly property – all your savings... But now all light has gone. The sound of falling earth is different, more muffled, with the coffin lid already covered. And yet... the lid itself, you recall, may not be very secure, fastened as it typically is with crude wooden nails. In a supreme effort of will, you gather all your last strength, clench your fists, and…

Meanwhile, above ground, the story unfolds as follows:

> On leaving the churchyard, when their work was done, [the gravediggers] still heard [the woman's] cries and moans. They at once hurried off to her husband, who was surrounded with guests, drinking to the memory of the deceased. Having related what had taken place, the matter was discussed by the guests and the neighbours, who soon came rushing in, and it was finally resolved *nem. con.* that an evil spirit had taken possession of the deceased, and that in order to prevent her walking at night and disturbing the people it was absolutely necessary to distinter her and drive an aspen stake through her body. The [village] sent a deputation to the priest, asking permission to disinter the body and perform this superstitious rite, deemed necessary in all such cases. The pope, horrified, hurried off to the churchyard, and had the body disinterred in the hope of saving a life, but superstition had already got its victim – the woman was dead, but unmistakable signs showed she had struggled hard to escape from the most horrible death the human mind can conceive.

This is a true story. The incident occurred in Russia in autumn 1888, in a region called Volhynia. What does it tell us? Clearly, that in Russia in the late nineteenth century, trying to escape from a mistaken live burial was no safer than in Bulgaria or in parts of Greece. An evil spirit has animated the 'corpse', which must accordingly be staked. Other details are a little harder to interpret. Were villagers really expecting her to walk only *at night*? This may of course imply that in such cases, the consequent panic catalysed nightmares, thus giving the impression that this person was 'walking at night' into people's bedrooms. And yet… did no one wonder that her cries and pleas from the coffin sounded both oddly human and oddly rational? If she had escaped the burial and the staking, what, exactly, would they have expected to see? A vampire zombie? An ordinary – if traumatised – woman in a shroud? Would the sole rational figure of the priest have been able to save her? In this case, he might, though we should note that the abbreviated phrase in Latin expands to *'nemine contradicente'*, which itself means 'no one dissenting'. And, as we will see in a few moments, being the sole voice of rational opposition in such circumstances could itself be fatally dangerous, even if you were an ordained priest.

In fact, the easiest way to begin tackling these questions is to look at another, grimly similar Russian tale from spring 1890:

A very lurid light has just been thrown upon the life and superstitions of the Russian peasantry by the perpetration of a gruesome crime in the name of what they take to be Christianity. A rich popular farmer died rather suddenly in the village of Sooroffsky. He had been seen in the enjoyment of excellent health on Thursday, and was found dead in his bed on Friday morning. He was prayed for and duly 'waked', after which he was carried to the grave, almost all the inhabitants of the village, inclusive of the priest, following him to the churchyard. Just as the body was being lowered, the lid, which had been fastened rather loosely with wooden nails, began to rise up slowly and detach itself from the coffin, to the indescribable horror of the friends and mourners of the deceased. The dead man was seen in his white shroud stretching his arms upwards and sitting up. At this sight the gravediggers let go the cords, and, along with the bystanders, fled in terror from the spot. The supposed corpse then arose, scrambled out of the grave, and, shivering from the cold (the mercury was two degrees below zero fahrenheit) made for the village as fast as his feebleness allowed him. But the villagers had barred and bolted themselves in against the 'wizard', and no one made answer to the appeals he made, with chattering teeth, to be admitted; and so, blue, breathless, trembling, he ran from hut to hut, like a rat in a burning room, seeking some escape from death. At last fortune seemed to favour him, and he chanced on a hut the inmate of which was an old woman who had not been to the funeral, and, knowing nothing of his resurrection, had left her door unbarred. He opened it and entered, and going up to the stove seemed as if he would get inside it, if he could. Meanwhile, the peasants gathered together, armed themselves with poles and stakes of aspenwood, the only effectual weapons in a fight with a 'wizard', and surrounded the cabin. A few of those whose superstition was modified by faith in the merits of modern improvements also took guns and pistols with them, and the door being opened the attack of these Christians against this 'devil's ally' began. The miserable man, dazed by all that had happened that morning, and suffering from cold and hunger, was soon overpowered, and his neighbours, with many pious ejaculations, transfixed him ... with holy aspen stakes to the ground in the court before the hut.

When things had reached this point the priest, who had recovered somewhat from his terror, came upon the scene, with a half-developed idea that perhaps after all the alleged corpse had been plunged in a lethargic sleep and might recover and live as before. But he found the unfortunate man pinned down to the earth with the aspen pales, with no manner of doubt about his death. The police superintendant (Stonovoy), who lived close by, then arrived, and also saw the murdered man, and made inquiry into the manner of his death. The peasants had gone to their daily work, leaving the body, according to the requirements of the superstition prevailing in Russia, until sundown, when they intended to draw out the stakes and throw the corpse into a bog.[29]

Even for hardened vampire hunters, this tale is so far beyond the bounds of ordinary credibility as to seem unreal. Stretching the muscles of our overworked imaginations one more time, however, let us try to imagine being a child in Sooroffsky on this memorable day. You see a dead man arising from his coffin. All the adults around him, priest included, flee in stupefied terror from this demon. Huddled for some time in breathless urgent debate, they sharpen stakes and swarm en masse to the old woman's house. A struggle; blows; sickening cries... And, after the man has been staked into the ground, he is left there *all day*, for any home-dwelling women or children to see, until unfastened and thrown into a nearby swamp.

It perhaps goes without saying that this made a strong impression on you. What we should also emphasise is how it probably *formed* your beliefs and fears for life. What you felt was not horrified sympathy for this desperately luckless man (who, a few hours since, had been both wealthy and popular). What you felt was that, for your elders to do this, there must be very, very dark and evil possibilities lurking around you. Your own father, a man who had faced and frightened off a pack of wolves one winter, had hurtled away from that grave with the rest of them...

Amongst a multitude of questions, certain key ones beg to be answered. First: just how common were such incidents? Second: how likely was it that anyone would stand up for the luckless man or woman who had found themself attending their own funeral? And thirdly, a cluster of related queries: what did the uncanny dead, and the uncanny living ('wizards' or witches) mean to these Russian peasants? How, indeed, did these people understand death itself?

Feeling that I have earned a brief rest after these traumas, I am going to retire temporarily to the shelter of fireside and samovar, and place our tour group in the capable hands of an expert guide.

Back in the 1990s, the anthropologist Elizabeth Warner was questioning Russian peasants on matters such as these. Happily, she did not hear of recent stakings in the villages of Zhukovo or Maevo, where she was staying, in the north of the country.[30] But she certainly did get the impression that live burials must have been all too common within living memory. Talking to an informant who was considered an authority on funeral rites, and who in his younger days often prepared the dead for burial, Warner asked him how death was ascertained. Answers: 'If the person wasn't breathing that meant he was dead.' You used a mirror above the lips; if it remained clear, then he or she was dead. 'How else would you tell?' asked the villager, with disarming assurance and simplicity. 'You look at him. He's not moving, that's all.' When questioned about checking for a heartbeat, her informant responded dismissively. This was beyond their scope, and – after all – even a normal heartbeat could be difficult to hear.[31]

This might well indicate that villagers were keen to get the dead underground as fast as they could. And it certainly suggests that an alarming number of Russian peasants woke up in their coffins, in many cases failing to attract any attention, and thus going uncounted in the tally of mistaken burials. (Cold must often have aggravated the problem: this was evidently a factor in the case of a suddenly awakened 'dead' tramp, reported privately to me by an embalmer some years ago.)

There does seem to have been some medical debate about uncertain deaths, and some exhumations. Yet the results of these could be grimly ironic. Most obviously, the person in the grave would in most cases be dead, and thus could not answer back. In 1880 the scholar M. Zabylin described 'the custom of disinterring any "suspicious" corpse: "a suspicious corpse (wizard) would be dug up by the whole village, and sometimes they would find him lying face down. This would give them fresh reason for thinking him a wizard, whereas in actual fact it could be he was just "false-dead", suffering from lethargic sleep, and had woken up later in his grave"'.[32] It is no good for us to here shake our heads at the seeming perversity of the peasant explanation, any more than it is to object to those irrational villagers who saw non-decomposition as a sign of vampirism, and decomposition as a sign that the vampire was eating itself and other corpses... What you believe often conditions what you see, and if you believe it strongly enough to stake one of your late friends, then no one is going to convince you that this 'wizard' was merely a live man trying to escape from mistaken burial.

More, in a few moments, about wizards and suspicious corpses. First, that other burning question from Russian vampire territory: If you gained attention from your coffin, was *anyone* going to help you? The answer seems to be that there was some element of luck involved. One or two local priests may have been unusually enlightened. Witness 'a horrible case of burial alive' which occurred in autumn 1894 'at Liuban, not far from St Petersburg. A peasant girl, named Antonova, had presumably died, and, after the usual services, was being buried, when the gravediggers were startled by sounds from the coffin. Instead of instantly breaking it open, they rushed off to find a priest or doctor, and when these officials arrived and broke open the shell the unhappy inmate was already the corpse she had been supposed to be. The body was half-turned in the coffin, the left hand, having escaped its bandages, being under the cheek.'[33]

Meanwhile, just in case the odds were not stacked against you heavily enough as you hammered on your coffin lid, wishing to hell that you had bought one of those Bateson patented life revival devices when the salesman called, there was another in-built superstition raising them that bit higher – especially from the point of view of your village priest. For in 'Vyatka province ... it was widely believed not only that people could revive after being pronounced dead but that the death of twelve priests would follow upon such a reawakening, so that a priest who discovered such a revived "corpse" in his church would feel obliged to kill him.'

Other Russian beliefs about death bring us back into some familiar territory. Warner tells of a liminal period between death, burial, and the fortieth day following the death. The person's soul would depart this world forever only after the fortieth day. 'During this transitional time, and particularly in the three days before the funeral, when the corpse lay at home in its coffin*, watched and prayed over day and night, many people believed there was some small risk that the deceased could be revived. This gave rise to many Russian tales, particularly from the north ... about corpses rising from the dead to terrify or harass the living, notably the grieving widow, or, in the case of vampires, to devour livestock and human beings.' Here we meet an overt belief in vampires, founded on the notion that the corpse was only 'slightly dead' in those two earliest stages. Not only that, but the asterisk links to Warner's note, explaining that 'Orthodox (though not Old Believer) practice requires an open coffin at this stage'. Even in the 1990s, when Warner was quizzing contemporary Russians, coffins were still watched in this way in some remoter rural areas.[34] Did that open coffin imply that – as in Romania and Macedonia – the corpse itself was somehow watching the proceedings of mourners?

Warner further adds that, in traditional Russia, witches and wizards often had a particularly hard time dying, and sometimes could not do so unless people removed part of the roof above the deathbed. This, she explains, related to a longstanding death custom: 'in Medieval Russia it was common, among both peasants and princes, to remove a corpse through the roof, thus avoiding contamination of the exit used by the living.' Clearly this habit was a Russian form of the 'corpse door', closely echoing the Italian habit of making a hole in one's roof – and possibly also involving a belief that the soul left through this exit, before the body was manoeuvred through it. Warner found that 'by the nineteenth century ... this custom was retained, by and large, as a vestigial form only ... being reserved for those suspected of witchcraft.' Her informants still recalled the custom, and one in particular knew precisely which part of the roof should be removed to hasten the death of a wizard.[35]

The reason for all these precautions would often be serious indeed. Warner tells of how a dead wizard was said to have returned to his home and, 'after gnawing his way through the door into the house' would 'throw himself upon the cradle, if there is one. He sucks the baby's blood, then turns to any other living creatures in the house.' Although here we meet vampiric bloodlust, we also find this demon possessed of the kind of general, indiscriminate voracity which caused vampire corpses to eat themselves, their graveyard neighbours, or apples, nuts and grapes. Warner adds elsewhere that, 'while the *revenants* of north Russian tales tended to devour the whole body of their victims, flesh and blood together,' those of southern parts and the Ukraine 'more usually drank blood'.[36]

Warner further explains that 'the Russian peasants have, from ancient times, divided their dead into two major categories. On the one hand are the "natural" dead who die of old age at the time appointed by God. On the other are the "unnatural" or "unclean" dead, sometimes referred to as *mertvyak* (living dead/revenant) or *zalozhnye pokoiniki* ... literally the "set aside" dead.' In the nineteenth century this latter group was still very large, and included 'all those who had died prematurely, that is before the expiry of the time span allotted to them at birth.'[37] The souls of such people were left in limbo until this timespan had expired, and their bodies were often rejected by the earth. 'Although many of this category of the dead may have been good Christians and had died prematurely through no fault of their own, all had the potential for "walking" after death.'[38]

As Warner rightly notes, many of these people were no more blameworthy than those Greeks who had simply been born on the wrong day. For, until around 1910 the 'unclean dead' might be those who had been drowned, lost in the forest and frozen, or struck by lightning. They were often left to rot unburied, or buried on the spot where they died.

What does this tell us, then, about that rich man from Sooroffsky in 1890? Clearly, a crucial point was that he had 'died' so suddenly, with no apparent cause. This may already have been on people's minds before his unexpected revival. They may, for example, have intended to open the grave at some later point, to ensure that he was really dead, and not 'walking'. At any rate, this once 'popular' man quickly underwent a dramatic transformation, being branded as a 'wizard', staked, and then – in a manner typically reserved for the 'set aside' dead – thrown into a bog even while his fresh grave lay there untenanted.

This, then, was an unusual kind of Russian wizard. There is no evidence that he had such status in his lifetime. But the category itself, as we have seen, was well-known – indeed, probably universally recognised. A *koldun* was a wizard or sorcerer; and *baba*, generally used for 'peasant woman' meant in narrower usage the village wise woman. Certain men and women had this capacity for good or evil magic. Sometimes healers of people and animals, they were revered and feared. Most villages seem to have had at least one such figure. They were very well known into the 1920s and '30s (with one of Warner's older informants citing in detail the exploits of a wizard named Anton) and still existed to some extent in the 1990s.[39] Again, writing in the 1930s, Koenig found that to the south in the Ukraine: 'Among the most dangerous of supernatural beings are the vampires, the ghosts of deceased witches and wizards.'

In many ways the *koldun* and the *baba* resemble the witch of Derekuoi, or the many 'cunning folk' who performed magical services for money across Britain, right through and probably beyond the nineteenth century. In Canewdon in Essex, for example, a male 'wizard', George Pickingale, was regarded with considerable awe or terror by many fellow villagers, who bribed or appeased him in various ways until his death in 1909.[40] From the point of view of Russian peasants, probably the two most important things about the *koldun* or *baba* were, simply, that they were both unusual and powerful.

As we have seen, all across the world, being just one of these things gave you a good chance of a deviant burial after death. And Russia was no exception.

> There are many nineteenth and early twentieth century accounts of the torments of witches and wizards at death, and their propensity for 'walking' … In the past, those suspected of witchcraft were generally buried, or reburied after exhumation, with the addition of an aspen stake plunged through their heart, in the reverse of the normal position, that is facing downward into the earth in the expectation that this would prevent them from moving back to the surface.[41]

Given what we have seen about the importance of nightmares in both witch and vampire cultures, it would be surprising if some of these exhumations were not prompted by such uncanny nocturnal visits (or 'walkings'), especially given the high chance that what you already feared was much more likely to then stalk into your dreams.

Heretics and Scapegoats

Given how many people had the potential to rise from their graves, it seems that almost any Russian village must have had some experience of at least one revenant. But we have not yet exhausted the list of uncanny suspects. The early 20th-century Russian scholar, P. P. Efimenko, tells of 'the *eretiki*', a group which

> roamed around at night in villages, captured people, and ate them. The *eretiki* were not alive, but dead. Therefore, if they really got on the nerves of the people, the people gathered at the grave of the one who was known as a sorcerer during his lifetime, opened it up with stakes, took out the *eretik* who was lying with his face downwards, and burned him in a bonfire or pierced his back with an aspen stick. The person … who was called a sorcerer (*koldun*) would become an *eretik* after his death, if he walks around at night and begins to eat people…

As so often, a quick thumb through our Vampire Code Book is required to make sense of this. For surely, even in Russian Vampire Country, no one was actually *eaten* in the night? In reality, the phrase must have meant something like 'sucked out their life'. This itself would then divide into two classes of attack. First, the *eretik* had made an assault which *felt like* someone sucking out your life – namely, a nightmare. Second, the *eretik* was simply chosen as scapegoat for an 'attack' which caused a sudden, inexplicable death. Glancing back at the quotation with these two hypotheses in mind, we notice the crucial phrase, '*if* he walks around at night...' Like so many other vampires, the Russian revenant is *useful*: if something happens, then he offers you a ready-made explanation, and a solution.

Taking Efimenko's words alone, we might imagine that the *eretik* was merely another name for the *koldun*, or wizard. But Felix J. Oinas, the modern scholar who cites Efimenko's discussion, found that in Siberia and the Russian north, the vampire and the heretic had merged into a single, hybrid figure. Posing a question which also applies to North America, Oinas asks: 'How are we to explain the curious fact of the existence of the notion of "vampire" among [the Great Russians], and the lack of a special term for it?' The answer, Oinas argues, is that 'the beliefs pertaining to vampires were transferred to heretics and the term "heretic" was also extended to include vampire.' Being no longer needed, the more precise vampiric *upyr* 'faded away in the sixteenth–seventeenth centuries'.

Oinas believes that this hybrid Russian demon was partly inspired by official, educated treatment of religious dissenters. Unable to comprehend the 'theoretical basis of the struggle ... against heresy' ordinary Russians could only witness the 'hysterical campaign waged against the heretics', with its 'brutal imprisonments and executions'. What could these people have done? Nothing less, the peasants believed, 'than the greatest sins imaginable – killing of Christians, drinking their blood, and eating their flesh – just as the vampires were believed to do.' This ironic or perverse reasoning nicely echoes what that hypothetical Russian child might have felt in Sooroffsky – someone treated so badly just *had* to be very, very wicked...

Hacking his way through the tangled thickets of popular belief which had grown up around the *eretiki*, Oinas found that they were related to two other Russian vampire types. Closely linked to the *eretiki* were the *inovercy* – holders of different faiths who for a long time were treated like the 'unclean dead' and buried in degraded sites, away from the graves of good Christians. Like the vampires of Zărneşti, Galicia or Metschin, these deviant corpses could also be blamed for bad weather.

> Occasionally the deceased *inovercy* were considered to have caused prolonged droughts, as the 'unclean' dead did. In order to bring rain, their graves were opened, and the corpses were abused. A leader of the sect of Flagellants, Samborov, was buried with his adherents on Sionsk mountain (in the Saratov province) in the seventeenth century. During a drought it was decided to exhume his body and throw it into the Volga River. They found, however, only a deep hole where the grave had been – so deep that even the longest rope could not reach the bottom. There was no trace of Samborov – he had vanished into the inferno. It was said that at night black dogs ran barking out of Samborov's grave.[42]

Come 1868, Oinas found, this weather magic was still occurring in the Tarascansk district of Russia – where, after a prolonged drought, people 'dug the coffin of a member of the sect of Old Believers, who had died last December, out of the churchyard, after which one of them opened the coffin, and raising the corpse struck it on the head, saying "Give us rain." At the same time several other peasants poured water on the body; it was then replaced in the coffin, and buried again in its old place in the churchyard'. Unknowingly signalling a typical link between sorcerers and heretics, the British press report on this case adds that, 'in other parts of Russia the peasantry believe that a drought is caused by witches keeping the rain in tubs, and this superstition has proved fatal to many old women who were believed to be the witches.'[43]

Variations of the practice were also seen, sometimes but not always involving water. In summer 1891 the Criminal Sessions Court at Samara tried six people, and sentenced them 'to imprisonment for terms of various duration up to four months for deliberately disinterring the body of a woman who had died of intoxication, and floating it down the Volga as a means of causing rain.'[44] In this case, the suspect life and death of the alcoholic would have been relevant, as may the link between death by fluid and recent drought.

A slightly later incident broadens out this weather scapegoating in an intriguing way. In late August 1899 a British paper reports on 'the government of Samara, in Russia' having

suffered for some time from great heat and an unprecedented spell of dry weather. In the minds of the moujiks [peasants] both the heat and the drought were due to some local incident, and at last, says a Moscow correspondent, the report was spread about the district of Bugulma that the corpse of a lately buried peasant had turned itself over in its coffin. A village meeting decided that the husband of the dead woman should be made to open the grave and restore the corpse to its proper position, as the moujiks believed that this would bring the long-desired rain. As the widower refused, the whole parish at once proceeded to open the grave, and great was the astonishment to find that the corpse was in the same position as on the day of interment. In another village in the district of Bugulma some moujiks opened the grave of a peasant who had lately been buried, and then poured water over the corpse, in the opinion that this was the best method of bringing rain.[45]

We have no clues as to why that second corpse should have been considered suspect, although it may simply have been because this was the last person buried in the village. But in the first case, where the lone dissenting widower is easily over-ruled by all of his neighbours, we can at least make an educated guess as to the underlying logic. If everyone really was astonished at the unmoved corpse they discovered, then they had presumably used the procedure at least once before – and, on that occasion, found that it *had* turned over.

Warner found that beliefs about the unclean dead and drought were indeed so widespread and deep-rooted as to put that one hostile widower into a very small minority. Behind what look like typical anti-vampire treatments of the 'unclean dead' (cutting the corpse in pieces, for example, or cutting off its legs to prevent it walking) lay essentially pagan beliefs about moisture and the earth.[46] On one hand these suspect dead were themselves voraciously hungry and thirsty – and when their teeth were emphasised (sometimes even being made of steel) it was probably to indicate their flesh-tearing powers, rather than the incisive puncturing of veins. On the other hand, it was also believed that the 'pure' earth, being essentially animate, became angry when unclean bodies were buried in it, and produced frost or drought as a result.[47] Such bodies must accordingly be buried in unclean places – the choice of the swamp for that luckless man in Sooroffsky would have had very solid traditional support in much of Russia.

Lest anyone remains in doubt about the majority view in such areas, or the pagan irreverence for either burial or religious orthodoxy, we can look at one final case from the early twentieth century. You may just want a stiff drink in your hand before we begin. On and after 9 August 1905, two British papers told of how,

> at Svino Krivza, in the Crimea ... the people had ascribed the prolonged drought which has ruined their crops this season to the death of a certain old man who had been regarded as an 'opyr' or wizard, no rain having fallen since his burial in March last. According to the popular superstition it was necessary, in order to appease the sorcerer's spirit, that his remains should be exhumed at midnight, and after being sprinkled with holy water by a priest, replaced in the grave. Accordingly on Sunday night a procession of villagers, headed by boys and girls carrying torches, and accompanied by fiddlers and flautists playing dismal dirges, set out for the cemetery. The body of the dead wizard was duly exhumed, and placed in a sitting posture against a tree, around which forty or fifty of the peasants danced a weird dance to the accompaniment of the village musicians.

Even at this stage the affair is a vivid one. The ritual, with its children (think of the impression this would make on a young mind), solemn music and dancing, is both strikingly well organised and thoroughly communal. Nor does the sober ceremony seem to have been in any way affected by the state of a corpse which had been in the earth for at least four months, some of which would have been very warm ones. But now, things turn nasty.

> In the midst of the curious ceremonial Father Constantin, the village pope, arrived. The villagers, thinking he had come to consummate the ceremonies by pouring holy water on the corpse, hailed him with joyful greetings. To their surprise and disappointment, however, the priest not only declined to assist in the affair, but upbraided them for their superstition and their sacreligious barbarity. The crowd at this grew indignant. Some among them who were under the influence of vodka, shouted that he was the real wizard, as the spirit of the dead man had entered into his body. The priest was accordingly seized, and despite his shrieks for mercy, was hurled by four of the men into

the reopened grave, the remains of the corpse being flung in after him with earth and stones. In the morning the police commissary, apprised by two women who had witnessed the affair, despatched a body of men to the spot. The pope was brought up out of the grave and given over to two doctors, who for more than an hour tried to restore him to animation, but failed, death having evidently been brought about by suffocation and shock.[48]

Having downed our drink, and recovered some degree of equanimity, we find that a little reading between the lines here goes quite a long way. Firstly: so vehement is the communal feeling about Constantin's refusal that he himself is considered demonised and radically dangerous. Even allowing for the alleged drunkenness of the villagers, we can fairly guess that he was hurled into the grave more out of terror than from vengeful spite. He had, simply, to be made safe for the good of the village. And secondly, to that brief diagnosis of death through shock and suffocation, we must add the small detail of shock and suffocation horribly compounded by the immediate proximity of a corpse at least four months old.

Besides the details we have just considered, the incident also stands as the most sharply memorable example of something we have witnessed time and time again in our journeys up Greek mountains, over Romanian plains and into remote forest villages, anywhere between Wroclaw and Varna. For most people, in most of history, there was nothing but magic. And if your village priest, with his precious Christian niceties, happened to stand in the way of those beliefs... One final little possibility is no less chilling than any of the above. Notice that just two women out of the whole village troubled to report the interment of Father Constantin. What if they had not? Russia is a big country. It may well be, then, that other priests met a similar fate, without anyone bringing in the police, and without any news of the matter reaching the outside world.

We are about to leave Russia for New England. Before we do so, however, we should take a brief look at one especially distinctive version of the vampire, found by Oinas in the northern Russian district of Olonec. This is the *erestun*: 'a living vampire who, outwardly a good peasant, pursues his vampiristic activity among the village people like a wolf in a sheepcote.' These vampires derived from evil sorcerers – people who were known to 'seize the moment when a neighbour is near his death and, as soon as the soul has left the body ... enter the deceased. After that, unpleasant things happen to the family.'

So far, all this is pretty familiar. But Oinas' source adds that there are also Russian '*erestuny* who "transform themselves", i.e. acquire another person's face and endeavour to sneak into their own or into another family.' This demon outwardly lives the life of 'a good peasant'. But soon 'people in the family or in the village begin to disappear one after another; the *erestuny* devours them. In order to destroy the transformed sorcerer, it is necessary to take the whip used for a heavily loaded horse and give him a thorough thrashing. Then he will fall down and give up his ghost.' Even once dead, this demon must suffer the usual vampire treatment, being staked between the shoulders to prevent his return.[49]

Here we clearly have another version of the 'live vampire' type. But what on earth can it mean? Firstly, 'disappear' is evidently some kind of synonym for 'die'. The multiple deaths are presumably due to one more (misunderstood) outbreak of contagious disease, and the vampire is typically used as scapegoat for the fatalities. In what sense, though, does the *erestun* 'acquire another person's face'? This, I confess, puzzled me for some time. At first glance this looks like the stuff of a thousand horror films – the person you *thought* you knew (your own father, sister, brother) is suddenly *something else*; alien; possessed... What this means in reality, though, is almost certainly some kind of mental illness. Their body, their face look just the same, but they are inexplicably different...

In such cultures insanity could often be seen as more or less demonic. In this context, indeed, any heretical religious views suddenly expressed by the changed person would probably have had especially grave significance. And clearly, the situation was serious enough to require very serious treatment. The possessed man or woman was quite literally whipped to death. As well as adding this appalling fate to our list of horrors inflicted on living scapegoats, we can also add it, more precisely, to all the countless abuses heaped onto the physically and mentally abnormal.

10

Versions of the Vampire (II): New England

The Fair Speechless Queen of the Grave

Plymouth County, Massachusetts, 1807. Five men stand around a coffin. The smell of freshly turned earth, pungent with the early morning dew, fills their nostrils. Cutting horizontally through the trees, the first rays of sunlight strike one of the group, his face gaunt and deathly pale. At the feet of this vampiric-looking young man the coffin lies smeared with damp earth, and the silver lines of snails or slugs. The other four men, distinctly healthier, and sweating heavily despite the morning chill and the hovering steam of their breath, have just jammed four muddy spades into the soil behind them.

The gaunt young man now nods, and 'displacing the flat lid' of the coffin the others lift the covering from the face of the corpse, revealing 'what they had indeed anticipated, but dreaded to declare.' Eyes locked irresistibly, they now see 'the visage of one who had been long the tenant of a silent grave, lit up with the brilliancy of youthful health. The cheek was full to dimpling, and a rich profusion of hair shaded her cold forehead ... while some of its richest curls floated upon her unconscious breast. The large blue eye had scarcely lost its brilliancy, and the livid fullness of her lips seemed almost to say, "loose me and let me go".' For a few seconds more the men appear spellbound, paralysed in this zone between life and death. A robin drops onto the handle of a spade. Five breaths come at once, clustering white vapour above the coffin. And then, finally, an all-too familiar sound breaks the stillness. The pale young man begins to cough.

Two weeks later he is dead. He has been sick for some time, and the ritual we have just witnessed was meant to save him. Ironically, it may have hastened his demise. This little vignette is just one of the darkly glittering gems of American vampire lore rooted out by the painstaking labours of Michael E. Bell, veteran folklorist and author of *Food for the Dead*.[1]

His title itself derives from this particular episode of New England vampire ritual. For the anonymous eyewitness who left us the words quoted above also left us a striking poem inspired by his experience:

> O fair was her cheek, as I knew it.
> When the rose all its colours there brought;
> And that eye, – did a tear then bedew it?
> Gleam'd like the herald of thought.
> She bloom'd, though the shroud was around her,
> Locks o'er her cold bosom wave,
> As if the stern monarch had crown'd her,
> The fair speechless queen of the grave.
> But what lends the grave such a lusture?
> O'er her cheeks what such beauty had shed?
> His life blood, who bent there, had nurs'd her,
> *The living was food for the dead!*[2]

This kind of educated response to New England vampirism seems rare indeed. Even before we come to the poem we have a strange sense of quasi-erotic voyeurism ('rich profusion of hair ... large blue eye'), the young girl's body catching the lacquered shine of some lost pre-Raphaelite masterpiece, or recalling that mid-Victorian vampire poem, *Lautrec*, whose female revenant 'yearn'd/Upon some fearful thing to feed'.[3]

One would give a great deal to know just who this ambivalent and poetical bystander was. For once, even Bell could not find out, and it remains unclear if our poet was one of the four men who dug up the coffin, or if there were in fact six assembled that morning. What we do know is that the gaunt young man was the girl's brother. He and his sister came, originally, from a family of fourteen children. They lived 'in that almost insulated part of the State of Massachusetts, called Old Colony or Plymouth County, and particularly in a small village adjoining the shire town' – a place where one could find 'the relicks of many old customs and superstitions'. Our anonymous author, writing in 1822, adds that, 'there was, fifteen years ago, and is perhaps at this time, an opinion prevalent among the inhabitants of this town, that the body of a person who died of a consumption, was by some supernatural means, nourished in the grave ... [by] some one living member of the family; and that during the life of this person, the body ... [retained], in the grave, all the fullness and freshness of life and health. This belief was strengthened by the circumstance, that whole families frequently fell a prey to this terrible disease.'

Those last words are no exaggeration. By the time that those men assembled at the girl's grave she, aged around 16, was the fourteenth member of her family to have been buried. Only her mother and brother remained alive. No modern parent would need telling that the death of a child is the biggest conceivable trauma they could face. Children should not die before their parents. As Keith Richards said, of the death of his son Tara, 'You don't get over these things ... Now it's a permanent cold space inside me.'[4] We can now begin to see why the anti-vampire rituals of New England were so enduring.

As Bell explains:

from the late eighteenth century and continuing into the mid-twentieth century, various combinations of the following measures were employed by Americans desperate to halt the relentless onslaught of consumption: removal and burning of vital organs—particularly the heart—sometimes, ingesting the ashes; burning the entire corpse, sometimes inhaling or standing in the smoke; turning the corpse face down and reburying it; searching for, and destroying (sometimes by burning), a vine found growing from the corpse; removing the shroud from the mouth of the corpse; rearranging the bones, especially the skull, of the corpse.[5]

The turning of the corpse was the remedy employed in Plymouth County in 1807, in the case of the deathly young beauty. Bell adds that, in summer 1788, a religious minister from Massachusetts, the Reverend Justus Forward, removed the lungs and liver of his mother-in-law, Mrs Dickinson, for similar reasons. On this occasion they were not burned, but reburied in a separate container, a practice 'unique in the American tradition'.[6]

The vampire beliefs of New England offer us an especially striking case of scapegoating. As so often, the living blamed the dead for death. Yet here, throughout all the wealth of evidence so doggedly unearthed by Bell, we never once find an insider using the word 'vampire'. We have the beliefs, and the practices, without the name. At one level, it is easy enough to understand why there had to be some kind of scapegoat. Consumption was an epic killer. In the northeast especially, where bitter winds combined with damp, it was for decades the biggest cause of early death, accounting for around 25 per cent of fatalities caused by disease.[7]

Yet, as we have seen, anti-vampire rituals were most likely to work only against *psychosomatic* problems. They were effective against conversion disorders, nightmares, and the Vampire Poltergeist. Otherwise, any apparent cures were the result of luck or accident. So, when people were using the vampire as scapegoat for a ruthless killer such as consumption, why did they not get discouraged by repeated failures? There are three broad answers. One is that, by definition, the germs of tuberculosis naturally killed off people in the same family. People did not understand that they should isolate the first victims, and to some extent could not do so anyway, with perhaps sixteen people occupying the same modest house. So it made a certain warped sense to believe that the vampire was indeed feeding on its own family.

Two: it is particularly likely that, under this merciless onslaught, the survivors wanted to give themselves at least some sense of *power*. As in so many other cases back in Europe, those who stood watching the grim smoke of the burning heart at least felt that they were doing something, rather than waiting in hopeless passivity for the next funeral. They may also have felt some relief from guilt – something which is, after all, a complicated emotion, often defying the apparent logic of a given situation.

Having said this, we need to take the third point no less seriously. For this is one which makes very clear that those unearthing and mutilating their sisters, brothers, mothers, fathers, wives, or husbands also had quite precise reasons for doing so. The dead were indeed held to be feeding on the living. To do this, they did not need much of a body. They did not need to leave the grave and visit you at night. All they needed was some sign of life. The key culprit was a heart which seemed to contain blood. But the liver and lungs, as we have seen, were also potential vampires themselves. This belief, then, involves the idea that something can feed on you *at a distance*. Just what can this mean? As we will see, for all the strangeness of the notion, it is one which links the supposedly backward natives of Rhode Island or Vermont, through a dark and powerful occult current, back to the sick men and women who had once thronged around Christ in the bright dust of Palestine, almost 2000 years before.

Before we move on through some of the key episodes detailed by Bell, we can remind ourselves of the ironic force of such belief in the case of that girl's terrified brother. The original 1822 account tells us that, 'in two weeks the brother, shocked with the spectacle he had witnessed, sunk under his disease. The mother survived scarcely a year, and the long range of sixteen graves, is pointed out to the stranger as an evidence of the truth of the belief of the inhabitants.' Just what did the brother die of? Probably of consumption. It is clear that he already had this when he stood at his sister's graveside, and it could perhaps have been the kind of 'galloping consumption' which carried off its victims with particular swiftness.[8] But the writer is quite emphatic about the role of shock, strongly implying that the trauma of the grave scene had hastened the brother's death. What might this tell us? Was there some element of voodoo death in this case? We have seen at length how powerful this kind of fatalistic belief can be; and that a version of it can even operate in a modern cancer ward, upon a victim with a wholly mistaken diagnosis.

There must, then, have been some chance that the brother faded faster just because, gazing down on that eerily preserved face, his worst fears were confirmed. Trying to put ourselves in his shoes, we find ourselves caught in a strange economy of life, death and terror – for, staring at the uncanny life-in-death of his sister, he now *knows* where his own life has gone. Not only that, but such is his terror at that moment that the dead girl all but literally sucks more life from him as he stands, weak with fatalistic horror. Like so many other victims of vampirism or voodoo, he goes home and makes up his mind to die. Perhaps, if the girl had looked less full of life he would have lingered on for a few more weeks. As we will see, the surviving relatives in such cases had their own way of explaining the evidently failed ritual.

Mercy Brown

Among the many remarkable episodes of North American vampirism discovered by Bell, the case of Mercy Brown seems to be the most famous. This may be because it occurred so recently, or because the girl's grave has survived in identifiable form. And again, it probably does not hurt that Mercy herself, unlike the otherwise vividly portrayed girl above, actually has a name. Certainly we can see evidence of how the definite site, and the relatively recent date have helped shape a tradition. When Bell went to interview Everett Peck, last known descendant of the Brown family, in November 1981, this veteran Rhode Islander told him of how families would visit the area around the Brown cemetery, for annual public events at the adjacent church and community hall. At such times, 'we were instructed by our ... mother ... when we were playing, "Don't go over the wall and don't go where that rock is. Stay away from there. Don't you touch it, now, because of this awful thing that took place years ago".'[9]

Just what was that 'awful thing'? The key to it lies in the Browns' family history. In December 1883 Mary Eliza, wife of George T. Brown, a 'respected farmer in Exeter, Rhode Island' died of consumption. Seven months later his 20-year-old daughter, Mary Olive, suffered the same fate. A few years later George's only son, Edwin, showed symptoms of the disease. Like others, he was sent away to what his family hoped would be a kinder climate, the increasingly popular health resort of Colorado Springs. But overall he grew worse, and after two years returned to Rhode Island. By the time that he and his wife climbed off the midnight train from Boston on 23 February 1892, his sister, Mercy Lena Brown, had already died of the disease. Afflicted by 'galloping consumption', Mercy was buried in January, aged just 19.[10]

Mercy had been attended in her last illness by a Dr Metcalf. In early March, Metcalf was visited by an unnamed young man who stated that 'Edwin A. Brown ... was in a dying condition from the same disease, and that several friends and neighbours fully believed the only way in which his life could be saved was to have the bodies of the mother and the two daughters exhumed in order to ascertain if the heart in any of the bodies still contained blood, as these friends were fully convinced that if such were the case the dead body was living on the living tissue and blood of Edwin.' Dr Metcalf sent him away, telling him that this belief was 'absurd'.

But the man presently returned to Metcalf. He now 'told the doctor that Mr Brown, the father, though not believing in the superstition himself, desired him to come up to satisfy the neighbours and make an autopsy of the bodies.' Accordingly, on Wednesday morning, 17 March, 'the doctor went as desired to what is known as Shrub Hill Cemetery, in Exeter, and found four men who had unearthed the remains of Mrs Brown, who had been interred four years' (in reality, nine, as Bell found). 'Some of the muscles and flesh still existed in a mummified state, but there were no signs of blood in the heart. The body of the first daughter, [Mary] Olive, was then taken out of the grave, but only a skeleton, with a thick growth of hair, remained.'

Finally 'the body of [Mercy] Lena, the second daughter, was removed from the tomb, where it had been placed till spring. The body was in a fairly well preserved state. It had been buried two months. The heart and liver were removed, and in cutting open the heart, clotted and decomposed blood was found, which was what might be expected at that stage of decomposition. The liver showed no blood, though it was in a well preserved state. These two organs were removed, and a fire being kindled in the cemetery, they were reduced to ashes, and the attendants seemed satisfied. The lungs showed diffuse tuberculous germs.'[11]

Decades later, young Everett Peck was still all too familiar with the rock where this burning took place. By that stage the ritual had become, to Peck's mother, 'that awful thing'. And yet, ironically, famed as the Mercy Brown case has become, and violently indignant as educated outsiders could be in response to such practices, George Brown himself *did not believe* in the superstition. Despite this, it was essentially George Brown who persuaded the still more reluctant doctor to conduct the autopsy. Why? As Bell points out, he almost certainly 'wanted to save the last remnant of his family. He could not rest knowing that he had not exhausted every possibility. How could he face the guilt if he said "no" and the epidemic continued? Brown and his community seemed aware that the disease could be transmitted from person to person, even though they did not understand how that occurred. So, there was an unspoken, tacit obligation to his family and his community to stop the contagion by whatever means were available'.

'It is clear,' Bell continues, 'that George Brown did not believe anyone in his family was a vampire. In characterizing the motivation for his course of action, we would be on firmer ground by substituting for "belief" one or more of the following terms: hope; desire; acquiescence; assent; possibility. These may be related to the concept of belief, but certainly do not require its existence.'[12]

Noting that Eddie Brown himself died on 2 May 1892, Bell is no less shrewd in arguing that, 'folk medicine is successful because it treats the community along with the patient. The patient is not regarded as an autonomous organism requiring a cure.' Rather, 'he or she is an integral part of a community, and a death is a loss to the community, a disturbance to the normal rhythm of life.' In such a situation, where 'the practitioner must reunite and heal the broken community,' George Brown, Bell concludes, 'realized what role he was being asked to play and why. He knew that no one else could give his son, his family, and his community what they required ... Singled out by circumstance to be a folk healer, he reluctantly assented. There was nothing magical in George Brown's pragmatic decision'.[13]

If we remained in any doubt about the power of communal needs and pressures, we might remind ourselves just how small and closely interwoven this place was. It numbered less than 1000 people, and the return of just two of them constituted a *news story* in the local paper (which is how we know that Eddie Brown and his wife got off that midnight train the 23rd of February). And we are about to get a no less powerful reminder of the strength of a vampire community, when we join the watching crowds on Woodstock Green, Vermont, in June 1830.

The Burning on Woodstock Green
In about 1884 the folklorist Jeremiah Curtin spoke to an old lady in New England. She told him that, 'fifty-five years before our conversation the heart of a man was burned on Woodstock Green, Vermont.' This man, she explained,

> had died of consumption six months before ... A brother of the deceased fell ill soon after, and in a short time it appeared that he too had consumption; when this became known the family determined at once to disinter the body of the dead man and examine his heart. They did so, found the heart undecayed, and containing liquid blood. Then they reinterred the body, took the heart to the middle of Woodstock Green, where they kindled a fire under an iron pot, in which they placed the heart, and burned it to ashes.

Curtin adds that 'the old lady who told me this was living in Woodstock at the time, and said she saw the disinterment and the burning with her own eyes.'[14]

In the realms of folklore, one brief conversation can be a very precious thing – now and then the single open door through which you can still glimpse some otherwise unimaginable scene from decades past. In this particular case, however, the old lady's recollection prompted Bell to track down a longer written report, printed in Woodstock's local paper in 1890. And from this we find that what the speaker omitted was no less startling than what she said.

The incident seems to have occurred about the middle of June 1830, and 'the name of the family concerned was Corwin ... near relatives of the celebrated Thomas Corwin, sometime Senator in Congress from Ohio'. With the brother of the dead man taken sick, several local doctors, Dr Joseph A. Gallup, Dr Burnwell, Dr John D. Powers, Dr David Palmer, Dr Willard, and several others 'all advised the disinterment ...being clearly of the opinion that this was a case of assured vampirism. Only there was a slight controversy between Drs Gallup and Powers, as to the exact time that the brother of the deceased was taken with consumption. Dr Gallup asserted that the vampire began his work before the brother died. Dr Powers was positively sure that it was directly after.'[15] No less striking than the involvement of all these doctors is the social standing of those present at the ritual destruction of the heart.

'The boiling of the pot on Woodstock Green, spoken of by the old lady, was attended by a large concourse of people. The ceremonies were conducted by the selectmen, attended by some of the prominent citizens of the village' including 'the Honourable Norman Williams, General Lyman Mower, General Justus Durdick, [and] B.F. Mower', who were all 'men of renown, sound minded fathers among the community, discreet careful men'. Once the heart was burned to ashes, 'a hole ten feet square and fifteen feet deep was dug right in the centre of the park where the fire had been built, the pot with the ashes was placed in the bottom, and then on top of that was laid a block of granite weighing seven tons, cut out of Knox ledge. The hole was then filled up with dirt, the blood of a bullock was sprinkled on the fresh earth, and the fathers then felt that vampirism was extinguished forever in Woodstock.'.[16]

Yet it seems that the fathers were in fact a little too confident. For eight or ten years after that strange cremation, something was still stirring beneath the placid turf of the village green. Around this time, 'some curious minded persons made excavations in the Park' to find the pot.

They dug down fifteen feet, but found nothing. Rock, pot, ashes and all had disappeared. They heard a roaring noise, however, as of some great conflagration, going on in the bowels of the earth, and a smell of sulphur began to fill the cavity, whereupon, in some alarm they hurried to the surface, filled up the hole again, and went their way. It is reported that considerable disturbance took place on the surface of the ground for several days, where the hole had been dug, some rumblings and shaking of the earth, and some smoke was emitted.[17]

As Bell himself emphasises, the Woodstock Green burning of 1830 is especially startling, even by the standards of New England vampirism. It is utterly, almost defiantly public, and involves the relations of a US senator, and several doctors, all of whom actively promote the ritual (rather than, as with Metcalf, grudgingly assisting in it). Gallup, Bell points out, had a degree from Dartmouth College, was the author of an 1815 medical treatise on epidemic diseases, and acted as lecturer at Vermont University.[18] Had a time machine pitched any one of us onto the outskirts of this gathering that summer, we could have been forgiven for thinking, at first glance, that we were looking at some dignified ritual of the Town Fathers (and noting, in passing, that one or two looked remarkably like their near-contemporary, Abraham Lincoln). Yet, as we edged through the well-dressed crowd, nostrils wrinkling curiously at this potent unfamiliar smoke, we would find the bystanders gazing down on a burning human heart; and would later be rewarded by the sight of sweat-coated men wrestling a colossal slab into a colossal hole, before presently scattering animal blood as if at some pagan sacrifice. In some ways this curious mixture is almost as darkly strange as the supposed 'cults of vampires' which opportunistic US media claimed were 'roaming the New England countryside' after first publication of *Food for the Dead*.

And the satanic rumblings...? Bell wonders if this later addition was perhaps not some kind of Christian moralising overlay, bringing in the Devil precisely so as to compensate for the pagan qualities seen on that June day of the burning.[19] Whatever the truth of this later rumbling echo in Vermont, there seems to be no doubt about the granite slab itself. This staggering feat makes some of the vampire destructions of Europe look almost lazy or slapdash by comparison. More typically, North American rituals seem to have been relatively practical and minimal. One case which partially rivals the trouble taken with the granite slab, however, occurred in Rhode Island in 1827.

We glimpsed the incident in Chapter Five. A slightly fuller account tells us that the girl's father was a Captain Levi Young of Connecticut, who married Annie Perkins, and began farming in Foster, Rhode Island. Later, 'his oldest daughter, Nancy, a very bright and intelligent girl, at an early age became feeble in health and died of consumption on April 6th, 1827, aged nineteen.' Before Nancy's death, the second daughter, Almira, had gone into a very rapid decline, showing no response to expert medical treatment. Mr Young, we are told, 'was a very worthy and pious man and wished to do everything possible to benefit his family, and he had the sympathy of all his friends and neighbours.' Accordingly, a short time after Nancy's death, 'in the summer of 1827, the neighbours and friends at Mr Young's request, came together and exhumed the remains of Nancy, and had her body burned while all the members of the family gathered around and inhaled the smoke from the burning remains' as a cure. The cure failed. Almira died 19 August, aged 17; a son, Olney, followed her in December 1831; and two other children died in 1836 and 1843, aged 26 and 25 respectively.[20]

The Jealous Vampire Bride

'It was the month of February and good sleighing. Such was the excitement that from five hundred to one thousand people were present.' For once, the crowds and the excitement were not generated merely by the snow or the sleighing. So far as we can tell, they were crowded around the workshop of the blacksmith, Jacob Mead, in the town of Manchester, Vermont. Inside, a human heart was being burned to ashes in the forge. Behind this typically pragmatic and efficient mode of destruction – memorable, if not quite stylised – there lay a particularly strange story.

Some time before those crowds assembled in winter 1793, a Captain Isaac Burton had married a woman called Rachel Harris. Soon after the marriage Rachel went into decline, 'and after a year or so died of consumption. Captain Burton after a year or more married Hulda Powel.'. Hulda was actually the stepsister of Rachel, both women having had the same father, Esquire Powel. But like Rachel, Hulda also 'became ill soon after they were married.' When she was 'in the last stages of consumption, a strange infatuation took possession of the minds of the connections and friends of the family. They were induced to believe that if the vitals of the first wife could be consumed by being burned in a charcoal fire it would effect a cure of the sick second wife.' They therefore 'disinterred the first wife who had been buried about three years. They took out the liver, heart, and lungs, what remained of them, and burned them to ashes on the blacksmith's forge of Jacob Mead.' One of Jacob's relatives, Timothy Mead, a leader of the town, 'officiated at the altar in the sacrifice to the Demon Vampire who it was believed was still sucking the blood' of Hulda. 'This account,' our author adds, 'was furnished me by an eye witness of the transaction.'[21]

This tale, of a dead wife avenging herself on her living replacement, seems to be unique in the bloodstained pages of North American vampire lore. And it reminds us, once again, of that recurring question: 'human vampire, or vampire zombie?' Rachel certainly seems to have some degree of perceived agency, intention, even personality, by comparison with some of her more anonymous revenant cousins.

What of the watching crowds? By now we know well enough that real vampirism was often a hard-headed matter. We should not too quickly assume that people reacting to it had their imaginations tickled in the manner of Victorian readers of *Dracula*, or later cinema-goers. But 500 is an especially large number of people, and 1,000 still more. Indeed, as Bell discovered through a 1791 census, if there really were 1,000 people gathered in the snow as Rachel's heart crisped to ash, then virtually the whole town had turned out for the event: its population two years since had numbered just 1,276 people (and the spare 300 might well have been accounted for by housebound babies and servants, along with the very sick or infirm).

Were some of these milling onlookers drawn out by the particular details of the Burton case? We should remind ourselves that this was a small town, in an era when feminism was not so much as a word, and when even as a half-formed concept it brought torrents of vituperation, elsewhere, on the head of Mary Wollstonecraft, from men and women alike. One thing which earned Wollstonecraft such hatred was her ability to see how many women were more or less complicit in their own oppression. Forced to live up (or down) to the image that bigoted men had of them, many had all but become their own stereotypes. So... if you were a fairly average woman in Vermont in 1793, with not very much to talk about, then dark whisperings in the butcher's or baker's as to Burton's rashly hasty second marriage, and the jealous vengeance of the slighted Rachel, might well help to enliven your life in the long winter evenings. When Bell alerts me to the fact that Hulda was said to be 'not as good-looking as Rachel' this possibility looks all the more plausible. And while I remember, anyone who decides to enliven our winter evenings by shooting the B-movie version of this, complete with Hulda and Rachel tastefully embracing in their shared tomb, well – you owe me a good seat at the premiere.

Interestingly, the imputed motive of post-mortem jealousy would be found, almost a century later, over in more classic vampire territory. The British press reported, in April 1892, that at Homoliez in Hungary 'several bodies of men had recently been found with their heads cut off. An investigation was made by the police, and it turned out that these mutilations had in every instance been committed by young men who were betrothed to the widows of the decapitated persons. The husbands had died a natural death, and their widows believed that [if] they married a second time their first husbands would reappear and destroy their wedded happiness. Hence they had persuaded their new bridegrooms to decapitate their deceased partners.'[22] Notice that these new suitors are as yet only 'betrothed' to the widows. This might well indicate that the husbands have died fairly recently, and that their bodies and souls are therefore typically perilous, in their as yet only slightly dead condition. We can well imagine, too, that in such a setting these widows could be all too liable to nervous or guilty bouts of sleep paralysis, and associated visits from the jealous dead.

The Vampire's Self-Sacrifice

Whatever was passing through the minds of these chilled multitudes as Rachel's heart was seared like a three-year-old steak on those red-hot coals, it seems clear that no one attempted to put a stop to the proceedings. Here, more than anywhere in surviving New England histories, the ritual was a thoroughly communal affair. By definition there must have been numerous respectable and relatively educated people present. If any had misgivings, they were nonetheless absorbed, like George Brown a century later, into that communal organism so shrewdly described by Bell.

But in a case which seems to have occurred in the following year, 1794, the power of vampire beliefs was attested with memorable force by just a single individual – a young girl living in Harvard, Massachusetts.

When that fell destroyer, consumption, broke into a family circle and began to bear away its victims in slow but sure succession, humiliating the most self-confident physicians with a sense of their impotence, there often came to light a strange delusion—the vulgar belief that if the heart of one who had died with that disease were burned, and the members of the household inhaled the fumes from it, they would escape the doom hanging over them. There is a well-attested tradition that about a century ago, in a consumptive-stricken family of Harvard already bereft of eight or more of its youth, a dying girl extracted from friends a solemn promise that her heart should be consumed for the benefit of her sisters, and her last wish was duly carried out. One of these sisters at least survived to acknowledge to her inquisitive granddaughter, who heard this tradition, that the story was essentially true.

As Bell notes when citing this account (penned by Henry Nourse around 1894), we have here a particularly poignant scrap of New England history. We have seen that communities in Europe could employ pre-emptive stakings by way of precaution. And from Barber we have heard of the 'automatic vampire piercing device' (patent pending). But in terms of someone *asking*, in life, to be treated as a vampire after death, this brave anonymous girl seems to be rivalled only by that Romanian Count who extracted a similar promise as he faced death in Paris in 1874.

The comparison is instructive. On one hand, the Harvard girl rivals a man from one of the most famed vampire heartlands ever known. On the other, she offers a check to any snobbish observer who might think that such noble precautions were indeed the honourable preserve of the titled aristocracy. Nor was this dying girl coerced by those around her. Rather, the 'solemn promise' she demanded shows us how seriously she took this, implying that she feared her wish might be disobeyed through family sentiment. It is of course just possible that the girl was also afraid for herself – that she imagined some kind of grey post-mortem limbo, buried alive and sustained by a parasitic body which her mind or soul disowned.

We have now surveyed several New England vampire cases in fairly memorable detail. In following pages we are going to try and shift from the 'what' to the 'why'; to try and place these potentially bewildering events and beliefs in a wider and more meaningful light. To begin solving the puzzle, however, we need to look first at another incident, offering us an unusual clue. Let us imagine that this one can is being filmed for contemporary cinema.

New England Nightmares?

The sound of surf on rocks. Through the darkness the pale splash of the breakers comes into focus. In the night sky the stars shine with an almost violent clarity, the only source of light for many miles. The camera sweeps in past Montauk Point and Long Island Sound. Presently a ghostly shape looms out of the darkness – the white clapboards of a large house. We hover, a moment, outside an upper window. Inside, the very atoms of the air are wild with terror. A bedroom, with three beds in rows. In the outer two, just motionless heads and blanketed bodies. In the centre, we zoom down into the eye of the storm of bristling fear which galvanises the room. A young girl lies as if pinned to the bed by unseen hands, her eyes gaping at some invisible horror, her chest heaving, gasping for breath. Minutes pass. In the nervous glitter of her eyes the unseen demon is reflected as surely as in a mirror. Finally, she snaps upright. Her body shakes. Her face runs with sweat. And five seconds later, she begins to scream.

The date, 1799. The place, Exeter, Rhode Island. The time, deepest night. And the haunted house belongs to a prosperous New England farmer by the name of Stukeley Tillinghast. Apparently nicknamed 'Snuffy Stuke' because of his typical 'homespun jacket of butternut brown', Stukeley was married to Honor, who, like so many other stoic wives of this region and era, bore fourteen children. The haunting we have just witnessed was no idle bad dream, and the afflicted girl was one of several sisters to suffer it. In 1799 Stukeley buried four of his children. Presently another child fell sick. At this point Stukeley took decisive action.

'A consultation was called with the most learned people, and it was resolved to exhume the bodies of the six dead children. Their hearts were then to be cut from their bodies and burned upon a rock in front of the house.' Several neighbours were called in to assist – among them the Wilcoxes, Reynolds, Whitfords, Mooneys, and Gardners.

> With pick and spade the graves were soon opened, and the ... bodies were found to be far advanced in the stages of decomposition. These were the last of the children who had died. But the first, the body of Sarah, was found to be in a very remarkable condition. The eyes were open and fixed. The hair and nails had grown, and the heart and the arteries were filled with fresh red blood. It was clear at once to these astonished people that the cause of their trouble lay there before them ... her heart was removed and carried to the designated rock, and there solemnly burned. This being done, the mutilated bodies were returned to their respective graves and covered. Peace then came to this afflicted family, but not, however, until a seventh victim had been demanded ... No longer did the nightly visits of Sarah afflict his wife, who soon regained her health. The seventh victim was a son ... He was too far gone when the burning of Sarah's heart took place to recover.[23]

Once again, this ritual was a communal affair. Not only that, but if the phrase 'designated rock' was not imposed by the writer (who penned the account in 1888) then this community had clearly incinerated other human organs in the past. But had they ever seen anything quite like Sarah? Even for people not highly sensitive to the behaviour of the Undead, the fact that all the recent corpses were decayed, while the *oldest* looked eerily alive, must have been grimly arresting. Just what, though, were the 'nightly visits' from which Honor Tillinghast now recovered?

The account also tells us that, apart from Sarah, each one of the sick children exhibited 'one symptom ... of a startling character' before they died: 'This was the continual complaint that Sarah came every night and sat upon some portion of the body, causing great pain and misery. So it went on'. Presently, 'the mother also ... complained of these nightly visits of Sarah. These same characteristics were present in every case after the first one.' The characteristics were, of course, those of sleep paralysis nightmares.

Bell is cautious about this possibility himself, wondering if Sidney Rider (the author of 1888) had 'embellished the narrative'.[24] And Bell has certainly shown that Rider was unreliable in some areas – he dated the incident about 1776, not 1799; and claimed that six rather than four children died in the one year; while 'the seventh victim' in fact seems to have been not a son (as Rider claims), but a daughter. For all this, one element which *does* seem trustworthy is the description of nightmare symptoms. First, it does not seem to have been added for the sake of dramatic effect; the details given are consistent with the nightmare, but are not luridly embroidered (there is no talk of 'evil', for example). Second: if Rider was, as Bell believes, 'employing a literary convention', it is rather odd that he did not use the actual term 'nightmare' (or even 'incubus').

Another way of approaching this question is to address Bell's puzzlement at a motif which appears unique in the records of New England vampirism. Why do no *other accounts* ever mention nightmares? To answer this, we need to remind ourselves of the role which vampire nightmares played back in Europe. In many cases, Europeans had nightmares because they *already* feared a vampire: someone had recently died; others were sick; perhaps poltergeist activity had begun... This cause of European nightmares is, crucially, founded on the different kind of vampire beliefs held in Greece, Romania, and so forth. These people believed that vampires did *leave their graves* to menace the living. By contrast, New Englanders did not. The corpse, or just a vital organ, could feed from its coffin, at a distance. With this difference in mind, we see two plausible reasons why nightmares are absent from New England accounts. One is that there were less of them, precisely because people did not *expect* the corpse to come to their room at night. The other is that those which did occur were not automatically linked to the vampire – again, because people did not expect it to leave its grave.

To this central point we can add some other supporting details. Most obviously, as stated above, after the exhumations and burning of Sarah's heart, the mother, Honor Tillinghast, found that the nightly visits ceased; and she 'soon regained her health'. Clearly, then, she did not have consumption. Her illness was psychosomatic and, as so often in such cases, it now stopped because she expected it to stop. We can also remind ourselves that the disturbed sleep patterns known to provoke nightmares would be all too likely in the children, who indeed were suffering from consumption. And, as Bell points out, one key symptom of consumption is a weight on the chest when lying down. On one hand, this does not simply 'explain' the complaints of the Tillinghast children, who talked of Sarah sitting on 'some portion of the body' – not just the chest. But on the other it *could* explain why consumptives who had nightmares did not report them, or think them to be the work of a revenant; they were, after all, used to feeling this kind of pressure at night. One other point is, if more conjectural, at least worth raising. By 1799 all the girls in the family were well over 13. Here as elsewhere, via that remarkable process to which any modern houseful of women can soberly attest, they would probably have all menstruated at the same time. In an already nervous household, this can hardly have calmed down those wracked by nightmares.[25]

Before we leave the haunted threshold of the Tillinghast house we should return to one of the more puzzling questions raised in opening pages. Time after time, given the grim efficiency of consumption as a killer, such rituals must have failed. But... did they? Was that always how it felt to those involved? Whether or not the seventh victim of the Tillinghast family was a son or daughter, it seems clear that he or she 'was too far gone when the burning of Sarah's heart took place to recover.' And so, the ritual had failed, here, only because it was performed *too late*. The seventh death does not persuade the community to abandon such acts, but is indeed likely to convince them, in other cases, that they should act *sooner*. And here they had all the more reason to think that. For in one sense the burning had worked. It cured Honor, who now 'regained her health'. Looking at the affair another way, we can further see how the power of belief shaped reality. The seventh death did not prove them wrong. It proved them right – they had all seen the uncanny life of Sarah's corpse, so long dead, and yet with fresh blood in its heart. If she was still 'alive' after all those deaths, then her only possible source of food would have seemed to be that seventh sick child.

Notice, finally, that we have here an echo of that mass vampire destruction that lit up the countryside around Serbian Medvegia in 1732. True, the Tillinghast family rituals were not quite so spectacular. They did not burn eleven corpses. But they did mutilate seven members of their own family. And, if they had thought it necessary, they would probably have burned seven Tillinghast hearts.

This case, then, gives us one valuable clue as to how certain New England vampire beliefs were produced, sustained, or aggravated. But there are other elements needed to gain a fuller sense of how these beliefs worked. As so often with magical notions, we will find ourselves taking some surprising journeys in order to access and understand the buried logic involved.

The Power of Life

When relating to Curtin that memorable scene upon Woodstock Green, the old lady also supplied him with another morbid gem. She told of how her uncle, 'a physician of good standing and repute, was present, with other physicians, at the opening of a grave in the town of Malone, New York … A "bone augur" had been observed making its way through one of the grave mounds in the church-yard, increasing in height day by day … They dug through the earth to the coffin below, finding that the augur had bored its way through the coffin lid. The lid was removed, and the people found that the "bone augur" was growing out of the heart of a man buried some time before.'[26]

What was a bone augur? Simply, a vine or root growing out of a corpse or a grave. ('Augur' itself does not mean 'plant', but in this context probably 'omen'.) The Malone tale is just one variant of a widespread superstition about vines, corpses and death. Discussing the case of the Spaulding family (again from Vermont), Bell cites an account which explains: 'it was said that a vine or root of some kind, grew from coffin to coffin, of those of one family, who died of consumption, and were buried side by side … when the growing vine had reached the coffin of the last one buried, another one of the family would die'.[27] To combat this, the surviving family should break the vine, and also burn the vital organs of that most recent corpse.

The uncanny tale of the sprouting heart tells us something important about how such a community viewed life in its most basic sense. First, a vine growing from a corpse was probably yet one more warning: that corpse was not yet *fully dead*. Second, life was a raw, brute, irreverent force. Such people were not interested in the evil *intentions* of the corpse, of some stylised undead persona which delighted in sheer malice for its own sake... They were alert, simply, to the dangers of life feeding on life; and the fact that this could occur with a vine as well as with a human body must only have confirmed the rawly tenacious impersonality which they believed to be at work.

American Magic

Until Bell's seminal work on the vampirism of New England, one of the chief sources for this topic was a short article published by a man called George R. Stetson. In 1896, just months before genteel readers clasped their trembling hands around copies of *Dracula*, Stetson cites a number of New England vampire exhumations. Withholding names, he tells of one which occurred in 'a well-to-do and ... intelligent family' in a seashore village near the fashionable resort of Newport. Just as with Bell's findings, the real culprit for death was consumption. In this case – which occurred 'some years' before 1896, it was generally believed that the afflicted family had saved living members by 'exhumation and cremation of the dead'.[28]

Stetson also spoke to a mason from the same village. At this point 'a hale, hearty, and vigorous man of fifty', the mason in his youth had lost two brothers to consumption. After the death of the first, and with the second fallen sick, their father had been advised to exhume the first son. The sick brother had objected to this, and had presently died (being fed on, it was believed, by the first dead child). When the mason himself became sick, the second dead son was disinterred, and blood was found in the heart. This was cremated, and the mason recovered. The man emphasised to Stetson that his father had seen 'the arterial blood' in the suspect corpse. He added that local doctors did not believe in the idea, although 'many others did'. Similarly, when questioned as to the logic of the cure, 'he could suggest nothing and did not recognise the superstition even by name'. The name was almost certainly 'vampire' or 'vampirism', given that Stetson's article was titled 'The Animistic Vampire in New England'. Stetson cites another case which, as Bell agrees, was almost certainly the Mercy

Brown affair, and refers to four villages in which ten separate families have conducted exhumations.

But the most interesting thing about Stetson is not his data, so much as his attitude to it. He is violently, almost wildly indignant at these barbaric superstitions. Hear him now, in full swing on the atavistic failings of Rhode Island. It is a place 'distinguished by the prevalence of this remarkable superstition – a survival of the days of Sardanapalus, Nebuchadnezzar, and of New Testament history in the closing years of what we are pleased to call the enlightened nineteenth century. It is an extraordinary instance of a barbaric superstition outcropping in and coexisting with a high general culture'. In this benighted region 'agriculture is in a depressed condition and abandoned farms are numerous', the area being 'the tramping ground of the book agent, the chromo peddler, the patent-medicine man and the home of the erotic and neurotic modern novel. The social isolation away from the larger villages is as complete as a century and a half ago ... while the agricultural and economic conditions are very much worse.' 'It is perhaps fortunate,' he adds presently, 'that the isolation of which this is probably the product, an isolation common in sparsely settled regions, where thought stagnates and insanity and superstition are prevalent, has produced nothing worse.'[29]

Just the briefest glance at these lines shows us a man utterly traumatised by the beliefs of his fellow Americans. Stetson flails around wildly and inconsistently for causes, talking of 'sparsely settled regions' just moments after he has noted that Rhode Island has the largest population per square mile of any state in America. Equally, his irrelevant blather about erotic novels necessarily presupposes literacy, and therefore some degree of education. Overall, he seems not just bewildered, but positively repelled by these almost subhuman beings. And what bothers Stetson most is his sense that this kind of superstition is *not* just the peculiar preserve of New England. He is forced also to recognise that it is impossible 'to force a higher culture upon a lower' – meaning, in so many words, that all of America is composed of essentially two classes: the enlightened and the superstitious.

Stetson was certainly not alone. In 1854 a journalist had described the exhumation and burning of two dead brothers, Lemuel and Elisha Ray, in Jewett City, Connecticut. The belief inspiring this, he states, 'tasks human credulity. We seem to have been transported back to the darkest age of unreasoning ignorance and blind superstition, instead of living in the 19th century, and in a State calling itself enlightened and Christian.'[30] The same kind of shell-shocked indignation was heard time and again in the nineteenth century when the educated were confronted with some chance glimpse of the usually hidden beliefs and habits of the rest of humanity.

And, at a glance, these certainly were startling. Back on the European continent, people were drinking blood as medicine at beheadings in Germany and Scandinavia until around 1870. In Britain, they were consuming powdered skull as a medical remedy until at least the 1860s; while in the twentieth century we have the enduring witch beliefs of Edwardian Essex, and the voodoo inflicted on Devon villagers by a Widow Yelston around 1949... Just outside your door or your carriage there was a whole alternative reality which stubbornly refused to be tamed by the powers of civilisation.

It was clearly this failure of civilisation which especially goaded Stetson. For those living in the nineteenth century the persistent delusions of the superstitious were a direct attack on one's own powerful ideology – the notion that progress, education and culture in general would slowly but inevitably raise everyone into an enlightened state. But one other reason for such violent indignation was rather more indirect and ironic. It was precisely that, on the whole, the educated had not a clue what was going on in the minds and lives of the uneducated. Accordingly, when some chance horror of popular culture did reach them, they reacted as if they had encountered someone from another planet. To put it another way: the quasi-vampiric exhumation rituals of New England looked all the odder because most outside observers failed to realise that they were just one part of a whole dense web of overlapping popular superstitions.

By careless oversight, the ordinary people of Texas or Kent or Pennsylvania did not considerately leave behind large books entitled 'All the Mad Stuff we Believed and I'd Bet you'd Kill to Know About in Later Years'... But what we have managed to find out still offers one broad conclusion. For most people, superstition *was* the way. The supposed witches murdered in Texas in 1860, and Arizona in 1952, were just two of many. As for medicine: Bell discovered reports from 1857 about a quack doctor, A. L. Nugent, operating in Concord, North Carolina. Nugent was found to have stolen from their graves the bodies of the two young daughters of an influential Concord citizen, and it presently transpired that he had exhumed sixteen corpses, in Concord and elsewhere, to make medicine. He believed, for example, that a tonic made from boiled human liver could cure diseases of the liver. It is likely that Nugent would have been lynched before he could have been brought to trial; but he apparently took his own life by poison once he realised that he had been found out.[31]

Transferring the Forces of Life

When we see the vampire rituals of New England in this context, they already start to look less marginal than they might otherwise do. That is, rather than a bizarre phenomenon on the fringes of 'civilised life', they seem like one more activity within a broad and durable web of magical behaviour. Not only that, but the exhumation rituals also connect quite precisely with certain magical habits in particular. For such practices are based on the idea that the force of life can be *transferred* from one body to another: in such cases, from the living to the not-quite-dead.

Compare that belief to other scraps of popular medicine from the era. As W. J. Hoffman explains, when a contagious disease is prevalent, one should put sliced onions in one's rooms, 'in the belief that the infectious matter would be absorbed, and not affect the occupants.' In Clinton County, anyone bitten by a snake would be 'immediately taken to the nearest house, where a chicken is secured, cut in two, and the warm bleeding surface of one of the halves placed upon the wound. It is believed the poison is quickly extracted...' Someone suffering from warts should 'rub the warts with a piece of bone and replace it where found. Whosoever picks up the bone subsequently will have the warts transferred to his own hands.'[32]

The most basic underlying logic of these treatments (all from Pennsylvania) is that disease or poison can be *transferred*. The idea is undoubtedly one of the oldest, most widespread, and most durable pieces of popular magic or medicine. Both the onion remedies and the use of a chicken were common treatments for plague in Shakespeare's England. As with the animate corpse, the notions underpinning these cures went back around 2,000 years, to the New Testament and the famous healing career of Jesus Christ. Here the most obvious transfers are positive ones: from the body of Christ or St Paul to the sick. Powerful healing forces cross from one body to another – and in some cases through another physical medium, as when Paul, evidently too busy to treat all his patients in person, touches himself with 'handkerchiefs and aprons' and has these passed to the sick.

There is also a hint that those thronging around Christ for cures in Palestine believed that they could transfer their diseases *to* him.

> But as he went the people thronged him. And a woman having an issue of blood twelve years, which had spent all her living upon physicians, neither could be healed of any, Came behind him, and touched the border of his garment: And immediately her issue of blood stanched. And Jesus said, Who touched me? When all denied, Peter and they that were with him said, Master, the multitude throng thee and press thee, and sayest thou, Who touched me? And Jesus said, Somebody hath touched me for I perceive that virtue is gone out of me. And when the woman saw that she was not hid, she came trembling, and falling down before him, she declared unto him before all the people for what cause she had touched him, and how she was healed immediately. And he said unto her, Daughter, be of good comfort: thy faith hath made thee whole; go in peace
>
> (Luke 8.42–48).

This makes it very clear that Christ himself believed potent healing forces were transferred from his body ('virtue is gone out of me'). What is not at first so clear is the possibility that the woman was furtive for a precise reason: namely, because she was trying to transfer her disease *to* Christ. If this was the case, she probably believed that he was sufficiently powerful (as his other cures attested) to absorb it without being harmed.[33]

In light of these parallels, the indignant complaint of that journalist of 1854, reeling at such 'unreasoning ignorance and blind superstition ... in a State calling itself enlightened and *Christian*' looks rather ironic. Would Christianity have even been established if superstitious men and women around Christ had not believed in the possibility of seemingly irrational cures? Stetson, by contrast, is for once accurate when he sees the New England rituals as 'a survival of the days of Sardanapalus, Nebuchadnezzar, and of New Testament history.' Yet the logic of transfer is not all that is needed to fully comprehend the anti-vampire rites of Rhode Island or Vermont. Two other pieces of the puzzle are required. One is the animate corpse. And the other is transfer *at a distance*.

Versions of the Animate Corpse

Let us start with some more popular cures. Another for warts (writes Hoffman) required you to 'steal a piece of fresh meat – beef being more beneficial – rub it upon the wart and bury it at a cross-road. As the meat decays the wart will disappear.' If you really must try this at home, then the beef cure is less anti-social than ones which require you to give your warts to someone else. In the above case, only the beef suffers. Why? Almost certainly because it is considered to be in some sense only *slightly dead*. Hence the precise requirement for *fresh* meat – this kind of detail matters, as does preference for beef, probably considered especially absorbent.

And the slightly dead human corpse comes more directly into view when we are told that, 'if anyone suffering from corns takes a small piece of cotton cloth, rubs it over the [corns] and hides it, unobserved, in a coffin with a body about to be buried, the corns will leave him.'[34] Here you choose a corpse because, while this avoids afflicting a living person, the slightly dead body still has sufficient life to absorb the corns. Meanwhile, a collection of popular American medical recipes made in 1837 explained that 'birth marks were removed by rubbing them with the hand of a corpse or the head of a live eel, three mornings in a row.' Here the link between a live (and probably absorbent) creature, and a slightly dead corpse is especially clear. The 'three mornings' may in the circumstances have implied the belief that the corpse would be fully dead after three days. Corpse stroking, notes Mary Beith, was also a persistent treatment for scrofula in the nineteenth century in the Scottish highlands and islands; and the belief itself, if not the practice, was still known in Indiana circa 1950.[35] All those examples involve a simple reversal of the logic underlying Bell's 'food for the dead'. Rather than the corpse feeding on you, you are giving it something to eat, and getting rid of that something in the process.

From another angle, the habits of a family preparing a corpse for burial also suggest that many ordinary Americans in the northeast recognised the lingering vitality of their dead. When studying these customs, Gary Laderman found that 'the body of the deceased would remain in the home for a period of one to three days and be constantly under surveillance, especially at night. It was placed in a designated room of the house,' often with 'white cloths covering mirrors'. To preserve the corpse for this period a vinegar-soaked cloth might be laid on the face, or ice used in very warm weather.[36]

It is possible that such constant surveillance was meant to prevent theft of the corpse by those supplying bodies for medical dissection. But other details suggest that the vigilance was motivated by a sense of the persistent life of the body, and its possible vulnerability to spiritual rather than physical harm. Covering of mirrors could in some cases have still denoted the dangers surrounding the lingering, mobile soul. And most notable of all is the outer span of three days. Was this again an indication of the need to protect the body, while it was only *slightly* dead?

One other hint at the animate corpse comes from a much later, and more direct, source. As we saw, a key surviving authority on the Mercy Brown case was a descendant of the family, Everett Peck. When interviewed by Bell in 1981, Peck stated that, 'when they dug up Mercy ... she had turned over in the grave.'[37] This may not have been true. For the newspaper account of the affair Bell found stated, as we saw, that she was actually in a tomb at this point, awaiting a spring burial (presumably when the frozen ground had thawed enough to permit grave-digging). For our purposes, however, what actually happened does not matter so much as what Peck believed. For he goes on:

> When I was younger, a lot of people was buried and they never was embalmed. Today, you're dead when you're in the ground, because if you're not, they finish killing you when they embalm you. Years ago, you wasn't embalmed. You're dead, you're dead; and you're down in the ground, buried. And then ... then, you know, a natural death doesn't happen in a few minutes. It sometimes takes years. For an example, your fingernails and your hair ... will still grow. Hair will grow and so will fingernails. Now, when this Mercy Brown was buried, there was no embalming. It's possible she weren't quite dead when they put her in there. Why was she turned over? Everything today is different than it was years ago.[38]

Just what did Peck mean by these intriguingly ambiguous remarks? There is certainly some sense that Peck is not talking, here, about the straightforward processes of decay as understood by modern biochemistry. First, we have that tantalising phrase 'they finish killing you'. And next, 'it's possible she weren't quite dead...' Now, this in another context could simply mean, 'she was buried alive'. But does it? If so, why talk about growth of hair and fingernails, which Peck almost certainly thinks occur *in a corpse*? Finally, we have to consider the possibility that Peck is here sketching out some curious space halfway between ordinary post-mortem chemistry, and the full-blown animate corpse of European vampire lands. He may well have believed that Mercy 'turned over' because this is the kind of thing that an animate corpse can do.

Action at a Distance

We now have a much clearer picture of the kind of beliefs in which the vampire rituals of New England were logical and necessary. Powerful forces could be transferred between living bodies, or between bodies thought to be alive. What was not understood, of course, was the sad reality of illness or disease: giving it to someone else does *not* actually take it away from you.

The final piece in our puzzle is perhaps the strangest, hardest one for us to really absorb. For, unlike the treatments seen here, which worked by immediate contact, the New England corpse was understood to feed on the living *without ever leaving its grave*. Clearly, people believed this. A few words on the traditions behind this notion of action at a distance should help to make this idea at least slightly less alien to us.

One basic point to recall is that, in the late nineteenth century and after, millions of ordinary people in Europe and North America took action at a distance very seriously indeed. It was, quite simply, the basis of much witchcraft. We have seen that in the Allegheny Mountains around this time, fear of a witch could be general, potent, and even fatal. Hoffman found that in Pennsylvania in the late 1880s there were still witches, some of whom 'even go so far as to profess the power of producing good or evil effects upon absent persons, regardless of distance.'[39]

In the case of corpse medicine, however, family bonds were evidently held to promote the vampiric actions of the corpse, from the distance of its grave. Writing on this topic, Bell quotes an 1869 text which tells of how, 'during the last winter, a young man named Henry Cole, a resident of Jay Hill, Maine, died of consumption, being the second one in the same family to fall a victim to this great scourge of New England. Another member of the family, Frederick, a brother of Henry, is now supposed to be in the last stages of consumption, and in order to stay the ravages of the disease the body of Henry has been disinterred for the purpose of removing and burning the heart.' This, the writer explains, was 'supposed to be a sovereign remedy, the popular theory being that there exists between blood relations a sympathetic link which death does not entirely sever, and which, unless interrupted, oftentimes works injury to the living and sometimes results in death.'[40]

If we step back a moment, we might well feel that this is one more particularly uneconomical explanation for processes that should really have been staring you pretty hard in the face. Rather than a half-dead brother or sister or child sucking your life away from their grave, your problems were arising very directly in your own house, as one sick person gave germs to another. And yet the popular theories of New England had one strong advantage. They allowed you to gain some sense of power, by knowing how to act against the ravenous corpse.

It is true that if a wife was 'feeding' on her living husband, or vice versa, the blood relation theory could not apply. But it is notable that in most cases the process was held to be operating between children. And even that slightly anomalous episode of 'the jealous vampire bride' involved two women who shared the *same father*. Did the notion of child feeding on child also fit the facts in more subtle, unstated ways?

Everyday Action at a Distance: Strange, but True...

Recall that, before being decimated by consumption, these were usually large families, containing ten or more children. On one hand, then, there may well have been some general, routine family tensions – a kind of contagion of mood among 12 or 14 people in a smallish house – which supported the notion of a particular bond among family members. More concretely and precisely, if the house contained two or more girls aged 11 upwards, then you had a good chance of observing a quite striking process of 'secret sympathy', as all females of the right age began to menstruate more or less in synchronicity. Beyond that, there was a form of action at a distance occurring around you which we ourselves have only recently begun to understand in its full power and detail. This was the effect of the moon on living bodies. There is now medical evidence to suggest that 'lunacy' is not merely an outdated astrological myth; psychotic acts do seem to rise at the time of the full moon. This effect operates regardless of any cloud cover, suggesting that the cause is the moon itself, rather than people's reaction to seeing it. While the action of the moon on tides is itself well-known, what has only recently been studied is its related action on aquatic lifeforms. Lyall Watson cites a study which found that if you moved oysters from the shores of Long Island to Chicago, they seemed to lose their ability to open (to absorb food) at high tide. But in fact, after a short interval of adjustment, what they had actually done was shift their internal clocks, so that they now opened when the tide *would have* flooded their new home, had it been a tidal area. Another study found that potatoes were essentially able to calculate the phases of the moon, and adjust their metabolic rate accordingly.[41]

This, then, is some quite powerful and quite precise action at a distance. And some of it was exactly the sort of thing that our New Englanders (all rural, and some coastal) would have recognised. Agricultural practices and beliefs relating to the moon (some of which are still used by wine producers) are very old and very widespread. You needed no laboratories, microscopes, or science grants to pay careful attention to the apparent phases and changes of growth around you. All you needed was a tradition, and the simple fact that your livelihood – if not your next meal – depended on the keenness and success with which you monitored nature.

At one point in *Food for the Dead*, Bell notes how the origins of New England vampire beliefs have been dubiously associated with Native Americans. Treating this notion with the scepticism it deserves, he argues that, 'making one scapegoat, Native Americans, responsible for the introduction of another scapegoat, vampires, seems an unjustified expansion of blame.'[42] Although this habit may not have been widespread, it offers a sharp reminder of how New England vampire beliefs might threaten notions of white Christian Anglo-Saxon superiority. In some cases, anti-vampire rituals were popular, unlearned affairs. But in others they involved the support and sanction of qualified medical doctors, town fathers, and the relatives of congressmen...

Stepping back a little, then, we are faced with a startling side of white Christian history which some modern white Americans may well be very keen to forget. In 1867, one racist journalist derided proposals for negro suffrage, claiming that, two years after black southern slaves were freed, the chief result was their 'steady retrogression ... towards the barbarism from which the Dutch and English traders rescued their forefathers,' before going on to make lurid assertions about the cannibalism of Louisiana voodoo.[43] Even as he did so, there were people who, like that old lady interviewed by Curtin, recalled the burning of a human heart and scattering of bullock's blood on Woodstock Green, *c.*1830, in the clear broad daylight of eminent Christian respectability. Elsewhere, those believing themselves 'food for the dead' were committing cannibalism by way of cure, swallowing the ashes of their own relations.

All this is a very different version of white American history or identity to the one many modern Republicans would like to see recalled or taught. Indeed, those Republican senators from Oklahoma who in February 2015 voted to ban the state's Advanced Placement History courses because they teach 'what is bad about America' would doubtless want this added to their list of Embarrassing Historical Facts.[44] And, so far as we know, no one was ever so much as cautioned, let alone prosecuted, over the many instances of grave desecration or corpse mutilation which these beliefs provoked.

For most people, across most history, there was nothing but magic. Turning, finally, to look at the other vampires of history, we will find that this rule holds good there also. In our own supposedly rational modern world, however, human blood drinking can be equally surprising.

CONCLUSION

The Other Blood Drinkers

The numerous vampires which have stalked through these pages have typically shown scant respect for modern aesthetics or stereotypes. Fat, shabby, and often guileless, they have also failed, in many cases, to drink blood. The truth seems to be, not so much that vampires like drinking blood, but rather, that we like the idea of vampires drinking blood. For some dark reason we have selected and amplified this trait from a larger mosaic of qualities – many of which are now wholly forgotten. Why does blood drinking secretly appeal to us?

To answer this question, we need to look at those who have done it, and who still do. For most of history, blood has been drunk for magical reasons, as medicine, and (in cases of desperation) as food. It has at times been a powerful bonding agent; at others the ultimate form of terrorism, aggression or revenge. Vampire murderers have drunk blood, and in subsequent reports have usually been described or treated as lunatics. The truth may be, however, that their madness is in part continuous with the behaviour of other blood drinkers – ones whose vampirism is ultimately transgressive, though not criminally so.

Every week, all over the world, educated people drink blood in public, highly organised religious ceremonies. They do this as a form of celebration, and one which seems to bind them together as a special kind of group: such is the impression given by the name of this ceremony, known as 'Communion'. The sect which promotes this ritual vampirism is a large and powerful one. It is called the Catholic Church. The ceremony is also emphatically magical – ordinary wine is actually *changed into* the blood of the sect's deity during the event.

This ritual is a perfect example of the unstable intensity associated with the drinking of human blood. For, as Bill Ellis explains, the ritual was one of various factors which initially made Christians a severely marginalised and demonised group:

> Details of the initiation of neophytes are as revolting as they are notorious. An infant, cased in dough to deceive the unsuspecting, is placed beside the person to be initiated. The novice is thereupon induced to inflict what seem to be harmless blows upon the dough, and unintentionally the infant is killed by his unsuspecting blows; the blood – oh, horrible – they lap up greedily; the limbs they tear to pieces eagerly; and over the victim they make league and covenant; and by complicity in guilt pledge themselves to mutual silence.

Cited by the early Church Father Tertullian (*c.*150–220AD), this hysterical moral panic goes on to detail the incestuous orgies Christians enjoyed once inflamed with vampiric bloodlust.[1] In certain basic senses this early (per)version of the Eucharist exactly matches its official successor. In both cases blood drinking is powerful. In both cases it is transgressive. And in both cases those two qualities work to bind the group with a force which tamer rites could not emulate.

There must be many reasons why the Catholic Church remains as powerful as it does, despite its proven role in multiple cases of rape and child abuse. One of these reasons is the secret appeal of a bizarrely magical custom. Like so much of early Christianity, the Catholic Church was founded on magic, and the appeal of magic. We must keep all of these qualities in mind as we track the sanguinary footprints of human vampires into the twenty-first century.

Let us shift now from those abstract qualities to something more immediate and sensuous.

> And how did it taste? Fancy the richest cream, warm, with a tart sweetness, and the healthy strength of the pure wine that 'gladdeneth the heart of man!' It was a draught simply delicious, sweeter than any concoction of the chemist, the confectioner, the winemaker, it was the very elixir of life itself ... it is ... rosy life, warm and palpitating with the impulse of the warm heart's last palpitation; it is ruddy, vigorous, healthful life – not the essence but the protoplasmic fluid itself ... No other earthly draught can rival such crimson cream, and its strength spreads through the veins with the very rapidity of wine.

Writing in 1875, this anonymous American journalist was in fact referring to a glass of fresh bullock's blood, consumed on a visit to a Cincinnati slaughterhouse – a place where a kind of medicinal blood drinking was still practised, by consumptives in particular, just as it was in the Shambles of Paris around the same time.

For in 1879 those suffering 'affections of the lungs, a general wasting away of the body, and other diseases' could be found at the slaughterhouse of La Villette in Paris, where 'every morning between the hours of eight and nine, from a hundred to a hundred and fifty invalids ... present themselves to claim their matutinal glass of blood'. With these patients being mainly female, any privileged 'maids or matrons of high degree' would be taken to a special reception room, where they could be seated along with attending relatives. Already well-organised in that sense, the Blood Clinic of Paris also showed a certain broad nod toward scientific precision, given that a patient would take the life source of cow, sheep, pig or bullock, depending on their particular condition.

At this time, it was less than twenty years since that people could be seen drinking blood at execution scaffolds in Germany, Austria and Scandinavia. This medicinal use was especially popular as a cure for epilepsy, and dated back to at least 1600. There, as in the shambles, the blood was 'imbibed as hot as the patient can take it.'[2] Allowing for differences in region, we seem here to witness a shift from a magical to an increasingly scientific kind of blood medicine. We also see blood being used in part as a kind of food. This could even explain why most of those present in La Villette were female: among the working classes especially, this was still an era when any meat in short supply would be naturally reserved for adult men of the household, so that a glass of blood (price six sous) might have been the Poor Woman's Steak of the day.

Official or unofficial drinking of animal blood has probably been far more common than documentary records might suggest. Writing in the 1980s, Norine Dresser found that men working in a US slaughterhouse routinely drank cow's blood; while an American woman named Donna considered herself a vampire due to drinking animal blood – a habit she had learned from a neighbouring butcher who befriended her in her lonely youth.[3]

In a few cases, such people developed a taste for blood which ultimately ran out of control. In April 1876 the *Duluth Weekly Tribune* described how, among those Americans 'drinking blood as a remedy for disease' two had gone on to drink human blood. Meanwhile, in

Britain in 1888, the eminent psychiatrist George H. Savage told of how, 'I once had under my care a young musician who had worked hard at a foreign conservatoire, and passed from moodiness to madness; he visited the city abattoire', where he 'obtained and drank hot blood from the slaughtered animals. This was after a few days stopped, but fortunately he was watched, for he was seen to try to decoy children to his rooms, and he owned to me that he wished to have their blood, as blood was his life, and his life was that of a genius.'[4] How many others slid from animal vampirism to human, and from blood as physical power, to blood as a kind of psycho-tonic?

A more extreme form of blood as food was seen countless times throughout the nineteenth century, during the many shipwrecks of the era. On 6 September 1884 a German ship *Montezuma* dropped anchor in Falmouth and deposited three unscheduled passengers, Captain Tom Dudley, Edmund Brooks, and Edwin Stephens, first mate. Sailing a yacht, the *Mignonette*, to Australia, the men had been wrecked by a storm on 5 July and forced into a smaller boat, with 17-year-old cabin boy Richard Parker. It later transpired that Stephens and Dudley had colluded to cut Parker's throat, 'caught the gushing blood in ... tins, and divided it between them.' In the subsequent trial, Stephens and Dudley were ultimately pardoned, after initially receiving death sentences. This must in part have been because 'the unwritten law of the sea' admitted how common such cases of desperate survival really were.

What seems to have been forgotten is how common it was to drink blood (usually of those already dead) as much as to eat your fellow passengers. Aboard HMS *Blonde* in 1826, there were some particularly striking Vampire Ethics. After being wrecked by gales near the Sandwich Islands in early February, the shell of this boat struggled on with the familiar horrors of death and madness slowly whittling down the survivors. By 6 February, each man or woman was on a ration of a quarter of a biscuit per day. By early March, it seems that those who died were being routinely vampirised, as the log records state of a dead boy, John Jones, 'threw the last named overboard, his blood being bitter'.

Also among the dead was one James Frier, a young man 'who was working his passage home under a promise of marriage to Ann Saunders, the female passenger'. Saunders, 'when she heard of Frier's death, shrieked a loud yell, [and] then snatching a cup from Clerk (the Mate), cut her late intended husband's throat, and drank his blood, insisting that she had the greatest right to it.' A scuffle now ensued with Clerk, 'and the heroine ... got the better of her adversary, and then allowed him to drink one cup to her two!'

Here we can only touch on the terroristic drinking of blood – something I have termed 'exo-vampirism', as a counterpart to the 'exo-cannibalism' practised by a tribe against its sworn enemies. Although associated with the primitive New World, exo-vampirism in fact occurred in Europe too. Spanish soldiers were said to have drunk the blood of Dutch citizens fleeing the besieged town of Naarden in 1572; and various people to have drunk the blood of Royalist soldiers and aristocrats in and after the French Revolution of 1789.

More recently, US war reporter Dexter Filkins offers a pithy summary of the psychology of vampiric revenge. Reviewing Filkins' 2008 book *The Forever War*, Lee Hamilton tells of how 'an Islamic Army of Iraq insurgent, Abu Marwa' had killed 'two Syrian members of Al Qaeda to avenge the murder of his uncle'. He then delivered 'their blood in vials to his widowed aunt. "She drank the blood of the Syrians," Abu Marwa says. "You see. We were for revenge. She was filled with rage".'[5]

In that case, perhaps the power of blood partly cancels the power of rage or grief. But in the earlier ones, there is a much clearer and more familiar vampire motive. 'Exo' denotes 'outsiders'. Again, blood drinking is about identity. It reasserts the identity of the oppressed against their oppressors. At the same time, it violently annihilates the identity of those vampirised, by denying their most basic boundaries or human rights.

Even the briefest glance at such behaviour shows us how strangely the magic acids of human blood dissolve ordinary rules, patterns or relationships. To drink even a few mouthfuls of it is to somehow absorb or triumphantly encompass your enemy. And matters are no less strange when we turn to more positive cases of blood-bonding.

In 1567 Thomas FitzGerald of Glin Castle, Ireland, was hung, drawn and quartered by the English. Afterwards, 'his mother, legend has it, seized his severed head, drank his blood, and walked, surrounded by a vast keening concourse, carrying his dismembered body to be buried at Lislaughtin Abbey.'[6] This seems not to have been the only case of funerary- or endo-vampirism spurred by English atrocities in Ireland. Another was seen at a Limerick execution in 1577, and yet another at Rathcormac, during the Tithe Wars of 1834.

At a cold distance, we cannot hope to fully dissect the psychology of such actions. But we might well suspect that the felt transgression of blood drinking echoed the extremity of both violence and loss. And it is also hard not to sense that by using blood to radically cross ordinary boundaries, those who drank it here were seeking to cross the harsh boundary between life and death.

Elsewhere, cases of positive and consensual blood drinking were markedly sexual. One Monday in autumn 1720, for example, 'a gentleman and a lady came in a Hackney coach to a surgeon's in Leadenhall Street, where both being bleeded, they drank each other's blood out of the porringers, paid a guinea, and went away about their business.'[7] Writing in 1893, the Austro-German psychiatrist, Richard von Krafft-Ebbing, described being visited by a married man with many scars on his arms. Krafft-Ebbing learned that when this man 'wished to approach his wife, who was young and somewhat "nervous", he first had to make a cut in his arm. Then she would suck the wound, and during the act became violently excited sexually.'[8] This tale, unearthed by one of *Dracula*'s recent editors, J. P. Riquelme, seems to describe a kind of spontaneous sexual blood-sucking, rather than one more self-consciously inspired by either vampire folklore or fiction.

At one level, we see here a shift from grim necessity to the luxuries of privileged self-definition. At another level, we witness a more radical change: from cosmic magic to personal magic. During the eighteenth century, older religious powers were increasingly redirected into the Romantic self. Where 'charm' had once been a demonic spell, it was here the more narrowly social and psychic mystery of sexuality. Versions of this darkly transgressive vampirism have now been appearing in fiction for over 200 years, from Carl Grosse's German novel, *Der Genius*, through John Polidori's 1819 tale 'The Vampyre', down to Stephanie Meyer's *Twilight* and beyond.[9]

The success of these two centuries of vampotainment returns us to that central question: why do so many of us like the idea of people drinking blood? Part of the answer echoes the contrast seen time and again throughout these pages: where once there was fear, now there is boredom. The idea of blood drinking is exciting, just as vampires are exciting. But perhaps there is also a more precise reason. We now live in a world where so many of the things which people *actually* drink are adulterated, diluted, or substituted: decaffeinated coffee; skimmed milk, rice milk, soya milk; fizzy drinks drained of sugar and laced with artificial sweeteners; even, in a sense, all the branded, bottled water which has been subtly alienated from streams, rivers, lakes or rain. Against that, and against an ever-increasing market in sterilisation and sanitisation, we have blood: secret, primal, rawly essential... To drink this, to imagine drinking it, is perhaps for some a rebellion against all those alienated and inessential fluids; a kind of Darwinian communion with our own biological life forces.

Casting our eyes across 2,000 years of blood drinking, we seem to have a spectrum of necessity or urgency. At one end, the extreme physical desperation of the shipwrecked; at another, the personal identity of sexual or Catholic vampires. In between, we have the perceived necessity of blood as medicine: for epilepsy, or to sustain and re-energise the lives of the aged. In her 1989 book, *American Vampires*, Norine Dresser details versions of blood drinking running across this spectrum. One woman becomes violently sexually excited when sucking her own blood, and later redirects this behaviour during vampiric sex with her husband. Others more tamely drink blood from sterilised lancet piercings, in decidedly non-Gothic surroundings.

Perhaps most interesting of all, however, is a woman named Kristin. For Kristin explicitly claimed to get something physical from drinking *human* blood in particular. Stating an intriguingly seasonal variation in her need for blood (one cup per week in winter, but a pint or more in summer) she told Dresser that the blood 'makes her feel energized, full of life, satisfied', and that animal blood would not produce this effect. She was also convinced that vampirism had run in her family, and that she had inherited a condition which made her pale, caused bright sunlight to hurt her eyes, and obliged her to wear sunglasses during daylight. Not only that, but in a scientifically tinged revision of vampiric contagion, she claimed her bites transmitted her condition to donors through something she called 'a "V" cell'.

Although most of these beliefs are clearly derived from vampotainment, it may well be that human blood did make Kristin feel 'energised [and] full of life'. For, as researcher Jana Britton has found in recent years, there is an extremely small group of people who consider human blood to be a medical necessity, not a lifestyle choice. Often termed 'medical sanguinarians' or 'sanguivores', these people believe themselves to have a physiological condition which makes human blood essential to their well-being. Some identify with 'vampirism'. Others do not, and are extremely publicity shy. At least one is supposed to survive on nothing except human blood. What appears to unite sanguinarians is their preference for human over animal blood. Like the fictional vampires of *Twilight*, they will drink the latter as a substitute, at times when human blood is not available. 'Donors' (adds Britton) 'are often partners', and sanguinarians will usually train in phlebotomy.

Thinking about this more broadly, we have to admit that it echoes certain modern attitudes to milk. A small group of people will drink only human milk (or, for example, eat breast milk ice-cream) on the basis that we are biologically designed for this, but not for cow's milk. It might also be added that sanguinarian drinking of animal blood has its own special difficulties. This blood needs to be filtered, to remove potential parasites. Whether they are drinking animal blood or human blood, sanguinarians clearly go to quite a lot of trouble. In the second case, they need a donor, and the donor must be not only safe but willing.

Do sanguinarians actually have an unrecognised medical condition? Britton cites very low blood pressure, and lower body temperature and pulse rate as common, though not universal symptoms. Does this condition require the drinking of blood, rather than, say, an iron tonic? Finally: does it require the drinking of specifically *human* blood? As Britton emphasises, it is difficult to answer these questions in the absence of mainstream medical research on the problem. Sanguinarians, she adds, do not want to consult doctors about a condition so stigmatic; and medicine itself is either shy of the ridicule such research would attract, or uninterested in a minority so small as to offer negligible pharmaceutical profits.

Some further light has been shed on these questions by the research of John Edgar Browning, who studied self-identifying vampire communities 'in 2009–2011 in the New Orleans metropolitan area, and ... in 2011–2013 in Buffalo, New York'. Browning found that 'blood drinking ... vampires feel energised or otherwise better than they would if they were to sustain themselves on regular food alone, like fruits, fish, and vegetables (which they eat too).' He stressed that 'the vampires I met' were 'competent and generally outwardly "normal" citizens. They performed blood-letting rituals safely and only with willing donors and participated regularly in medical exams that scarcely (if ever) indicated complications from their feeding practises.'

This last detail is more important than it might seem. If you or I were to consume human blood on a regular basis, we would stand a good chance of suffering iron toxicity. As Dr Steve Schlozman of Harvard University kindly informs me, iron toxicity can 'cause muscle spasms, seizures, confusion, and death'. The absence of these problems (whether felt by the blood drinker, or measured by medical tests) would suggest that the human blood diet of sanguinarians is actually rebalancing a physiological deficiency of some kind. Britton too confirms that those she has interviewed have not suffered toxicity effects. The obvious test for sanguinarians would seem be to the alternating blind supply of animal and human blood. Would they feel equally 'satisfied, energised, and healthy' if they drank animal blood which they believed to be human? Yet again, medicine is so far uninterested in running such tests.

What we can say is that, in the long view, any perceived or actual demonisation of sanguinarians is far from unique in the history of blood drinking. For it is hard to imagine a group more severely and hysterically marginalised than the early Christians of Tertullian's day. Popular belief held that they murdered infants and drank their blood, and after this inflammatory appetiser, gorged themselves in orgies of incestuous lust with their own mothers, fathers, brothers or sisters. Later, Christians took one central feature of this moral panic and transformed it into the most solemn rite of the Catholic Church, a religious group which (in 2017) had an estimated 1.26 billion members. Here as elsewhere, blood drinking tilts unstably from being intensely negative to intensely positive. In reality, like so many other magical beliefs or entities, it is neither good nor bad, but powerful.

Select Bibliography

Where a name is not specified as a source in my text, the incident in question is usually cited from a contemporary newspaper account. All Greek accounts from *c.*1960 are derived from *The Dangerous Hour*. All details concerning Lefkada kindly supplied by Katherine Skaris.

Books

Abbott, G. F., *Macedonian Folklore* (Cambridge: Cambridge University Press, 1903).

Adler, Shelley, *Sleep Paralysis: Night-mares, Nocebos, and the Mind-Body Connection* (New Brunswick: Rutgers University Press, 2011).

Alexiou, Margaret, *The Ritual Lament in Greek Tradition* (Lanham: Rowman & Littlefield: 2002).

Argenti, Philip P., and H. P. Rose, *Folklore of Chios*, 2 vols (Cambridge: Cambridge University Press, 1949).

Badone, Ellen, *The Appointed Hour: Death, Worldview, and Social Change in Brittany* (Berkeley: University of California Press, 1989).

Barber, Paul, *Vampires, Burial, and Death: Folklore and Reality* (New Haven: Yale University Press, 1988).

Barrow, Bob, *Inside the Mani: A Guide to the Villages, Towers and Churches of the Mani Peninsular* (Stoupa: Matthew Dean, 2006).

Beith, Mary, *Healing Threads: Traditional Medicines of the Highlands and Islands* (Edinburgh: Polygon, 1995).

Bell, Michael E., *Food for the Dead: On the Trail of New England's Vampires* (Middletown, Conn.: Wesleyan University Press, 2011).

— *Vampire's Grasp* (forthcoming).

Blum, Richard and Eva, *The Dangerous Hour: The Lore of Crisis and Mystery in Rural Greece* (London: Chatto & Windus, 1970).

Bond, John, *An Essay on the Incubus* (London, 1753).

Bondeson, Jan, *A Cabinet of Medical Curiosities* (London: I.B. Tauris, 1997).

Calmet, Augustin Dom, *Dissertations upon the apparitions of angels, dæmons, and ghosts, and concerning the vampires of Hungary, Bohemia, Moravia, and Silesia* (Paris, 1746).

Camporesi, Piero, *The Incorruptible Flesh: Bodily Mutation and Mortification in Religion and Folklore*, trans. Tania Croft-Murray (Cambridge: Cambridge University Press, 1988).

— *The Magic Harvest: Food, Folklore and Society*, trans. Joan Krakover Hall, (Cambridge: Polity, 1993).

Clancy, Susan, *Abducted: How People Come to Believe They Were Abducted by Aliens* (Harvard UP, 2005).

Clarkson, Michael, *The Poltergeist Phenomenon* (New Jersey: New Page Books, 2011).

Danforth, Loring M., and Alexander Tsiaras, *The Death Rituals of Rural Greece* (Princeton UP, 1982).

Dresser, Norine, *American Vampires: Fans, Victims and Practitioners* (New York: Vintage, 1990).

Elliott, J. K. (ed), *The Apocryphal New Testament: A Collection of Apocryphal Christian Literature in an English Translation* (Oxford: Oxford University Press, 1993).

Knight, Bernard, *Lawyer's Guide to Forensic Medicine* (London: Cavendish Publishing, 1998).

Lawson, J. C., *Modern Greek Folklore and Ancient Greek Religion: A Study in Survivals* (Cambridge: Cambridge University Press, 1910).

Linder, Keith, (ed. Richard Sugg), *The Bothell Hell House: Poltergeist of Washington State* (CreateSpace, 2018).

MacDermott, Mercia, *Bulgarian Folk Customs* (London: Jessica Kingsley, 1998).

Macnish, Robert, *The Philosophy of Sleep* (Glasgow, 1827).

Melton, J. Gordon, *The Vampire Book: The Encyclopedia of the Undead* (Visible Ink Press, 2010).

Merridale, Catherine, *Night of Stone: Death and Memory in Russia* (London: Granta, 2000).

Mitchell, Caroline, *Paranormal Intruder* (CreateSpace, 2013).

Paxton, Frederick S., *Christianizing Death: The Creation of a Ritual Process in Early Medieval Europe* (Ithaca: Cornell University Press, 1990).

Perkowski, Jan, *The Darkling: A Treatise on Slavic Vampirism* (Ohio: Slavica, 1989).

Roll, William, and Valerie Storey, *Unleashed: Of Poltergeists and Murder: The Curious Story of Tina Resch* (New York: Paraview, 2004).

St Clair, S. G. B. and Charles A. Brophy, *Twelve Years' Study of the Eastern Question* (London: Chapman and Hall, 1877).

von Schertz, Karl Ferdinand, *Magia Posthuma* (Moravia, 1704). As Niels K. Petersen points out, the title page of this edition incorrectly gives 1706 as date of first publication.

Stoker, Bram, *Dracula*, ed. J. P. Riquelme (New York: St. Martins, 2002).

Sugg, Richard, *The Secret History of the Soul: Physiology, Magic and Spirit Forces from Homer to St Paul* (Cambridge Scholars, 2013).

— *Mummies, Cannibals and Vampires: The History of Corpse Medicine from the Renaissance to the Victorians* (Routledge, 2015).

— *A Century of Supernatural Stories* (CreateSpace, 2015).

— *A Century of Ghost Stories* (CreateSpace, 2017).

— *Fairies: A Dangerous History* (London: Reaktion Books, 2018).

Summers, Montague, *The Vampire: His Kith and Kin – A Critical Edition*, ed. John Edgar Browning (Berkeley: Apocryphile Press, 2011).

— *The Vampire in Europe: A Critical Edition*, ed. John Edgar Browning (Berkeley: Apocryphile Press, 2014).

Wachtel, Nathan, *Gods and Vampires: Return to Chipaya*, trans. Carol Volk (Chicago: University of Chicago Press, 1994).

Waller, John, *A Treatise on the Incubus, or Nightmare* (London, 1816).

Watson, Lyall, *Supernature: A Natural History of the Supernatural* (London: Sceptre, 1973).

Weismantel, Mary J., *Cholas and Pishtacos: Stories of Race and Sex in the Andes* (Chicago: University of Chicago Press, 2001).

Wilby, Emma, *Cunning Folk and Familiar Spirits: Shamanistic Visionary Traditions in Early Modern British Witchcraft and Magic* (Brighton: Sussex Academic Press, 2005).

Wise, Jeff, *Extreme Fear: The Science of Your Mind in Danger* (Basingstoke: Palgrave, 2009).

Wright, Dudley, *Vampires and Vampirism* (London: William Rider & Son, 1924).

Zopfius, John Heinrich, *Dissertation on Serbian Vampires* (Halle, 1733).

Articles and Websites

Baldick, Chris, 'Promiscuous Pluralism', *Times Literary Supplement*, 27 Sep 1985, 1066.

Barber, Paul, 'Forensic Pathology and the European Vampire', *Journal of Folklore Research* 24.1 (1987): 1–32.

Bell, Michael E., 'American Vampires and the Ongoing Ambiguity of Death', *Kritikos* 10 (2013), http://intertheory.org/bell.htm.

du Boulay, Juliet, 'The Greek Vampire: A Study of Cyclic Symbolism in Marriage and Death', *Man* 17.2 (1982): 219–238.

Bower, Bruce, 'The Stuff of Nightmares', *Cosmos*, 5 January 2010.

Browning, John Edgar, 'The Real Vampires of New Orleans and Buffalo: a research note towards comparative ethnography', *Nature*, 24 March 2015.

Burr, Malcolm, 'Notes on the Origin of the Word Vampire', *The Slavonic and East European Review* 28.70 (1949): 306–307.

Canessa, Andrew, 'Fear and Loathing on the Kharisiri Trail: Alterity and Identity in the Andes', *Journal of the Royal Anthropological Institute* 6.4 (2000): 705–720.

Cannon, Walter B., 'Voodoo Death', *American Anthropologist* 44.2 (1942): 169–181.

Cornélissen, G., P. Grambsch *et al*, 'Congruent Biospheric and Solar-Terrestrial Cycles', *Journal of Applied Biomedicine* 9 (2011): 63–102.

Davies, Owen, 'The Nightmare Experience, Sleep Paralysis, and Witchcraft Accusations', *Folklore* 114.2 (2003): 181–203.

del Campo, Edgar Martín 'The Global Making of a Mexican Vampire: Mesoamerican, European, African, and Twentieth-Century Media Influences on the Teyollohcuani', *History of Religions* 49.2 (2009): 107–140.

Dempsey, Corinne G., 'Lessons in Miracles from Kerala, South India: Stories of Three "Christian" Saints', *History of Religions* 39.2 (1999): 150–176.

Durham, Edith M., 'Of Magic, Witches and Vampires in the Balkans', *Man* 23 (1923): 189–192.

— 'Whence Comes the Dread of Ghosts and Evil Spirits?' *Folklore* 44.2 (1933): 151–175.

Eberly, Susan Schoon, 'Fairies and the Folklore of Disability: Changelings, Hybrids and the Solitary Fairy', *Folklore* 99.1 (1988): 58–77.

Ellis, Bill, 'De Legendis Urbis: Modern Legends in Ancient Rome', *Journal of American Folklore* 96.380 (1983): 200–208.

Feilberg, H. F., Feilberg, 'The Corpse-Door: A Danish Survival', *Folklore* 18.4 (1907): 364–375.

Gallant, Thomas, 'Peasant Ideology and Excommunication for Crime in a Colonial Context: The Ionian Islands (Greece), 1817–1864', *Journal of Social History* 23.3 (1990): 485–512.

Galt, Anthony H., 'Magical Misfortune in Locorotondo', *American Ethnologist* 18.4 (1991): 735–750.

Golden, Richard M., 'American Perspectives on the European Witch Hunts', *The History Teacher* 30.4 (1997): 409–426, 416.

Hamilton, Lee H., 'Outside the Green Zone, the Human Dimension', *The New York Times*, 12 September 2008.

Henderson, Lizanne, 'The Survival of Witchcraft Prosecutions and Witch Belief in Southwest Scotland', *Scottish Historical Review* 85.219 (2006): 52–74.

Hendricks, George, 'German Witch Mania', *Western Folklore* 23.2 (1964): 120–121.

Hickey, Sally, 'Fatal Feeds? Plants, Livestock Losses and Witchcraft Accusations in Tudor and Stuart Britain', *Folklore* 101.2 (1990): 131–142, 139.

Hoffman, W. J., 'Folk-Medicine of the Pennsylvania Germans', *Proceedings of the American Philosophical Society*, 26.129 (1889): 329–352.

Hogg, Anthony, '6 Reasons Why You Shouldn't Buy An "Antique" Vampire Killing Kit' http://vamped.org/2014/10/31/6-reasons-why-you-shouldnt-buy-an-antique-vampire-killing-kit/

— www.thevampirologist.wordpress.com

Keyworth, David, 'Was the Vampire of the Eighteenth Century a Unique Type of Undead-corpse?', *Folklore* 117.3 (2006): 241–260.

Koenig, Samuel, 'Beliefs Regarding the Soul and the Future World Among the Galician Ukrainians', *Folklore* 49.2 (1938): 157–61.

— 'Supernatural Beliefs among the Galician Ukrainians', *Folklore* 49.3 (1938): 270–76.

— 'Beliefs and Practices Relating to Birth and Childhood among the Galician Ukrainians' *Folklore* 50.3 (1939): 272–287.

— 'Mortuary Beliefs and Practices Among the Galician Ukrainians', *Folklore* 47.2 (1946): 83–92.

Laderman, Gary, 'Locating the Dead: A Cultural History of Death in the Antebellum, Anglo-Protestant Communities of the Northeast', *Journal of the American Academy of Religion* 63.1 (1995): 27–52.

Lee, Demetrocopoulou, 'Folklore of the Greeks in America', *Folklore* 47 (1936): 294–310.

— 'Greek Accounts of the Vrykolakas', *Journal of American Folklore* 55.217 (1942): 126–132.

Leinweber, David Walter, 'Witchcraft and Lamiae in "The Golden Ass"', *Folklore* 105 (1994): 77–82.

Madrigal, Alexis, 'The Dark Side of the Placebo Effect: When Intense Belief Kills', *The Atlantic*, 14 September 2011.

Maple, Eric, 'The Witches of Canewdon', *Folklore* 71.4 (1960): 241–250.

Mitchell, Stephen A., 'Witchcraft Persecutions in the Post-Craze Era: The Case of Ann Izzard of Great Paxton, 1808', *Western Folklore* 59 (2000): 304–328.

Murgoci, Agnes, 'Customs Connected with Death and Burial among the Roumanians', *Folklore* 30.2 (1919): 89–102.

—'The Vampire in Roumania', *Folklore* 37.4 (1926): 320–349.

Ó Gilláin, Diarmuid, ‹The Leipreachán and Fairies, Dwarfs and the Household Familiar: A Comparative Study›, *Béaloideas* 52 (1984): 75–150.

Oinas, Felix J., 'Heretics as Vampires and Demons in Russia', *Slavic and East European Journal* 22.4 (1978) 433–441.

Oliver-Smith, Anthony, 'The Pishtaco: Institutionalized Fear in Highland Peru', *The Journal of American Folklore* 82.326 (1969): 363–368.

Park, Katharine, 'The Life of the Corpse: Division and Dissection in Late Medieval Europe', *Journal of the History of Medicine and Allied Sciences* 50 (1995): 111–132.

Petersen, Niels K., www.magiaposthuma.blogspot.com

Porter, J. Hampden, 'Notes on the Folk-Lore of the Mountain Whites of the Alleghanies', *American Folklore* 7.25 (1894): 105–117.

Puhle, Annekatrin, 'Ghosts, Apparitions and Poltergeist Incidents in Germany between 1700 and 1900', *Journal of the Society for Psychical Research* 63.857 (1998–99): 292–304.

Roscoe, J., 'Magic and its Power', *Folklore* 34.1 (1923): 25–44.

Samper, David, 'Cannibalizing Kids', *Journal of Folklore Research* 39.1 (2002): 1–32.

Simpson, Jacqueline, 'Repentant Soul or Walking Corpse? Debatable Apparitions in Medieval England', *Folklore* 114.3 (2003): 389–402.

Stone, Jon, Roger Smyth, Alan Carson, Steff Lewis, Robin Prescott, Charles Warlow and Michael Sharpe, 'Systematic Review of Misdiagnosis of Conversion Symptoms and "'Hysteria'"', *BMJ* 331.7523 (2005): 989–991.

Sugg, Richard, 'The Hidden History of Deviant Burials', *History Today*, February 2017.

Terbovich, John B., 'Religious Folklore among the German-Russians in Ellis County, Kansas' *Western Folklore* 22.2 (1963): 79–88.

Vukanović, T. P., 'Witchcraft in the Central Balkans I: Characteristics of Witches', *Folklore* 100.1 (1989): 9–24.

Warner, Elizabeth A., 'Russian Peasant Beliefs and Practices concerning Death and the Supernatural Collected in Novosokol'niki Region, Pskov Province, Russia, 1995. Part I: The Restless Dead, Wizards and Spirit Beings' *Folklore*, 111.1 (2000), 67–90.

— 'Russian Peasant Beliefs and Practices concerning Death and the Supernatural Collected in Novosokol'niki Region, Pskov Province, Russia, 1995. Part II: Death in Natural Circumstances' (*Folklore*, 111.2 (2000): 255–81.

— 'Death by Lightning: For Sinner or Saint? Beliefs from Novosokol'niki Region, Pskov Province, Russia', *Folklore* 113.2 (2002): 248–259.

— 'Russian Peasant Beliefs Concerning the Unclean Dead and Drought, Within the Context of the Agricultural Year', *Folklore* 122.2 (2011): 155–175.

Welch, F. B. 'The Folk-Lore of a Turkish Labour Battalion', *Annual of the British School at Athens* 23 (1918–19): 123–125.

Wilson, Katharina, 'The History of the Word Vampire', *Journal of the History of Ideas*, 46 (1985): 577–583.

Wright, A. R., 'Public Right of Way Believed to Be Created by the Passage of a Corpse', *Folklore* 39.3 (1928): 284–285.

Notes

Introduction: Vampire Terror

1. St Clair spent more than two years in Bulgaria on his own before meeting Brophy on a visit to Paris. The two returned to Bulgaria together, where they spent a further 18 months (*Twelve Years' Study of the Eastern Question* (London: Chapman and Hall, 1877), v–vi).

2. This timing is a rough guess. In many cases a funeral may even have happened much sooner after death. One rural Greek interviewed in around 1962 had 'heard my grandmother saying that in the old days people were buried as soon as they had died' (*Dangerous Hour*, 72). Twenty-four hours was still the standard span on the island of Evia in the 1980s (*see*: Juliet du Boulay, 'The Greek Vampire: A Study of Cyclic Symbolism in Marriage and Death', *Man* 17.2 (1982): 219–238, 227).

3. *A Cabinet of Medical Curiosities* (London: I.B. Tauris, 1997), 99, 101. Doctors unsure if death had really occurred would cut or burn a corpse on the soles of its feet, and thrust long needles under its toenails. For further details *see* ibid, 96–121. For a particularly vivid example of live burial, see *Hampshire Advertiser* , 20 December 1845, 7. This describes the fate of a Mrs Blunden, buried alive around 1700, despite her corpse having been watched above ground for a full five days.

4. Harry Ludlam, *Ghosts Among Us: Eyewitness Accounts of True Hauntings* (London: Janus, 1995), 30–32.

5. *Dangerous Hour*, 71.

6. 'ΠΕΡΙ ΑΛΙΒΑΝΤΩΝ. Part I·, *Classical Review* 40.2 (1926): 52–58, 52; italics mine.

7. Anon, *The British Review* 16.32 (1820), 475.

8. *Travels in Montenegro* (London: Richard Phillips, 1820), 48–49.

9. Barber, *Vampires*, 62.

10. Quoted in: Montague Summers, *The Vampire in Europe: A Critical Edition*, ed. John Edgar Browning (Berkeley: Apocryphile Press, 2014), 229–30.

11. Cited in: J. C. Lawson, *Modern Greek Folklore and Ancient Greek Religion: A Study in Survivals* (Cambridge: Cambridge University Press, 1910), 369.

12. Though the village is real, 'Ambéli' is itself a pseudonym.

1. What, When and Where

1. http://www.theguardian.com/world/shortcuts/2013/jul/16/meaning-vampire-graves-poland

2. Barber, *Vampires*, 78–79.

3. T. J. Westropp, 'A Study in the Legends of the Connacht Coast, Ireland' *Folklore* 28.2 (1917): 180–207, 207.

4. 'Repentant Soul or Walking Corpse? Debatable Apparitions in Medieval England', *Folklore* 114.3 (2003): 389–402, 390.

5. *The Living Mountain* (Edinburgh: Canongate, 2011), 88.

6. S. O. Addy, 'Head of Corpse Between the Thighs', *Folklore* 12.1 (1901): 101–102. Sheila Monaghan at the church has kindly supplied exact date of renovations, and confirms that the piece of the coffin lid can still be seen on the wall in the entrance porch today.

7. Christine Dell'Amore, '"Vampire" Picture: Exorcism Skull Found in Italy', *National Geographic*, 10 March 2009.

8. BBC News, 6 June 2012: http://www.bbc.co.uk/news/world-europe-18334106

9. *John Bull*, 1 March 1824.

10. Anon, 'Burial Face Downwards to Prevent the Return of the Ghost', *Folklore*, 27.2 (1916): 224–25.

11. *See*: Katharina Wilson, 'The History of the Word Vampire', *Journal of the History of Ideas*, 46 (1985): 577–583, 580–81. In this 1688 usage certain merchants are denounced as 'the vampires of the public, and riflers of the kingdom'. After long debate about its origins, 'vampire' is now almost universally agreed to be of Slavic origin, and Jan Perkowski claims that it is found in this form in a manuscript dated to 1047 (Perkowski, *The Darkling* (Ohio: Slavica, 1989), 22). On etymology, see also: Malcolm Burr, 'Notes on the Origin of the Word Vampire', *The Slavonic and East European Review*, 28.70 (1949), 306–307.

12. We also find 18th-century accounts of vampirism in the *Magia Posthuma* (1706) of Charles Ferdinand de Schertz.

13. *The Devil is an Ass* (1641), 3–4. The possibility of having a body of air, though ruled out here by Satan, was accepted by many. It is found in Donne's poem, 'Air and Angels'. See also Henry More, *The Immortality of the Soul* (1659), 293.

14. The *Complete Sermons of John Donne*, ed. George R. Potter and Evelyn M. Simpson, 10 vols (Berkeley and Los Angeles: California University Press, 1953–62), VII, 257.

15. Donne seems to credit the Old Testament story of the apparition of Samuel to Saul (even if this was itself, in his words, 'unlawful'); see *Sermons*, VII, 375, and also *Biathanatos* (1644), 202–3. In three instances when he does refer to ghosts in any detail, Donne presents them as creatures which *lack* bodies. Thus in a private letter he tells Sir Henry Wootton that 'when letters have a convenient handsome body of news, they are letters; but when they are spun out of nothing, they are nothing, or but apparitions, and ghosts, with such hollow sounds, as he that hears them, knows not what they said' (*Letters* (1651), 121, nd). Cf, similarly, *Sermons* V, 199, and *Sermons*, II, 83.

16. *Three Books of Occult Philosophy*, trans. J[ohn] F[rench] (1651), 483. French, who translated other Continental works under the signature 'J. F.' at this time, was a medical doctor, and this translation is dedicated to another doctor, Robert Childe (b1r–b2r). Notably, this would later be cited in the context of early modern vampire incidents by Henry More.

17. For some reason Summers dates this incident as occurring around 1730 (*Vampire in Europe*, 159).

18. Hubener had been described by the German author and physician Job Fincelius, who worked, aptly enough, at Wittenberg University, fabled home of Doctor Faustus. And More got his tales from a work by the famed Italian philosopher, Pico della Mirandola. *See*: *An Antidote Against Atheism* (1655), 209. Pico's complete works were published at Basle in 1572, and Donne – who cites him in his *Essays on Divinity* – was just the sort of person to have read them all (*See* R. C. Bald, *John Donne: A Life* (Oxford: Clarendon Press, 1970), 28).

19. Cited in Lawson, *Modern Greek Folklore*, 365. This is backed up by, first, a story from Zacynthos of a man punished for murder by being turned into a *vrykolakas* after death. By 1910, Lawson could state that he had 'remained so for a thousand years'. A little

more reliably, we have a reference to revenants from the Bishop of Antioch, who died in 1599 (Lawson, 409, 403).

20. *The Present State of the Greek and Armenian Churches, anno Christi 1678* (1679), 277–78. As early as about 1413, we hear of a body which resembled the Greek revenant, being wholly uncorrupted long after death. But this, which was seen in the time of Sultan Mehmed I (1413–1421) was inert, and did not menace the living (*see* Abbott, *Macedonian Folklore*, 212–13).

21. These famed cases can themselves be dated back to a little before the 18th century. Calmet had been slightly preceded by a now lesser-known author, John Heinrich Zopfius, who produced a *Dissertation on Serbian Vampires* in 1733. Moreover, Calmet himself also describes the events as not merely recent occurrences, but ones supposedly known 'for about sixty years past' in the regions he cites (*Dissertations upon the apparitions of angels, dæmons, and ghosts, and concerning the vampires of Hungary, Bohemia, Moravia, and Silesia* (1759), 180).

22. *True Briton*, 3 July 1799.

23. Later, they can also be found puncturing the veins of certain Ukrainians (*see*: Samuel Koenig, 'Supernatural Beliefs among the Galician Ukrainians', *Folklore* 49.3 (1938): 270–76, 272).

24. John Hooper, *The Guardian*, 2 July 2004.

25. Piero Camporesi, *The Incorruptible Flesh: Bodily Mutation and Mortification in Religion and Folklore*, trans. Tania Croft-Murray (Cambridge: Cambridge University Press, 1988), 36–43.

2. Vampire Stories

1. 'Was the Vampire...?', 245–47.

2. For other reports of wandering corpses in the UK, France, and Germany, *see*: Darren Oldridge, *Strange Histories: the Trial of the Pig, the Walking Dead, and Other Matters of Fact from the Medieval and Renaissance Worlds* (London: Routledge, 2005), 57–61.

3. Calmet, *Dissertations*, 196–97.

4. Dudley Wright, *Vampires and Vampirism* (London: William Rider & Son, 1924), 87.

5. *See*, for example, the reprint in an Australian paper (*Warwick Argus*, 27 March 1897).

6. In some accounts Stanacka, or Stanoska, is said to be Jowiza's daughter.

7. A similarly large-scale exhumation occurred in April 1755 in Upper Silesia, where thirty bodies were unearthed (*Whitehall Evening Post or London Intelligencer*, 10 April 1755).

8. There has indeed recently been some effort to capitalise on the village's uncanny history. However, it has not been possible to find the original grave and although there is still a Plogojowitz (in Serbian, Blagojević) family, it is not certain that they are descendants of Peter, for which uncertainty they may well be grateful.

9. Summers, *Vampire in Europe*, 150.

10. It is worth adding that severe trauma of another kind (i.e., asphyxiation) causes ejaculation in the living. This has been seen, most commonly, in male felons when hanged.

11. On the overlap between strigoi and witches, see Ronald Hutton, *The Witch: A History of Fear, from Ancient Times to the Present* (London: Yale UP, 2017), 194-5.

12. *The Independent*, 28 October 2007.

13. *The Independent*, 27 October 2007.

3. The Free Range Vampire

1. Cf. Barber, *Vampires*, 2.

2. Summers, *The Vampire: His Kith and Kin – A Critical Edition*, ed. John Edgar Browning (Berkeley: Apocryphile Press, 2011), 30.

3. Keyworth, 'Was the Vampire…?', 244.

4. Murgoci, 'Vampire', 327.

5. On keyholes see Murgoci, 'Vampire', 334.

6. Nicholas K. Papacostas and N. W. Thomas, 'Animal Folklore from Greece', *Man* 4 (1904): 119–122, 120.

7. Demetracopoulou Lee, 'Greek Accounts of the Vrykolakas', *Journal of American Folklore* 55.217 (1942): 126–132, 127. Cf.du Boulay, 226, noting that the Greek vampire comes in any guise, human or animal; and N. W. Thomas, who notes that, c.1901 in Greece, 'black dogs or pigs seen about midnight or before cockcrow are regarded as demons or vampires' ('Animal Superstitions', *Folklore* 12.2 (19091): 189–94, 191).

8. Murgoci, 'Vampire', 323. Murgoci adds that in Siret, however, the soul was conceived of in more rarefied terms as a little light.

9. Murgoci, 'Vampire', 329.

10. On the passing through closed doors, *see* Lee, 'Folklore of the Greeks in America', 304. On keyholes and straw, see George

Stetson, 'The Animistic Vampire in New England', *American Anthropologist* 9.1 (1896): 1–13, 3.
11. 'Supernatural Beliefs among the Galician Ukrainians', *Folklore* 49.3 (1938): 270–276, 271.
12. M. Edith Durham, 'Of Magic, Witches and Vampires in the Balkans', *Man* 23 (1923): 189–192, 190.
13. Lee, 'Greek Accounts', 132, 129.
14. Barber, *Vampires*, 126.
15. *Dissertations*, 284.
16. Cited by Barber, *Vampires*, 126.
17. *The Star*, 11 April 1874, citing Ralston, *Russian Folk Tales*.
18. *Vampires*, 52–53.
19. *Daybreakers*, dir. Michael and Peter Spierig, 2009.
20. *Dangerous Hour*, 76.
21. Murgoci, 'Vampire', 327–28. Barber notes that 'various granular substances are put into graves ... in order to hinder the revenant, and these include millet, sea sand, mustard seeds, oats, linen seeds, carrot seeds, and poppy seeds' (*Vampires*, 49). It may be that some of the accounts seen by Barber are effectively abstracted versions of the basic desire to provide food.
22. Lee, 'Greek Accounts', 130. George here also seems to imply that the vampire might be bribed with food: 'They go to his grave, and I don't know what they throw to him, and he stops coming out.'
23. *Vampire*, 267.
24. Lee, 'Greek Accounts', 127. Cf.Barber, *Vampires*, 100, on the lack of reference to blood-drinking in Serbian vampirism.
25. Lee, 'Folklore of the Greeks in America', 303.
26. Barber, *Vampires*, 65.
27. Cited by Summers, *Kith and Kin*, 30. Allacci himself does seem a little surprised at these daylight assaults, given his use of the word 'actually'.
28. Du Boulay, 226.
29. *Modern Greek Folklore*, 368.
30. *The Star*, 19 April 1887; Murgoci, 'Vampire', 341–43.

4. How to Make a Vampire
1. Emma Wilby, *Cunning Folk and Familiar Spirits: Shamanistic Visionary Traditions in Early Modern British Witchcraft and Magic* (Brighton: Sussex Academic Press, 2005), 13; Mrs John Borland, 'Some Kerry Notes', *Folklore* 31.3 (1920): 234–237, 235.

2. Cited by Summers, *Kith and Kin*, 30.

3. *Dangerous Hour*, 72. On the precise analysis of the appearance of a decaying body, *cf.* Lawson, who also notes many Greek curses along the lines, 'may the earth reject thee' (*Modern Greek Folklore*, 370, 395).

4. On Mehmed's reign, see: Jason Goodwin, *Lords of the Horizon: A History of the Ottoman Empire* (Picador, 2003), 327.

5. Abbott, *Macedonian Folklore*, 212–13. Cf. Lawson, *Modern Greek Folklore*, 399–400.

6. Joseph Brown, *Eastern Christianity and the War* (1877), 34.

7. 'Peasant Ideology and Excommunication for Crime in a Colonial Context: The Ionian Islands (Greece), 1817–1864', *Journal of Social History* 23.3 (1990): 485–512, 493.

8. On vampires and church festivals, *see also:* W. H. D. Rouse, 'Folklore from the Southern Sporades', *Folklore* 10.2 (1899): 150–185, 173.

9. Barber, *Vampires*, 30–31. For more on the caul, see Murgoci, 'Vampire', 329–30.

10. Philip P. Argenti and H. P. Rose, *Folklore of Chios*, 2 vols (Cambridge: Cambridge University Press, 1949), I, 244–5.

11. Matthew Schofield, 'In Romania, Pre-emptive Strikes on "Vampires"', *Seattle Times*, 31 March 2004 http://seattletimes.com/html/nationworld/2001891951_vampires31.html

12. *The Star*, 19 April 1887.

13. Barber, *Vampires*, 33. Again, the notion of wind or air as themselves animate is by no means limited to uneducated or magical cultures. The *ruach* of the Old Testament, the *thymos* of Homer, and the *pneuma* of the New Testament were all closely associated with the soul or the divine. For further details, *see:* Richard Sugg, *The Secret History of the Soul: Physiology, Magic and Spirit Forces from Homer to St Paul* (Cambridge Scholars, 2013).

14. 'The Folk-Lore of a Turkish Labour Battalion', *Annual of the British School at Athens* 23 (1918–19): 123–125, 123–4. This man and one other were supposed to be able in life to change into dogs, hares and especially cats. It is telling that part of the belief surrounding the men was evidently inspired merely by their being typically 'accompanied by several cats which lived in their houses'.

15. *Cf.*also Durham, 'Of Magic, Witches and Vampires', 189–192, 189, on the cat taboo in Montenegro, *c.*1920.

16. Barber, *Vampires*, 33.
17. Lee, 'Greek Accounts', 130–131, 128.
18. Anne Ross, *The Folklore of the Scottish Highlands*, (London: Batsford, 1976), 108.
19. Leland L. Duncan et al, 'Fairy Beliefs and Other Folklore Notes from County Leitrim', *Folklore* 7.2 (1896): 161–83, 181. For a Japanese version of this belief, *see*: W. L. Hildburgh 'Some Magical Applications of Brooms in Japan', *Folklore* 30.3 (1919): 169–207, 197.
20. 'Greek Vampire', 225–26.
21. Barber (*Vampires*, 19) notes that in some cases people were buried just in a shroud, without a coffin.
22. Du Boulay, 'Greek Vampire', 226.
23. Personal communication from Katherine Skaris.
24. Frederick S. Paxton, *Christianizing Death: The Creation of a Ritual Process in Early Medieval Europe* (Ithaca: Cornell University Press, 1990), 21. Calmet notes the same thing on the authority of the Church Father, Origen (*Dissertations*, 20).
25. John 11.39–44.
26. *See*: *The Apocryphal New Testament: A Collection of Apocryphal Christian Literature in an English Translation*, ed. J. K. Elliott (Oxford: Oxford University Press, 1993), Acts of Peter, 'The Gardener's Daughter', 398–9; Acts of John, v.62–86, 328–335.
27. Given that the Lazarus miracle appears in *only* John's gospel, we indeed have to take seriously the idea that for Mark and Luke the idea was just too much to swallow. As for Matthew...? Perhaps he meant to write it down but forgot. He, after all, was perfectly happy with the idea of several saintly zombies bursting their graves and wandering about the city after Christ's crucifixion: '... and the earth did quake, and the rocks rent; and the graves were opened; and many bodies of the saints which slept arose; and came out of the graves after his resurrection, and went into the holy city, and appeared unto many' (Matthew 27.51–3).
28. Ricaut, *Present State*, 277.
29. Katharine Park, 'The Life of the Corpse: Division and Dissection in late Medieval Europe', *Journal of the History of Medicine and Allied Sciences* 50 (1995): 111–132, 117. Cf. ibid, 116, on the Italian preference for corpse matter from Egyptian mummies, not recently dead bodies.
30. 'The Life of the Corpse', 115.

31. *Cf.* F. S. Copeland on how, in Slovakia, 'the soul of a wicked person, notably that of a warlock or witch' would leave its grave forty days after death and haunt humankind ('Slovene Folklore', *Folklore* 42.4 (1931): 405–446, 428).

32. Du Boulay, 'Greek Vampire', 226. On the relationship between Greek 'loosing' and 'binding' and the New Testament, *see* Lawson, 397.

33. Du Boulay, 'Greek Vampire', 222. In Ambéli this notion over-rode that concerning preserved corpses. The villagers did not believe that a preserved corpse was a universal mark of vampirism.

34. Du Boulay, 'Greek Vampire', 232.

35. *Dangerous Hour*, 69.

36. This last post-mortem period is commemorated by various rituals: 'At this service the family prepares koliva with sugar and hands them out to all that have attended the service. I asked about the significance of sugar in the koliva and my grandmother told me that sugar generally signifies joy, but in funerals it signifies a burial sheet ... In addition, in the first 40 days of mourning no one is allowed to bring any cake or sweets to the house of the mourned; they only eat biscuits or semolina cake (halva). After the spirit goes on to heaven, they can then eat sugar again' (Katherine Skaris, personal communication).

37. Warner, 'Russian Peasant Beliefs and Practices concerning Death and the Supernatural Collected in Novosokol'niki Region, Pskov Province, Russia, 1995. Part II: Death in Natural Circumstances' (*Folklore*, 111.2 (2000): 255–81, 265.

38. 'Beliefs Regarding the Soul and the Future World Among the Galician Ukrainians', *Folklore* 49.2 (1938): 157–61,158–59.

39. Barber, *Vampires*, 190.

40. Danforth and Tsiaras, *Death Rituals*, 38–39.

41. Du Boulay, 'Greek Vampire', 224. *Cf.*(ibid.) the fact it is 'this word and never that meaning simply "to die" (*pethaíno*), which is used about this last moment'. For other indications that the soul was something, or somewhere (on earth) during or after death, *see also*: 'Death and Burial', 98; 'Greek Vampire', 232; 'Russian Peasant Beliefs': 70, 268–9; 278, fn 17; Catherine Merridale, *Night of Stone: Death and Memory in Russia* (London: Granta, 2000), 51.

42. W. H. D. Rouse, 'Folklore Firstfruits from Lesbos', *Folklore* 7.2 (1896): 142–161, 146.

43. Barber, *Vampires*, 48.

44. 'Mortuary Beliefs and Practices Among the Galician Ukrainians', *Folklore* 47.2 (1946): 83–92, 84.

45. *See* R. B. Onians, *The Origins of European Thought* (Salem: Ayer, 1987), 171–3. Citing Frazer, Onians (172) also finds something similar among the Society Islanders.

46. Danforth and Tsiaras, *Death Rituals*, 38–39.

47. Alexiou, *Ritual Lament*, 37.

48. Warner, 'Russian Peasant Beliefs and Practices concerning Death and the Supernatural Collected in Novosokol'niki Region, Pskov Province, Russia, 1995. Part I: The Restless dead, Wizards and Spirit Beings' *Folklore*, 111.1 (2000), 67–90, 72. None of Warner's present-day informants feared the dead or had strong beliefs in the possibility of their return (70–1). For more on Russian vampires and revenants, *see* Felix J. Oinas, 'Heretics as Vampires and Demons in Russia', *Slavic and East European Journal* 22.4 (1978) 433–441, 437, 433.

49. Alexiou, *Ritual Lament*, 38. In Canada around 1918 'an old lady of English extraction' offered a loose echo of such fears, stating that 'fretting or weeping near a corpse will disturb its rest' (F. W. Waugh, 'Canadian Folklore from Ontario', *Journal of American Folklore* 119.32 (1918): 4–82, 26).

50. Helkiah Crooke, *Microcosmographia* (1615), 516; Robert Burton, *The Anatomy of Melancholy* (1621), 29.

51. 'A Treatise of the Soul', in *The Works of Sir Walter Raleigh*, ed. William Oldys and Thomas Birch, 8 vols (Oxford: University Press, 1829), VIII, 571–591, 588.

52. *The Diary of Ralph Josselin 1616–1683*, ed. Alan Macfarlane (Oxford: Oxford University Press, 1991), 113–114.

53. 'Death and Burial', 98.

54. Katherine Skaris, personal communication.

55. W. R. Paton, 'Naxian Superstitions', *Folklore* 4.2 (1893): 257.

56. Koenig, 'Beliefs regarding the Soul', 158. In the Hebrides at the start of the twentieth century, 'a bowl of water is sometimes placed in a bed from which a corpse has been removed, the reason given being that the corpse may be thirsty' (A. Goodrich-Freer, 'More Folklore from the Hebrides', *Folklore* 13.1 (1903): 29–62, 6). This must surely be a confused reference not to the corpse (which after all is no longer in the bed), but the soul. Occasionally, there were rituals designed to prevent the soul

being ejected from the house too soon. Dust or sweepings thrown out at time of death, for example, could risk 'ejecting the soul of the deceased' (Paton, 'Naxian Superstitions', 257; Ellen Badone, *The Appointed Hour: Death, Worldview, and Social Change in Brittany* (Berkeley: University of California Press, 1989), 61. For others, no less strikingly, 'if anything that was in the house at the moment of death is put outside, the soul will be forced to wander without peace until it has collected all the objects touched by its last breath' (ibid., italics mine). For a different version of the dust custom, *see* Merridale, *Night of Stone*, 50.)

57. 'Russian Peasant Beliefs Concerning the Unclean Dead and Drought, Within the Context of the Agricultural Year', *Folklore* 122.2 (2011): 155–175, 167.

58. *Dangerous Hour*, 69.

59. Samuel Koenig, 'Mortuary Beliefs', 84.

60. Koenig, 'Beliefs Regarding the Soul', 157–8.

61. Murgoci, 'Death and Burial', 92. For similar habits in Slavic culture, *see*: Barber, *Vampires*, 33. The 'practice of throwing open the windows ... before death for the purpose of easing the departure of the soul,' E. Bendann notes, 'was resorted to' in England in 1890, 'upon the death of a dignitary of the Church of England' (*Death Customs: An Analytical Study of Burial Rites* (New York: Alfred A. Knopf, 1930), 59). On the door custom in mid-twentieth century England, *see*: B. A. [sic], 'Death and Burial Customs – Broughton, Hampshire', *Folklore* 61.2 (1950): 103–4, 104. For the idea that a corpse doubled in a mirror would cause another death, *see* Barber, 33; Roy Palmer, *The Folklore of Warwickshire* (London: Batsford: 1976), 100.

62. Murgoci, 'Death and Burial', 92.

63. A further empirical notion may also be lodged within the custom. A mirror could look like a means of exit, and therefore be perilous in a way that a wall was not. In 1962 one Greek informant could still state: 'Some people think that it is bad luck when a mirror breaks because it can have your soul and then, when it breaks, you will die' (*Dangerous Hour*, 78). On mirrors and death ritual in southern Ireland in the nineteenth century, *see*: Duncan et al, 'Fairy Beliefs', 161–83, 181.

64. A related belief noted by the officers was that, when going to the fountain, everyone must 'throw some water out of every bucket ... as some elementary spirit might otherwise be floating on the

surface of the water, and, not being thrown out, take up his abode in the house, or enter into the body of any one who drank from the vessel'.

65. On Brittany, *see* Badone, *Appointed Hour*, 61–62. Badone notes that the mirror custom was recorded there as late as 1984. Merridale (*Night of Stone*, 57) notes that the soul of a child could be bound 'to earth for ever' in Russian peasant culture, if its mother were to lay out the body and weep excessively over it while doing so.

66. Piero Camporesi, *The Magic Harvest: Food, Folklore and Society*, trans. Joan Krakover Hall, (Cambridge: Polity, 1993), 14. For other possible motivations for such temporary openings, *see* Warner, 80–81; and Merridale, *Night of Stone*, 50.

67. Waugh, 'Canadian Folklore', 26.

68. Fr. John B. Terbovich, 'Religious Folklore among the German-Russians in Ellis County, Kansas' *Western Folklore* 22.2 (1963): 79–88, 87.

69. Feilberg, 'The Corpse-Door: A Danish Survival', *Folklore* 18.4 (1907): 364–375, 363.

70. H. T. Browne notes that in Northern Ireland people had in the past similarly used 'the feet-first exit [and] the roundabout route to the graveyard' to 'confuse the spirit, so that it could not easily find its way back' ('County Antrim Folklore To-day' *Ulster Journal of Archaeology* 3.1 (1938): 208–214, 210–11.

71. Summers, *Vampire in Europe*, 142.

72. A broader version of the corpse-door precautions can still be found on the island of Lefkada, where, 'after a funeral, anyone that has attended has to go to a restaurant or coffee shop before returning home. If they do return home, there is a pitcher of water outside the front door which they use to splash water on their face in a backwards motion three times, before entering the house; this is so they don't bring death with them to their homes' (Katherine Skaris, personal communication).

73. Murgoci, 'Death and Burial', 95–96. *Cf.*Clodagh Tait, *Death, Burial and Commemoration in Ireland, 1550–1650* (Basingstoke: Palgrave, 2002), 38, on the average gap (3.3 days) between death and burial in early modern Ireland.

74. As Michael Bell shrewdly points out, it was probably also important for the corpse to know that the rituals were being properly carried out, so as to assist its post-mortem repose.

75. *Macedonian Folklore*, 199.
76. Koenig, 'Beliefs Regarding the Soul', 157.
77. *Evening News* (Portsmouth), 9 April 1903.
78. W. H. Thornton, *Reminiscences of an Old West Country Clergyman*, ed. Duff Hart-Davis (Ludlow: Excellent Press, 2010), 20–21.
79. Oddly enough, those carrying a corpse any distance through much of England could meet with the same problems as seen in Hungary; this was because, for a long time it was believed that the passage of a corpse over private land automatically created a permanent public right of way. Landowners might therefore refuse passage. In turn, this sometimes meant extremely long journeys (in one case a 5 mile detour around a mountain with the coffin) which might then give rise to the kind of accident described by John Hobbs. For just two articles among several, *see*: A. R. Wright, 'Public Right of Way Believed to Be Created by the Passage of a Corpse', *Folklore* 39.3 (1928): 284–285; B.A., 'Death and Burial Customs. Broughton, Hampshire', *Folklore* 61.2 (1950): 103–104.
80. Barber, *Vampires*, 42.
81. Murgoci, 'Vampire', 329.
82. 'Hypothesis Concerning Soul Substance Together with Experimental Evidence of The Existence of Such Substance', *American Medicine*, April, 1907.

5. Vampire Scene Investigation

1. The span of this general depression remains a matter of debate, with some authorities pushing the boundaries back to the 13th or 14th century, and some ending it around 1750 (see Brian Fagan, *The Little Ice Age: How Climate Made History 1300–1850* (New York: Basic Books, 2000), 49, 48)). Jean M. Grove states: 'The Little Ice Age lasted from 1300–1850 and was worldwide' (*Little Ice Ages: Ancient and Modern*, 2 vols (London: Routledge, 2004), II, 642).
2. Barber, *Vampires*, 119.
3. Barber, *Vampires*, 109.
4. Barber, *Vampires*, 40.
5. *Countess Dracula: the Life and Times of the Blood Countess, Elisabeth Báthory* (London: Bloomsbury, 1997), 228.
6. *Voyage into the Levant* (1701), cited by Barber, 22.
7. *John Bull*, 15 June 1844.

8. 'Greek Accounts',132.
9. Lee, 'Folklore of the Greeks', 304. In 1942 she now believed that such bodies were preserved 'by the kind of water in the soil' ('Greek Accounts', 132).
10. On the Tyrol, *see* Summers, *Vampire in Europe*, 160.
11. *Daily Gazetteer*, 6 September 1738.
12. *Food for the Dead*, 29.
13. *The Phantom World*, ed. Henry Christmas, 2 vols (London: 1850), II, 56–59.
14. *Dissertations*, 285.
15. *Preston Guardian*, 22 September 1855.
16. Barber, *Vampires*, 126.
17. Cited by Barber, *Vampires*, 126.
18. *Cf.* Barber, *Vampires*, 116.
19. *See*: Nicholas Wade, 'Does Man Alone have Language? Apes Reply in Riddles, and a Horse Says Neigh', *Science* 208.4450 (1980): 1349–1351.
20. Barber, *Vampires*, 69–70.
21. In parts of Greece the 'light-shadowed' were still believed to exist in the 1960s, and were sensitive not just to vampires but to exotica in general (*see*: *Dangerous Hour*, 110–111).
22. Summers, *Vampire in Europe*, 173, citing *Daily Telegraph*, 15 February 1912.
23. *See*: Samuel Koenig, 'Beliefs and Practices Relating to Birth and Childhood among the Galician Ukrainians' *Folklore* 50.3 (1939): 272–287, 277.
24. Barber, *Vampires*, 48.
25. Barber, *Vampires*, 53.
26. Daniel McLaughlin, 'A Village Still in Thrall to Dracula', *The Observer*, 19 June 2005.
27. http://www.courrierinternational.com/article/2011/09/13/pour-echapper-aux-vampires-rien-ne-vaut-les-vieilles-recettes.
28. Matthew Schofield, 'In Romania, Pre-emptive Strikes on "Vampires"', *Seattle Times*, 31 March 2004 http://seattletimes.com/html/nationworld/2001891951_vampires31.html
29. Gabriel Ronay, 'Vampire Slayer Impales Milosevic to Stop Return', *The Herald*, 10 March 2007 http://www.heraldscotland.com/vampire-slayer-impales-milosevic-to-stop-return-1.829326 *Cf.* also: Hugo Rifkind, 'Serbian vampire hunters', *The Times*, 8 March 2007, 12.
30. Milosevic was 64 when he died.

31. Barber, *Vampires*, 49.
32. *Bulgarian Folk Customs*, 68. *Cf.* also Feilberg, who notes that flax seeds might be strewn around a house after a death, because any spirit trying to re-enter would have to count them all before it did so, and Koenig, who found poppy seeds used for the same reason in the Ukraine.
33. *Food for the Dead*, 138–39.
34. For a recent example, see Yusuf Sonmez, the Turkish doctor labelled 'Doctor Vampire' after his alleged involvement in black market organ transplants (*Mummies, Cannibals and Vampires: The History of Corpse Medicine from the Renaissance to the Victorians* (Routledge, 2015), 422–27).
35. Barber, *Vampires*, 64.
36. *Food for the Dead*, 9.
37. Murgoci, *Food for the Dead*, 22.
38. *History Natural and Experimental* (1638), 363–65. This work first appeared in Latin in 1622.
39. Barber also notes that, if you were born with a caul, your parents would keep it, dry it, and later crumble it into your food as prevention against possible vampirism (Barber, *Vampires*, 31).
40. The irony is especially sharp, given how durable the Blood Libel proved in Russia. When another such fabrication led to a trial in Austria-Hungary in 1883, at least one British paper reported the story in a notably irresponsible way (*see*: 'Murder of a Girl by Jews. Revolting Revelations', *The Dundee Courier*, 18 May 1883).
41. *Food for the Dead*, 169–70.
42. *Lloyd's Weekly Newspaper*, 28 May 1871.
43. Barber, *Vampires*, 64.
44. Melton adds that, 'the first such kit was alleged to have been produced by Nicolas Plomdeur, a gun maker in Liege, Belgium, in the mid-19th century. His kit included a real pistol made in the shape of a Latin cross, a silver bullet, a wooden spike, powder flask, and a clove of garlic' (*The Vampire Book: The Encyclopedia of the Undead* (Visible Ink Press, 2010), 519).
45. http://starweb.mercermuseum.org/starweb/MercerCollections/servlet.starweb
46. *See*: http://doaav.blogspot.co.uk/2010/07/scoop-on-vampire-hunting-kits.html*See*, also, Anthony Hogg, '6 Reasons Why You Shouldn't Buy An "Antique" Vampire Killing Kit' http://vamped.org/2014/10/31/6-reasons-why-you-shouldnt-buy-an-antique-

vampire-killing-kit/ (Many thanks to Anthony for sending this one over.)

47. *Dangerous Hour*, 75–76. The same man also notes that mercenary Greek priests even sold 'a medicine' supposed to make corpses 'dissolve easily'.
48. Barber, *Vampires*, 72.
49. Barber, *Vampires*, 35–36.
50. Murgoci, 'Vampire in Roumania', 326.
51. Barber, *Vampires*, 53.
52. Wright, *Vampires and Vampirism*, 87.
53. *Dissertations*, 214.
54. Barber, *Vampires*, 73.
55. Barber, *Vampires*, 73.
56. Barber, *Vampires*, 25, 73.
57. *The Independent*, 28 October 2007.
58. Stetson, 'Animistic Vampire', 10.
59. Barber, *Vampires*, 70–71.
60. *Western Times*, 27 June 1913.
61. *Phantom World*, II, 209–10.
62. Murgoci, 'Vampire in Roumania', 326.
63. Barber, *Vampires*, 76.
64. *See*, for example, the case of the shoemaker of Breslau (Barber, *Vampires*, 12–13).
65. *Modern Greek Folklore*, 374.
66. Du Boulay gives the word *zimatáo* for this sense of 'boiling' ('Greek Vampire', 226).
67. Interestingly, this kind of ritual could also be found in very different territory around the same time. The Luo tribe of Kenya, as studied by Evans-Pritchard, had similar fears and similar solutions. If someone had been made sick by a corpse, they might dig up the bones and burn them, then throwing the ashes into a marsh. Or, more simply, they might just pour boiling water through a hole in the culprit's grave (E. E. Evans-Pritchard, 'Ghostly Vengeance Among the Luo of Kenya' *Man* 50 (1950): 86–87, 86).
68. Du Boulay, 'The Greek Vampire', 226.
69. Summers, *Vampire in Europe*, 168, citing *Neues Wiener Journal*, 10 June 1909.
70. Barber, *Vampires*, 102, 107. As Barber notes, ironically, the quicklime would in fact preserve the body.
71. Barber, *Vampires*, 74, 55.

72. Murgoci, 'Vampire in Roumania', 326.
73. M. S. R., 'Angels – demons – Spirits', *Englishwoman's Domestic Magazine*, no date, 178; Barber, *Vampires*, 54.
74. In Romania people would also bind the coffin with trailers of wild roses (Murgoci, 'Vampire in Roumania', 328).
75. MacDermott, *Bulgarian Folk Customs*, 67–68.
76. Charlotte Sophia Burne, *Shropshire Folklore: A Sheaf of Gleanings* (London: Trubner, 1883), 112.
77. *Shropshire Folklore*, 128.

6. Vampire Nightmares (I)

1. Nigel Hawkes, *The Times*, 14 November 1994, 16.
2. 'Active Sleep', *The Times*, 17 November 1994, 19.
3. In keeping with the body's circadian rhythms, lowest body temperature usually occurs at around 4.30am.
4. Owen Davies, 'The Nightmare Experience, Sleep Paralysis, and Witchcraft Accusations', *Folklore* 114.2 (2003): 181–203, 182.
5. *Sleep Paralysis: Night-mares, Nocebos, and the Mind-Body Connection* (New Brunswick: Rutgers University Press, 2011), 2.
6. Also writing quite recently, Susan Clancy has 20 per cent for SP with nightmare (*Abducted: How People Come to Believe They Were Abducted by Aliens* (Harvard UP, 2005), 35).
7. *Sleep Paralysis*, 35, 9, 13.
8. *The Philosophy of Sleep* (1838), 143.
9. *Sleep Paralysis*, 13.
10. 'The Dark Side of the Placebo Effect: When Intense Belief Kills', *The Atlantic*, 14 September 2011.
11. *Sleep Paralysis*, 12.
12. This is the hag, when maids lie on their backs,
    That presses them and learns them first to bear,
    Making them women of good carriage
    (Romeo and Juliet, 1.4, 92–4).
    'The hag' has been a standard name for the nightmare for centuries in a variety of cultures.
13. 'Nightmare Experience', 188–89.
14. *Philosophy of Sleep*, 149. Cf. Waller (*Treatise*, 68) who finds it relatively rare among women.
15. 'Nightmare Experience', 189. This last point may be true to some extent. But what Davies does not note is that pregnant women stop menstruating. John Bond, another Scottish physician, and author of the first full study of the nightmare in 1753, cites several

cases of women suffering nightmares before and after the general onset of menstruation – that is, in childhood or after menopause (*Essay on the Incubus*, 46–50). John Waller, a naval surgeon and author of a later (1816) treatise on nightmare, made the same point about pregnant women; and Macnish stated that 'people who were extremely subject to it in their youth, sometimes get rid of it when they reach the age of puberty' (Waller, *Treatise*, 66, 68; *Philosophy of Sleep*, 149). Although this last specifies no gender, the broad pattern looks pretty clear. The attacks can stop in women when they reach the age of menstruation, and are more likely to restart after this permanently ceases, or during pregnancy.

16. Lee, 'Greek Accounts', 127.
17. 'Nightmare Experience', 195. *Cf.* Adler, *Sleep Paralysis*, 26.
18. *Essay on the Incubus*, 71.
19. Waller, *A Treatise on the Incubus, or Nightmare* (London, 1816), 59–60.
20. 'Nightmare Experience', 182.
21. http://www.paranormalnews.com/article.aspx?id=120
22. *Sleep Paralysis*, 29, 17, 10, 8- 9.
23. *Sleep Paralysis*, 19; Margaret Kammerer, 'Night Frights', *The Times*, 18 Sept 1996, 19.
24. *Sleep Paralysis*, 137, fn2.
25. www.squidoo.com/sleep-paralysis-stories
26. Cited in: Rosemary Guiley, *The Encyclopedia of Vampires, Werewolves and Other Monsters* (Visionary Living: 2005), 211.
27. Thomas Bromhall, *History of Apparitions* (1656), 52.
28. Barber, *Vampires*, 16.
29. Warner, 'Russian Peasant Beliefs Concerning the Unclean Dead', 168.
30. Barber, *Vampires*, 185.
31. *Vampires*, 7.
32. Koenig, 'Supernatural Beliefs of the Galician Ukrainians', 272.
33. Du Boulay, 'Greek Vampire', 227, 226.
34. http://www.paranormalnews.com/article.aspx?id=120 (2001).
35. *Sleep Paralysis*, 17.
36. 'Nightmare Experience', 189.
37. Sadly, such working conditions are by no means a thing of the past in our globalised economy. When I first wrote this chapter, long before the FIFA revelations exploded in mid-2015, the scandal about labourer exploitation at the Saudi World Cup site offered a grim example. Adler, meanwhile, was able to link such

conditions specifically to nightmare among Thai construction workers employed in Singapore, Saudi Arabia, Iraq, Kuwait, and Brunei, labouring seven days a week, 12 hours a day 'for meagre wages', and treated 'almost like slaves'. Just over twenty years ago, these conditions seem to have brought on nightmare attacks so severe or so frequent that the victims actually died of them (*Sleep Paralysis*, 128).

38. 'Mortuary Beliefs', 86–87.
39. *Sleep Paralysis*, 13.
40. For more on this Andean vampire (usually called a 'kharisiri' or 'pishtaco') *see*: Andrew Canessa, 'Fear and Loathing on the Kharisiri Trail: Alterity and Identity in the Andes', *Journal of the Royal Anthropological Institute* 6.4 (2000): 705–720; Sugg, *Mummies, Cannibals and Vampires*, 157–164.
41. http://en.allexperts.com/q/Paranormal-Phenomena-3278/2012/1/dark-figures-4.htm; http://www.squidoo.com/sleep-paralysis-true-stories
42. http://www.godlikeproductions.com/forum1/message1866002/pg1
43. http://www.unexplainedmysteries.com/forum/index.php?app+blog&blogid=3085&showentry=24537
44. http://www.searchingforghosts.com/what-is-it.html
45. http://www.kajam.com/index.php?file=storydeatil&Id=77F18361-2334-47C2-BAF5-A0A3F9A39845
46. http://www.yourghoststories.com/real-ghost-story.php?story=8666
47. http://www.staceyandthedream.com/apps/blog/sleep-paralysis-and-cleaning
48. Calmet, *Dissertations*, 209.
49. *The Times*, 4 February 1785, 1.
50. *Phantom World*, II, 56–59.
51. Barber, *Vampires*, 18.
52. Barber, *Vampires*, 4.
53. *See* Keyworth, 'Was the Vampire...?', 259–60.
54. *Dracula* (New York: Dell, 1973), 313.
55. This idea goes back at least to Hippocrates (*c.*460BC). *See*: C. R. S. Harris, *The Heart and the Vascular System in Ancient Greek Medicine* (Oxford: Clarendon Press, 1973), 91.
56. *Sleep Paralysis*, 13.
57. Anthony H. Galt, 'Magical Misfortune in Locorotondo', *American Ethnologist* 18.4 (1991): 735–750, 738–39.

58. This matches what Adler found when interviewing the Hmong: 'I was surprised to find ... that 58% of the people I interviewed had had at least one nightmare' (*Sleep Paralysis*, 98).

59. 'OHS Expirence' [sic],http://paranormal.about.com/u/ua/ humanenigmasTell-Your-Story-About-Old-Hag-Syndrome.24.htm

60. answers.yahoo.com/question/index?qid=20100922233203AA sAWDS

61. Tom Peete Cross, 'Witchcraft in North Carolina', *Studies in Philology* 16.3 (1919): 217–287, 280.

62. http://www.squidoo.com/sleep-paralyis-stories

7. Vampire Nightmares (II): Dying of Fear

1. *Sleep Paralysis*, 1, 2, 45.

2. *Dissertations*, 209.

3. Waller, *Treatise*, 15, 16–17.

4. *Philosophy*, 138.

5. Jon Stone *et al*, 'Systematic Review of Misdiagnosis of Conversion Symptoms and "'Hysteria'"', *BMJ* 331.7523 (2005): 989–991, 989.

6. For just a handful of examples, *see*: Deodat Lawson, *Witchcraft at Salem Village* (1692); Eric Maple, 'The Witches of Canewdon', *Folklore* 71.4 (1960): 241–250, 244–45; Ronald Duncan, *Where I Live* (London: Country Book Club, 1954), 121–123.

7. Canon J. Roscoe, 'Magic and its Power', *Folklore* 34.1 (1923): 25–44, 32–33.

8. Walter B. Cannon, 'Voodoo Death', *American Anthropologist* 44.2 (1942): 169–181, 172.

9. For more on taboo (or *tapu*), *see*: Ross Bowden, 'Tapu and Mana: Ritual Authority and Political Power in Traditional Maori Society', *Journal of Pacific History* 14.1 (1979): 50–61.

10. 'Voodoo Death', 169. Cannon refers also to examples of voodoo death from British Guiana, Hawaiian Islands, and Haiti (175).

11. *Sleep Paralysis*, 119–20.

12. *Extreme Fear: The Science of Your Mind in Danger* (Palgrave, 2009), 64–78.

13. *Extreme Fear*, 71–72.

14. Durham, 'Whence Comes...?', 153.

15. Calmet, *Phantom World*, II, 56–58.

16. Barber, *Vampires*, 16, 17.

17. 'Greek Vampire', 226–27.

18. Barber, *Vampires*, 25.

19. Barber, *Vampires*, 16.
20. For just a handful of examples, *see*: *The Times*, 8 July 1811; *The Liverpool Mercury*, 14 January 1814; *The Derby Mercury*, 7 March 1855; *Nottinghamshire Guardian*, 29 January 1864.. For much more on this subject *see*: Sugg, *A Century of Supernatural Stories* (CreateSpace, 2015).
21. *Lawyer's Guide to Forensic Medicine* (Cavendish Publishing, 1998), 242.
22. *Preston Guardian*, 9 March 1850; *The Times*, 28 July 1964.
23. *The Times*, 24 April 1958.
24. *Daily Mail*, 11 October 1968.
25. There is evidently room for error or confusion in some cases, where exact time of death is not clear, and delayed vagal inhibition deaths run close to the 12 hours of more rapid voodoo deaths.
26. *Sleep Paralysis*, 1, 94, 124–25, 102.
27. *Sleep Paralysis*, 130.
28. For just a handful of examples, *see*: James Carmichael, *News from Scotland* (1592); Anon, *A Strange Report of Six Most Notorious Witches* (1601); Anon, *The Trial, Condemnation and Execution of Three Witches...* (1682), 3; Richard Baxter, *The Certainty of the Worlds of Spirits* (1691), 105; Duncan, *Where I Live*, 121–123; Anne Ross, *Folklore of the Scottish Highlands* (London: Batsford, 1976), 67–8, 72–3; T.P. Vukanović, 'Witchcraft in the Central Balkans I: Characteristics of Witches', *Folklore* 100.1 (1989): 9–24, 9–11; Lizanne Henderson, 'The Survival of Witchcraft Prosecutions and Witch Belief in Southwest Scotland', *Scottish Historical Review* 85.219 (2006): 52–74, 60–61.
29. *See*: *Birmingham Daily Post*, 12 May 1893; *Derby Mercury*, 24 May 1893.
30. *Pall Mall Gazette*, 8 September 1900.
31. *The Standard*, 11 August 1900.
32. *Manchester Courier*, 3 July 1901.
33. *Yorkshire Telegraph*, 18 August 1902.
34. Dalya Alberge, *Guardian*, 23 January 2017.
35. Richard Sugg, 'The Hidden History of Deviant Burials', *History Today*, 21 February 2017.
Kindly commenting on this theory, Simon Mays noted that the tongueless corpse was buried in a site which began to be used as a cemetery only when it became too waterlogged for habitation.

36. *Evening News*, 6 September 1904.
37. Ralston, *The Star*, 11 April 1874.
38. Sir James Frazer, *Balder the Beautiful* (1913; repr. Library of Alexandria, 1935), section 17.
39. Frazer, *Balder the Beautiful*, section 17.
40. 'Fatal Feeds? Plants, Livestock Losses and Witchcraft Accusations in Tudor and Stuart Britain', *Folklore* 101.2 (1990): 131–142, 139.
41. Richard M. Golden, 'American Perspectives on the European Witch Hunts', *The History Teacher* 30.4 (1997): 409–426, 416. For the best recent overview of witchcraft globally and historically, see Hutton, *The Witch* (2017).
42. In England, witchcraft prosecutions were outlawed in 1736; in Switzerland only in 1794; and in southeast Germany, not until 1813.
43. W.B. Carnochan, 'Witch-Hunting and Belief in 1751: The Case of Thomas Colley and Ruth Osborne', *Journal of Social History* 4.4 (1971): 389–403; *Leeds Mercury*, 19 April 1860; *The Standard*, 11 November 1879.
44. Stephen A. Mitchell, 'Witchcraft Persecutions in the Post-Craze Era: The Case of Ann Izzard of Great Paxton, 1808', *Western Folklore* 59 (2000): 304–328.
45. George Hendricks, 'German Witch Mania', *Western Folklore* 23.2 (1964): 120–121.
46. David Smith, 'Ghanaian Woman Burned to Death for being a "Witch"', *The Guardian*, 29 November 2010; Emily Alpert, 'Murder charges filed after woman burned alive in Papua New Guinea', *Los Angeles Times*, 18 February 2013.
47. 'Notes on the Folk-Lore of the Mountain Whites of the Alleghanies', *American Folklore* 7.25 (1894): 105–117, 114.
48. www.trueghosttales./com/paranomral/has-anone-experienced-sleep-paralysis-like-me/
49. *Sleep Paralysis*, 27.
50. http://www.nhs.uk/conditions/Sleep-paralysis/Pages/Introduction.aspx (posted 16 October 2014)
51. *Sleep Paralysis*, 27–28.
52. *The New York Times*, 13 July 1999.
53. Bruce Bower, 'The Stuff of Nightmares', *Cosmos*, 5 January 2010.
54. E-mail communication, 19 September 2012.
55. *Sleep Paralysis*, 27.
56. Clancy, *Abducted*, 74, 105, 4–5.

57. D. P. Walker, *The Decline of Hell: Seventeenth Century Discussions of Eternal Torment* (London: Routledge, 1964), 39.
58. www.yourghoststories.com/real-ghost-story.php?story=8666
59. Kristoff, 'Alien Abduction? Science Calls it Sleep Paralysis'.
60. *Sleep Paralysis*, 22.

8. The Vampire Meets the Poltergeist

1. William Roll and Valerie Storey, *Unleashed: Of Poltergeists and Murder: The Curious Story of Tina Resch* (Paraview, 2004), 96.
2. MacDermott, *Bulgarian Folk Customs*, 67.
3. Lee, 'Greek Accounts', 129.
4. *Dangerous Hour*, 73.
5. Barber, *Vampires*, 25, citing Elwood Trigg.
6. *Modern Greek Folklore*, 369.
7. Wright, *Vampires and Vampirism*, 87.
8. Alan Murdie, 'Haunted Hotels', *Fortean Times*, 25 September 2014.
9. *See*, for example: Sitwell, *Poltergeists*, 167, 172; Roll, *Unleashed*, 40, 52–3: *Century of Ghost Stories,* numbers 29, 37, 60.
10. Sitwell, *Poltergeists*, 343. For more on fairy poltergeists, *see*: Sugg, *Fairies: A Dangerous History* (Reaktion Books, 2018).
11. *Twelve Years' Study*, 31–32.
12. *Haunted People*, 78.
13. Annekatrin Puhle, 'Ghosts, Apparitions and Poltergeist Incidents in Germany between 1700 and 1900', *Journal of the Society for Psychical Research* 63.857 (1998–99): 292–304, 298, 300.
14. Summers, *Vampire in Europe*, 175, citing *Observer*, 2 September 1923.
15. *Pera svrgnuo Savu Savanovića.* By Dušanka Novković Glas javnosti 26-04-2006.
    http://magiaposthuma.blogspot.co.uk/2007/09/kisilova.html
16. We will see several examples of these phenomena below. Anyone who wants to read up on poltergeists in detail should consult: Sacheverell Sitwell, *Poltergeists* (New York: Dorset Press, 1988); Harry Price, *Poltergeist over England* (Country Life, 1946); Caroline Mitchell, *Paranormal Intruder* (CreateSpace, 2013); Sugg, *A Century of Ghost Stories* (2017).
17. In the twentieth century, exorcisms featuring poltergeist phenomena have displayed nearly similar levels of violence to that reported from Pentsch. *See*: Carl Vogel, *Begone, Satan!* (Martino

Fine Books, 2013) for the 1928 exorcism of Anna Ecklund, in Iowa, and D. Scott Rogo, *Poltergeist Experience*, 209ff, for the exorcism of Douglas Deen in St Louis, in 1949. This last was to become the basis for William Peter Blatty's novel, *The Exorcist*.

18. E-mail communication from Caroline Coughlan (née Mitchell), 20 April 2014. For the full account of this case, *see*: Caroline Mitchell, *Paranormal Intruder* (CreateSpace, 2013). At the time of this long-running case Mitchell was a police officer. Incidents were witnessed by three fellow officers, whose statements appear in the book.

19. I have spoken with Keith on several occasions about his case. While it is by no means typical (the apparent agent being in his 40s), the poltergeist has followed him to various hotels during work-related travel. It has also persisted after he moved house. His book-length account of the affair has been published as *The Bothell Hell House* (CreateSpace, 2018).

20. Clarkson, *Poltergeist Phenomenon*, 103–6.

21. *Nottingham Evening Post*, 1 March 1906.

22. Sitwell, *Poltergeists*, 305; Geoff Holder, *Poltergeist Over Scotland* (Stroud: History Press, 2013), 10.

23. Clarkson, *Poltergeist Phenomenon*, 29, 167–8.

24. William G. Roll, *The Poltergeist* (New York: Paraview), 160–61.

25. http://www.stornowaygazette.co.uk/lifestyle/lifestyle-leisure/strange-freak-in-tolsta-chaolais-1-118250

26. Holder, *Poltergeist over Scotland*, 124–26.

27. Roll, *Unleashed*, 213.

28. Germaine Cornélissen *et al*, 'Weak Magnetoperiodism rather than Socio-Photo-Thermoperiodism Characterizes Human Terrorism', *Health and Education in the 21st Century* (2007): 77–85. http://www.chronobiology.narod.ru/magnetoperiodism.html

29. *See*: Halberg, Cornélissen, et al, 'The Incidence of Sudden Cardiac Death in Austria', *Scr Med* 80.4 (2007): 151–156; Franz Halberg, Germaine Cornélissen et al, 'Personalized Chronobiologic Cybercare', *Journal of Applied Biomedicine* 9 (2011): 1–34, 10.

30. Joseph Lovering, 'Catalogue of Auroras Observed … after the Year 1838', *Memoirs of the American Academy of Sciences* 10.1 (1868): 1–8, 7.

31. The OED's first example is from a dictionary of 1796. See also Charlotte Smith, *Marchmont*, 4 vols (1796), III, 257.

9. Versions of the Vampire (I)

1. Cited by Keyworth: 'Was the Vampire...?', 256.
2. Corinne G. Dempsey, 'Lessons in Miracles from Kerala, South India: Stories of Three "Christian" Saints', *History of Religions* 39.2 (1999): 150–176, 166; Edgar Martín del Campo, 'The Global Making of a Mexican Vampire: Mesoamerican, European, African, and Twentieth-Century Media Influences on the Teyollohcuani', *History of Religions* 49.2 (2009): 107–140, 107–110.
3. W. R .S. Ralston, cited in: *The Star*, 19 April 1887.
4. MacDermott, *Bulgarian Folk Customs*, 68.
5. Koenig, 'Supernatural Beliefs', 272, 274.
6. E. E. Evans-Pritchard, 'Ghostly Vengeance Among the Luo of Kenya' *Man* 50 (1950): 86–87.
7. James E. Crombie, 'Shoe-Throwing at Weddings' *Folklore* 6.3 (1895): 258–281, 275–6.
8. *See* Andrew Canessa, 'Fear and Loathing on the Kharisiri Trail: Alterity and Identity in the Andes', *The Journal of the Royal Anthropological Institute* 6.4 (2000): 705–720, 705–6.
9. Anthony Oliver-Smith, 'The Pishtaco: Institutionalized Fear in Highland Peru', *The Journal of American Folklore* 82.326 (1969): 363–368, 363–4; Nathan Wachtel, *Gods and Vampires: Return to Chipaya* (Chicago: University of Chicago Press, 1994), 73–74.
10. On the bells, *see* Wachtel, *Gods and Vampires*, 74.
11. David Samper, 'Cannibalizing Kids', *Journal of Folklore Research* 39.1 (2002): 1–32, 15; Wachtel, *Gods and Vampires*, 53.
12. *See*: Samper, 'Cannibalizing Kids'; Wachtel, *Gods and Vampires*, 82–88.
13. Wachtel, *Gods and Vampires*, 87, 53–67.
14. *Dangerous Hour*, 72.
15. *Dangerous Hour*, 74.
16. Barber, *Vampires, Burial, and Death*, 9.
17. *Dangerous Hour*, 73–74.
18. *Reminiscences of Athens and the Morea* (London: John Murray, 1869), 162–64.
19. Fermor, *Mani: Travels in the Southern Peloponnese* (London: John Murray, 2004), xi, 86–99.
20. Bob Barrow, *Inside the Mani: A Guide to the Villages, Towers and Churches of the Mani Peninsular* (Stoupa: Matthew Dean, 2006).
21. 'An Historical Study of the Werwolf in Literature', *PMLA* 9.1 (1894): 1–42..

22. Barber, *Vampires*, 73.
23. http://www.shroudeater.com/cparis.htm
24. Barber, *Vampires*, 30–31.
25. Leatherdale, *Dracula: The Novel & the Legend: A Study of Bram Stoker's Masterpiece* (Aquarian Press, 1985), cited by: Chris Baldick, 'Promiscuous Pluralism', *TLS* 27 Sep 1985, 1066.
    Diarmuid Ó Giolláin, 'The Leipreachán and Fairies, Dwarfs and the Household Familiar: A Comparative Study', *Béaloideas* 52 (1984): 75–150, 113.
26. *See*, for example: Susan Schoon Eberly, 'Fairies and the Folklore of Disability: Changelings, Hybrids and the Solitary Fairy', *Folklore* 99.1 (1988): 58–77, 60, 64–69.
27. T. P. Vukanović, 'Witchcraft in the Central Balkans I: Characteristics of Witches', 12.
28. *Vampires, Burial, and Death*, 31.
29. *The Leeds Mercury*, 14 March 1890, citing British *Daily Telegraph*.
30. These are part of Pskov province, near the town of Novosokol'niki.
31. Warner, 'Russian Peasant Beliefs', 73–74.
32. Warner, 'Russian Peasant Beliefs', 74.
33. *Reynold's Newspaper*, 7 October 1894.
34. Warner, 'Russian Peasant Beliefs', 73, 70–71, 87.
35. Warner, 'Russian Peasant Beliefs', 80–81.
36. Warner, 'Russian Peasant Beliefs Concerning the Unclean Dead and Drought, Within the Context of the Agricultural Year', *Folklore* 122.2 (2011): 155–175, 170–71.
37. This idea now seems bizarre. In fact, a number of educated people held a version of it in the 16th- and 17th-centuries (*see*: *Mummies, Cannibals and Vampires*, 181–82).
38. Warner, 'Russian Peasant Beliefs', 75.
39. Warner, 'Russian Peasant Beliefs', 78–80.
40. Eric Maple, 'The Witches of Canewdon', *Folklore* 71.4 (1960): 241–250.
41. Warner, 'Russian Peasant Beliefs', 78.
42. Oinas, 'Heretics as Vampires and Demons', 438–39.
43. *Preston Guardian*, 1 August 1868.
44. *Leamington Spa Courier*, 4 July 1891.
45. *Huddersfield Daily Chronicle*, 25 August 1899. Bugulma is in southeast Russia.
46. Warner, 'Unclean Dead', 158.
47. Warner, 'Unclean Dead', 168, 165.

48. *Penny Illustrated Paper and Illustrated Times*, 19 August 1905. A report in the *Aberdeen Daily Journal* on 9 August indicates that the incident occurred on Sunday 6 August.
49. Oinas, 'Heretics as Vampires and Demons', 434.

10. Versions of the Vampire (II): New England

1. Bell's dating of 1807 is approximate; the quoted author was himself writing in 1822 (*Food for the Dead*, 269–72).
2. *Food for the Dead*, 272.
3. John Payne, *Poetical Works* (London: Private Printing, 1902), 260.
4. *Life* (London: Weidenfeld and Nicholson, 2010), 386.
5. Michael Bell, 'American Vampires', http://intertheory.org/bell.htm
6. Bell, 'American Vampires', http://intertheory.org/bell.htm
7. *Food for the Dead*, 29.
8. *Food for the Dead*, 271–2, 20, 29–30.
9. *Food for the Dead*, 8.
10. *Food for the Dead*, 33–34, 20.
11. *Food for the Dead*, 20–21, citing anonymous Rhode Island newspaper report.
12. *Food for the Dead*, 36–37.
13. *Food for the Dead*, 38.
14. Jeremiah Curtin, 'European Folk-Lore in the United States', *Journal of American Folklore* 2.4 (1889): 56–59, 58.
15. *Food for the Dead*, 204. Here the atypical terms 'vampire' and 'vampirism' have been imposed by the educated newspaper writer.
16. *Food for the Dead*, 204–5. Knox ledge was a granite quarry, named after Timothy Knox, who was a sometime student of Harvard, and allegedly the first settler in Windsor County, Vermont, in 1765. (Paul T. Hellmann, *Historical Gazetteer of the United States* (Routledge, 2005), 2001).
17. *Food for the Dead*, 205.
18. *Food for the Dead*, 206.
19. *Food for the Dead*, 210.
20. *Food for the Dead*, 136, 142, citing Casey Tyler, article for *Pawtuxet Valley Gleaner*, 1892.
21. *Food for the Dead*, 215–16. On Timothy's status, *see* 217. Sharp-eyed readers may have noted that the words 'altar', 'sacrifice', and (most of all) 'Vampire' are unusual in such

accounts. This is because the written version of the story derives from a Judge Pettibone, who Bell believes penned it between 1857 and 1872 (*Food for the Dead*, 216).

22. *The Huddersfield Daily Chronicle*, 20 April 1892.

23. *Food for the Dead*, 65–67, citing Sidney Rider, 1888.

24. *Food for the Dead*, 70.

25. A case of corpse exhumation found by Michael Bell does seem to have involved nightmares. In 1886 the coffin of a young girl in the Roman Catholic cemetery in Birmingham, Connecticut, was opened, and all pins removed from her hair and her shroud; this apparently being due to 'a strong superstition among the Irish people that if a corpse is buried tied or with pins or with even a knot at the end of the thread that sews the shroud the soul will be confined to the grave for all eternity, and that the persons guilty of the blunder will be disturbed by the restrained spirits while on earth.' One of the women removing the pins explained to a bystander that she herself 'had been bothered for two nights previous by the ghost of the girl' (*Syracuse Herald*, 21 February 1886: 'Opening a Grave: On Account of a Strange Superstition about the Tying of a Shroud').

26. Curtin, 'European Folk-Lore in the United States', 58.

27. *Food for the Dead*, 219–20.

28. Stetson, 'Animistic Vampire', 8.

29. Stetson, 'Animistic Vampire', 7–8, 10.

30. *Food for the Dead*, 158–59.

31. 'Vampire's Grasp', chapter six, MS. Many thanks to Michael for sending this on pre-publication.

32. Hoffman, 'Folk Medicine', 332, 342, 345.

33. The Greek word translated as 'virtue' (and also, tellingly, as 'power') was *dunamin*, as in 'dynamic'.

34. Hoffman, 'Folk Medicine', 344, 335.

35. Mary Beith, *Healing Threads: Traditional Medicines of the Highlands and Islands* (Edinburgh: Polygon, 1995), 170; Violetta Halpert, 'Folk Cures From Indiana', *Hoosier Folklore* 9.1 (1950): 1–12, 9.

36. Gary Laderman, 'Locating the Dead: A Cultural History of Death in the Antebellum, Anglo-Protestant Communities of the Northeast', *Journal of the American Academy of Religion* 63.1 (1995): 27–52, 33.

37. *Food for the Dead*, 19.

38. *Food for the Dead*, 9.
39. Hoffman, 'Folk Medicine', 330.
40. 'Vampire's Grasp', chapter seven.
41. Lyall Watson, *Supernature: A Natural History of the Supernatural* (London: Sceptre, 1973), 35–36, 40–41.
42. *Food for the Dead*, 236–40, 240.
43. British correspondent of the London *Standard*, 1 January 1867.
44. *See*: http://rt.com/usa/233947-oklahoma-ban-advanced-placement-history/

Conclusion: The Other Blood Drinkers

1. 'De Legendis Urbis: Modern Legends in Ancient Rome', *The Journal of American Folklore* 96.380 (1983): 200-208.
2. *Aberdeen Weekly Journal*, 9 October 1879.
3. *American Vampires: Fans, Victims, Practitioners* (New York: Vintage, 1990), 28–29.
4. *Aberdeen Weekly Journal*, 6 October 1888.j
5. Lee H. Hamilton, 'Outside the Green Zone, the Human Dimension', *The New York Times*, 12 September 2008. Notably, when Marwa vowed revenge his aunt's response was: 'Ashrab min Dambum' – an Arabic phrase 'often invoked and rarely acted upon', and meaning, 'I will drink their blood' (http://archive.today/bv1Iw).
6. Christopher Buckley, *But Enough About You: Essays* (New York: Simon & Schuster, 2014), 94.
7. *Applebee's Original Weekly Journal* (London), 24 September 1720.
8. *Dracula*, ed. J. P. Riquelme (New York: St. Martins, 2002), 396–97, cit. *Psychopathia Sexualis* (1893).
9. *Der Genius*, also known as *Memoirs of the Marquis of Grosse*, was published serially in German from 1791–95. Appearing in English as *Horrid Mysteries* in 1796, it influenced Jane Austen and Thomas Love Peacock, among others.

Index

Also available from Amberley Publishing

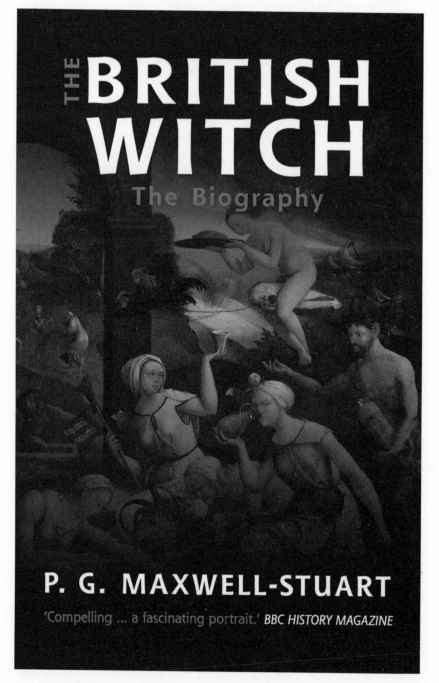

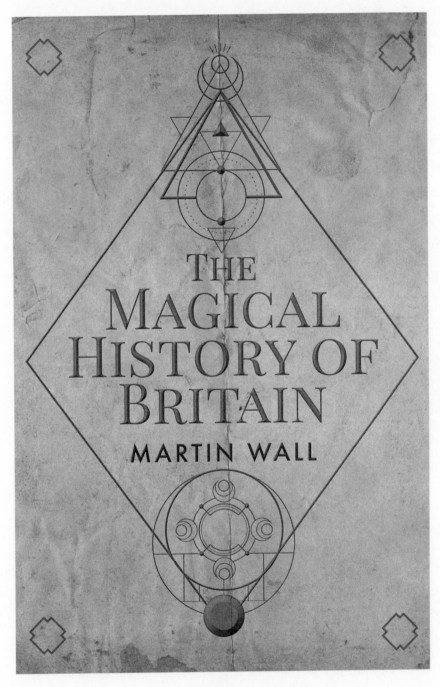